Key Houses of the Twentieth Century

Plans, Sections and Elevations

Colin Davies

Key Houses of the Twentieth Century

Plans, Sections and Elevations

Colin Davies

W. W. Norton & Company
New York • London

Design and drawings copyright © 2006 by Laurence King Publishing
Text copyright © 2006 by Colin Davies

For information about permission to reproduce selections from this book,
write to Permissions, W. W. Norton & Company, Inc., 500 Fifth Avenue,
New York, NY 10110

Manufacturing by C&C Offset Printing Co., Ltd
Project managed by Henrietta Heald
Book design by Godfrey Design www.godfreydesign.co.uk
Drawings by Adrian Scholefield
Picture research by Claire Gouldstone

Library of Congress Cataloging-in-Publication Data

Davies, Colin, 1929–
    Key houses of the twentieth century : plans, sections, and elvations
    Colin Davies.—1st ed.
       p. cm.
    Includes bibliographical references and index.
    ISBN-13: 978-0-393-73205-4 (pbk.)
    ISBN-10: 0-393-73205-3 (pbk.)
    1. Architect-designed houses—Designs and plans. 2. Architecture,
Modern—20th century—Designs and plans. I. Title.
    NA7126.D38 2006
    728'.370222—dc22

                                          2006016248

W. W. Norton & Company, Inc.,
500 Fifth Avenue, New York, N.Y. 10110
www.wwnorton.com

W. W. Norton & Company Ltd.,
Castle House, 75/76 Wells Street, London W1T 3QT

0 9 8 7 6 5 4 3 2 1

Contents

Introduction

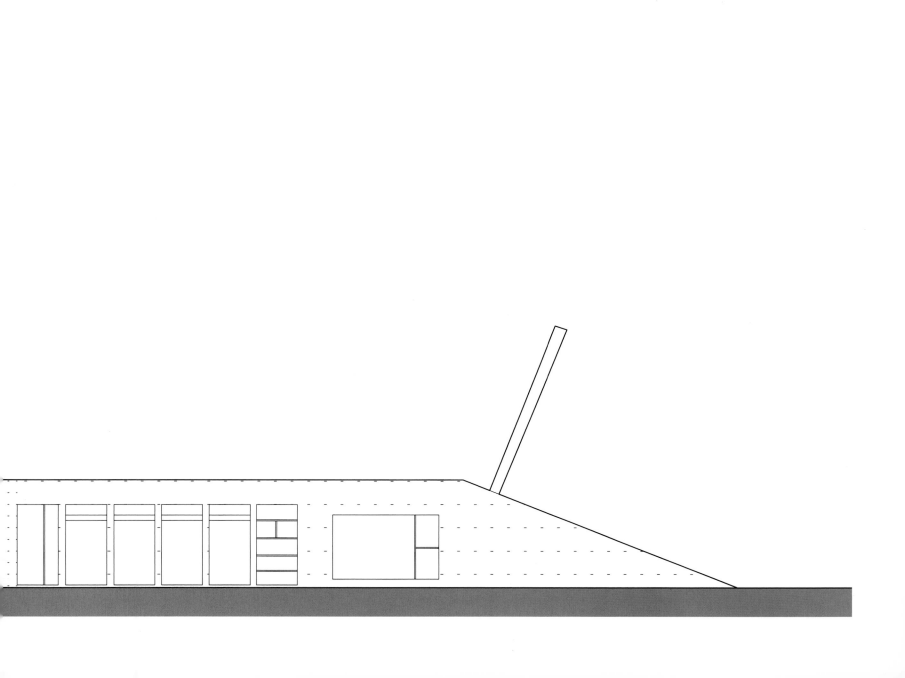

Villa Savoye

The individual, architect-designed house is a distinct category of artistic and cultural production, comparable perhaps to the landscape painting, the documentary film or the romantic novel. The fact that houses in general also perform a practical function – are, in fact, essential to survival in most parts of the world – may lead us to look at them in a different light. We might be tempted, for example, to include among the 'key houses of the twentieth century' examples of vernacular or mass-produced houses – the American tract home, the English cottage or the Swedish summer house. Surely these 'ordinary' houses have had more effect on the daily lives of most people than any of the 'special' houses in this book. In a comprehensive global history of the twentieth-century house, the individual architect-designed house would be hardly more than a footnote.

But this book does not aim to provide a comprehensive global history. It deals with something more limited but no less interesting: the relatively small selection of houses that form what might be termed the artistic canon. The

houses in this book are the famous houses, the houses that, for one reason or another, have been widely published and have found their way into architectural history books.

The canon, in architecture as in any art, is an imperfect thing, full of distortions and injustices. But that doesn't mean it is isn't useful. In fact, it is essential to the progress of the art. Without it, architectural conversations – in books and exhibitions, in offices and conference rooms, and most of all in schools of architecture – would be greatly impoverished. The canon is the pool of shared knowledge that unites architects all over the world and gives them their collective identity. When an architect says the words 'Villa Savoye', another architect immediately sees a picture in his mind and at the same time recalls a dozen other conversations, in lecture rooms, over drawing boards or in front of computer screens. A thorough knowledge of canonical buildings, not just their names and their portraits but their detailed anatomy, is essential to every serious architect and architecture student. This book provides the means to acquire and maintain that

Lovell Beach House

Lovell Health House

Barnsdall House

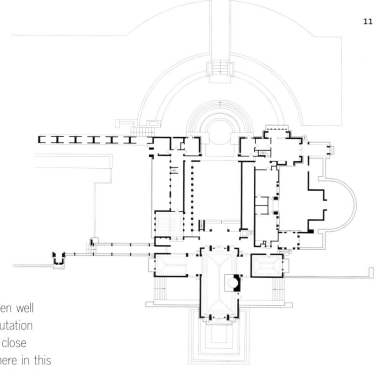

Barnsdall House

knowledge. It is concerned only with houses, but houses are the laboratories of architecture, where new and experimental ideas are tested and the art is carried forward. A history of twentieth-century houses is a condensed history of twentieth-century architecture.

Admission to the canon obviously depends on the quality and originality of the work in question. Unimaginative or incompetent examples are not usually celebrated by architectural history. But quality and originality are not the only criteria for admission. The authorship of the piece is often an important consideration. Any house designed by an acknowledged genius such as Le Corbusier, for example, is likely to become canonical, while a brilliantly original house by an unknown architect may well escape history's attention. For this reason, the representation in this book of works by 'form-givers' such as Le Corbusier, Frank Lloyd Wright and Ludwig Mies van der Rohe is far greater than could be justified by the sheer volume of their work. The works are included because they are unquestionably canonical.

The canonical architects were often well known to one another, not only by reputation but also by personal contact and even close friendship. One can start almost anywhere in this collection of houses and, working outwards, plot a global web of architectural allegiances. Take, for example, the four Los Angeles houses of the 1920s. Two of them had the same client, Dr Philip Lovell, and the other two had the same architect, Frank Lloyd Wright. Dr Lovell's wife was a friend of Aline Barnsdall, the client of one of the Wright houses. Rudolph Schindler, the architect of the **Lovell Beach House** (pages 50–51), and Richard Neutra, the architect of the **Lovell Health House** (pages 68–69), were both Austrians and had long been friends and colleagues. And both of them had worked for Wright on the **Barnsdall House** (pages 40–41), Schindler as a supervising architect and Neutra as a garden designer. Neutra had also designed the garden of the Beach House.

Before they had come to America, both Schindler and Neutra had been taught by the great Austrian proto-Modernist Adolf Loos, two

Tugendhat House

Chamberlain Cottage

of whose houses, the **Moller House** (pages 60–61) and the **Müller House** (pages 74–75), are included in this book. Loos's famous theoretical essay 'Ornament and Crime' was published in French in 1920 in the magazine *L'Esprit Nouveau*, which was edited by Le Corbusier. Le Corbusier had worked for Peter Behrens in Berlin, as had Walter Gropius and Mies van der Rohe. Both Gropius and Mies were directors of the Bauhaus school, which produced several famous architects, including Marcel Breuer, who emigrated first to England and then to America, where he joined Gropius at Harvard University and designed several houses including the **Chamberlain Cottage** (pages 102–103). Harry Seidler was one of Breuer's students and worked on the design of the Chamberlain Cottage before emigrating to Australia and designing a house for his mother in the Breuer style, the **Rose Seidler House** (pages 110–11), arguably thereby changing the course of architectural history in that country. And so it goes on – an old boys' network perhaps, but a living, growing organism rather than a lifeless statistical survey.

All artistic canons, indeed all art histories, depend to some extent on networks of this kind. They also favour certain styles and movements, sometimes disproportionately to their popularity or the extent of their influence at the time. In twentieth-century architecture the style favoured in this way was Modernism. Most historians would agree that Modernism was the characteristic style of the century. Consequently, there are more Modernist houses in this book than could be justified on a purely statistical basis. Other styles are often named in relation to Modernism – pre-Modernist (Edwin Lutyens's **Orchards**, pages 24–25), Postmodernist (the **Vanna Venturi House**, pages 142–43), or neo-Modernist (Eisenman's **House VI**, pages 160–61).

Before the Second World War, Modernism was an avant-garde European style represented by a tiny fraction of total building output. But then a few Modernist pioneers such as Gropius and Mies emigrated to America to escape from Nazi Germany and were welcomed by leaders of architectural taste such as Philip Johnson and Henry Russell Hitchcock. It is partly as a result of

Pavillon de l'Esprit Nouveau

Orchards

Vanna Venturi House

this cultural transfer that those earlier émigrés, Schindler and Neutra, began, with hindsight, to seem important and were duly admitted to the canon. After the war, corporate America adopted Modernism and its influence grew to become an orthodoxy, like Christianity after its adoption by the Roman Empire.

Modernism was a progressive movement, more interested in invention than tradition. The machine and the products of the machine were its inspiration. It wanted to re-found architecture on rational, functional grounds and transform society by resolving the conflict between everyday life and mechanized industry. But the house was, and is, the last and strongest bastion of tradition. The domestic realm is deeply conservative, which is why Le Corbusier's concept that the house should be 'a machine for living in' remains provocative to this day. Many of the houses in this book are essays in the reconciliation of modernity with domesticity. It is in these designs that the drama is played out. And because the canon favours the new and the different, it is usually modernity that dominates.

Eight of the houses in this book are by Le Corbusier and all of them are architectural provocations. The **Pavillon de L'Esprit Nouveau** (pages 48–49) and the **Weissenhof House** (pages 56–57) were both built for exhibitions and therefore had no clients in the usual sense. They were prototypes for possible mass-production. The pavilion is what we would now call a 'module' that can be stacked up to form a multi-storey apartment block. But Le Corbusier's houses for wealthy clients, such as the **Villa Savoye** (pages 80–81) and the **Villa Stein–de Monzie** (pages 54–55), were no less revolutionary. For all his propagandizing about the industrial age, Le Corbusier was an artist, not a technologist. In the morning he painted his Purist still-lifes and in the afternoon he designed houses that also came to be known as 'Purist'. They were not so much machines for living in as works of art for living in. In them, the Modernist style came into sharp focus for the first time. Open plans, reinforced-concrete structures and plain, geometrical forms were not new entirely new in 1927, but these were houses, not factories or

Rose Seidler House

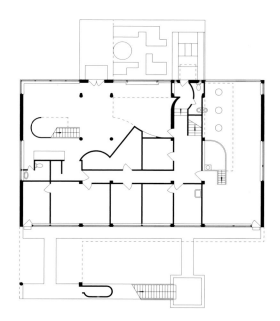

Villa Stein–de Monzie

High and Over

Wolf House

art schools or office buildings. The Purist villas became enormously influential. English Modernist houses of the 1930s, such as Amyas Connell's **High and Over** (pages 72–73) and Edwin Maxwell Fry's **Sun House** (pages 88–89), would have been inconceivable without the influence of Le Corbusier. Denys Lasdun's House in **Newton Road** (pages 98–99) is practically a copy of Le Corbusier's Villa Cook.

Later, during the 1960s and 1970s, the New York Five, including Michael Graves (**Hanselmann House**, pages 146–47), Peter Eisenman (**House VI**, pages 160–61) and Richard Meier (**Douglas House**, pages 162–63), produced a body of work that is, in effect, a homage to early Le Corbusier. By this time, however, Le Corbusier himself had moved on, leaving Purism behind in order to explore the architectural potential of rougher materials and more rugged forms in houses such as the **Villa Shodan** (pages 130–31) and the **Maisons Jaoul** (pages 132–33). These in turn became reference points for other architects such as Louis Kahn and Tadao Ando.

As we have seen with Schindler and Neutra, the artistic canon sometimes works retrospectively. Fascination with Le Corbusier's mature architecture makes us want to know where it came from and to look for its origins in earlier work. The **Villa Schwob** of 1917 (pages 34–35) is certainly no masterpiece of Modernism – it is more a neoclassical oddity – but our understanding of Le Corbusier would be the poorer without a knowledge of it.

Mies van der Rohe was a very different architect from Le Corbusier, though no less an artist and no less a Modernist. Mies's architecture was more austere and intellectual, less instinctive and emotional, and it follows, perhaps, that the domestic realm was more resistant to it. The **Wolf House** (pages 58–59) and the **Lange House** (pages 62–63) are both in some sense partial realizations of the Brick Country House project of 1923, which is more an abstract spatial composition than a believable home. The **Tugendhat House** (pages 78–79) is also a development from another design, the famous Barcelona Pavilion, a purely ceremonial and

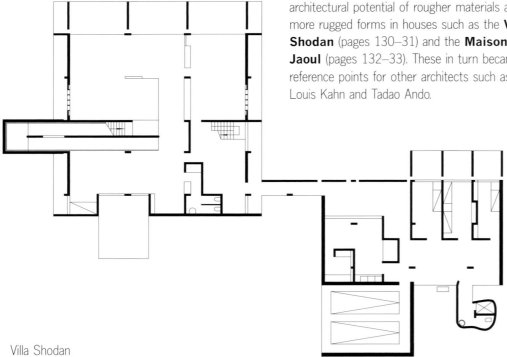

Villa Shodan

Villa Schwob

Douglas House

symbolic building. But there is one Mies house which has become, as it were, the head of a large extended family. It is the **Farnsworth House** of 1951 (pages 112–13). In the extreme simplicity and refinement of this building, we see most clearly what is often the true function of the individual architect-designed house: to represent an architectural idea in as pure and perfect a form as possible. The Farnsworth House encapsulates all the major themes in Mies's architecture: its structural clarity, its spatial flexibility, its transparency in both literal and conceptual senses, and its essential classicism.

The many descendants of the Farnsworth House include Philip Johnson's **Johnson House** (pages 108–109), which was actually completed before the Farnsworth, the California 'Case Study' houses by Craig Ellwood and Pierre Koenig (pages 120–21 and 134–35), Ronnie Tallon's house in Dublin (pages 152–53) and Norman Foster's **Cho en Dai House** in Kawana, Japan (pages 212–13). But there are reflections of the Farnsworth to be glimpsed in other, less obvious works, such as Jørn Utzon's own house in

Hellebaek (pages 118–19) or even Shigeru Ban's **Furniture House** (pages 218–19).

The Farnsworth House also illustrates a kind of guilty secret in the canonical history of the architect-designed house: the fact that perfectly satisfied clients are rather rare. Of course, some clients were true patrons and willing collaborators in the creation of a work of art. Louis Kahn's clients, for example, seemed to be willing to become his students and to forgive their teacher when he disappeared for months to work on more important projects. But many, like Edith Farnsworth, were resentful at being forced to pay more than they had intended for a house they didn't like. Le Corbusier and Frank Lloyd Wright were particularly ruthless in this respect, which is perhaps a rather negative reason for their prominence in the canon.

For many architects, the way to overcome the client problem was to design a house for themselves. About one quarter of the houses in this book, from Peter Behrens's 1901 house in Darmstadt (pages 22–23) to Ma Qingyun's house for his father near Xi'an (pages 232–33), were

Farnsworth House

Cho en Dai House

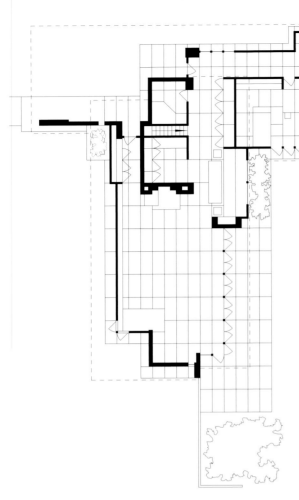

designed by architects either for themselves or for close relatives. What this demonstrates, perhaps, is that for ambitious architects a house is not so much a dialogue with a client as a projection of their future careers as designers.

As far as architectural history is concerned, the Modernism of Le Corbusier and Mies and their followers dominates the century. And yet it has failed to win the hearts of the general public. It has remained a minority passion. A cynic might say that the reason that the canon features so many architects' own houses is that nobody else wanted them. European Modernism is both the architectural profession's greatest success and its greatest failure. But the 'Modernism', if such it can be called, of the third of the great form-givers, Frank Lloyd Wright, is different.

Wright was building important buildings long before the start of the century and for him European Modernism was a late-coming rival. It was Wright's genius that he could invent new forms that seemed always to have been there. He somehow cancelled out the normal opposition between tradition and modernity, and his

architecture was welcomed by ordinary people not with a suspicious frown but with a spontaneous smile. We encounter him first in the **Robie House** (pages 32–33), the epitome of the Prairie Style, though its suburban Chicago site is very far from any prairie. It has all the spatial freedom of a Le Corbusier villa without any of the off-putting austerity. It uses new materials, such as steel and concrete, and new forms, such as long cantilevered roofs, but it is also homely and hearth-centred. There is nothing traditionally classical or Gothic about it, yet it does not reject ornament.

It is some measure of the fertility of Wright's architectural imagination that the five of his houses included in this book are all in completely different styles, even when, like the Barnsdall House and the **Ennis House** (pages 42–43), they are close in time and space. **Fallingwater** (pages 92–93) is the most famous and most spectacular of them, but perhaps in the long run the most important is the **Jacobs House** of 1936 (pages 90–91), a modest family home for people who, though not

Villla Dall'Ava

Fisher House

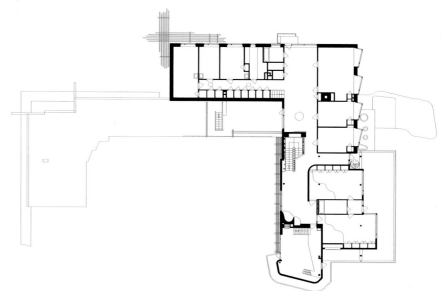

Villa Mairea

poor, were certainly not rich. It is what Wright called a Usonian house. Usonia was his name for an imagined America, an America as it might have been if he had designed it. The Usonian houses were uncompromisingly modern but they were cheaply built using a rationalized system of construction in natural materials such as brick and wood. The Jacobs House is that very rare thing: an architect-designed modern house that appeals to popular taste. You can find bits of the Jacobs House all over suburban America, from the open-plan kitchen and the built-in wardrobes to the patio and the car port.

To describe Wright's architecture as an alternative to European Modernism would be a gross solecism. He would have put it the other way around. But the architecture of another influential form-giver, Alvar Aalto, is sometimes listed, with Hans Scharoun and others, under the heading 'the alternative tradition'. Aalto's great contribution to twentieth-century architecture was a questioning of regularity and consistency. These are qualities normally assumed to be quintessentially architectural. They are almost

what the word 'architecture' means. Aalto gloried in inconsistency and irregularity: the juxtaposition of forms and materials that seemed to represent different worlds. His **Villa Mairea** (pages 94–95) is the perfect example, with its non-congruent upper and lower floors, its overlapping spaces and its columns all different – single, double, triple; steel, wood, concrete. Aalto's style was personal and inimitable, but the intuitive freedom of his compositional method surely made possible a variety of Post- or late-Modernist styles, from the serious-minded regionalism of José Antonio Coderch's **Casa Ugalde** (page 116–17) to the playful form-juggling of Frank Gehry's **Winton Guest House** (pages 192–93). Even the urbane Dutch houses of the last decade of the century, such as Rem Koolhaas's **Villa Dall'Ava** (pages 206–207) and Ben van Berkel and Caroline Bos's **Möbius House** (226–27), owe a debt to Aalto and Scharoun.

The individual architect-designed house is often a prototype on which to test new ideas and new technologies. This function is particularly evident in those houses loosely termed High

Robie House

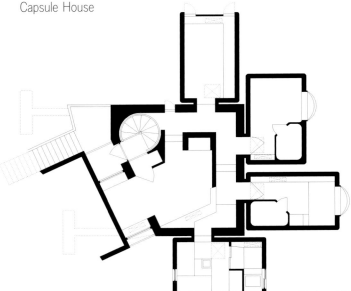

Wichita House

Tech, which try to break the common association of domesticity with traditional or natural materials and see the house as an industrial product. When Michael and Patty Hopkins built their steel and glass house in Hampstead in 1977, the **Hopkins House** (pages 174–75), it was to be their main home and their studio, but more importantly it was to be the ideological foundation of their new architectural practice. That practice went on to great success and for a while the Hopkinses were the British establishment's favourite architects (though, ironically, they soon outgrew the High Tech style).

Thirty years earlier, another designer couple, Charles and Ray Eames, had built themselves a similar 'manifesto house', the **Eames House** (pages 106–107), to which the Hopkins House owes an obvious debt. The idea was to make a house out of standard industrial components taken straight from manufacturers' catalogues. It would be the realization of that recurring dream of the twentieth century: a house that could be mass-produced like a car. But the Eames House remained a one-off, a design classic and an

inspiration for decades to come, but a non-starter in true commercial and industrial terms. Perhaps the Eameses never intended to start mass-producing houses. Soon after building their house, they abandoned the practice of architecture in order to concentrate on furniture design, exhibitions and films.

Richard Buckminster Fuller certainly did intend to mass-produce houses. His **Wichita House** (pages 104–105) was meant to take over the production lines of the Beech Aircraft factory when the war was over and military aircraft were no longer needed. The product was advertised and the orders started to flood in, but then Fuller seemed to get cold feet and called a halt to the project with only two prototypes built. The Wichita House did nothing to ease the postwar American housing shortage but it deserves its place in the canon because of the many new ideas and new technologies that it proved could work. Fuller's influence on the High Tech architects of the 1980s was profound, matched only by that of Jean Prouvé, who built a house for himself out of mostly metal

Maison Prouvé

components left over from previous aborted projects, the **Maison Prouvé** (pages 124–25). It was a kind of High Tech bricolage, machine-like but human.

In the 1960s, Kisho Kurokawa became fascinated by the architectural potential of prefabricated living pods or capsules. The Archigram group in England had followed the same line of thought in projects such as the famous Plug-in City, but Kurokawa built a real piece of plug-in city in his Nagakin Capsule Tower of 1972. Two years later, he built himself **Capsule House K** (pages 166–67) – an extremely rare example of the one-off 'prototype' coming after the full-scale application of the idea.

In hindsight, it may seem reasonable to apply the label 'pre-Modernist' to those houses of the first decade of the twentieth century in which an older tradition still lives and breathes. But of course it is a distortion of history. In truth, there is little in Edwin Lutyens's **Orchards** (pages 24–25), Charles Voysey's **Hollybank** (pages 26–27) or Charles Rennie Mackintosh's **Hill House** (pages 28–29) that can be said to

anticipate the coming of the Modernism (though many historians, including Nikolaus Pevsner himself, have tried to see it that way). But this doesn't mean that those traditional houses represented a stylistic dead end. They had a profound influence on the everyday domestic architecture of the twentieth century. The English suburban villas of the 1930s owed almost everything to Voysey and still form the bedrock of British architectural taste. But the more vigorous, more progressive line of development came from a different place and had somewhere else to go. It is that progressive line that is favoured by architectural history, forming the artistic canon and providing the contents of this book.

Eames House

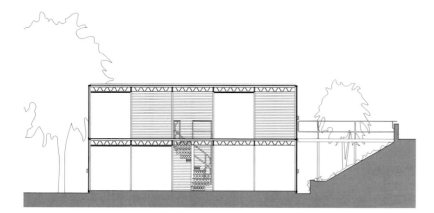

Hopkins House

Buildings

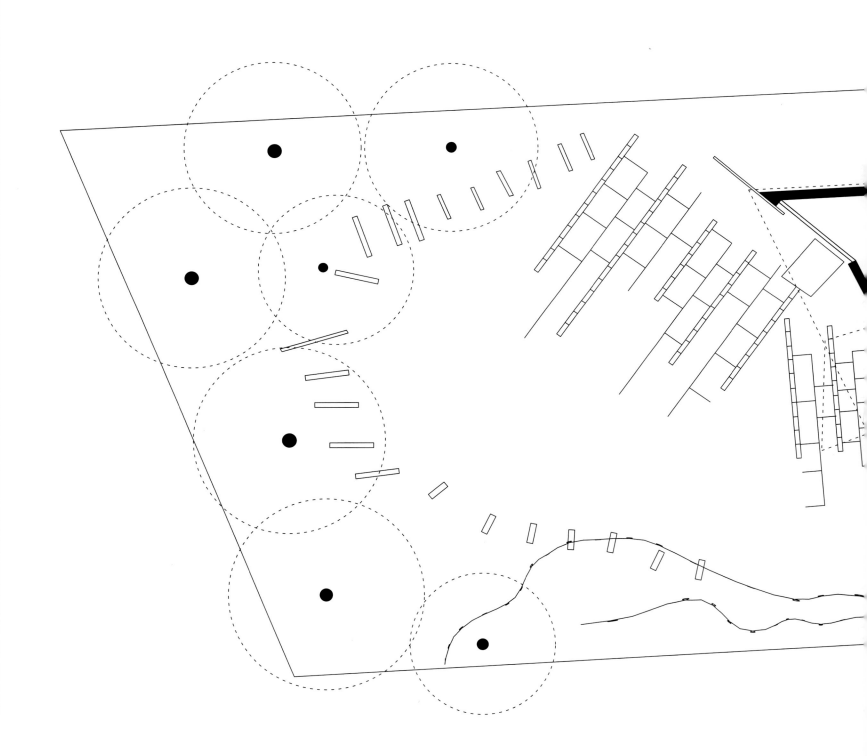

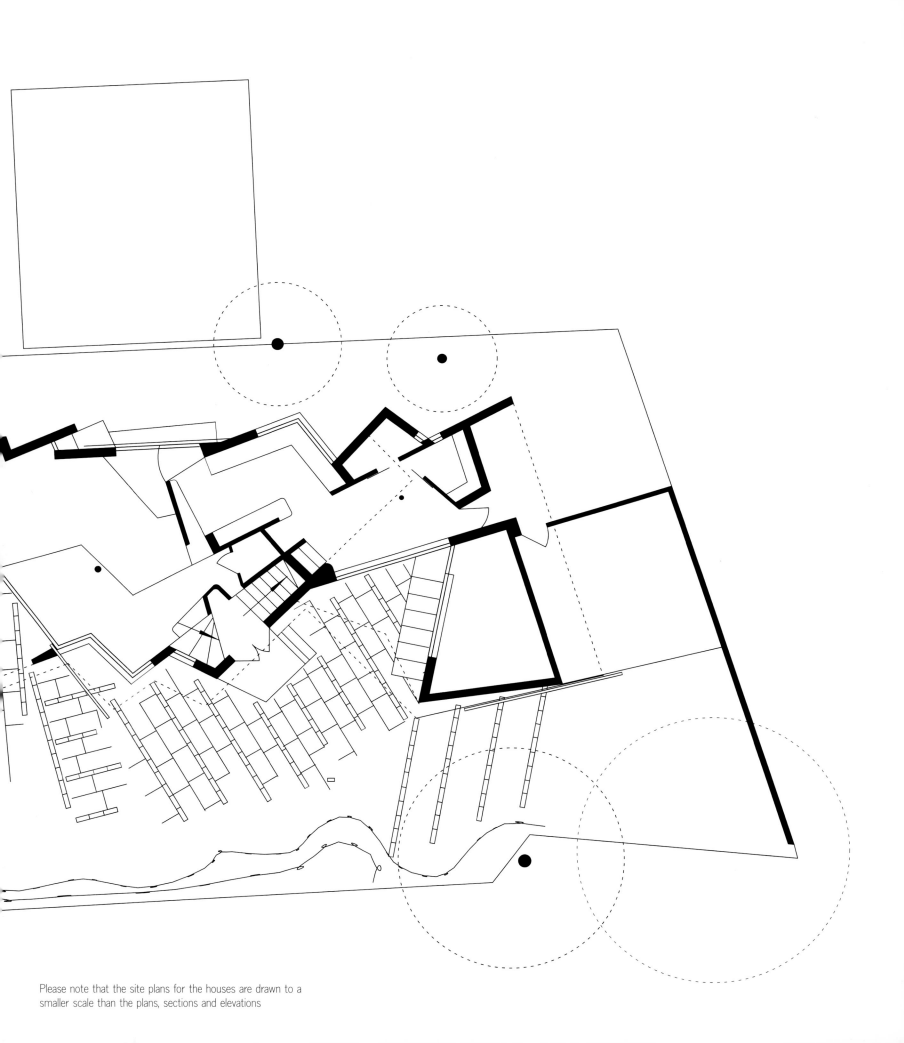

Please note that the site plans for the houses are drawn to a
smaller scale than the plans, sections and elevations

Behrens House

Peter Behrens, 1868–1940

Darmstadt, Germany; 1901

Peter Behrens began his career as a painter, but in the 1890s he started to experiment with the applied arts – glassware, ceramics, furniture and graphics – successfully exhibiting his work in Berlin and Munich.

In 1899 he was invited to join an artists' colony in Darmstadt, founded by the local Grand Duke to enhance the prestige of the city and encourage local industry. There were seven artists in the colony and each was provided with a house on a hill called Mathildenhöhe near the old town. Six of the houses were designed by the Austrian architect Joseph Maria Olbrich, a leading exponent of *Jugendstil*, or Art Nouveau style, but Behrens designed his own house, the most elaborate and expensive of them all. It was his first architectural work. He had never had any formal architectural training, but a privileged background and a private fortune proved to be adequate substitutes.

The Behrens House is vaguely Art Nouveau in style, but its upright form, its steep pyramid roof, its gables and its dormer windows are not markedly different from those of many other bourgeois German houses of the period. An unusual feature is the bold marking of the white stucco façades with pilasters and ogee arches

in dark green glazed bricks. Viewed from the north or entrance side, the house appears to be two storeys high, but from the garden side it is obvious that there are service rooms (including the kitchen) in the basement, and guests' and children's rooms in the attic.

The main event of the interior is the suite of ground-floor rooms designed for stylish living and entertaining. In the entrance hall, an operatically sweeping stair faces a large opening with two steps down into the music room, a rather dark, solemn space with marble-clad walls and black or grey furniture, including a grand piano. The plan is square and the ceiling is raised so that the room is almost a cube. Another large opening in the adjacent wall is flanked by Egyptian-style figures holding crystal lamps and contributing further to the generally funereal atmosphere.

Through the opening, the dining room is a deliberate contrast: brightly lit by a big bay window, with white furniture and panelling and a red carpet. A door in the corner leads out onto a small terrace and flight of steps down into the garden. Upstairs on the first floor, Behrens' study and its adjoining library extend upwards into the roof with half-timbered sloping ceilings.

Like many architects' own houses, the Behrens House was an advertisement and a manifesto as much as a home. It formed part of the Darmstadt colony's first major exhibition in 1901, and Behrens produced a special coloured brochure for visitors. He designed almost every element of the house: furniture, wall and floor coverings, light fittings, curtains, even cutlery and crockery. It is, to use the composer Wagner's term, a *Gesamtkunstwerk*, or total work of art.

Behrens and the other members of the colony believed that they were creating a new kind of art, the art of daily life. Later, the Modernists took this idea and made of it a radical new style. Behrens played a key part in this development, not least because his architectural office in Berlin employed three of the great names of 20th-century architecture: Walter Gropius, Ludwig Mies van der Rohe and Le Corbusier.

1 Ground Floor Plan

1 Entrance
2 Cupboard
3 Hall
4 Music room
5 Dining room
6 Ladies' room

2 Elevation

3 First Floor Plan

1 Bedroom
2 Bathroom
3 Gentleman's study
4 Library

4 Section A–A

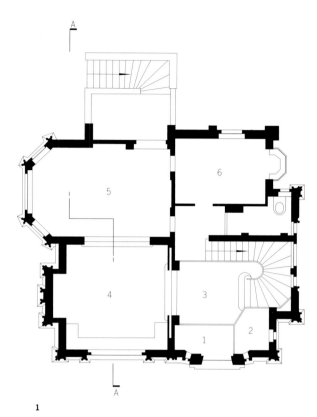

1

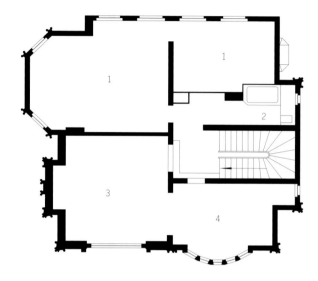

3

2

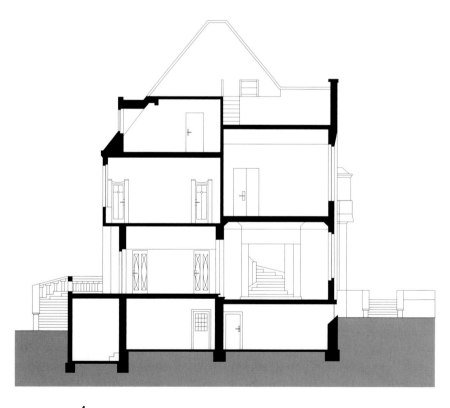

4

Orchards

Edwin Lutyens, 1869–1944

Surrey, UK; 1902

It was Edwin Lutyens more than any other architect who carried forward the English Arts and Crafts tradition of Philip Webb and Richard Norman Shaw into the twentieth century. Lutyens brought a new freedom and inventiveness to the style, but for the first 15 years of his career, from 1890 onwards, his chief source of inspiration remained the English domestic architecture of the sixteenth and seventeenth centuries. Orchards, with its coursed rubble walls, oak-framed windows and picturesque brick chimneys, might easily be mistaken for an Elizabethan farmhouse. The clients were Sir William and Lady Julia Chance, who first encountered their architect at the top of a ladder supervising the construction of a house, Munstead Wood, for their future neighbour, the celebrated gardener Gertrude Jekyll. They liked what they saw and promptly engaged both Lutyens and Jekyll to design their new house and garden.

Orchards looks larger than it actually is because its plan is composed of relatively narrow, single-aspect wings wrapped around a courtyard. The west side of the courtyard cannot properly be described as a 'wing' since it consists only of a single-storey loggia of semicircular stone arches. All the main rooms — hall (or drawing room),

dining room and study — are on the ground floor of the south wing, opening onto a sunny terrace. The east wing is mostly the domain of the staff, and the north wing is divided by the carriage entrance, with Lady Julia's painting and sculpture studio to one side. Two seemingly ad hoc extensions — a small enclosed service yard to the east and a stable block to the north — contribute to the building's air of relaxed practicality. It was this lack of ostentation that so much impressed the German diplomat Hermann Muthesius, who chose Orchards to represent Lutyens's work in his influential 1904 survey *Das Englische Haus*.

A masterly use of materials, a satisfying rightness of proportion and a hundred delightful details make this not just a pseudo-vernacular house but a work of art. The walls are of yellowish Bargate stone, enlivened with courses of tiles laid flat, Roman fashion. Roofs are steeply pitched to show off large areas of the same red tiles, punctuated by chimney stacks turned through 45 degrees to emphasize their verticality, and by diminutive dormers, including a fake one above the carriage entrance. Other windows are expansively arranged — either in continuous ribbons, such as the ones that wrap around the porch at first-

floor level, or with double rows of casements in important rooms. The big, triple-layer bay window of the studio, with its own hipped roof, was repeated on a larger scale in the main hall of the slightly later Deanery Gardens in Berkshire.

The garden is as important as the house, but the relationship between the two is informal, almost accidental-looking. The dining room opens onto an arcaded loggia tucked under the south-east corner of the building, facing a small terrace. From here the view over the Surrey countryside is spectacular. A short flight of steps in the corner of the terrace leads down to the so-called Dutch garden; this is a piece of symmetrical outdoor architecture resembling the remains of a ruined chapel made into raised flowerbeds and paved walks. Beyond lies the croquet lawn and to the left the big walled kitchen garden with elaborate arched entrances, which again seem to suggest the presence of an earlier, larger agricultural establishment. It is all a kind of fiction, but the world it creates is nevertheless seductive.

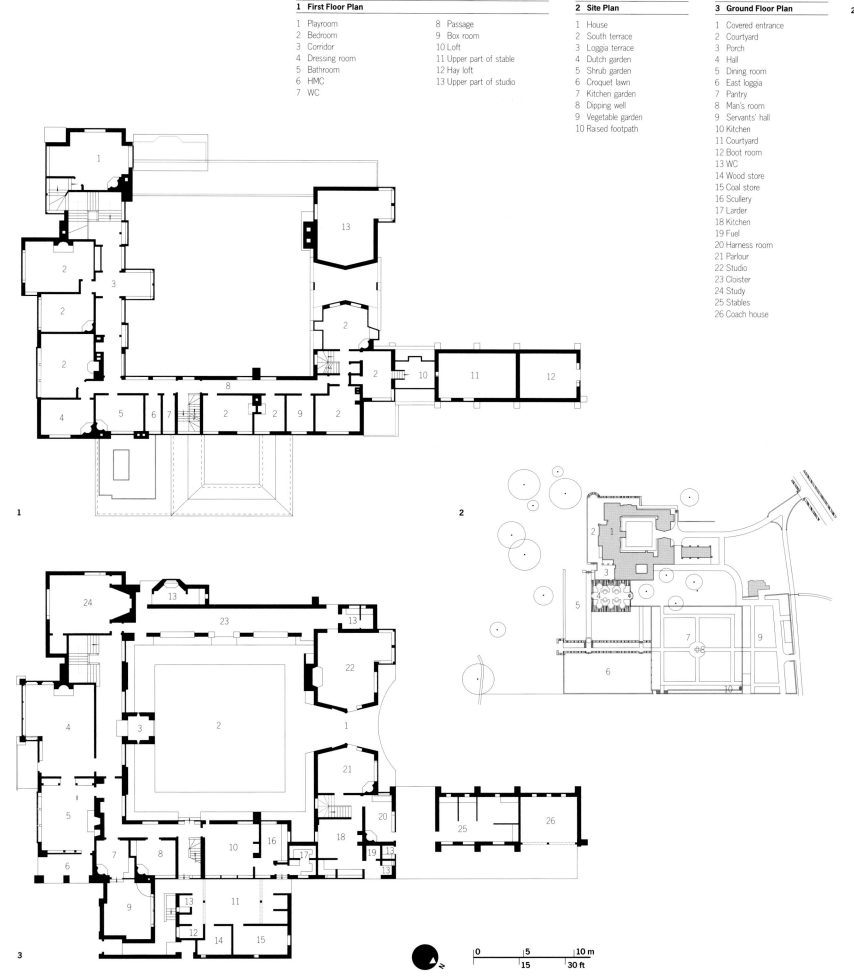

1 First Floor Plan

1 Playroom
2 Bedroom
3 Corridor
4 Dressing room
5 Bathroom
6 HMC
7 WC

8 Passage
9 Box room
10 Loft
11 Upper part of stable
12 Hay loft
13 Upper part of studio

2 Site Plan

1 House
2 South terrace
3 Loggia terrace
4 Dutch garden
5 Shrub garden
6 Croquet lawn
7 Kitchen garden
8 Dipping well
9 Vegetable garden
10 Raised footpath

3 Ground Floor Plan

1 Covered entrance
2 Courtyard
3 Porch
4 Hall
5 Dining room
6 East loggia
7 Pantry
8 Man's room
9 Servants' hall
10 Kitchen
11 Courtyard
12 Boot room
13 WC
14 Wood store
15 Coal store
16 Scullery
17 Larder
18 Kitchen
19 Fuel
20 Harness room
21 Parlour
22 Studio
23 Cloister
24 Study
25 Stables
26 Coach house

0   5   10 m

15   30 ft

Hollybank

Charles Voysey, 1857–1941

Chorleywood, Hertfordshire, UK; 1903

The productive phase of Charles Voysey's career was short, and he designed only a few, mostly quite modest houses, but the style of those houses was so accurately attuned to the taste of the English middle class that it became the very image of the nation at home. A watered-down version of the style was reproduced tens of thousands of times in the 1920s and 1930s by the speculative developers who built suburbia.

'Metroland' was the name given to that part of suburbia that stretched north out of London along the Metropolitan railway line. Voysey himself lived at its outer limits, just ten minutes' walk from Chorleywood station, in a house called The Orchard that he designed in 1899. Next door, some distance away along the same lane, he built Hollybank for a local doctor, incorporating a consulting room and a waiting room. It displays most of the essential Voysey features: roughcast walls with corner buttresses, steeply pitched roofs, big gables, stone-dressed windows with leaded lights, and chimneys placed wherever they are needed, apparently artlessly but somehow completing the composition. It looks innocent, as if constructed by a local craftsman in a local style, but in fact it is full of artifice. The informality is

carefully gauged, the result of countless small artistic judgments and precise specifications: the colour of the roof tiles, the thickness of the tiled string courses separating the elevations, the shape of the chimney pots, the angle of the buttresses.

The Orchard has a long front elevation with gables at each end, but Hollybank is smaller and shorter, as if the central section had been taken away and the gables pushed together. This creates a potentially uneasy duality, making Hollybank look like two semi-detached houses, an impression reinforced by the two front doors, one for the surgery and one for the house. Yet, by attention to detail, Voysey avoids a conflict and creates a satisfying whole. The gables are the same size, but the front doors are different; the windows are asymmetrically disposed (those on the second floor are a later addition) and the main roof rises up between the gables to tie them together.

Inside, the plan is casual and cottage-like. The main living room is also the entrance hall. One corner is taken out for a draught lobby, as if this were some ad hoc adaptation, and at the other end of the room an arched opening leads to the main staircase. This is hardly an efficient plan. Circulation space takes up about one third of

the room, and the corner staircase necessitates a long corridor on the first floor. But, for Voysey, the feel of the spaces took priority over diagrammatic clarity. The mixture of functions is deliberate. The floor of Delabole slate seems to say 'hall', while the green-tiled fireplace seems to say 'living room'. This ambiguity is not a Postmodern joke; it is a refusal to let domestic life be pigeonholed. Arches have an important role. The doorway to the service corridor is arched, and the wall between the hall and the staircase is pierced by a pair of lunettes above the picture rail. There is also a big arched recess for bookshelves to the right of the fireplace. There is no structural logic to these arches but they soften and humanize the space. Versions of them are being constructed right now in ordinary houses all over England.

Voysey liked to design every detail of his houses, from the cast-iron fireplaces and built-in washstands in the bedrooms to his favourite red curtains, sewn exactly in accordance with his specification. It is paradoxical that such an obsessive control of detail should result in such a relaxed and comfortable interior.

1 Northwest Elevation

2 Southeast Elevation

3 First Floor Plan

1 Bedroom
2 Dressing room
3 Box room
4 Bathroom
5 WC

4 Southwest Elevation

5 Ground Floor Plan

1 Hall
2 Dining room
3 Lavatory
4 Consulting room
5 Dispensary
6 Waiting room
7 Kitchen and scullery
8 Larder
9 Coal cellar
10 Garage
11 Yard

6 Northeast Elevation

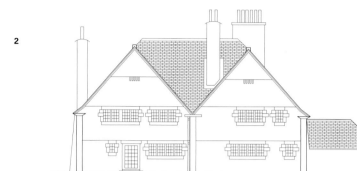

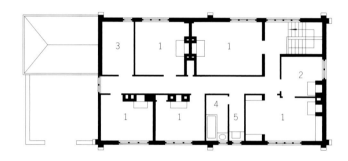

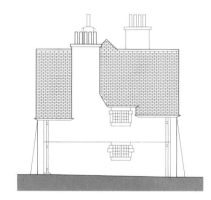

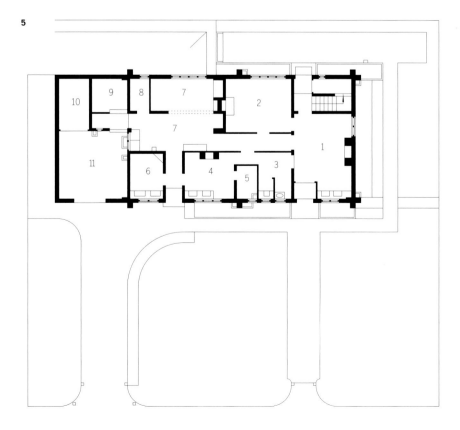

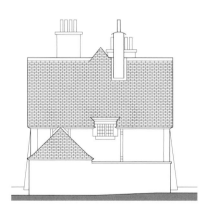

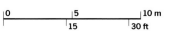

Hill House

Charles Rennie Mackintosh, 1868–1928

Helensburgh, Dunbartonshire, UK; 1904

The architecture of Charles Rennie Mackintosh is like an elegant Art Nouveau bridge between the nineteenth-century Gothic Revival and twentieth-century Modernism. It was influenced by the Scottish tower-house tradition and the English Arts and Crafts school, as well as the international Art Nouveau movement, of which Mackintosh was an honoured and important member. But it is also a kind of abstract art that looks forward to Cubism in painting and Functionalism in architecture. Somehow Mackintosh managed to design buildings that were traditional and new at the same time — like his masterpiece, the Glasgow School of Art, which combines stone walls and arched openings with huge metal-framed studio windows that might have been borrowed from a German factory.

Mackintosh designed only three important houses: Windyhill at Kilmacolm, Renfrewshire, completed in 1899; the House for an Art Lover, a design that won second prize in an international competition in 1901 but was not built until 1999, in Glasgow; and Hill House in upper Helensburgh, which was completed in 1904, has been well preserved and is now one of the best places to see the Mackintosh style in the flesh. The

Hill House client was Walter Blackie, a prominent Glasgow publisher, who was introduced to Mackintosh by his art director, Talwin Morris.

The house stands on a south-facing slope with panoramic views over the River Clyde, and the main entrance is at the narrow, west end. Immediately, the visitor is confronted by an elevation that could only have been designed by Mackintosh. The separate parts are conventional enough — a gable, a recessed porch, a couple of chimneys, a scattering of small windows, and a larger bay window at first-floor level — but the way in which they are grouped turns the whole composition into proto-Modernist sculpture.

The larger chimney, which is battered on one side, stands proud of the gable wall, bringing with it sections of wall on either side to form a strikingly asymmetrical figure. The bay window is also asymmetrical, glancing left towards the river.

This is more than simply informality; it is a new abstract language. And there can be no doubt that Mackintosh was consciously creating this effect. Why else would he take the harling right up to the edges of the forms, omitting the normal stone quoins and copings? The whole house is composed in a similar way, from the inside out,

but with an eye to picturesque effect. The eastern half is given over almost entirely to the staff and the children, who occupy a version of a tower house, three storeys high, with many a gable, chimney and projecting bay. There is even a spiral staircase in a 'baronial' turret tucked into the re-entrant south-east corner.

The main rooms in the western half — library, drawing room and dining room — all face south over the terrace and are ranged along a generous hallway with the main staircase on the north side. Each room, including the hallway, has a distinctive character. This is not just a question of decoration — the white walls, stencilled pink roses and spindly black furniture for which Mackintosh is well known as an interior designer — but a question of space. The large bay window in the drawing room, for example, seems like a flat-roofed afterthought from the outside — but inside, with its built-in seat and low bookcases, it gently invites you to pause, sit and read.

1 Second Floor Plan

1 Kitchen
2 Bathroom
3 Bedroom
4 Tank room
5 Living room/school room
6 Attic

2 First Floor Plan

1 Storage
2 Kitchen
3 Bathroom
4 Dressing room
5 Master bedroom
6 Exhibition room/bedroom
7 Interpretation room/
dressing room
8 Living room/night nursery
9 Study/day nursery
10 Bedroom/night nursery
11 Bedroom

3 Ground Floor Plan

1 Entrance
2 Cloakroom and WC
3 Library
4 Hall
5 Storage
6 Drawing room
7 Dining room
8 Pantry
9 Office
10 WC
11 Kitchen
12 Tea room
13 Shop

4 Section A–A

5 South Elevation

6 North Elevation

7 West Elevation

8 East Elevation

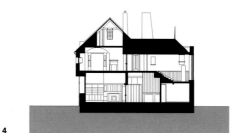

4

1

5

6

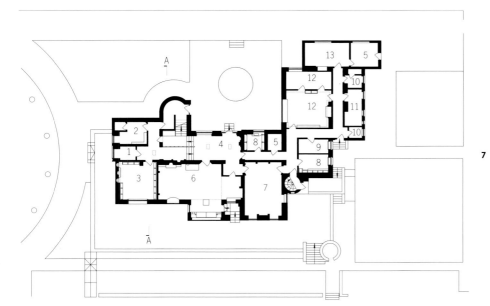

2

7

3

8

0   5   10 m

15   30 ft

Gamble House

Charles and Henry Greene, 1868–1957 and 1870–1954

Pasadena, California, USA; 1908

Before they qualified as architects, Charles and Henry Greene studied woodwork, metalwork and toolmaking at the manual training school of Washington University. The brothers were not simply designers but craftsmen too, and as the influence of the English Arts and Crafts movement gathered strength in the USA in the early years of the twentieth century, they fell under its spell. They were familiar with the works of John Ruskin and William Morris, but their knowledge was in their hands as well as their heads. Early experiments with the standard Colonial styles soon gave way to tougher, more honest buildings, the products not of pictorial representation but of an intimate dialogue between man and materials.

Yet the Gamble House does not look remotely English. From a distance, it vaguely resembles a Swiss chalet or perhaps a palatial log cabin, but close up, where the carpentry is visible, the strongest influence seems to be traditional Japanese architecture. The Greenes never went to Japan, but they probably saw and studied the Ho-o-den temple exhibited at the Chicago World Expo of 1893, which is said also to have influenced Frank Lloyd Wright. In the Gamble House, a Japanese-style post-and-beam structural system is cleverly combined with the simpler and lighter American balloon-frame method.

The external walls are softwood-framed and shingle-clad – no different in principle from the humblest shack – but attached to this basic core at first-floor level are three sleeping porches that resemble master carpenters' demonstration pieces. Two are propped up on stout double posts and the third is bracketed off in a corner of the ground-floor living room. Every post, beam, joist, purlin and rafter is visible in these structures, and every joint is enjoyed for its tectonic expressiveness. Projecting rafter ends are shaped and rounded, and balustrades are lovingly caressed by the craftsman's hand, though in form they are as plain as ranch fences.

But it is the main supporting structures that look most Japanese: parallel queen post trusses with subtly tapered struts and booms, or bracketed columns vaguely reminiscent of Torii temple gates. The sleeping porches are integrated with the rest of the house by their shared use of the shallow-pitched, many-gabled, generously overhanging roof. They read as rooms without walls rather than as outgrowths or extensions.

Japanese influence continues inside the house. The sumptuous front-to-back entrance hall is lined in rich red teak panelling and dominated by the large, but nevertheless bonsai-like, stained-glass oak tree that spreads its branches from the front door into side panels and fanlights. Most rooms have prominent picture rails, creating a strip of wall below the ceiling that corresponds to the decorative rammas of the traditional Japanese house. In the cruciform living room, the queen post trusses reappear to define bays in two arms of the cross: an inglenook on one side and a bay window overlooking the garden terrace on the other. In Mr Gamble's study, warm teak gives way to sober oak, and for once a vaguely English feature appears in the form of an almost gothic brick fireplace.

On the first floor, hardly less sumptuous bedrooms are spatially transformed by their adjacent sleeping porches. On the top floor, a single large attic room with windows all around serves as a kind of wind tower to promote healthy ventilation throughout the house, but it is also a good place from which to view the nearby valley of Arroyo Secco and the San Gabriel mountains beyond.

1 First Floor Plan

1 Bedroom
2 Linen room
3 Cupboard
4 Sleeping porch
5 Covered balcony

2 Attic Floor Plan

3 Ground Floor Plan

1 Hall
2 Dining room
3 Butler's pantry
4 Kitchen
5 Screened porch
6 Cold room
7 Cupboard
8 Bedroom
9 Living room
10 Den
11 Terrace

4 Basement Plan

1 Storage
2 Laundry
3 Vegetable room
4 Coal bin
5 Cellar

5 Section A–A

6 Elevation

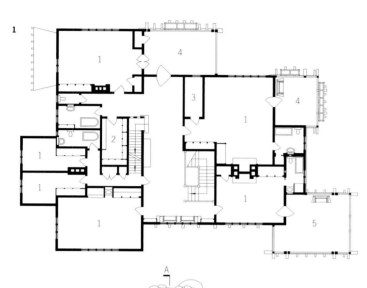

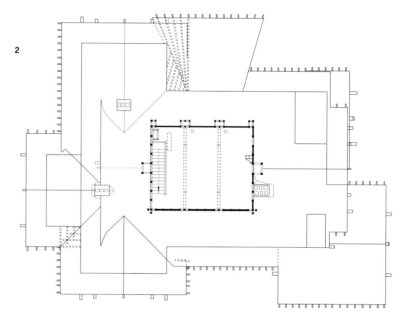

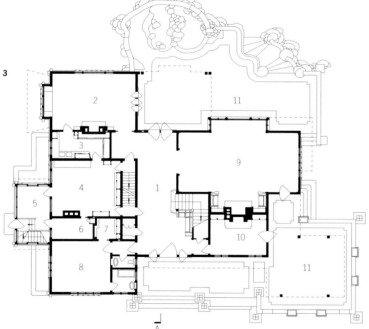

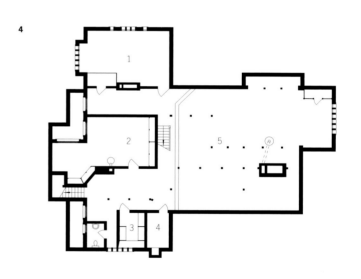

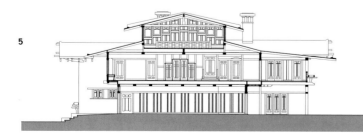

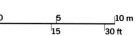

Robie House

Frank Lloyd Wright, 1867–1959

Chicago, USA; 1909

Last and best of Frank Lloyd Wright's 'Prairie' houses, the Robie House seems designed for the open plain rather than the narrow street-corner lot that it occupies in the Chicago suburb of Hyde Park. When first built, its exaggeratedly horizontal form must have seemed a weird apparition among its conventionally upright neighbours. It has no façades, no ordinary external walls or windows, and no front door. It practically fills its site; what little open space remains is gathered into the overall stratified composition by dwarf walls and planters. Horizontality is further emphasized by stone sills, window heads and copings, and by thin Roman bricks with raked-out horizontal mortar joints.

Wright's compositional method at this time was to arrange symmetrical forms in asymmetrical clusters. The basis of the composition is a long, apparently symmetrical, two-storey block with a very shallow pitched roof cantilevered out to an improbable extent at both ends. At first-floor level on the south side, facing the road, 14 french windows open onto a cantilevered balcony like the deck of a ship. The balcony casts a deep shadow over more french windows on the ground floor. The symmetry is an illusion since the raised terrace at the west end, over a semi-basement, is

balanced by the wall of the open service yard at the east end. But symmetry is only one factor in a more complex equation. Above the main block, a third, bedroom storey, complete with windows, balconies and hipped roofs, creates the off-centre cross axis that sets the whole composition in motion. On one side, a huge chimney emerges to anchor all the horizontal planes below. Lower down at the east end of the building, another hipped roof covers the three-car garage and staff wing.

But how do we get in? The main entrance is at the back of the building, at the end of a long footpath between the main block and the northern site boundary. Bypassing the billiard room and playroom that occupy most of the ground floor, we cross the rather dark entrance hall and climb the central staircase to emerge into one of the great domestic interiors of the twentieth century: a long, low room like a ship's salon, brightly lit by those 14 south-facing french windows. The space is divided into living and dining zones by the hearth — always for Wright the symbol of family life and attachment to the earth. Its freestanding brick chimney is a massive presence but not an obstruction, allowing us to pass either side and see the whole length of the ceiling through a

rectangular opening at the top. The ceiling is divided into panels, each equipped with two types of electric light: glass globes on either side of the raised central area, and concealed bulbs behind wooden grilles in the lower areas at the sides. At each end of the long space, triangular bay windows create intimate sitting and dining areas. These bays are scarcely visible from the outside, so deeply overshadowed are they by the vast cantilevering roofs. Such roofs cannot be built in timber; in fact, they are supported by two hidden steel roof beams that extend along the whole length of the main block.

Frederick C. Robie worked in the family bicycle-manufacturing business and had plans to break into the rapidly growing market for automobiles. But then his father died leaving crippling debts, his wife left him and he was obliged to sell the house in 1911, a mere two years after its completion. It is still in good repair and is open to the public.

1 Section A–A

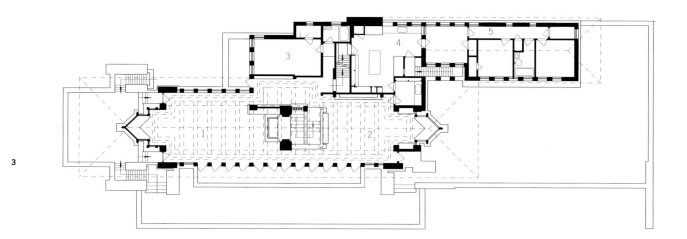

2 Second Floor Plan

1 Bedroom
2 Master bedroom

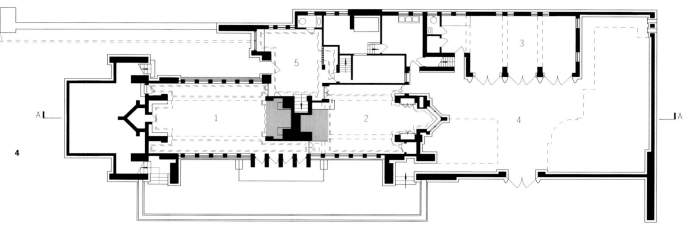

3 First Floor Plan

1 Living room
2 Dining room
3 Guest room
4 Kitchen
5 Staff quarters

4 Ground Floor Plan

1 Billiard room
2 Playroom
3 Garage
4 Service yard
5 Entrance hall

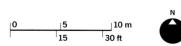

Villa Schwob

Le Corbusier, 1887–1965

La Chaux-de-Fonds, Switzerland; 1917

Before he became Le Corbusier and the greatest Modernist architect of the twentieth century, Charles Edouard Jeanneret pursued a brief and not very professional career as a local architect in his Swiss home town of La Chaux-de-Fonds. He designed six houses in the town, including one for his parents. None of them shows any hint of the Modernism to come, but the last one, the Villa Schwob, is stranger and more original than its rather conventional predecessors. It was also the only one that the mature Le Corbusier was proud to call his own.

The Schwobs were a cultured local family who had grown rich from watchmaking. They knew Jeanneret's parents' house and wanted something similar but bigger. Jeanneret was fresh from his inspiring travels around Europe, including the Voyage d'Orient, and he was determined to make an architectural fresh start with this important commission. He strained for originality in every detail – and the effort is obvious, resulting in a clumsy complexity.

The core of the composition is a two-storey box, square on plan, almost a cube if the height of the basement is included. The box is intersected symmetrically by a church-like form with rounded ends or apses that project too far on either side to be mere bay windows. Two more forms are added to this core: a flat-roofed third floor, set back behind shallow roof terraces, and a narrow, three-storey entrance and staircase block forming the street frontage on the north side. These additional forms threaten the identity of the apsed box, which is therefore provided with a large cornice to reassert its outline. Critics have read much into the bizarre street elevation, with its blank square panel like a cinema screen. Colin Rowe, for example, sees it as the prototype of many provocatively flat façades in Le Corbusier's later work, from the Villa Stein (see pages 54–55) to the monastery church at La Tourette.

Inside the house, the main spatial event is a double-height salon lit by a very large window in the south elevation. On the ground floor, the apses on either side contain a dining room and a games room, and at the garden end the leftover corners of the box are filled by a library and a *coin de feu*. Upstairs, the apses are occupied by the two main bedrooms. The only views down into the salon are from a balcony across the north end and little grilled spyholes set in otherwise blank oriels adjacent to the big window. There are more bedrooms and rooms for staff on the top floor. Functions seem have been assigned to spaces arbitrarily so that the whole plan resembles an ad hoc internal adaptation of a rigidly symmetrical external form. The kitchen could not be made to fit and had to be hidden behind the garden wall to the right of the main entrance.

The dominant external material is high-quality yellow brickwork, but this is an infill to a reinforced-concrete frame – one of the earliest domestic applications of this technology. In 1916 Jeanneret was already promoting his Domino House concept as the answer to postwar reconstruction. Some of the Domino sketches include features reminiscent of Villa Schwob, but it was the drawing of the naked structure that became the Modernist icon.

1

5
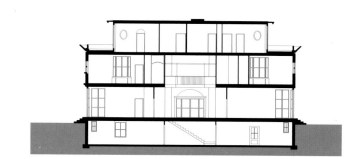

2
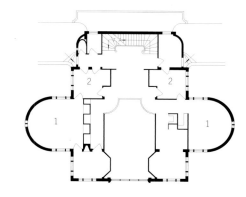

6
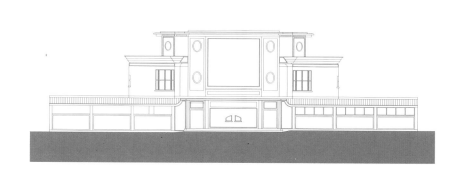

3
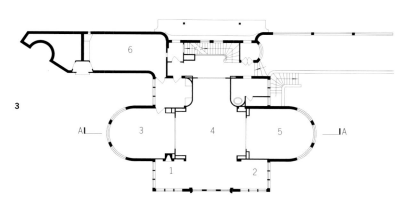

7

4
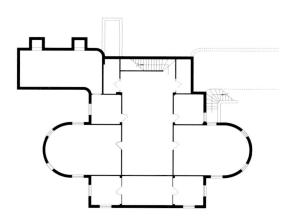

8
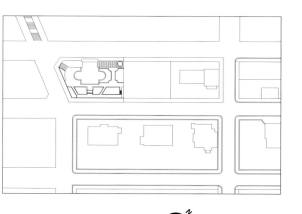

Villa Snellman

Eric Gunnar Asplund, 1885–1945

Djursholm, near Stockholm, Sweden; 1917–18

Vernacular but also classical — and even, in its lightness and austerity, seeming to prepare itself for the coming of Modernism — the Villa Snellman is simple on the surface but complex and subtle underneath. No wonder it became a favourite reference point for Postmodernists of the 1980s.

Erik Gunnar Asplund called it 'an attempt to accommodate a modern house in a structure one and a half rooms wide'. The main, two-storey wing is a plain rectangle, divided longitudinally, with a living zone on one side facing the garden, and a circulation and service zone on the other side facing the entrance courtyard. Nothing could be simpler. At first sight the plans, with their slightly angled internal walls, resemble those of an old farmhouse. The single-storey servants' wing, set a few degrees off the right angle, reinforces the impression of an ad hoc adaptation and an unthinking adherence to a vernacular tradition. It is, in fact, all designed and deliberate.

The angled walls were a new invention. It was probably Ragnar Ostberg, the designer of Stockholm City Hall, then under construction, who first used angled walls in houses as a means of reconciling a functional interior with a symmetrical façade. In the Villa Snellman, however, the device seems designed not to solve an architectural problem but to create a sense of informality, a new kind of relaxed domestic space. The angled outer wall of the passage on the upper floor is a clever way to integrate awkward elements such as the spiral staircase to the attic, but the very subtle kink in the opposite wall can have no functional justification. It is the light touch of the artist.

The not-quite-circular upper hall is another artistic subtlety. The house was originally to have been built in stone, and in the plans of the earlier version the upper hall (really a living room) is a perfect circle. But with the change to timber, probably to save money, Asplund grasped the opportunity to create a freer, more organic shape. The circle in a square was a favourite Asplund form, and it is perhaps not too fanciful to see this upper hall as related to the great drum of his most famous work, Stockholm Public Library.

The subtleties of the plan are more than matched by the subtleties of the elevations. This is unmistakably a classical building. Most of the windows are small and square, and there are no columns or cornices, but the walls are decorated by some rather emaciated stucco swags. On the courtyard side these swags occur beneath the attic windows, but on garden side they occur between them. In both elevations a small lunette marks the position of the upper hall with its higher ceiling pushing up into the attic space.

These elevations can now be seen as very different — one consisting of four bays, the other of five. Moreover, the windows are not arranged symmetrically. On the garden side, looking from left to right, the first-floor and attic windows become further and further out of line with the ground-floor windows. On the courtyard side, all the windows are moved over to the right, as if being pushed by the staff wing.

Since there is nothing in the plan to explain these adjustments, some critics have read into them psychological meanings. In particular, the two doors standing side by side — the main entrance with its canopy and the French window of the lower hall — have been interpreted as an unsettling ambiguity. Asplund might or might not have intended this, but it was exactly the sort of thing the Postmodernists were looking for.

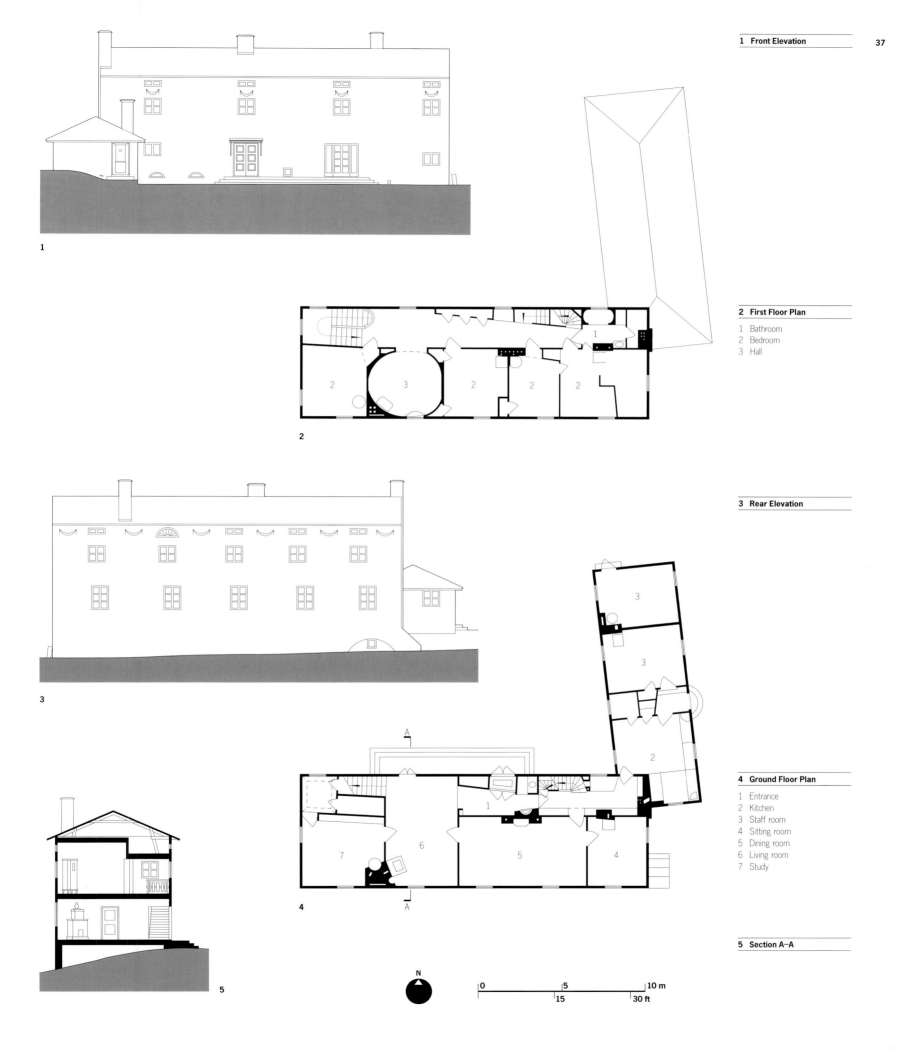

1 Front Elevation

2 First Floor Plan

1 Bathroom
2 Bedroom
3 Hall

3 Rear Elevation

4 Ground Floor Plan

1 Entrance
2 Kitchen
3 Staff room
4 Sitting room
5 Dining room
6 Living room
7 Study

5 Section A–A

N

0   5   10 m
  15   30 ft

Villa Henny

Robert van 't Hoff, 1887–1979

Huis ter Heide, The Netherlands; 1915–19

Robert van 't Hoff was born in Rotterdam in 1887 but received his architectural education in England, first at Birmingham School of Art and later at the Architectural Association in London. In the years before the First World War, he lived in Chelsea and designed several houses in the Arts and Crafts style, including one for the painter Augustus John. Then, in 1913, he received a gift from his father that changed his architectural outlook totally. It was a copy of the now famous Wasmuth portfolio of designs by Frank Lloyd Wright. So impressed was van 't Hoff by the revolutionary new architecture depicted in the portfolio that he immediately left for the USA, missing the Augustus John housewarming party.

While in America, van 't Hoff visited Wright himself and many of his buildings, including the Larkin Building in Buffalo, the Midway Gardens in Chicago and the Unity Temple in Oak Park. Returning to the Netherlands in 1914, he built a villa in Huis ter Heide, the Verloop Summer House, which, though more modest in scale, was somewhat similar in form to Wright's Prairie-style houses. But it was his next villa in Huis ter Heide, for an Amsterdam businessman called A. B. Henny, that architectural history has chosen to canonize.

The reason is that it was innovative in two ways: it was the first major building in Europe to show the clear influence of Wright, and it was built in a new material: reinforced concrete.

Unlike Wright's, van 't Hoff's designs tend to be rather stiff and formal. Villa Henny is a neat, contained object standing in the middle of a lawn with a small companion in the form of a square pool. Externally, it is symmetrical about both axes and the plan suffers from a slight awkwardness in its effort to preserve the symmetry. Half of the ground floor is taken up by an enormous south-facing living room dominated by a central fireplace and opening out onto a raised terrace. The rather narrow, axial entrance hall is on the north side, between service rooms that accommodate themselves to the given outline of the building as best they can. Upstairs, symmetry rules even more strictly. Bedrooms, bathrooms and studies slot themselves into a cross-in-square plan reminiscent of a Byzantine church.

It is in the treatment of the exterior that the influence of Wright and the structural potential of reinforced concrete come into play. Nothing is two-dimensional. The walls have re-entrant corners and set-backs in section, forming balconies on the

upper level and planting boxes below; the windows are all projecting bays made of rows of identical sashes in threes, fours and eights (not including the end returns); and the square, flat slab of the roof finishes the whole composition off with great panache, cantilevering out over the corners in a way that must have seemed very daring in 1919.

Having made his reputation with the Villa Henny, van 't Hoff joined the avant-garde De Stijl group, contributing articles to its journal and collaborating with Theo van Doesburg on several projects. He also became a communist and interested himself in the design of workers' housing, though few actual buildings resulted. In 1933, thoroughly disillusioned with architecture, he moved back to England to live in an anarchist commune. He died in the Hampshire village of New Milton in 1979.

1 First Floor Plan

1 Bathroom
2 Bedroom
3 Main bedroom
4 Hall
5 Study
6 Dressing room
7 Guest room

2 Ground Floor Plan

1 Entrance
2 Cloakroom
3 Kitchen
4 Sitting room
5 Study
6 Lobby
7 Storage
8 Living room
9 Terrace
10 Pond

3 South Elevation

4 West Elevation

1

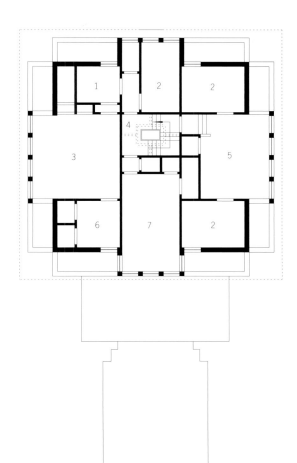

2

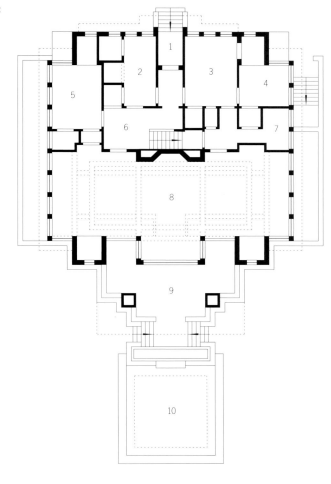

3

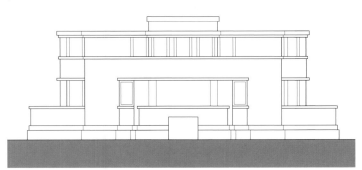

4

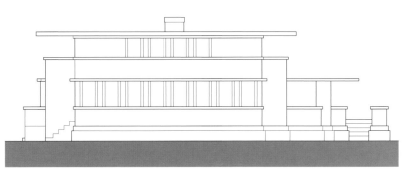

Barnsdall House

Frank Lloyd Wright, 1867–1959

Los Angeles, California, USA; 1917–21

Aline Barnsdall was a wealthy heiress, a theatre producer and – shockingly for the time – an unmarried mother. She moved from Chicago to Los Angeles in 1916 and three years later bought an entire city block of 14.5 hectares (36 acres) called Olive Hill. Her plan was to develop the site as a theatre colony, including a 1,250-seat theatre, apartments for artists and administrators, a cinema, a commercial strip on Hollywood Boulevard, and a large house for herself and her daughter. She wanted Frank Lloyd Wright, whom she had met in Chicago, to be her architect. It was not a good time to ask, however.

Wright's career in America had not yet recovered from the effects of tragedy and scandal in his personal life, and he was spending much of his time in Tokyo building the Imperial Hotel. When at last he produced a design, it marked a complete change of direction in his domestic architecture. The Prairie Style that had made his name in the Midwest was cast aside and a new theatrical romanticism made its first appearance – a style appropriate for a city of dreams.

The theatre colony idea was soon abandoned, but the Barnsdall House, popularly known as the Hollyhock House, went ahead. It stands in the middle of the site, at the top of the hill, arranged around a courtyard with the entrance on the northwest corner. The front of the house, however, is the symmetrical west wing facing the ocean, with the living room thrust forward in the centre. It is this dominant block, almost like a separate building, that proclaims the new style and dictates the architectural language of the rest of the house. Its elevations are divided into wall and roof zones of about equal height, separated by a plain cornice on which stands a row of the stylized hollyhocks that give the house its nickname.

Whereas the roofs of the Prairie houses had been shallow-pitched, elongated and overhanging, the roof here is flat and hidden by a high, battered parapet. In reality, this parapet is timber-framed and stuccoed, but it resembles solid stone, giving the building a monumental aspect. Ancient Mayan temples are usually cited as the inspiration for the form, although Wright seems never to have acknowledged the influence.

The living room is dominated by the fireplace – always for Wright a symbol of the family, but here perhaps tinged with irony given his own and his client's circumstances. It has a massive carved-stone overmantel lit by a rooflight, and a shallow pool in front of the hearth, but it is not placed on the main east–west axis as it might once have been. It has been moved to the south wall, leaving the way clear through to the courtyard. To anyone looking out across the courtyard, the east wing opposite takes the form of a bridge over a wide, low opening like a proscenium. And, sure enough, beyond the opening lies a little semicircular Greek theatre with a pool where the stage should be. But the whole courtyard is a kind of theatre. A prominent staircase in one corner encourages the 'audience' to explore the roof terraces, and the loggia roof in front of the living room serves as an elevated stage. House and garden are combined to form an ensemble more like a village than a house. In the southeast corner, Aline's and her daughter's bedrooms occupy a cluster of fantastical forms, variations on the Mayan theme with memories of the earlier style in the stained-glass windows and a timber-framed sleeping alcove.

Aline soon fell out with her architect, as many clients did, and she lived in the house for less than six years. It became the headquarters of the California Art Club, then was left vacant for a time in the 1940s, narrowly escaping demolition. It is now fully restored and open to the public.

1

2

3

1 Bedroom
2 Storage

4

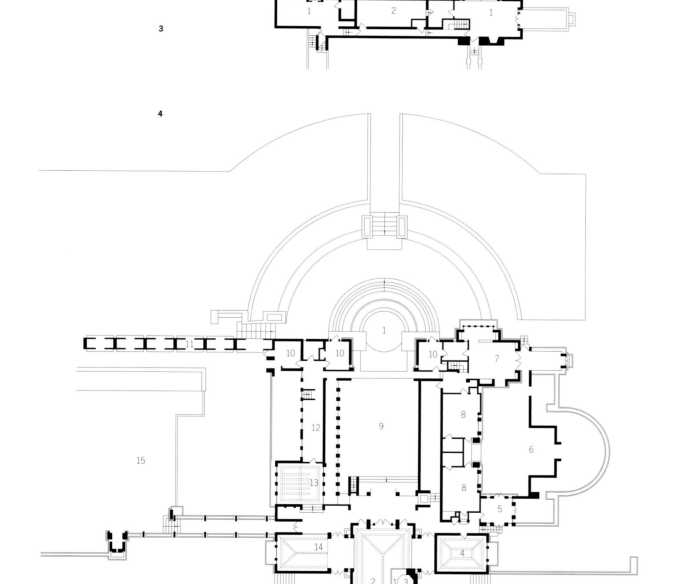

1 Pool
2 Living room
3 Fire
4 Library
5 Conservatory
6 Patio
7 Nursery
8 Bedroom
9 Garden courtyard
10 Staff rooms
11 Kennels
12 Kitchen
13 Dining room
14 Music room
15 Car court

0   5   10 m
15   30 ft

Ennis House

Frank Lloyd Wright, 1867–1959

Los Angeles, California, USA; 1923

The humble concrete block seems an unpromising medium for the creation of high architecture, but for a period during the 1920s Frank Lloyd Wright himself put his faith in it as the building technology of the future. He had moved his office from the Midwest to Los Angeles, and by 1921 had already launched his new West Coast style in the romantic, vaguely Mayan forms of the Barnsdall House (see pages 40–41). But in construction terms the style was skin deep, like a film set, and it fell short of Wright's commitment to nature and truth.

Wright had a vision of a new, solid, telluric architecture rising from the paved and sculpted earth in pyramid and ziggurat forms. Masonry was costly but concrete blocks could be standardized and mass-produced, and an ornamented block would be little more expensive than a plain one. At first – in the Alice Millard House, for example – the blocks were laid in ordinary mortar, but as the technology developed Wright introduced a more sophisticated steel-reinforcement system which knitted the blocks together in what he thought of as a kind of woven textile. In theory, the system required no mortar and could be used to make beams as well as walls and columns.

The Ennis House is the largest and most ambitions of the textile block houses. It is also the one that most clearly represents that vision of a new earth architecture. The half-acre site occupies the loop of a hairpin bend in Glendower Avenue as it winds its way up the foothills of the Santa Monica mountains. It is an eminence from which to view the city and on which to be viewed by the city. Little is known about the clients, Charles and Mabel Ennis, except that they made their money in the menswear business and were clearly socially ambitious. A shy and retiring couple would never have chosen such a site. The first impression of the house, viewed from below, is of a commanding cliff or rampart on which stands a cluster of squat, tapered and stepped masses. They are not quite pyramids or ziggurats, but they seem to owe their ancestry to some such ancient forms.

Everything is made of 40 cm (16 inch) square concrete blocks, either plain or ornamented with an asymmetrical relief pattern of interlocking squares. The lower ramparts or retaining walls are actually a separate structure, heavily reinforced and backfilled to create a level platform for the house. Wright's other block houses are mostly compact, upstanding structures, but the Ennis

House has a stretched-out, articulated plan that is held together by a spine in the form of an enclosed loggia 35 metres (100 feet) long overlooking the narrow garden on the north side. Inside, there is no escape from the blocks, which form the walls, the columns and even the flat ceilings. The main room is the dining room, a high formal space thrust forward to the edge of the rampart on the south side to take advantage of the best view over the city.

The Ennises fell out with their architect and supervised the later phases of the construction themselves. Wright could reasonably claim that the house as it was finished was not quite what he designed, although this does not excuse its overscaled and curiously undomestic character – more like a hotel or an embassy than a private house. Historically, however, it is of the first importance as an example of Wright's depth and breadth of vision, ranging from the pattern on a 40 cm (16 inch) block to a whole urban landscape.

1 Main Floor Plan

1 Dining room
2 Kitchen
3 Pantry
4 Hall
5 Living room
6 Cupboard
7 Bathroom
8 Study
9 Bedroom
10 Balcony
11 Terrace
12 Garden
13 Bridge over entrance

2 Lower Floor Plan

1 Entrance porch
2 Motor court
3 Garage

3 Section A–A

4 Section B–B

5 East Elevation

6 South Elevation

7 West Elevation

8 North Elevation

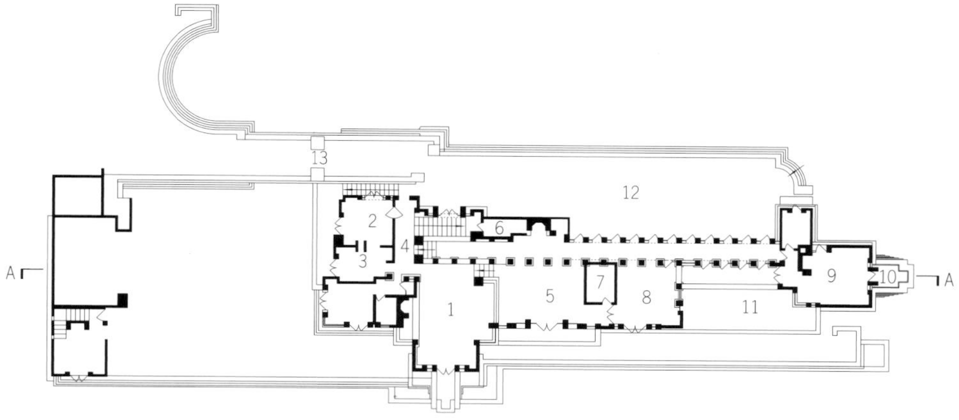

1

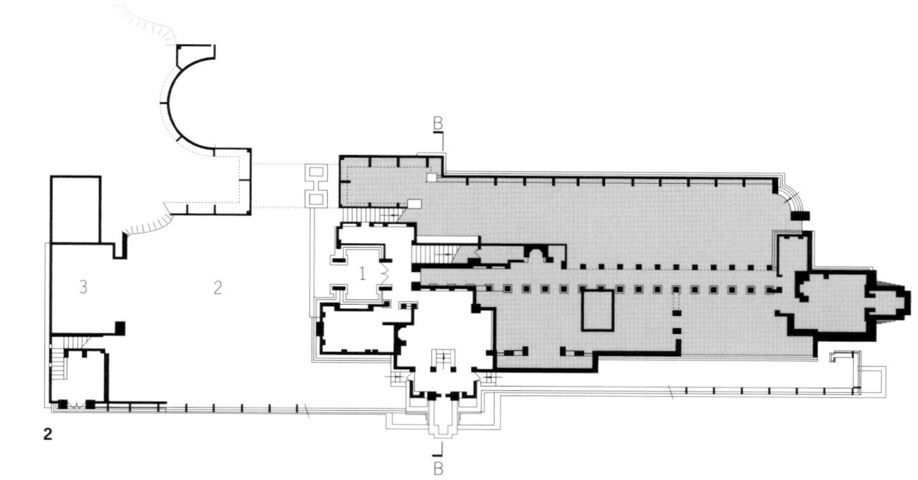

2

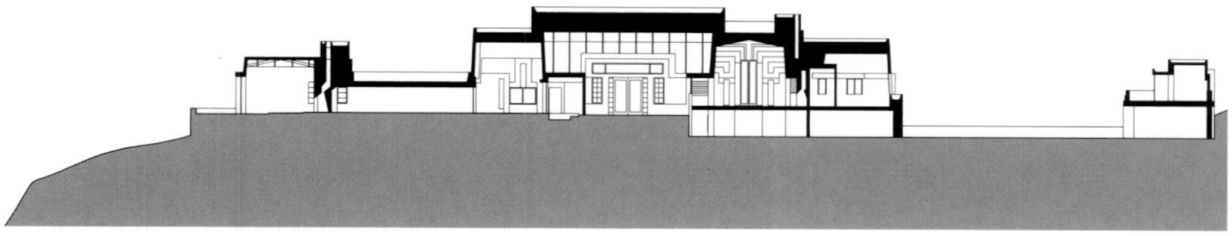

3

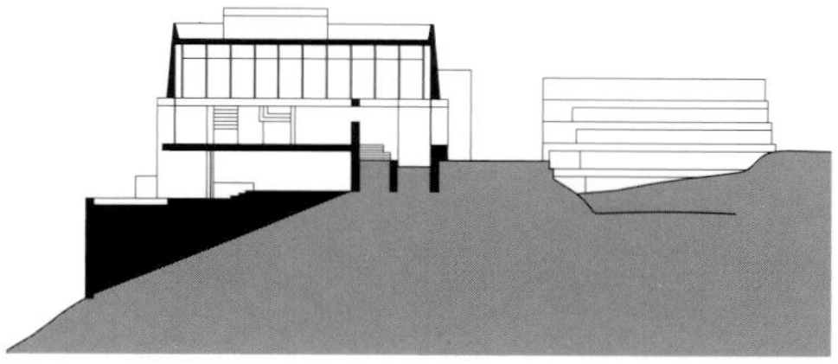

4

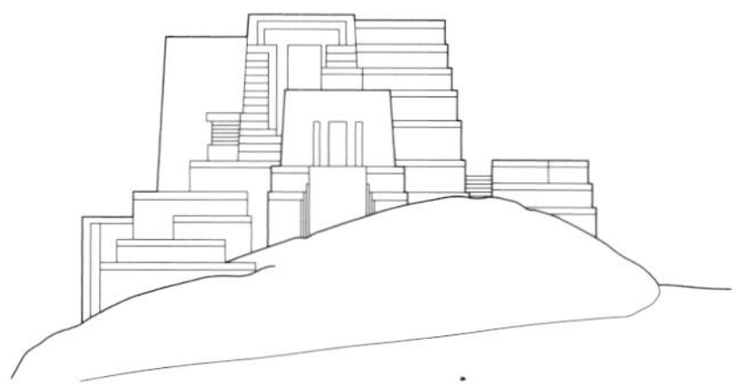

5

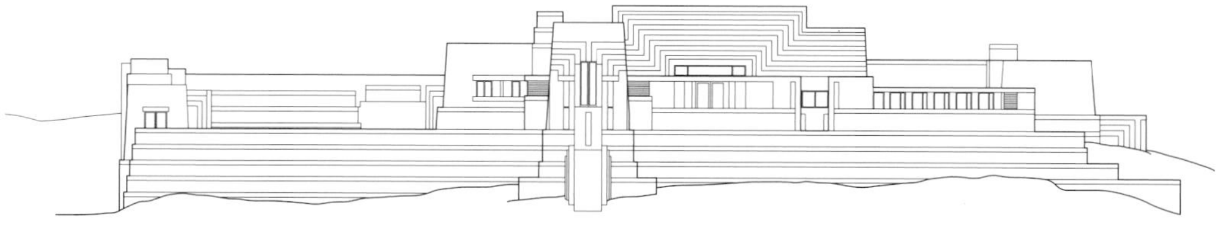

6

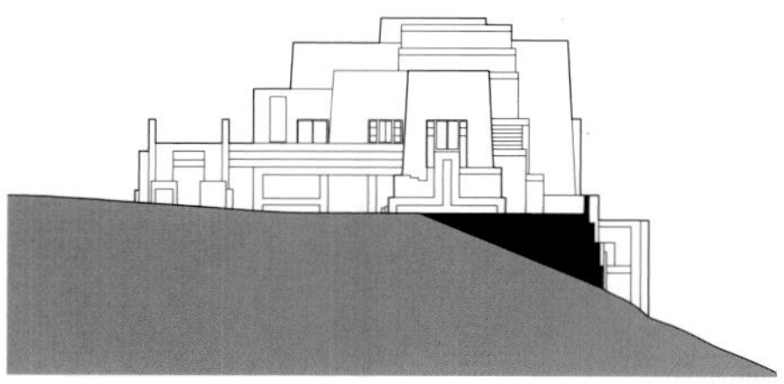

7

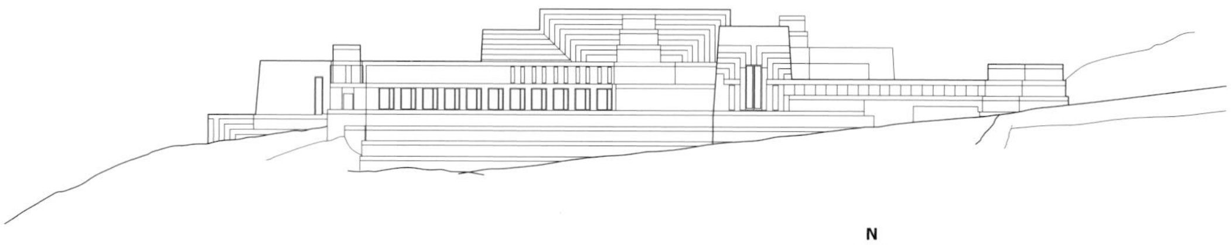

8

N

0 — 5 — 10 m
15 — 30 ft

Schröder House

Gerrit Rietveld, 1888–1964

Utrecht, The Netherlands; 1923–24

Imagine a world where the only forms are floating lines and planes, all at right angles, and the only colours are black, white, red, blue and yellow – in other words, a vast, three-dimensional painting by Mondrian. The Schröder house is a small sample of that world, a fragment of a global city of the future in which art and life are at last united. This was the vision of the De Stijl group of avant-garde painters and designers working in The Netherlands just after the First World War. Members included Theo van Doesburg, J. J. P. Oud, Robert van 't Hoff and, of course, Piet Mondrian.

Gerrit Rietveld, the co-designer of the Schröder House, joined the De Stijl group in 1919. He was mainly a furniture designer, and the previous year he had made an uncompromisingly 'elementarist' wooden armchair. It was unpainted, but some time in the early 1920s it received the Mondrian colour scheme that would make it famous as 'the red blue chair'.

Apart from furniture, Rietveld had designed a few shop and apartment interiors, but the Schröder House was his first complete building. The client was Truus Schröder-Schräder, a pharmacist by training but a progressive spirit and an art lover by inclination. When her lawyer

husband died, Truus Schröder-Schräder decided to begin a new life in a new house with her three young children. Rietveld might already have been her lover at that time. If he was not, he became so when they began to collaborate on the design of the house. The site was very ordinary – a left-over plot at the end of a terrace of brick houses – but it was right on the edge of town and looked out over open countryside. The view is now blocked by a motorway.

Although it shares a wall with the last house in the terrace, the Schröder House totally ignores its neighbours. The future has arrived, it seems to say, and the past has become irrelevant. It is composed not of walls and roofs but of abstract rectilinear planes, vertical or horizontal, painted white or grey. They are not made of concrete, as one might assume, but of rendered brick and timber. The planes seem to float – especially, for example, the front of the south-east-facing balcony and the roof that hovers over the fully glazed east corner. Linear elements such as mullions, transoms and steel columns are painted in stronger colours – black, red and yellow – as if to indicate that they are the stems from which the planes have grown. Windows are membranes of glass

stretched between the planes. Hinged sashes can be fixed in only two positions: shut or open at 90 degrees. There is no distinction between external and internal space. The planes and lines of the 'exterior' remain the same in the 'interior' – hard, painted surfaces with not a carpet or a curtain in sight. Furniture, much of which is built-in, speaks the same formal language. Wardrobes double as partitions, desks are extensions of windowsills, and beds are plain, boxed mattresses. On the lower floor, the plan is fairly conventional, with loadbearing walls forming distinct rooms, but on the first floor an ingenious system of sliding partitions either subdivides the space for daily living or opens it up for entertaining.

The house was a work of art, but it also served well as a home, and Truus Schröder-Schräder lived in it until her death in 1985. It survives now both as a building and as iconic image, a memory of a shining artistic vision. That vision proved less durable. Its end had already been signalled by 1924, when Mondrian fell out with van Doesburg because he had dared to put diagonal lines in his paintings.

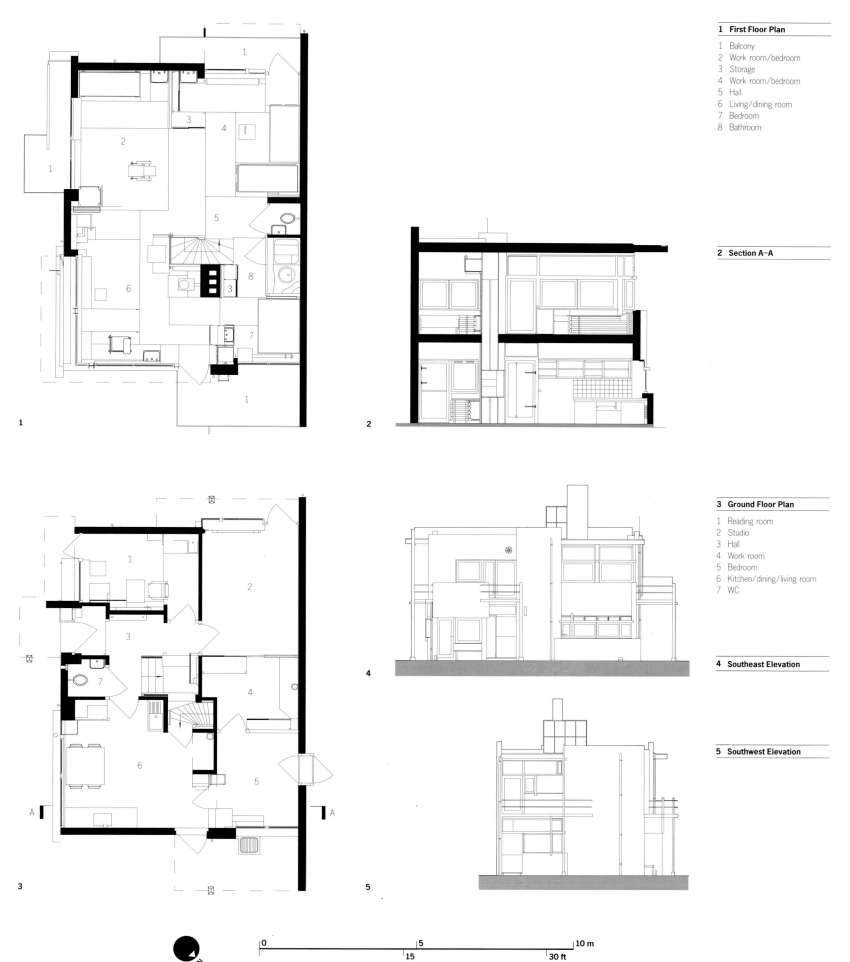

1 First Floor Plan

1 Balcony
2 Work room/bedroom
3 Storage
4 Work room/bedroom
5 Hall
6 Living/dining room
7 Bedroom
8 Bathroom

2 Section A–A

3 Ground Floor Plan

1 Reading room
2 Studio
3 Hall
4 Work room
5 Bedroom
6 Kitchen/dining/living room
7 WC

4 Southeast Elevation

5 Southwest Elevation

0   5   10 m

15   30 ft

Villas La Roche–Jeanneret

Le Corbusier, 1887–1965

Auteuil, France; 1925

By 1923, Charles Edouard Jeanneret, a provincial designer of classical and chalet-style houses, had moved to Paris and become Le Corbusier, a metropolitan Modernist of boundless ambition. One of his new friends was Raoul La Roche, a Swiss banker and a generous patron. La Roche owned a collection of modern paintings, including some by Le Corbusier, and he wanted a new house and gallery to house them, but he did not have a site to build on. Meanwhile, Le Corbusier had become interested in a development site in the Paris suburb of Auteuil. A complicated series of negotiations and feasibility studies eventually resulted in the building of two houses on an awkward corner of the Auteuil site, at the end of a private cul-de-sac. One of the houses was for La Roche, the other was for Le Corbusier's brother, Albert Jeanneret, and his new wife, Lotti Raaf.

Standardization and repetition were crucial concepts for Le Corbusier, who saw his one-off houses, if not as prototypes for mass production, at least as typological experiments. This might explain why, although the plans of the two houses are quite different, the middle part of their north-facing street façade is symmetrical, implying that they are a handed pair. On the south side, they are built right up to the site boundary, leaving no room for gardens at ground level and virtually ruling out any windows in the back wall. The top two floors are therefore carved out to form a shared lightwell rising from small patios at first-floor level. More generous gardens are provided on the fully accessible flat roof.

There are some subtly modulated domestic interiors, such at the triple-zone living room that takes up most of the top floor of the Jeanneret house, but it is in the gallery wing of the La Roche house that space becomes truly dynamic. This is an area designed for the contemplation of art but also for movement – the first of many Corbusian *promenades architecturales*. The journey begins at the front entrance in the recessed block that links house to gallery. Suddenly we are in a triple-height hall. A bridge passes over the entrance at first-floor level and a balcony is visible one level further up on the left side. A staircase in the corner leads up to a big landing from which there is a view into the street across a recessed balcony. From the landing, the bridge leads to the dining room of the house, but we choose instead to enter the double-height gallery, which is lit by high-level ribbon windows. A ramp rises from the far corner, following the gently concave wall on the left. Having ascended the ramp, we arrive on the balcony that could be seen from below. This is the library, and from here we can look back down at the bridge and the entrance beneath it. On the way, we may have seen some beautiful paintings, but we have also enjoyed a variety of stimulating spatial experiences.

The gallery wing is raised off the ground like a bridge and supported in the middle by a single circular column. This column is more than simply a structural member. It is a piloti, a symbol of the liberation of space. Add this to the free plans, the free façades, the ribbon windows and the roof gardens – and all the ingredients of the new architecture are now in place.

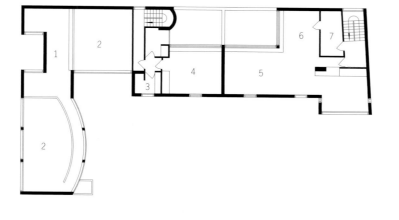

1 Second Floor Plan

1 Library
2 Void
3 WC
4 Bedroom
5 Living room
6 Dinning room
7 Kitchen

1

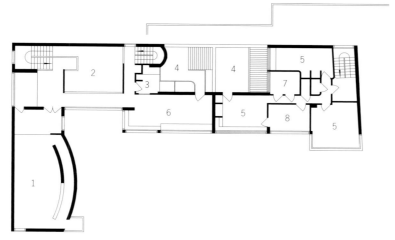

2 First Floor Plan

1 Gallery
2 Void
3 Office
4 Terrace
5 Bedroom
6 Dinning room
7 Bathroom
8 Studio

2

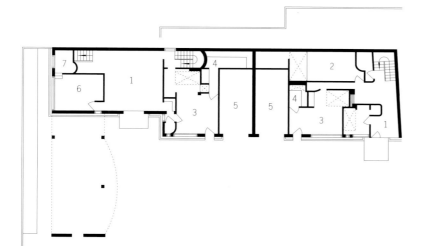

3 Ground Floor Plan

1 Hall
2 Studio
3 Dinning room
4 Kitchen
5 Garage
6 Bedroom
7 WC

3

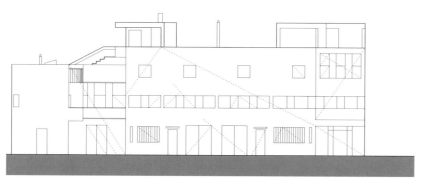

4 North Elevation

4

0   5   10 m
15   30 ft

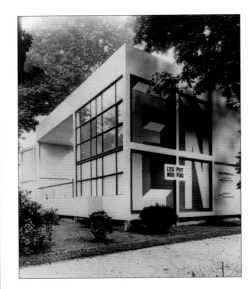

Pavillon de l'Esprit Nouveau

Le Corbusier, 1887–1965

Paris, France; 1925

When it was put to Le Corbusier that, as his contribution to the 1925 Exposition des Arts Décoratifs in Paris, he might design 'a house for an architect', he objected that his houses were for everyone. To prove it, he designed not simply a house but a whole new way of life, including artefacts of every size and scale – from a wine glass to a city for three million people.

The house itself was a stark box, posing a deliberate challenge to the slick superficiality of most of the other exhibits (this was the exhibition that launched Art Deco). It looked unfinished – and for a good reason. Although marketed as a standard detached suburban house, it had originally been conceived as an apartment to be mass-produced and stacked up in eight-storey blocks known as Immeubles Villas. These blocks, in turn, were the components of a project for a whole city known as the Ville Contemporaine. The Voisin car and aeroplane company had been persuaded to sponsor a special version of this project, using the same building types, including 18 enormous cruciform skyscrapers, for the redevelopment of the centre of Paris. Models and dioramas of the Ville Contemporaine and the Plan Voisin were displayed at the Exposition in

an extension to the house/apartment. The whole pavilion was named after the magazine that Le Corbusier edited with Amadée Ozenfant.

Once inside the stark box, visitors were presented with a complete reinvention of the domestic interior. The living room, inspired by a typical Parisian artist's studio, was double-height with a steel-framed industrial window. Bedrooms – or, rather, sleeping, bathing and dressing spaces – were accommodated on a gallery overlooking the living room. Dining space, kitchen and maid's room occupied the space under the gallery. The recessed corridor that would have given access to the dwelling in an apartment block was preserved both in the pavilion and in the advertised detached version, where it formed a sheltered entrance from the street. But the most exciting feature was the garden, a huge, double-height external room in which grew a large tree, poking its head through a round hole in the roof.

Le Pavillon de l'Esprit Nouveau may not have been a house for an architect, but it was a house for, in Le Corbusier's phrase, 'a cultivated man of today', and it was furnished in an austere and tasteful manner. Functional storage units designed by the architect himself were used to

define spaces, and Purist paintings were hung on the walls. Chairs were either of the standard bentwood Thonet type or leather-covered 'club' armchairs. A laboratory flask served as a vase, and tableware, including wine glasses, was chosen from the simplest and most common ranges.

The pavilion was finished late, missing most of the publicity attending the opening of the exhibition, and it stood for only nine months. It also far exceeded its budget, leaving Le Corbusier heavily in debt. Yet, like the equally temporary Barcelona Pavilion by Mies van der Rohe, it has become one of the beacons by which architectural history navigates. A replica built in Bologna, Italy, in 1977 is still used for exhibitions.

1

1 Elevation

2
1
4
3
3

2

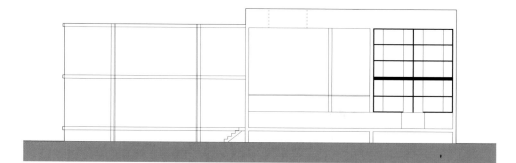

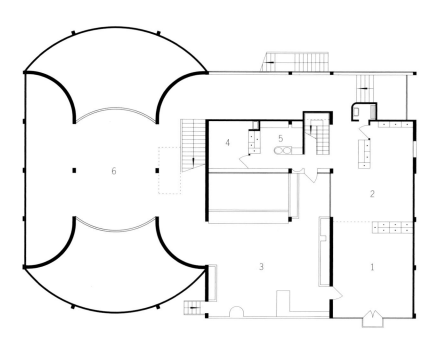

2 First Floor Plan

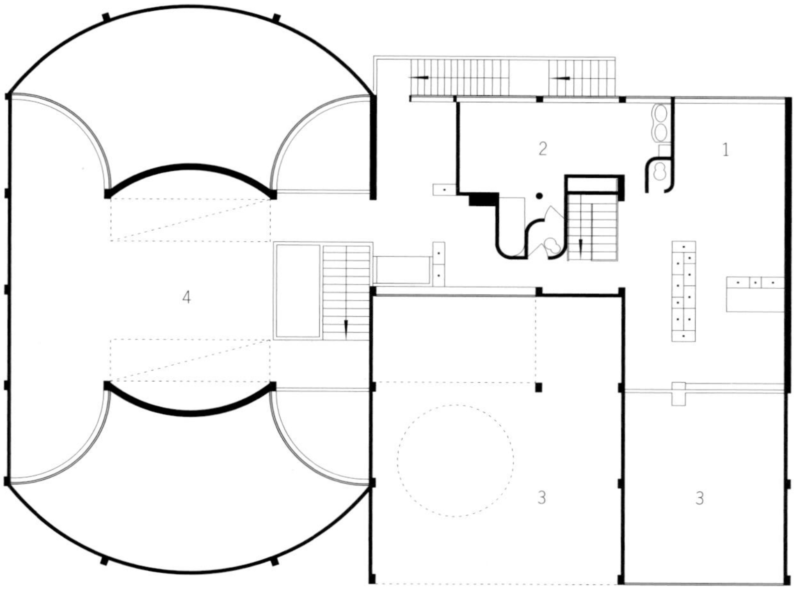

1 Bedroom
2 Dressing room
3 Void
4 Exhibition space

4
5
6
2
3
1

3

3 Ground Floor Plan

1 Living room
2 Dining room
3 Garden
4 Maid's room
5 Kitchen
6 Exhibition space

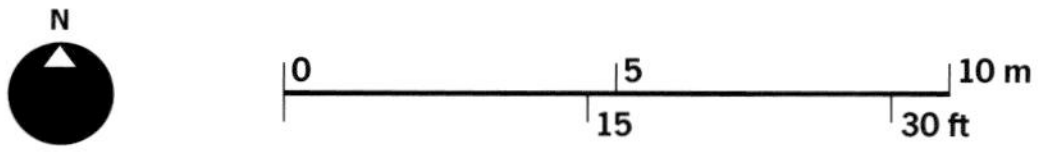

N
0
5
10 m
15
30 ft

Lovell Beach House

Rudolph Schindler, 1887–1953

Newport Beach, California, USA; 1926

Rudolph Schindler was 26 years old and already an experienced architect and engineer when in 1914 he left his native Austria to take up a job with a commercial practice in Chicago. He had trained under Otto Wagner and Adolf Loos, and his ambition was to work for Frank Lloyd Wright, whose Wasmuth portfolio had been an inspiration to progressive European architects and students of architecture since its publication in 1910. In 1918, after repeated pleas, Wright gave him a job and eventually sent him to Los Angeles to oversee the construction of the Barnsdall House (see pages 40–41). When that building was finished, Schindler stayed on and set up his own practice.

These biographical details convey the slightly awkward position that Schindler occupies in the history of Modernism. Despite his impeccable pedigree, he was removed from the mainstream — both physically, by his location in the culturally raw setting of the West Coast, and architecturally, by his association with Wright. When Henry Russell Hitchcock and Philip Johnson put on their famous 'international style' exhibition in New York in 1932, they left Schindler out, much to his annoyance. Not until the 1960s did his pioneering work begin to be acknowledged by architectural historians.

The Lovell Beach House is the building on which Schindler's revived reputation was based. Not surprisingly, it shows the influence of both Loos and Wright. 'Space architecture' was the phrase that Schindler used to sum up his design principles, echoing Loos's *Raumplan*. For Schindler it was space, rather than structure or function, that characterized the new architecture. It is rather surprising, therefore, and not typical of Schindler's work, that the most prominent feature of the house is its primary structure of five reinforced-concrete portal frames. But these are abstract and spatial rather than tectonic — not columns and beams as much as profiles cut out of notional sheets of concrete. Floors and roofs of exposed timber joists span simply between the concrete frames. This basic structure of frames and platforms is the essence of the house. Enclosing elements — large areas of glass and walls framed in lightweight metal — are secondary, and external spaces are as important as internal ones.

Apart from a garage and a shower cubicle, the ground floor is completely open, almost an extension of the beach, and intended as a play area for children and adults alike. On the first floor is the main living room, which is double-height and

overlooked by the second-floor gallery that gives access to the bedrooms on the north side. Each bedroom opens onto to an open-air sleeping porch sheltered by a cantilevered wooden canopy. Some critics have remarked that Schindler was never very good at designing staircases, and the Lovell Beach house seems to bear this out. Two staircases, one rather steep, the other very gentle, rise in opposite directions from the plinth that marks the main entrance on the north side. The gentle staircase rises to the big cantilevered balcony overlooking the ocean, on its way crashing through one of the portal frames and apparently endangering its structural integrity.

There is no doubting the inventiveness and boldness of the design, nor its appropriateness as a 'play house' in which to enjoy the healthy California climate. The client, Philip M. Lovell, was what might now be called a health guru, and has the distinction of being the patron of two canonical Modernist houses, the other being the Health House designed by Schindler's friend and compatriot Richard Neutra (see pages 68–69).

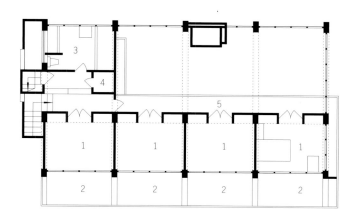

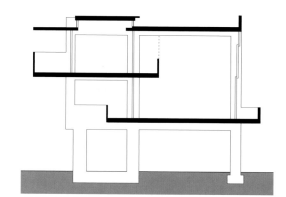

1 Second Floor Plan

1 Bedroom
2 Sleeping porches
3 Bathroom
4 Linen room
5 Balcony

1

2

2 Section A–A

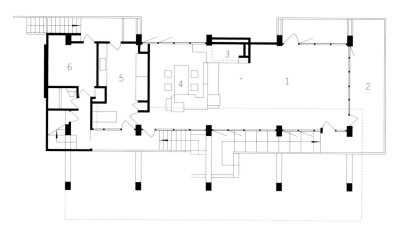

3

3 First Floor Plan

1 Living room
2 Balcony
3 Fireplace
4 Dining area
5 Kitchen
6 Maid's room

4

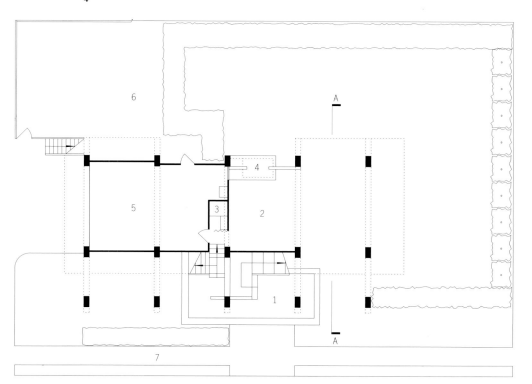

4 Ground Floor Plan

1 Main entrance
2 Playground sand
3 Shower
4 Fireplace
5 Garage
6 Garden
7 Pavement

N

0   5   10 m
15   30 ft

Bauhaus Staff Houses

Walter Gropius, 1883–1969

Dessau, Germany; 1927

The Bauhaus in Dessau, designed by Walter Gropius in 1925, is perhaps the most important of all early Modernist buildings. Its cubic forms, its curtain walls and its abstract, asymmetrical plan were uncompromising proclamations of the new style. The houses for the Bauhaus staff, sited some distance away in a wooded suburban street, resemble miniature Bauhauses – abstract and asymmetrical, they have big studio windows like curtain walls. There were originally seven houses: a director's house for Gropius himself and three pairs of semi-detached houses for senior masters and their families. When they were first built, some disapproval was voiced by socialist-minded staff members, who thought them too luxurious.

The director's house, which was bombed in the Second World War and no longer exists, was certainly not modest. It had a separate flat in the basement for a housekeeper, a guest suite on the first floor and a large studio. The interior, however, was a fairly straightforward arrangement of simple, boxlike rooms. There were no Corbusian ramps nor double-height spaces, and windows, though large, were holes-in-walls rather than continuous ribbons. The composition was cubic rather than planar. The L-shaped first floor was superimposed on the rectangular ground floor, which was in turn superimposed on a terrace or plinth. Walls sometimes coincided and sometimes didn't. The west wall, for example, was a single plane, but on the south side of the house the first floor oversailed the ground floor to cover the west end of the terrace.

One of the other houses was also bombed, but five survive and have been fully restored. They were presumably planned in pairs for economic reasons, though the cost saved by sharing a single wall could not have been great. Semi-detached houses usually have mirrored plans producing a symmetrical building. This would, of course, have created a static, classical effect quite foreign to the new style. The solution to this problem is ingenious. Each pair of houses is essentially made up of three blocks. A central block contains the living rooms on the ground floor and the studios on the first floor, divided by a party wall. On the north side, the first floor is cantilevered out and the studios are provided with very large windows. The other two blocks, containing the dining room and kitchen on the ground floor and the bedrooms on the first floor, are almost identical apart from the distribution of windows. To avoid the semi-detached symmetry, they are attached to diagonally opposite corners of the central block and one has been rotated 90 degrees. The result is a varied, eventful form, with many set-backs, overhangs, recesses and projecting balconies. Though advanced in form, the houses have quite conventional structures, mainly of loadbearing concrete block, rendered and painted.

Apart from Gropius, the original tenants were Laszlo Moholy Nagy, Lyonel Feininger, Georg Muche, Oskar Schlemmer, Wassily Kandinsky and Paul Klee. Each decorated his house in his own style, and a film was made about the art of living in the new architecture. Such a concentration of volatile creative spirits in one place was bound to cause discord, and there were many rows and flouncings-out. The turnover of residents was high. Not all lived like simple artisans. When Mies van der Rohe took over the director's house in 1930, he and his mistress, the interior designer Lilly Reich, employed a butler who wore white gloves.

In 1933 these examples of dangerously Bolshevik architecture were searched for weapons and explosives by Nazi soldiers, but by then it was clear that the Bauhaus ideal would have to be pursued elsewhere.

1 Site Plan

1 Director's house
2 Staff houses

**2 Director's House:
First Floor Plan**

1 Landing
2 Guest room
3 Roof terrace
4 Studio
5 Storage
6 Maid's room
7 Laundry
8 Bathroom

**3 Director's House:
Ground Floor Plan**

1 Hall
2 Living room
3 Dining room
4 Terrace
5 Bedroom
6 Kitchen
7 Service pantry
8 Food pantry
9 Bathroom

**4 Staff Houses:
First Floor Plan**

1 Landing
2 Studio
3 Bedroom
4 Balcony
5 Bathroom

**5 Staff Houses:
Ground Floor Plan**

1 Hall
2 Living room
3 Dining room
4 Terrace
5 Kitchen
6 Storage

1
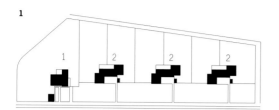

2
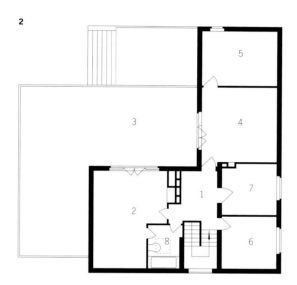

4
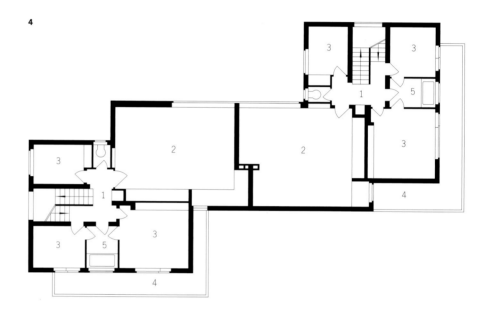

3
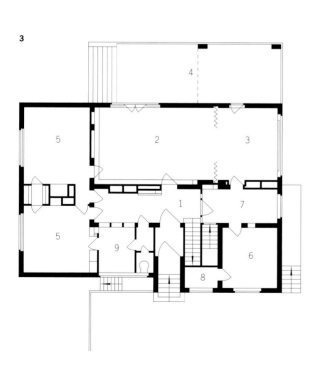

5
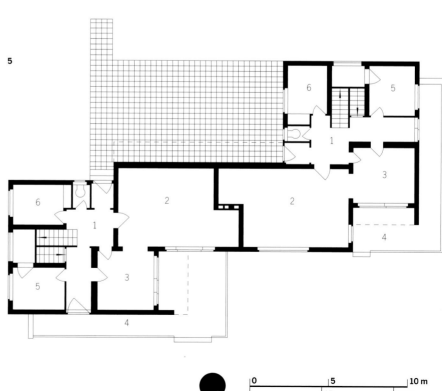

Villa Stein—de Monzie

Le Corbusier, 1887–1965

near Paris, France; 1927

In his seminal article 'The Mathematics of the Ideal Villa', Colin Rowe points out that the Villa Stein—de Monzie and Andrea Palladio's Villa Foscari of 1550–60 share the same overall proportions — eight units long by five and a half units deep by five units high — and the same structural layout — an ABABA pattern of single and double bays. We do not know for sure that Le Corbusier was paying conscious homage to Palladio, but the fact that his wealthy clients, Gabrielle de Monzie and her American friends Michael and Sarah Stein, holidayed together in the Steins' Renaissance villa outside Florence lends weight to the theory. For all its startling modernity, the Villa Stein—de Monzie is essentially a classical building.

The villa is also many other things, however. It is a development of the 'Dom-ino' structural principle, with beamless floor slabs supported on, and cantilevered from, slender columns. It is a deluxe version of the workers' apartment design demonstrated in the Pavilion de l'Esprit Nouveau (see pages 48–49) with its two-storey covered terrace. And it is a three-dimensional Purist painting — a collection of *objets-types* composed in a rectangular frame, with rounded staircases, bulging walls and oval columns substituted for

bottles, guitars and piles of plates. The plan is complex, with separate suites for the Steins and Madame de Monzie and a full complement of servants' rooms, but the precise configuration of partitions is less important than larger structural and spatial manipulations.

The Villa Stein—de Monzie stands far back on its long, narrow site — a symbol of modern life to be viewed through the windscreen of the car that has brought us the 19 km (12 miles) from the centre of Paris. The elevation facing the drive is as carefully composed as any Renaissance façade, but there is no modelling other than the drawbridge-like canopy over the main entrance and a balcony right up on the top floor that seems to have been cut out and folded down from the paper-thin wall. Two narrow ribbon windows extend across the full width, leaving no doubt that this is a lightweight screen, not a loadbearing wall.

The elevation facing the garden at the back is much more relaxed and human. Here the screen has been partially removed to reveal open spaces behind: a roof garden in which stands an oval form like a ship's funnel (originally Sarah Stein's painting studio with a viewing platform on top) and a two-storey covered terrace that reaches out into the

garden at first-floor level and lowers a staircase like a gangway. This terrace is overlooked by a balcony at second-floor level, which in turn is overlooked by the roof garden. No wonder the house's official name was 'Les Terrasses'.

Compared with these multi-level external spaces, the interiors are rather subdued. The main living space on the first floor is roughly Z-shaped, snaking around the kitchen and the terrace. Curved forms, such as the piano-shaped hole in the floor allowing a view of the entrance hall below and the curved partition defining the dining space, seem like afterthoughts. Le Corbusier, no doubt, saw these as necessary modern counterpoints to the underlying classical harmonies.

The house still exists but has been radically altered and converted into apartments.

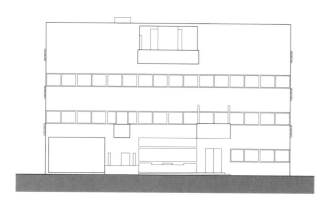

1
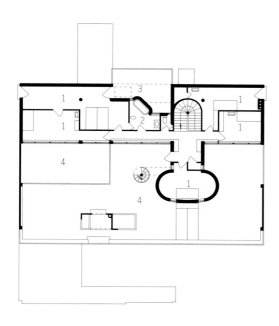

2
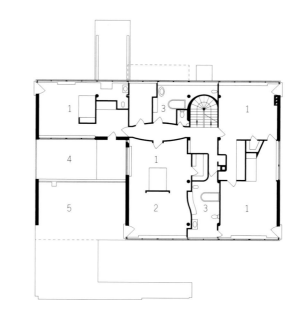

1 South Elevation

2 Section A–A

3
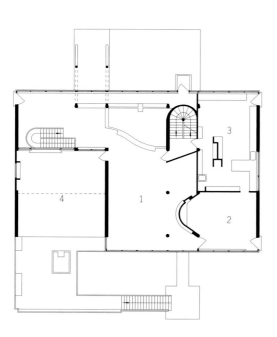

4

3 Third Floor Plan

1 Bedroom
2 Bathroom
3 Roof terrace
4 Void

4 Second Floor Plan

1 Bedroom
2 Dressing room
3 Bathroom
4 Roof terrace
5 Void

5

6
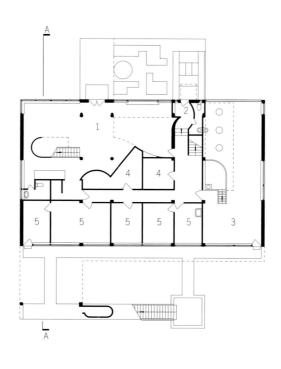

5 First Floor Plan

1 Living room
2 Dining room
3 Kitchen
4 Terrace

6 Ground Floor Plan

1 Entrance hall
2 Service entrance
3 Garage
4 Store
5 Staff room

N

0   5   10 m
0   15   30 ft

Weissenhof House

Le Corbusier, 1887–1965

Stuttgart, Germany; 1927

Le Corbusier designed two buildings for the 1927 Weissenhof housing exhibition in Stuttgart, a single house and double house. The single house is the more interesting because it is the only built example of a design that Le Corbusier had been developing since 1919: the Maison Citrohan. The name is a slightly obscure pun on Citroën, the car manufacturer, indicating that this is meant to be a house that resembles a car: popular, standardized and mass-produced.

With its plain white walls, external staircase and flat roof, the first version of the Maison Citrohan design looked more like a Mediterranean vernacular cottage than a product of mechanized industry, although its double-height living room lit by a big industrial window probably owed much to the typical Parisian artist's studio. The second version, exhibited at the 1922 Salon d'Automne, was more elaborate and modern-looking. The whole house was raised up on pilotis, indicating a reinforced-concrete frame structure, and the staircase was brought into the main volume.

In the Weissenhof house, the concept was further refined and smartened up for a show in which it would inevitably be compared with houses by an array of other prominent European Modernists, including Walter Gropius, Mart Stam, J. J. P. Oud and Ludwig Mies van der Rohe. Le Corbusier omitted the rather awkward projecting terrace that had been a feature of Citrohan 2, restoring a perfect shoebox form raised on two rows of five pilotis. The form is not symmetrical, however, because the staircase has been placed outside the columns, its presence signalled by a small balcony projecting from the front façade and doubling as a canopy over the main entrance.

As in the closely related Pavillon de l'Esprit Nouveau of 1925 (see pages 48–49), the double-height living room, or 'foyer', is overlooked by a gallery that accommodates the main bedroom and boudoir. But here the edge of the gallery is at a slight angle, and the upper and lower spaces are linked by a sculptural assemblage of functional objects – a fireplace, a chimney, a writing desk incorporated into the balustrade, and a curious suspended cube that defines the dining area.

There are two more bedrooms on the top floor, which is only half enclosed. The other half is a roof garden that has been treated as a room within the box, complete with a full-height external wall and an unglazed ribbon 'window'. Part of it is roofed in line with the staircase zone of the plan.

The idea of external spaces treated as rooms would be repeated on a larger scale in the Villa Savoye (see pages 80–81).

Several elements of this design became essential components of Le Corbusier's mature style. The 'five points of a new architecture' – free plan, free façade, pilotis, roof garden and ribbon windows – were first published in a brochure distributed by the builder of the Weissenhof house. Traces of the Maison Citrohan can be detected in most of the Purist villas of the 1920s, and the whole idea of a rectangular box with glazed ends can be seen in otherwise very different buildings such as the Maisons Jaoul (see pages 132–33) and the Millowners' Association building in Ahmedabad. Even the double-height apartments of the Unité d'Habitation in Marseilles are versions of the Maison Citrohan. The one thing it never became was a popular, standardized and mass-produced house.

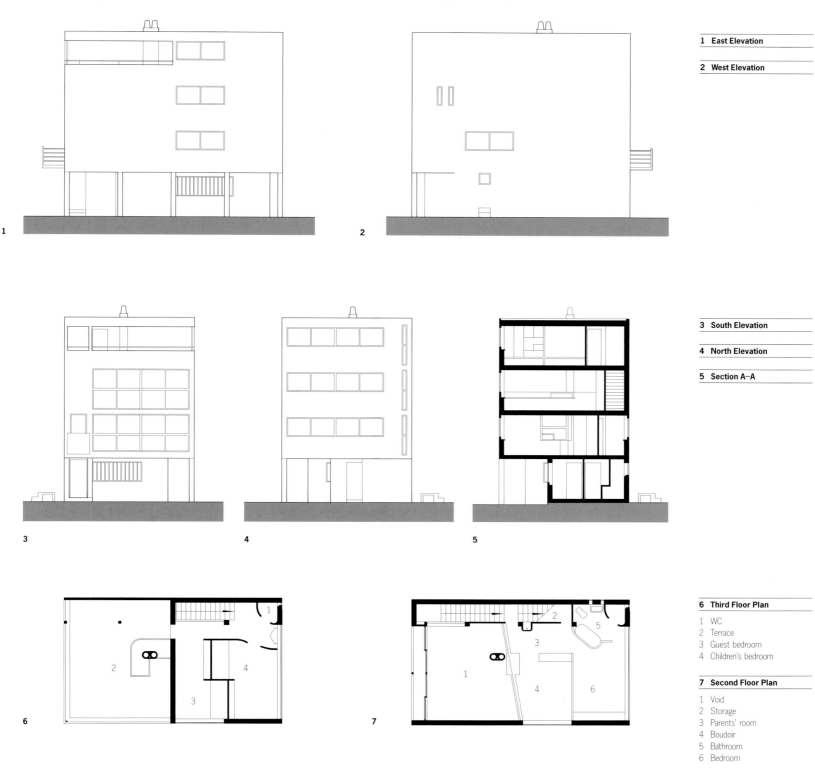

1   **East Elevation**

2   **West Elevation**

3   **South Elevation**

4   **North Elevation**

5   **Section A–A**

6   **Third Floor Plan**

1   WC
2   Terrace
3   Guest bedroom
4   Children's bedroom

7   **Second Floor Plan**

1   Void
2   Storage
3   Parents' room
4   Boudoir
5   Bathroom
6   Bedroom

8   **First Floor Plan**

1   Living room
2   Dining room
3   Kitchen
4   Maid's room

9   **Ground Floor Plan**

1   Boiler room
2   Coal store
3   Washroom
4   Storage

0   5   10 m

15   30 ft

Wolf House

Ludwig Mies van der Rohe, 1886–1969

Gubin, Germany (now Poland); 1927

Some of the best known and most influential buildings of the twentieth century were never actually constructed. One such is Mies van der Rohe's Brick Country House project of 1923. Only two drawings of it survive, a plan and a perspective. They are prints, not original drawings; they do not precisely correspond to each other, and the perspective was probably not drawn by Mies. Nevertheless, they have become iconic. The plan, in particular, seems to mark a conceptual breakthrough in early Modernist spatial design. It bears a closer resemblance to a painting than to a plan – specifically, a painting called *Rhythm of a Russian Dance* by Theo van Doesburg. A number of freestanding brick walls, arranged at right angles to one another, loosely define a group of merging or overlapping spaces. Three of the walls have been extended, as if by some centrifugal force, as far as the frame of the drawing and possibly beyond. The perspective indicates that some of the walls are two storeys high, that the roof is a flat slab, cantilevered in places, and that the external enclosure of the house is completed by floor-to-ceiling glass walls. Rooms seem to have been abolished and space flows into space with unprecedented freedom.

The Wolf House is the Brick Country House project redesigned under the sobering influence of a real client and a real site. The client was Erich Wolf, a wealthy Gubin factory owner. He was a progressive spirit and a collector of modern art, but a house without rooms was too advanced a concept even for him. What we have, therefore, is a compromise. Large German houses of this period were usually supplied with a dining room, a living room, a music room and a study. The Wolf House is no exception, but here the rooms flow into one another, not formally or axially through framed openings, but asymmetrically, in a stepped formation. Each space shares a wall surface with its neighbour so that it is hard to say where one ends and the other begins. And the space continues to flow out onto a large paved terrace resembling a fifth 'room'. The boundary between the dining room and terrace is blurred by a big cantilevered roof over full-height glass doors. The flowing-space effect is only partially realized, but there is no doubt that the Brick Country House project was always at the back of Mies's mind.

Flowing space, however, is not the only architectural theme of the Wolf House. It is also a dynamic, asymmetrical composition of solid cubic forms, piled up to three, or perhaps four, storeys. The largest of these forms is the base on which the house stands, stretching the full width of the narrow sloping site. This could be seen as a separate landscape element, designed to level off the slope and form the terrace, but it is also part of the house. Its retaining wall is built of the same brick and continues upwards on one side to form the external walls. From the terrace, the building steps back twice. There is a roof terrace over the living room, and the whole composition is crowned by the simple brick box containing the staff bedrooms. On the entrance side, the building has an austere, forbidding aspect. Large areas of perfectly laid brickwork are relieved only by a few small windows and the corner-cantilevered concrete balcony of the master bedroom that also serves as an entrance porch.

The Wolf House would have been as near as we could get to a built version of the Brick Country House. Sadly, however, we have to be content with drawings and photographs. It was destroyed during the Second World War and only fragments of the terrace remain.

1

1 Second Floor Plan

2

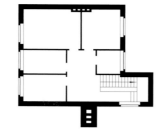

2 First Floor Plan

3

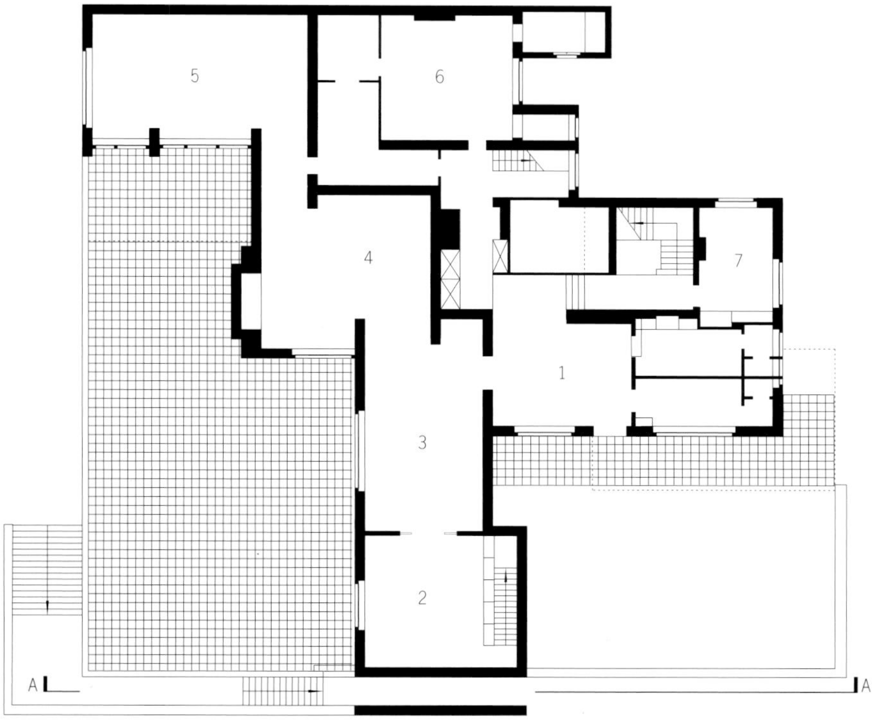

3 Ground Floor Plan

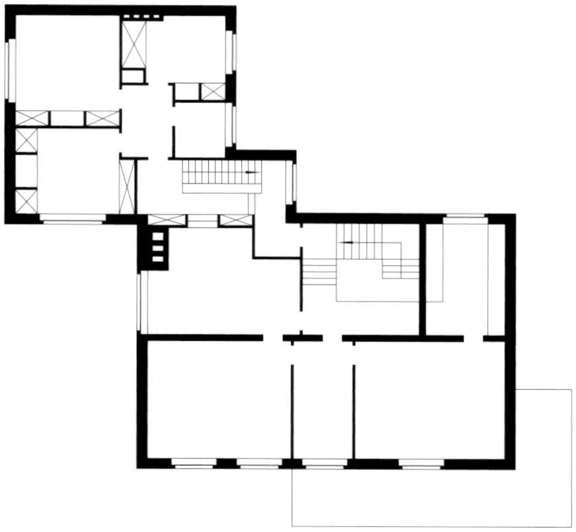

1 Entrance and stair hall
2 Study/library
3 Music room
4 Living room
5 Dining room
6 Kitchen
7 Parlour

4

4 Section A–A

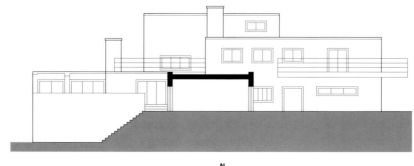

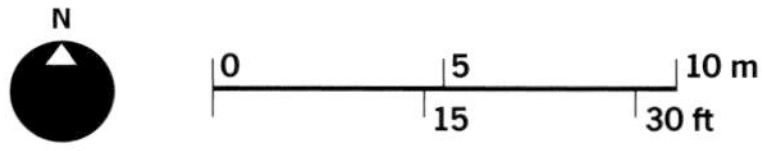

Moller House

Adolf Loos, 1870–1933

Vienna, Austria; 1928

Raumplan is the word used by critics to describe Adolf Loos's characteristic compositional method. Coined by Heinrich Kulka, Loos's first biographer, the term simply means designing in three dimensions, spatially rather than diagrammatically. Loos disliked plans and instead used models to work out his designs. The method allowed rooms of different sizes to have different ceiling heights and floor levels. In a rambling composition this would be easy to achieve, but Loos's houses are compact, urban, multi-storey buildings. Rooms are 'nested' together without hidden voids or false surfaces to mask the discrepancies in height and level. Spaces are always clearly defined as rooms but not always fully enclosed. Typically, small, low spaces look down into larger, higher ones, creating a complex interior, at once unified and articulated.

In the Moller House the main living area is divided into five separate but connected spaces: a central hall, a sitting alcove, a music room, a dining room and an external terrace. The dining room and terrace are four steps above the hall and music room, and the sitting alcove is higher still, housed in a box that cantilevers out to form a canopy over the main entrance. Open to the hall and lit by a long horizontal window, this

alcove 'supervises' both the interior spaces and the street outside. The critic Beatrice Colomina has seen a gendered meaning in this space. It is a reading or sewing window, suitable for the woman of the house (the man's study is adjacent to it on the same level but closed off), yet its occupant is also on display, as if in a box at the theatre. The relationship between the dining room and music room is also theatrical, although it is the everyday activity of the dining room rather than a musical performance that is raised on a stage. The stage analogy is heightened by the absence of any permanent steps linking the two spaces.

There is no single, top-to-bottom staircase serving all five levels of the house. Steps are introduced where necessary to serve the subtle spatial relationships of the *Raumplan*. The journey from the street entrance to the sitting alcove directly above it, for example, involves eight right-angled turns and three separate flights of steps, one of them a dog-leg with winders. The route passes through three separate rooms: a narrow entrance hall with a built-in bench, a cloakroom lobby on the half-landing, and the hall, which opens onto the music room. Something approximating to an ordinary staircase rises from the hall to the

bedroom floor above but stops short of the top floor and roof terrace, which are accessible only by means of a small spiral staircase.

Symmetry is an important secondary aspect of the *Raumplan* method, but it never dominates the composition. Although the street façade of the Moller House is perfectly symmetrical, the spaces immediately behind it are radically asymmetrical. And, although at first the garden façade seems asymmetrical, on closer inspection it turns out to be two symmetrical compositions welded together. Loos uses symmetry not as a diagrammatic framework but as a means of defining and stabilizing space.

The Moller House was built in a wealthy suburb of Vienna for the owner of a textile factory and his wife. It is now the Israeli consulate and is not open the public.

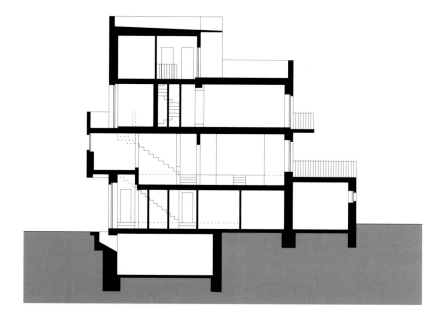

1

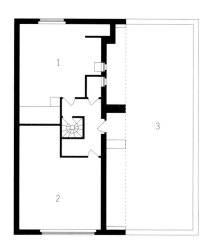

2

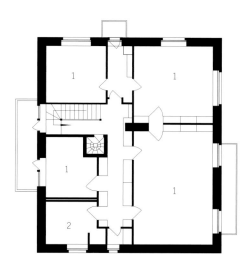

3

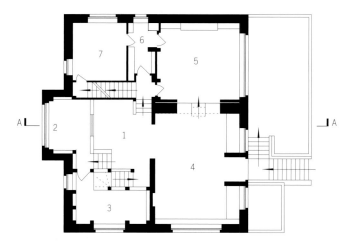

4

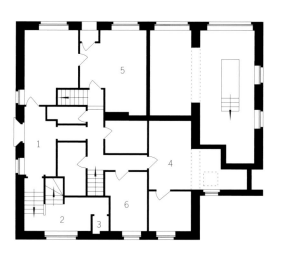

5

2 Third Floor Plan

1 Bedroom
2 Studio
3 Terrace

3 Second Floor Plan

1 Bedroom
2 Bathroom

4 First Floor Plan

1 Vestible
2 Sitting alcove
3 Library
4 Music room
5 Dining room
6 Servery
7 Kitchen

5 Ground Floor Plan

1 Entrance
2 Cloakroom
3 WC
4 Laundry
5 Caretaker's room
6 Staff room

Lange House

Ludwig Mies van der Rohe, 1886–1969

Krefeld, Germany; 1928

The Lange House has a brother next door: the Esters House, built at the same time and in the same style, but not an identical twin. Hermann Lange and Josef Esters were managing directors of a silk-weaving factory in Krefeld. Lange, the instigator of the joint project, was a member of the Deutsche Werkbund, a patron of Berlin's National Gallery and an important collector of modern art. His house therefore also served as a private gallery. Large areas of well-lit wall space were a basic need, which ruled out the radical openness and transparency of the Tugendhat House (see pages 78–79) or the Barcelona Pavilion, designed at about the same time.

The Lange House is also unlike those more ambitious Modernist exercises in that it is clad in, or rather hewn out of, heavy, red, English-bonded brickwork. The house has a monumental quality, but is far from monolithic. Cubic forms of different heights and widths are asymmetrically arranged, and the mostly hidden steel frame makes itself apparent here and there in cantilevered canopies and balconies. Large picture-windows puncture the brickwork on the garden side, but in the more functional north-west elevation, facing the road, windows gang together to form long ribbons.

Apart from the service wing at the north-east end, which has a garage and staff room at basement level, this is a two-storey house. The main entrance, a modest single door beneath a cantilevered canopy, opens into a small vestibule, which leads to the biggest, most important room, the 'living hall'. This is the main circulation space, giving access to the staircase in an alcove at one end, a generous dining recess and three smaller, enclosed living rooms (music room, parlour, study).

A contemporary photograph of the living hall shows it furnished with only four armchairs arranged around a coffee table well away from the walls. Clearly, the main function of this space was to display works of art, including paintings by Chagall and Kirchner, sculpture by Lehmbruck and several medieval madonnas. Art was displayed in the smaller living rooms too, but these also had the benefit of views over the garden terrace through almost-full-height windows.

The site slopes slightly to the south-east and the level garden terrace is defined by a low retaining wall. Terrace and house together form a simple rectangle on plan, as if they were two halves of the same structure, divided by the back wall of the house with its many set-backs. The

interlocking of interior and exterior is emphasized by virtual rooms defined by cantilevered balconies at each end of the house.

Set-backs occur in section as well as in plan so that most of the bedrooms on the first floor open onto roof terraces. The plan at this level is more functional, almost hotel-like, with its corridor circulation and six en suite bathrooms. Three of these are 'internal', but lit and ventilated by a narrow strip of clerestory windows over the lowered roof of the ribbon-windowed corridor.

Both the Lange and Esters houses survive in good condition and are used, appropriately, for art exhibitions.

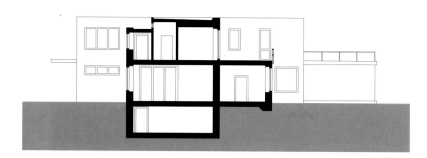

1

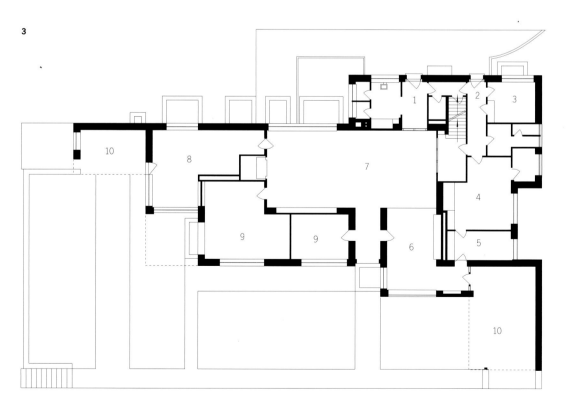

2

2 First Floor Plan

1 Staff bedroom
2 Bedroom
3 Bathroom
4 Storage
5 Laundry
6 Terrace

3 Ground Floor Plan

1 Entrance
2 Service entrance
3 Maid's room
4 Kitchen
5 Servery
6 Dining room
7 Living room
8 Study
9 Day room
10 Covered terrace

0	5	10 m
15	30 ft	

Wittgenstein House

Paul Engelmann (1891–1965) and Ludwig Wittgenstein (1889–1951)

Vienna, Austria; 1928

In 1925, Margaret Stonborough, an heiress and patron of the arts, commissioned Paul Engelmann to build a large house for her in Vienna. Engelmann, a pupil of Adolf Loos, set about designing a vaguely Loosian house with some classical details. It might never have come to the notice of architectural history had not Engelmann made the mistake of discussing the project with Margaret's brother, the philosopher Ludwig Wittgenstein.

Wittgenstein was a friend of Loos and had always been interested in architecture. He was unemployed at the time, having written his *Tractatus Logico-Philosophicus* and having recently been dismissed from his teaching job for abusing his pupils. He muscled in on the project without delay, beginning a collaboration which eventually, inevitably, led to the ending of his friendship with Engelmann. History could not have totally ignored a house designed by one of the great philosophers of the twentieth century, but it was not until the 1960s, when the house was threatened with demolition, that the world of architecture became genuinely interested in it.

Engelmann's design was almost complete when Wittgenstein took over, and the original basic layout survives in the final building. A collection of interpenetrating cubic forms — the tallest three storeys high — occupies an open site in an otherwise densely built-up district of Vienna.

Wittgenstein adapted the layout to conform to his own very personal architectural theories. The adaptations were not all improvements, and some of the subtleties of Engelmann's plan were lost. For example, he introduced an ugly, buttress-like block with a sloping glass roof to the back of the house to make room for his sister's private rooms, and he replaced Engelmann's understated Loosian staircase with a rather clumsy and intrusive glazed stair tower and lift. His detailed alterations are nevertheless fascinating. Engelmann used harmonic proportions and symmetry for the main spaces on the ground floor — hall, music room, dining room and library — but Wittgenstein refined these qualities to the point of obsession. Joints in the dark grey, artificial-stone floors were exactly aligned with doors and windows, and walls were thickened where necessary to preserve perfect symmetry. No skirtings, architraves or cover strips were allowed, so construction had to be totally accurate. No one seems to have cared much about the upper floors, which were more loosely planned for use by children, staff and Mr Stonborough.

Wittgenstein had trained as an aeronautical engineer in Manchester, UK, and therefore paid particular attention to anything mechanical or electrical. He designed radiators, air grilles, light switches, window frames and door handles, and even involved himself in the development of the lift mechanism that would be clearly visible in its glass tower. External openings were fitted with metal shutters that rose up from a slot in the floor, balanced by counterweights. Electric lights were bare bulbs mounted close to the ceiling and centred precisely. The overall effect is dignified, but cold and hard — a long way from the comfortable sumptuousness of a Loos interior.

The house is more a curiosity than a masterpiece, yet, despite its flaws and its divided authorship, critics have repeatedly returned to it seeking clues to the workings of a great mind. It has even been interpreted as a kind of built philosophical bridge between the *Tractatus* and the later *Philosophical Investigations*. It now houses the Bulgarian Cultural Institute.

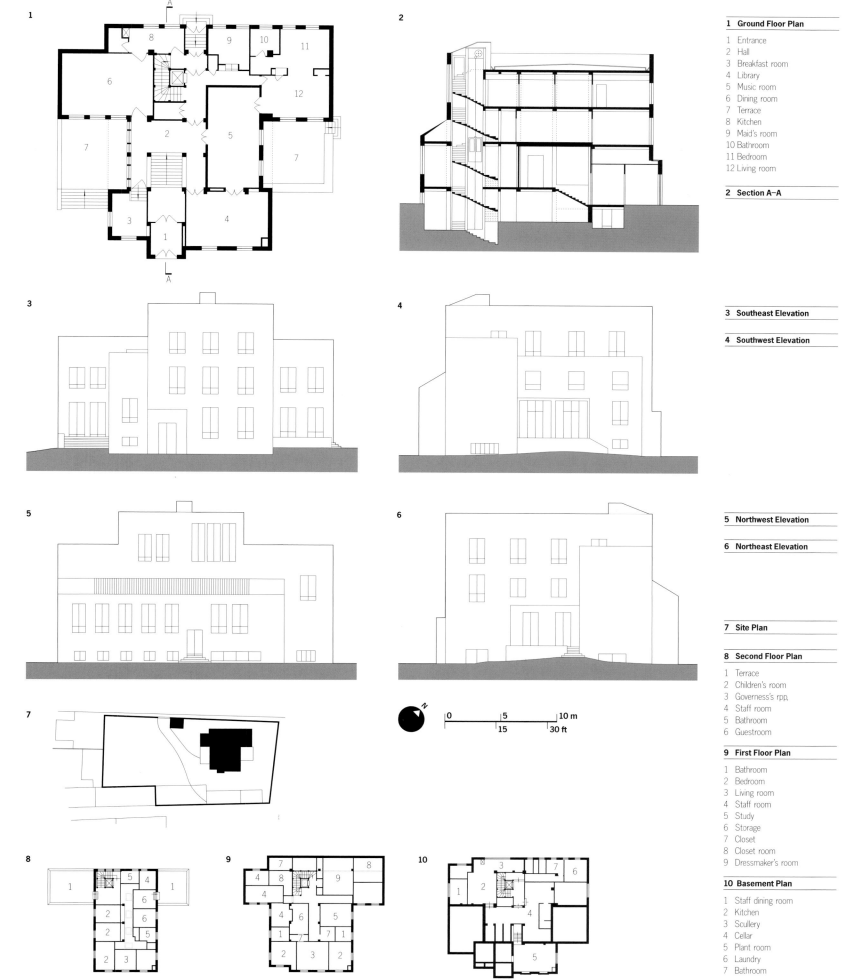

1 Ground Floor Plan

1 Entrance
2 Hall
3 Breakfast room
4 Library
5 Music room
6 Dining room
7 Terrace
8 Kitchen
9 Maid's room
10 Bathroom
11 Bedroom
12 Living room

2 Section A–A

3 Southeast Elevation

4 Southwest Elevation

5 Northwest Elevation

6 Northeast Elevation

7 Site Plan

8 Second Floor Plan

1 Terrace
2 Children's room
3 Governess's rpp.
4 Staff room
5 Bathroom
6 Guestroom

9 First Floor Plan

1 Bathroom
2 Bedroom
3 Living room
4 Staff room
5 Study
6 Storage
7 Closet
8 Closet room
9 Dressmaker's room

10 Basement Plan

1 Staff dining room
2 Kitchen
3 Scullery
4 Cellar
5 Plant room
6 Laundry
7 Bathroom

Melnikov House

Konstantin Melnikov, 1890–1974

Moscow, Russia; 1929

The house built by Konstantin Melnikov for himself and his family in an otherwise unremarkable residential street in Moscow has usually been seen as an eccentric aberration. It looks more like a church or a planetarium than a house, and critics have assumed that its interlocking cylinders perforated by lozenge-shaped windows must have mystical significance. There is some justification for this interpretation. Melnikov, the designer of the USSR pavilion at the 1925 Exposition des Arts Décoratifs in Paris, had strange ideas – for example, about sleep and the architecture of sleep. The bedroom of the Melnikov House originally had three tomb-like forms, sculpted in a smooth hard plaster and permanently fixed to the floor in a symmetrical arrangement. These served as beds for the parents and two children, screened only by a pair of short, fixed partitions. It must have looked like a set for a science-fiction film – the suspended animation bay of a spaceship, perhaps. All other furniture was banished on the grounds of hygiene. Clothes were stored in the large communal dressing room on the ground floor.

But, looked at another way, the house is perfectly rational. Melnikov only got permission to build it because the Moscow authorities were interested in its potential as a prototype. Its form arises from a logical analysis of the structural qualities of its main material: loadbearing brick. The cylinder is a very stable form, needing no buttressing, and the lozenge is the shape naturally created when openings in a brick wall are formed by corbelled 'arches' instead of lintels. A solid wall was thereby converted into a 'diagrid' frame using only bricks and mortar. Bricks were left uncut, with projecting courses to form a key for stucco or plaster. Far from being a whimsical decorative device, the perforated cylinder was a cheap, easy-to-build walling system with many applications. Floor structures are equally innovative. A plan of 9 metres (30 feet) in diameter made ordinary beams or joists uneconomical. Melnikov therefore devised an egg-crate frame of thin wooden planks halved together, stiffened and braced by floors and ceilings of tongue-and-groove boards orientated in different directions.

The house is also innovative in spatial terms, in section as well as on plan. The double-height first-floor living room, brightly lit by a big window facing the street, contrasts with the low, lozenge-lit bedroom on the same level in the other cylinder. The studio above the bedroom is also double-height, with three rows of lozenges and a gallery that gives access to the terrace on the living-room roof. The terrace overlooks the studio, which overlooks the living room, creating a nice balance between continuity and separation.

Arrangements for vertical circulation seem awkward and unresolved. A spiral staircase linking living-room and studio levels extends downwards via a straight flight to the off-centre entrance hall, and upwards via little more than a ladder to the gallery and roof terrace. But the logic of the plan becomes clear in two projects for workers' housing that Melnikov designed in the year the house was completed. What looks in the house like an ad hoc expedient becomes, in the projects, a regular rhythm of cylinders and spirals.

But the projects were never built and the system was never applied on a large scale. Ten years after the completion of the house, the Modernist Melnikov was forced to scratch a living from painting, having fallen from favour with a now firmly Socialist Realist architectural establishment. He was partially rehabilitated in the 1950s, and was still living in the house on his death in 1974.

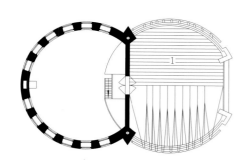

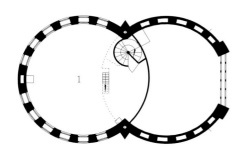

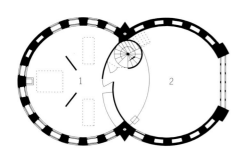

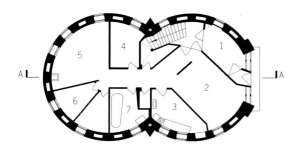

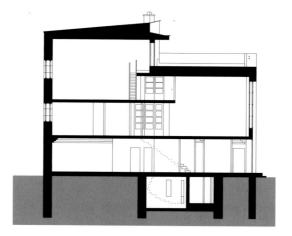

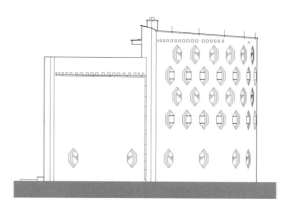

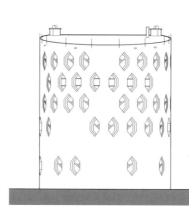

1 Roof Plan

1 Terrace

2 Section A–A

3 Second Floor Plan

1 Studio

4 East Elevation

5 First Floor Plan

1 Bedroom
2 Living room

6 North Elevation

7 Ground Floor Plan

1 Hall
2 Dining room
3 Kitchen
4 Utility room
5 Dressing room
6 Day room
7 WC

8 South Elevation

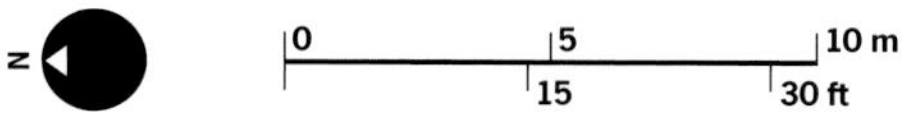

0   5   10 m

15   30 ft

Lovell Health House

Richard Neutra, 1892–1970

Los Angeles, California, USA; 1927–29

Healthy living was an important theme in 1920s Modernism; the new white architecture was a celebration of fresh air, sunshine and space for the liberated human body. And Philip Lovell was the high priest of healthy living. A physician from New York, he made a fortune in California from the promotion of callisthenics, vegetarianism and nude sunbathing. His wife, Leah, ran a progressive kindergarten. Lovell wrote articles on health and beauty in the *Los Angeles Times* and occasionally included hints on building healthy houses. When he came to build a big new house for his own family in the Hollywood Hills, it inevitably became a demonstration of his ideas. The Lovells had already employed Rudolph Schindler to design a house for them at Newport Beach (see pages 50–51). For their new house, they turned to another Austrian émigré, Schindler's friend and erstwhile partner, Richard Neutra.

The result was a house to rival the best products of the European avant-garde. Whereas the villas of Le Corbusier, for example, made their abstract forms and open plans out of messy materials such as insitu concrete and ordinary blockwork, the Health House was assembled from precision factory-made steel components. It has a

lightweight frame, with perimeter columns at very close intervals doubling as mullions for standard steel-framed windows. The floors and roof are supported by lattice trusses. Similar components were used in the Eames House 20 years later (see pages 106–107). The opaque walls are made of concrete sprayed onto metal mesh – a technique that Le Corbusier was experimenting with at about the same time.

The form of the house was every bit as advanced as its technology. What was new in 1928 was its 'subtractive' geometry. Viewed from the southwest, the plain rectangle of the roof defines the notional outline of a three-storey box dug into the hillside. Sections of the external wall are recessed from this outline, leaving the floors or roofs above apparently unsupported. Structurally this is achieved not by cantilevering the floors but by suspending them from cantilevered roof beams. On the lowest level, a deep recess accommodates a terrace and half of a swimming pool, but here the supporting structure becomes a delicate colonnade. Bands of white concrete break out of the box onto the hillside, becoming curving retaining walls and linking the house to Leah's kindergarten next door.

The main entrance is on the top floor, which also accommodates the bedrooms. Sleeping in the open air was an important part of Lovell's health regime, so every bedroom has an adjacent screened porch with long views over the city of Los Angeles to the south and the wild landscape of Griffiths Park to the north. From the entrance hall, a generous staircase leads down to a long, relatively narrow living space. Dining and library zones flank a main sitting area focused on a rustic fireplace, which perhaps shows the influence of one of Neutra's teachers, Frank Lloyd Wright, but looks incongruous in these clinical, almost institutional, surroundings. The staircase is unenclosed and the high, glass-walled, south-facing space that it occupies is one of the most photographed Modernist interiors of the century.

When the house was finished, Lovell proudly trumpeted it in his newspaper column and crowds came to visit. Many were repelled by its alien character, but the native architects took note and California Modernism took another step forward.

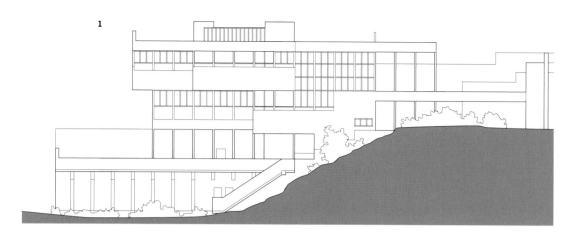

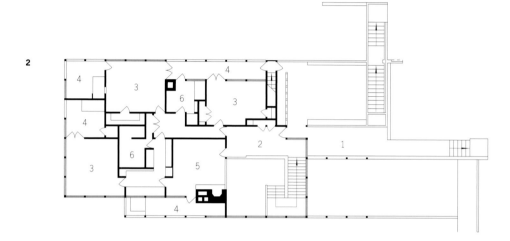

2 Entrance Level Plan

1 Entrance terrace
2 Entrance
3 Bedroom
4 Sleeping porch
5 Study
6 Bathroom

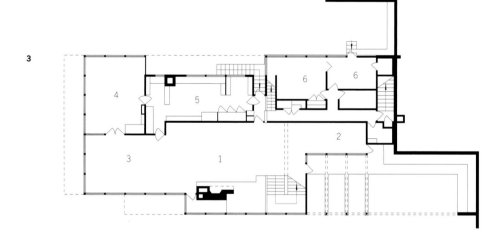

3 First Floor Plan

1 Living room
2 Library
3 Dining room
4 Porch
5 Kitchen
6 Guestroom

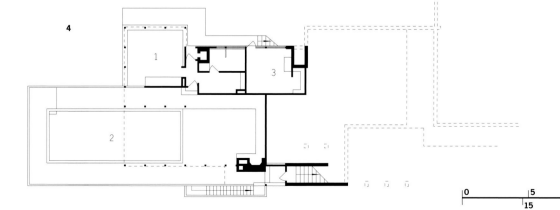

4 Ground Floor Plan

1 Porch
2 Pool
3 Laundry room

E1027

Eileen Gray, 1878–1976

Roquebrune–Cap Martin, France; 1924–29

E1027 was built by Eileen Gray for herself and the architectural critic Jean Badovici – hence the name: E for Eileen, 10 for Jean (J is the tenth letter of the alphabet), 2 for Badovici and 7 for Gray. No doubt the name was also meant to make the house sound like a car or an aeroplane, one of a range of industrial products, although in fact it took three years to build under the constant supervision of its designer. Gray was a modest and hesitant pioneer of Modernism, but pioneer she was. She was influenced by Le Corbusier, but by no means in thrall to him. The idea that a house was a machine for living in was foreign to her. She designed for the needs of human beings, not the imperatives of an abstract system.

Born into a Irish–Scottish family, Gray began her career as a furniture and textile designer in Paris. Her steel-framed chairs and geometrically patterned carpets showed architectural tendencies and it was natural that she should eventually want to build. She had travelled in the south of France as a young woman and returned there in search of a site. From a practical building point of view, a steep, rocky seashore with only a narrow track for access could hardly have been more awkward, but as a setting for a Modernist villa it was perfect.

The house is relatively small but arranged expansively with a free spatial flow from interior rooms to exterior terraces. A large, multi-purpose living room occupies a rectangular concrete box with full-height windows facing the sea across a wide balcony. The box is raised above the ground on pilotis, but because of the slope of the site it can be entered directly from a porch on the landward side. The balcony resembles the deck of ship, with a tubular-steel balustrade and a concrete companionway at one end, descending to the lower terrace.

At the east end of the building, the plan becomes rather complex, with kitchen, bathroom and study bedroom at living-room level, and guest room and staff room on the floor below. A spiral staircase connects the two floors and continues up to the flat roof. Gray said that the plan was designed to allow every occupant complete freedom and independence. 'There must be still the impression of being alone, and if desired entirely alone.' How much this was a reflection of her relationship with Badovici is a matter of speculation, but it explains why shared spaces such as the staircase and kitchen are minimized, while the bedrooms each have a private terrace.

The house is obviously the work of a furniture designer. Eileen Gray seems not to have made any real distinction between architecture and furniture, much of which is in what was then described as the 'camping' style. Wardrobes incorporate special compartments for different items of clothing; headboards are built into walls; and freestanding cupboards act as screens or room dividers. The overall effect is efficient, but also comfortable and caring.

There is a disturbing story attached to E1027, and it involves Le Corbusier. In 1938, by which time Gray was no longer living there, Badovici allowed Le Corbusier to adorn the house with eight large murals, including one that the artist said represented Badovici, Gray and their unborn child. Gray considered it a gross act of vandalism. Later, Le Corbusier built a little cabin for himself overlooking E1027, thereby destroying its privacy. He claimed to be an admirer of the house and of Gray's work in general, but that admiration seems to have been mixed with darker feelings. It was while swimming in the sea close to the house that Le Corbusier suffered a heart attack and died in 1965. Gray died in 1976. The house is currently being restored.

| **1** Section A–A | **2** South Elevation | **3** First Floor Plan | **4** Section B–B | **5** Lower Floor Plan | **6** West Elevation | 71 |

2 South Elevation

1 Entrance
2 Japanese room
3 Bedroom
4 Living/dining/kitchen
5 Terrace

3 First Floor Plan

1 Main entrance
2 Living room
3 Wardrobe
4 Shower
5 Alcove
6 Dining area
7 Terrace
8 Bar
9 Bedroom
10 Bathroom
11 Service entrance
12 Winter kitchen
13 Summer kitchen

5 Lower Floor Plan

1 Guest room
2 Servant's room
3 Heating
4 Workshop
5 Terrace under house
6 Shed

1

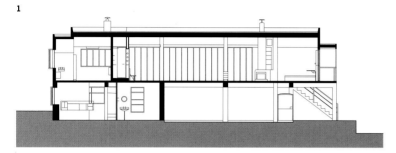

2

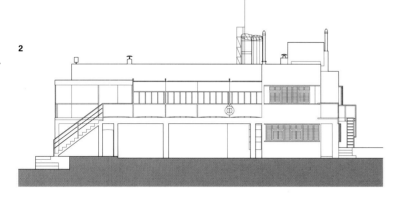

3

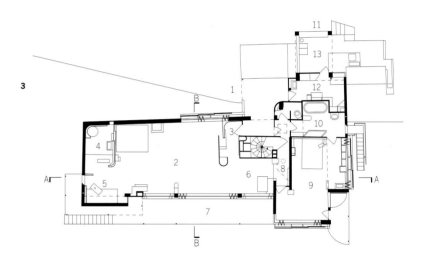

4

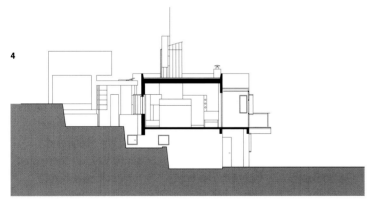

5

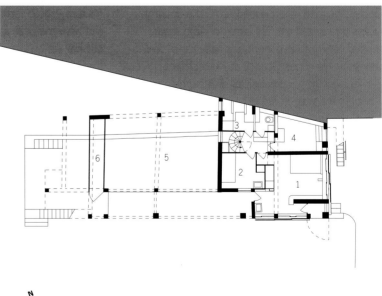

6

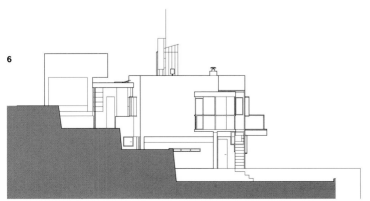

N

0   5   10 m
15   30 ft

High and Over

Amyas Connell, 1901–80

Amersham, Buckinghamshire, UK; 1930

Amyas Connell worked his passage to England from his native New Zealand as a stoker on a steamship in 1923. Three years later he was keeping very different company, having won a scholarship to study at the British School in Rome, whose director was Bernard Ashmole. In 1929, at the age of 35, Ashmole was appointed professor of classical archaeology at University College, London, and decided to build a country house for himself and his family in Amersham, a small town within commuting distance of the university. He chose Connell as his architect.

Given the circumstances of Ashmole's and Connell's meeting, it would have been reasonable to expect the house to be classical in style, or at least comfortably traditional. Not so. To the local people of Amersham, and in particular the planning authorities, High and Over was a shocker: a stark, white, concrete, flat-roofed, undecorated box with a Y-shaped plan. It was one of the first truly Modernist houses in England.

Le Corbusier was a strong influence. Connell and his fellow New Zealander Basil Ward (they later set up a partnership) had visited the 1925 Exposition des Arts Décoratifs in Paris, and been impressed by the Pavillon de l'Esprit Nouveau

(see pages 48–49). The little pavilion may have encouraged them to abandon tradition and embrace abstraction, but in every other respect it was very different from High and Over. The Amersham house is more an Italian Renaissance villa than a prototype for mass housing, with formal gardens extending the geometry of the plan out across the open hilltop site. It is an odd mixture – both formal and informal, symmetrical and asymmetrical, as if determined to be modern but not yet quite ready to let form flow naturally from function. The diagrammatic plan, with three wings radiating from a hexagonal core, is adapted in some rather clumsy ways to meet the domestic requirements. On the ground floor, the tripartite division – living room, dining room, library – seems sensible enough, although the servicing of the dining-room wing necessitates a single-storey kitchen extension and a long corridor on one side.

On the first floor, the master bedroom and the guest room get a wing each, with the staff bedrooms in the third, but there is no room for a staff bathroom, which has to be accommodated in an incongruously prominent position over the main entrance. On the top floor, symmetry breaks down completely. The children's bedrooms and a

night nursery occupy the staff wing, with a big day nursery in the top of the hexagonal core. Roofs of the other two wings are terraces shaded by elegant cantilevered concrete canopies.

But it is the hexagonal core that constitutes the principal spatial event of the interior. Two of its three free sides are occupied by the front and garden entrances. The third bulges out to accommodate the staircase, which is fully glazed over two storeys, bringing daylight into the heart of the house. A circular hole in the first-floor landing opens up a double-height space and makes a gallery from which to view an illuminated fountain. The house has a reinforced-concrete frame with rendered brick infill. Windows are mostly Corbusian ribbons, but with occasional vertical accents, like the almost traditional bay window in the master bedroom.

The house's Modernist features do not, in the end, seem to be fully developed. Perhaps, after all, this is an essentially classical house.

1 First Floor Plan

1 Bedroom
2 Dressing room
3 Bathroom

2 Second Floor Plan

1 Day nursery
2 Night nursery
3 Nurse's bedroom

3 Ground Floor Plan

1 Living room
2 Library
3 Dining room
4 Kitchen
5 Pantry

4 Site Plan

1

2

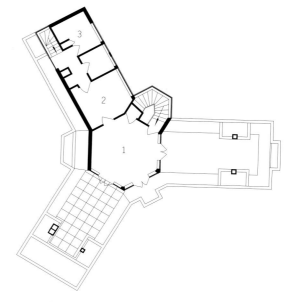

3

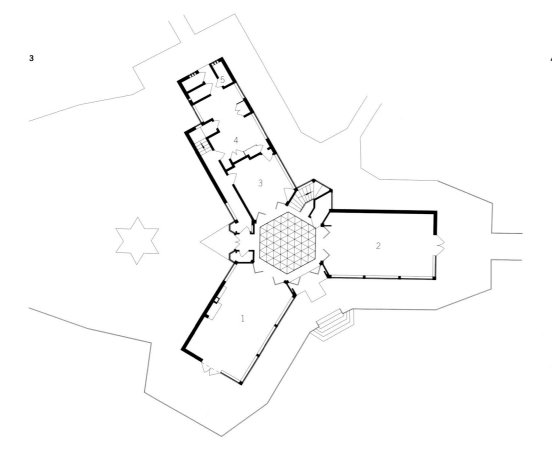

4

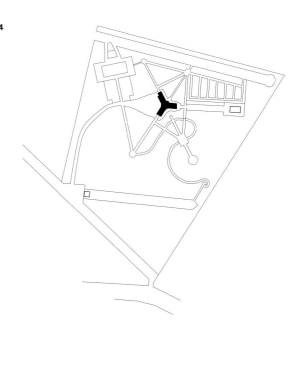

0   5   10 m

15   30 ft

Müller House

Adolf Loos, 1870–1933

Prague, Czech Republic; 1930

According to Kenneth Frampton, the Müller House represents 'the ultimate Loosian *Raumplan*'. It sits on a rather constricted, sloping site, among other detached houses in what was in the 1930s, and is again today, a well-to-do suburb of Prague. The exterior is extremely austere – a plain stuccoed box perforated by small windows – but there is a clue to the sumptuousness of the interior in the recessed entrance porch lined with Travertine stone. A short corridor leads to an entrance hall, which is small but classical in its proportions and symmetries. Behind the far wall, a short flight of steps leads up to a little formal threshold space that is the pivotal point of the whole plan.

Ahead lies the fine, high, rectangular living room, a double square on plan. Loos's fondness for symmetry is immediately apparent in the placing of the red-brick fireplace, the built-in sofa that answers it at the other end of the room, the three tall windows in the long external wall, and the paired ceiling lights.

. The symmetry is not tyrannical, however. We enter off-centre (but in line with the left-hand window) and the 'wall' through which we enter is an asymmetrical abstract composition, more void than solid. It is clad in streaky blue Cipolin marble,

which makes it more than just a wall, and though it is divided into three equal bays, each bay is different. To the right of the pivotal threshold, steps lead up to the dining room, which is open to the staircase and looks down into the living room through the end bay of the Cipolin wall.

Too wide to be accommodated in the main external box, the dining room projects beyond it, forming an external terrace for the bedroom on the floor above. Another flight of steps to the left of the threshold leads up to the Lady's Room. This little study, lined in lemon wood, has an even smaller sitting alcove at a yet higher level, from which you can look back over the living room through a discreet window resembling the spy-hole in the solar of an English medieval manor house. These combined living spaces can be seen as a single, convoluted spiral. The library next to the Lady's Room is in effect the man's room, lined in masculine mahogany, with a modern desk and leather chesterfields either side of a tiled fireplace. Bedrooms are arranged more straightforwardly on an upper floor reached by means of a top-lit, open-welled staircase in the middle of the plan. Loos designed all the built-in furniture, including wardrobes, dressing tables and bedside tables.

The client was a wealthy building contractor with a wife and one young daughter, so this was a household with more servants than masters. A completely separate service staircase, with an adjacent lift, rises from the basement utility rooms, up through the living and bedroom levels, to what ought in theory to be staff rooms on the top floor. In fact, one of these rooms was decorated in Japanese style and used by the family in conjunction with the large flat roof, which accommodated a swimming pool.

The house was lovingly restored in 2000, complete with surprising but apparently original bright yellow window frames, and is now open to the public.

1 Second Floor Plan

1 Bedroom
2 Roof terrace

2 First Floor Plan

1 Bedroom
2 Dressing room
3 Bathroom
4 WC

3 West Elevation

4 Upper Ground Floor Plan

1 Living room
2 Dining room
3 Servery
4 Kitchen
5 Lady's room
6 Library
7 From entrance hall

5 Section A–A

6 Lower Ground Floor Plan

1 Entrance
2 WC
3 Storage
4 Boiler room
5 Kitchen
6 Staff room
7 Garage

1

2

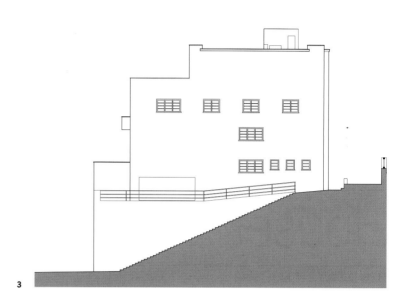

3

4

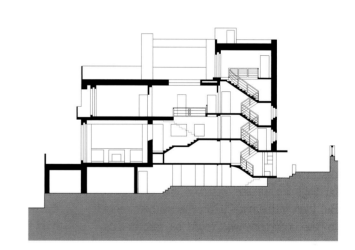

5

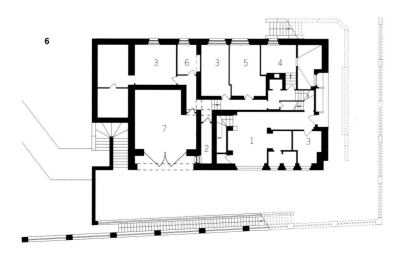

6

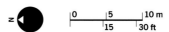

Houses at Am Rupenhorn

Hans Luckhardt, 1890–1954

Charlottenburg, Berlin, Germany; 1930

Early in their careers, the Luckhardt brothers, Wassili and Hans, were associated with the Glass Chain, a utopian correspondence group led by Bruno Taut. The group shared the poet Paul Scheerbart's vision of a new glass architecture that would unify the arts and transform the European city with buildings that were the modern equivalent of the medieval cathedral. Wassili's designs of the early 1920s for houses and public buildings are angular, crystalline and expressionist. But then, in the mid-1920s, the brothers seem to have undergone what might be described as an anti-religious conversion, and began to see the future in rational and productive rather than spiritual and mystical terms. By 1925, they had built an uncompromisingly abstract and cubic terrace of houses in the Dahlem district of Berlin that belonged firmly to the movement known as the *Neue Sachlichkeit*, or New Objectivity. The Dahlem terrace was built in traditional rendered brickwork, but it was not long before the brothers were experimenting with lightweight-steel frames.

The two steel-framed houses at Am Rupenhorn in Charlottenburg, Berlin, rival the early villas of Le Corbusier as clear statements of the new Modernist aesthetic. Both are plain white rectangular boxes, one parallel to the road, one at right angles to it, but they are variations on a single theme and can be considered together. They are somewhat reminiscent of the version of the Maison Citrohan that Le Corbusier built at the Weissenhof Siedlung in 1927, but they relate more subtly to their site, which slopes up from the road to the edge of a wood.

One way to cope with the slope would have been to raise the houses on Corbusian pilotis, sacrificing direct access to the ground from the main living rooms. The alternative — to dig them into the ground — would have compromised the purity of the white boxes. The design resolves the problem by creating an artificial ground level in the form of a paved terrace projecting forward from the top of the slope. Service functions such as kitchen, garage, chauffeur's room and storerooms are tucked under the terrace, and almost the whole of the first floor at terrace level is occupied by a single large living room. Bedrooms are on the floor above and there is a garden on the flat roof, defined as an external room by a pergola and a floating cornice borrowed from Le Corbusier. There are differences between the two houses, apart from their orientation. The house to the north is more elaborate, with a vertical slot over the main entrance, from which small balconies project, and a second, lower terrace on the north side, supported by a curved retaining wall. Both houses have lightweight-steel frames with identical column grids, dividing the box longitudinally into two unequal parts: a living zone, and a service and circulation zone.

The technology was advanced for the time. Photographs of the houses under construction show a relatively tidy site resulting from the mainly dry construction. The external wall is made of precast-concrete infill panels with a cork lining for insulation and an outer waterproof coating of render on steel mesh. Precast-concrete panels are also used for the floors, spanning between steel joists. Window and door frames are all steel.

Spatially, the houses are simple and rational, with none of the sculptural and dynamic qualities of Le Corbusier's villas. But these are more than just technical exercises. The main living room of the north house, for example, is extremely refined, with its library alcove defined by two freestanding columns, its almost classical lighting cornice, its freestanding radiators and its enormous, full-height sliding glass panels opening onto the terrace.

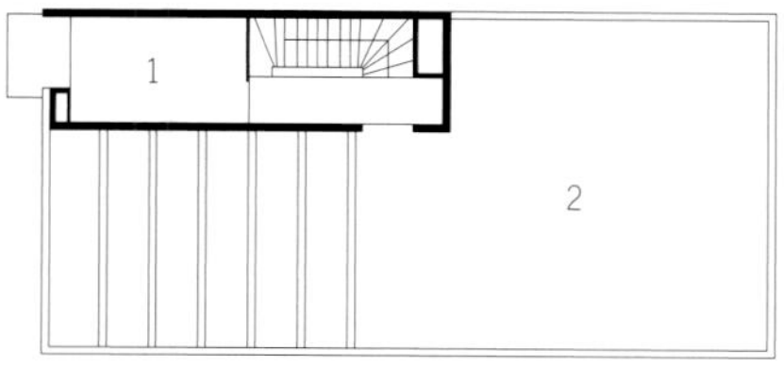

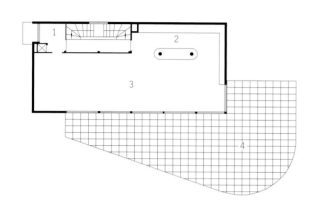

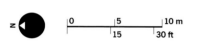

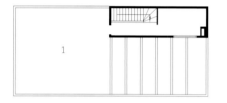

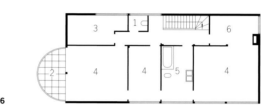

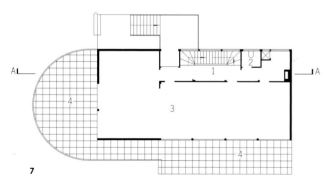

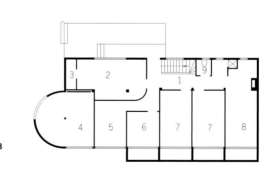

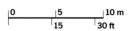

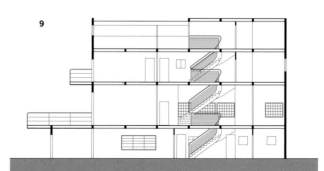

House 1

1 Second Floor Plan

1 Bedroom
2 Roof Garden

2 First Floor Plan

1 WC
2 Bathroom
3 Maid's room
4 Dressing room
5 Bedroom

3 Ground Floor Plan

1 Servery
2 Library
3 Living area
4 Terrace

4 Basement Plan

1 Hall
2 WC
3 Laundry
4 Plant room
5 Garage
6 Storage
7 Larder
8 Bathroom
9 Kitchen
10 Chauffeur's room

House 2

5 Second Floor Plan

1 Roof garden

6 First Floor Plan

1 Wc
2 Terrace
3 Maid's room
4 Bedroom
5 Bathroom
6 Dressing room

7 Ground Floor Plan

1 Hall
2 WC
3 Living room
4 Terrace

8 Basement Plan

1 Hall
2 Kitchen
3 Larder
4 Garage
5 Chauffeur's room
6 Laundry
7 Storage
8 Plant
9 WC

9 Section A–A

Tugendhat House

Ludwig Mies van der Rohe, 1886–1969

Brno, Czech Republic; 1928–30

'There is more to life than just looking at onyx walls and veneers of precious woods,' wrote the architecture critic Roger Ginsburger of the Tugendhat House in 1931. He was one of several critics who disliked what seemed to them more a furniture exhibition than a house. Its enormous single living space lacked any seclusion or privacy, and there were no walls to hang pictures on. But Grete Tugendhat and her husband Fritz disagreed. She was an intellectual, an early follower of the philosopher Martin Heidegger, and she loved the austerity of the house, its essential seriousness. 'I always wanted a modern house,' she said, 'with generous spaces and clear, simple forms.'

In plan and section the house is actually rather complex: three storeys high, on a steeply sloping, south-facing site, with the main entrance on the top floor. But its heart is the main living room on the middle floor, to which everything else is subservient. There are no changes of height or level in this room, simply an expanse of white linoleum answered by a flat plastered ceiling. On the south and east sides it is bounded by straight glass walls, or rather by the views through them – the first a long view over the garden to the Spielberg castle on the opposite hill, the second

a close-up view of pot plants in a narrow winter garden. The room is thus defined and adorned not by pictures of nature but by nature itself. On the north and west sides the enclosure is more complicated, with set-backs and alcoves that loosely define different uses: an entrance area, a study, a library, a space for a grand piano.

In the middle of the room, two extraordinary objects divide the space more purposefully: a semicircular wooden partition is wrapped around a dining table, and a screen of solid marble divides the remaining space roughly in half. These are the onyx walls and precious veneers that so irritated Ginsburger. Their strongly figured surfaces are, perhaps, fossilized versions of the living nature visible through the windows. They have their counterparts in the famous Barcelona Pavilion, designed at about the same time, as do the chrome-clad cruciform columns that measure out the space on a square grid. For this is a steel-framed building, although the frame is mostly concealed behind plaster and stucco.

Two sections of the south-facing glass wall, each 5 metres (16 feet) wide, can be lowered into the floor by electric motors. The openings line-up exactly with the wood and onyx screens. So what

resembles on plan a 'flexible' space is in reality subtly divided into distinct zones by columns, screens, furniture and window mullions, grouped symmetrically. A door at the west end of the south wall opens onto a paved terrace from which a broad flight of steps descends to the garden.

When the house was built, a large willow tree stood near the bottom of these steps, almost exactly opposite the dining area. The tree no longer exists, but it was shown on the original plans and was without doubt part of the design: the living natural pivot of the whole composition. The Tugendhat House is now preserved as an historic monument and museum.

1

1 East Elevation

2

2 North Elevation

3

3 South Elevation

4

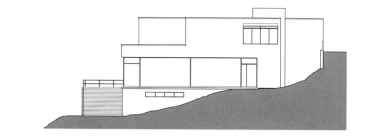

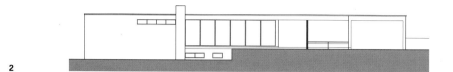

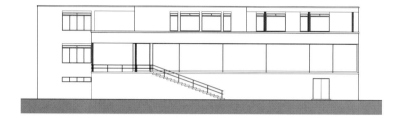

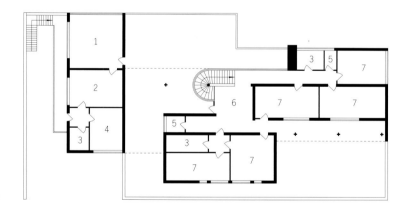

4 Second Floor Plan

1 Garage
2 Storage
3 Bathroom
4 Chauffeur's room
5 WC
6 Entrance
7 Bedroom

5

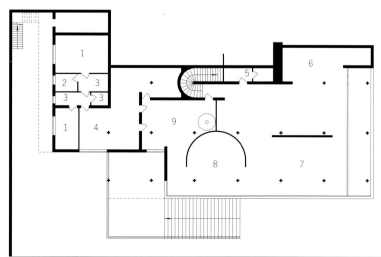

5 First Floor Plan

1 Staff room
2 Bathroom
3 Storage
4 Kitchen
5 WC
6 Study
7 Sitting area
8 Dining area
9 Servery

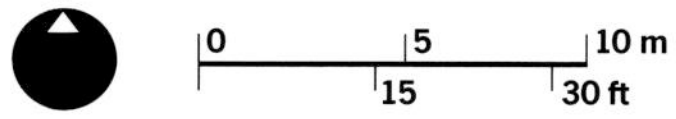

N
0
5
10 m
15
30 ft

Villa Savoye

Le Corbusier, 1887–1965

Poissy, France; 1931

Last and best of the Purist villas, the Villa Savoye was designed to show off the inventions that Le Corbusier had tested and refined in a dozen previous projects. What he had identified as the 'five points of a new architecture' – pilotis, roof garden, free plan, free façade, long windows – are all present, plus a couple more: pedestrian ramp and vehicle-turning circle. They are composed with the apparently effortless skill of a master in full command of his craft. After this he would move on to new tasks and new visions.

With a wealthy, open-minded client and an unrestricted site, the conditions were propitious for the creation of a masterpiece. This was Le Corbusier's first opportunity to design a large, truly freestanding villa, viewable from all sides. The basic arrangement of forms and spaces is very simple: a shallow box, almost square on plan, is provided with long windows on all four sides and raised off the ground on pilotis. The size of the box is dictated by two fixed factors: the maximum gradient of a pedestrian ramp and the minimum turning circle of a car. Like objects in a Purist painting, the ramp and the turning circle had to be included in the frame implied by the box. This restriction caused problems in the development

of the design, which was far too big for its budget (a normal situation for Le Corbusier). Cuts had to be made. The curvaceous screen wall that shelters the rooftop solarium and gives the villa its ship-like character is all that is left of the second-floor master bedroom suite in the original design.

It is remarkable how little of the space in the final building is fully enclosed and usable by the client. Discounting the garage and rooms for staff on the ground floor, the accommodation amounts to no more than a salon, three bedrooms, a boudoir, two bathrooms and a kitchen. These are all on one level, the piano nobile, most of the remainder of which is devoted to a terrace, treated as a roofless room, and an extension to the boudoir, which is roofed but open to the terrace.

It is the masterly way in which the spaces are combined that makes the design so fascinating. The ramp is the key. From the austere, factory-glazed entrance hall it rises in two stages to the piano nobile, where it steps out onto the terrace and rises another two stages to the solarium. Its companion, the spiral staircase, though a beautiful object, is for staff and short-cuts only. The proper way to enjoy the spaces is by means of the slow, continuous, ceremonial procession of

the ramp. Many delightful details enhance the enjoyment: the diagonal tiling of the entrance-hall floor, the all-glass wall that divides and unites the salon and the terrace, the tiled lounger in Madame Savoye's bathroom, the ship's funnel of the staircase enclosure, and the unglazed window in the solarium screen that ends the journey up the ramp with a perfectly framed view of the valley of the Seine in the distance.

Despite several attempts to reduce construction costs, the final contractor's bill was twice the original estimate. The building also suffered from numerous defects about which the client complained for years afterwards. In a better condition now than it ever was in the 1930s, it has become a place of pilgrimage for architects from all over the world.

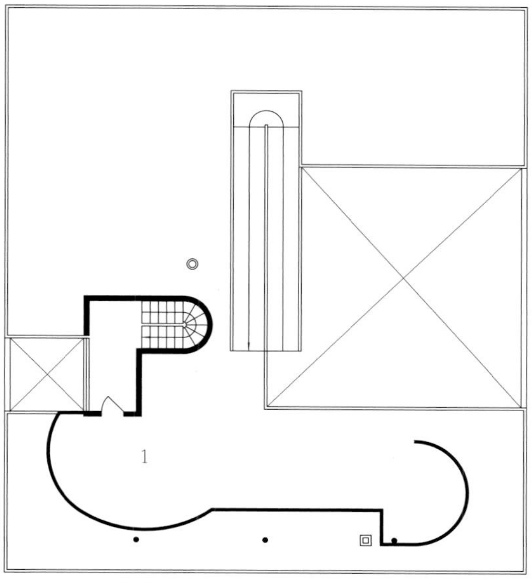

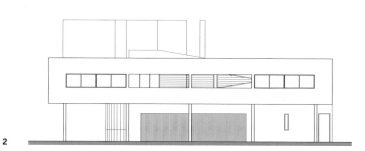

2 Northeast Elevation

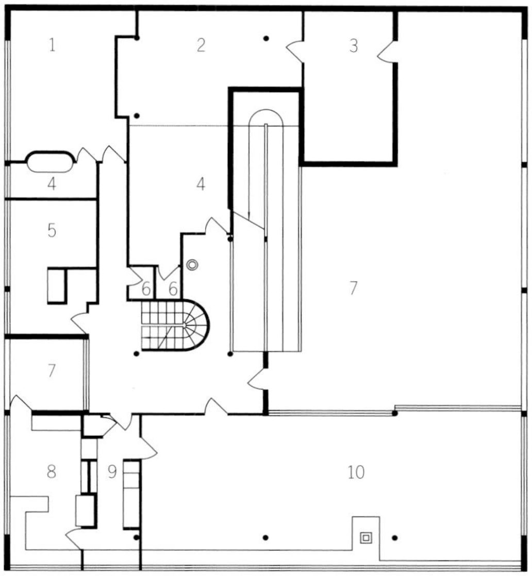

3 First Floor Plan

1 Son's room
2 Madame's room
3 Boudoir
4 Bathroom
5 Guest room
6 WC
7 Terrace
8 Kitchen
9 Pantry
10 Salon

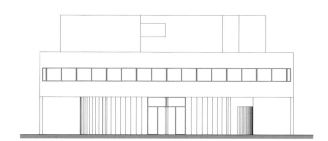

4 Southeast Elevation

5 Ground Floor Plan

1 Laundry
2 Chauffeur's room
3 Ensuite bathroom
4 Maid's room
5 Garage
6 WC

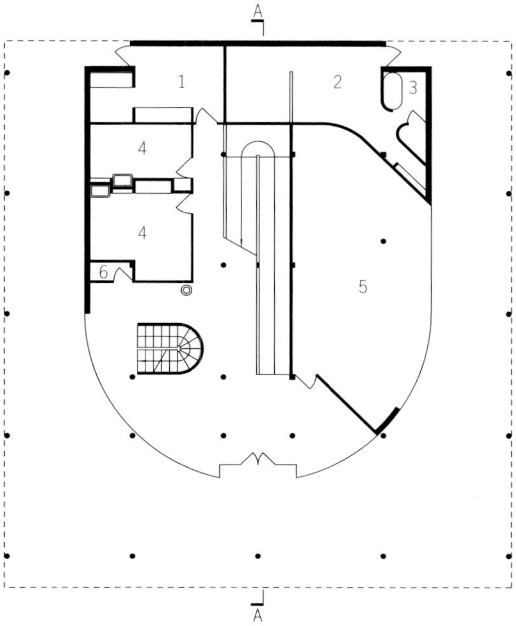

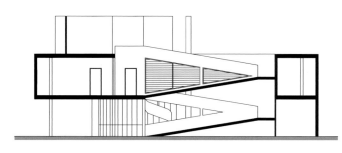

6 Section A–A

0 5 10 m
15 30 ft

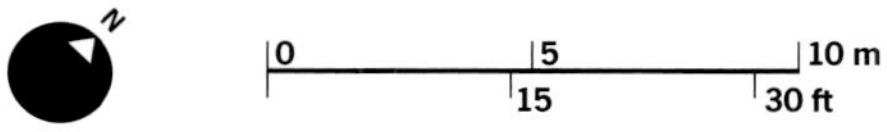

Aluminaire House

Alfred Lawrence Kocher and Albert Frey, 1885–1969 and 1903–98

Syosset (Plainview), New York, USA; 1930–31

To design a cheap, standardized, uncompromisingly modern house suitable for mass production was the dream of many an ambitious architect in mid-century America. Most projects progressed no further than the prototype stage, but a few, such as Konrad Wachsmann's Packaged House and Buckminster Fuller's Wichita House (see pages 104–105), have entered the history books because of the originality of their designs and the eminence of their designers. The Aluminaire House is perhaps not as famous as it should be, given that it is one of the earliest examples of the type.

It made its first appearance as a full-size prototype in the 50th Anniversary Exhibition of the New York Architectural League held at Grand Central Palace in April 1931. Contemporary accounts suggest that it was the only interesting exhibit in a rather dull show.

When the exhibition was over, the architect Wallace Harrison bought the house for his own use, dismantling it and re-erecting it on his estate in Long Island. The following year, Henry Russell Hitchcock and Philip Johnson chose to show photographs and drawings of it in their epoch-making International Style exhibition at the Museum of Modern Art in New York. It was

one of only two American houses included in the exhibition, the other being Richard Neutra's Lovell Health House (see pages 68–69).

But was it genuinely American? Its designer, Albert Frey, was a Swiss émigré who had worked for Le Corbusier in Paris between 1928 and 1930 and produced a full set of construction drawings for the Villa Savoye (see pages 80–81). With this in mind, it is easy to see the origin of certain features of Aluminaire. The six columns that are its only vertical supports are strongly reminiscent of the Domino House concept; the ground floor is open at the front, displaying two of the columns as pilotis; there is a partly covered roof garden; the walls are all non-loadbearing; and the windows are continuous ribbons except for the complete glass wall on one side of the double-height living room. All these features are borrowed from Le Corbusier's Purist repertoire.

Frey's partner, A. Lawrence Kocher, was a Californian who trained as architect but also worked as a teacher and journalist. He was managing editor of *Architectural Record*, and the Aluminaire House naturally featured in the magazine. An article that he wrote about site planning for suburban housing was illustrated

by an axonometric drawing showing Aluminaire houses grouped in alternative arrangements. It could easily be mistaken for Le Corbusier's Pessac housing estate, completed in 1929.

In one important respect the Aluminaire House is definitely not Corbusian: as its name suggests, it is made of metal rather than concrete. The structural frame is of aluminium and light steel, and the external walls are of insulation board on a wooden frame covered by thin sheets of corrugated aluminium. Aluminium was a relatively new material at the time and the whole idea of a metal house – a house like a car – gave it the futuristic look necessary to attract publicity and, perhaps, investment in production. Its designers reckoned that it would be economical if produced in tens of thousands. It never was, of course. It remained a single prototype. But it still exists, carefully restored, on the Central Islip campus of the New York Institute of Technology.

1 Second Floor Plan

1 Living room
2 Library
3 Lawn
4 Terrace

2 First Floor Plan

1 Living room
2 Dining room
3 Bedroom
4 Kitchen
5 Exercise room
6 Bathroom

3 Ground Floor Plan

1 Garage
2 Hall
3 Storage
4 Heater
5 Porch

4 West Elevation

6 South Elevation

5 East Elevation

7 Section A–A

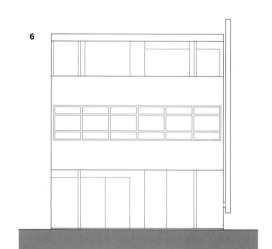

1

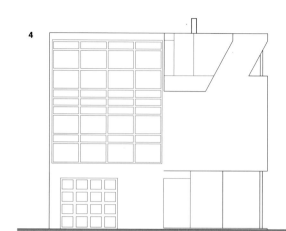

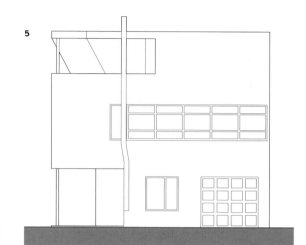

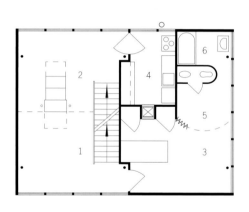

2

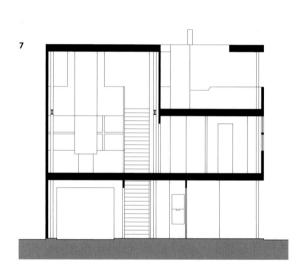

6

7

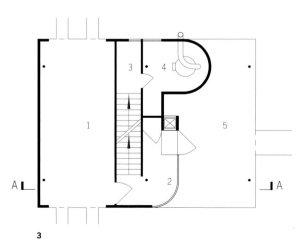

3

0   5   10 m
15   30 ft

Schminke House

Hans Scharoun, 1893–1972

Löbau, Germany; 1932–33

Hans Scharoun believed that architectural form and space should emerge from the requirements of the client's brief and the particular qualities of the site. In a sense, this was what all German Modernists of the 1920s and 1930s believed. But the movement was beginning to divide into two streams. One, represented by Ludwig Mies van der Rohe, tended towards abstraction and universality – a looser fit between form and function, and a wish to dominate the site. The other, represented by Scharoun and his mentor Hugo Häring, saw buildings as organisms that evolved to fit their functional and physical environments. Coming at the end of the first phase of Scharoun's career, the Schminke House represents an important stage in the development of 'organic' Modernism.

The site was next door to the client's noodle factory on the outskirts of Löbau, Germany. There were views to the north, away from the factory, and a slope down to a road along the eastern boundary, which ran at a slight angle to the north–south axis. These site conditions were determinants of the design. The view to the north presented a dilemma. Which way should the house face – towards the sun (and the factory) or towards the

view? Scharoun decided that the main living areas of the house should benefit from both sun and view. This suggested a long, narrow form, with windows on both sides facing precisely north and south. The house was therefore placed at an angle to the eastern boundary, which gave Scharoun the opportunity to make one of his favourite moves: introducing a non-right angle (in this case an angle of 26 degrees) into the plan.

It is this angle that gives the building its dynamic quality. Both the east and west ends of the house are angled but, more importantly, so is the main staircase, which rises directly from the entrance in a double-height hall. The form of this staircase acts like a welcoming gesture, indicating the big square opening into the living room. The south-facing windows of the living room form a relatively narrow horizontal ribbon, allowing the sunshine in but also keeping it under control. On the north side of the room, where there is no danger of uncomfortable solar-heat gain, a full-height glass wall looks out onto a terrace and the long view beyond. At its east end, the living room kinks left and becomes a glazed solarium, with a little conservatory or winter garden on the south side. The solarium is surrounded by the terrace,

which is cantilevered over the falling ground. On the floor above, the master bedroom is provided with an equally spacious terrace, sheltered by a big roof overhang supported on a single steel column. Three flights of steps link the terraces with each other and the garden, all of them set at the same angle as the main staircase.

The fact that Scharoun spent his childhood in the busy port of Bremerhaven might explain why the Schminke house looks so much like a ship. The terraces are decks, the external stairs with their metal handrails are companionways, and the rounded corners seem to have been shaped or profile-cut in sheet steel. There is even a porthole in the side wall of the entrance hall. In Scharoun's later, postwar work, the marine theme became less prominent, but the organic design method became even more radical. By the early 1960s, those two streams of Modernism had become completely different styles. Nothing could illustrate the contrast better than two Berlin buildings that stand almost side by side: Mies's National Gallery and Scharoun's Philharmonie.

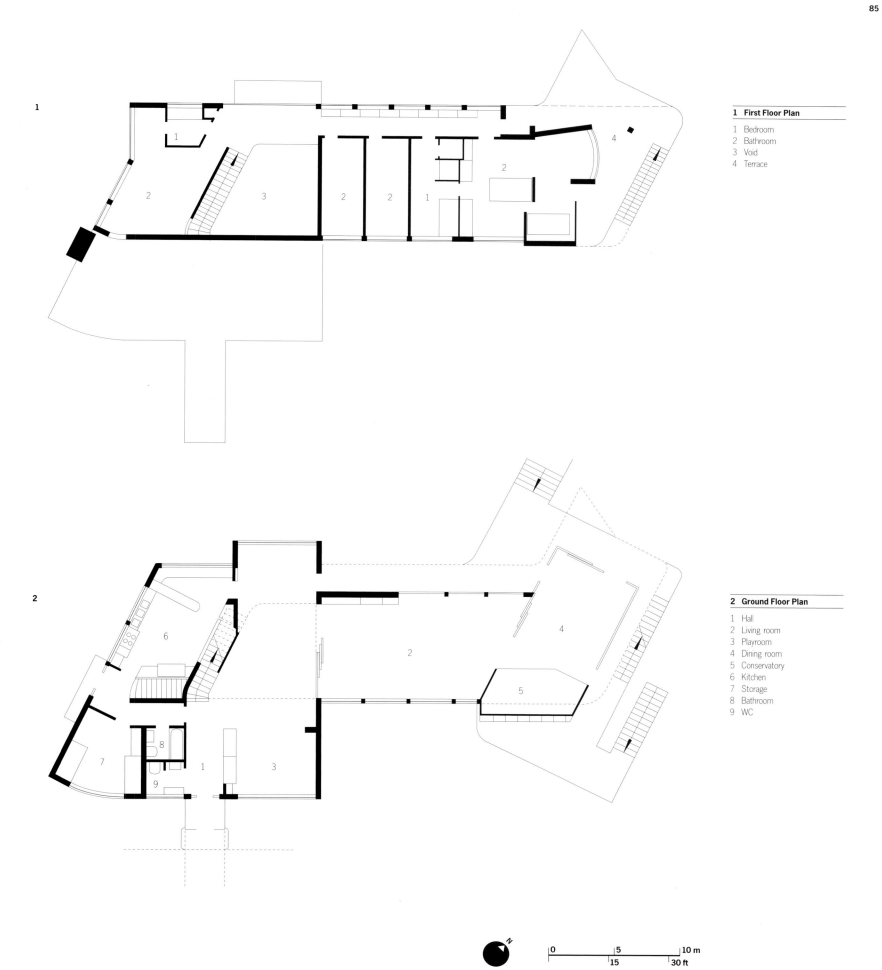

1

1 First Floor Plan

1 Bedroom
2 Bathroom
3 Void
4 Terrace

2

2 Ground Floor Plan

1 Hall
2 Living room
3 Playroom
4 Dining room
5 Conservatory
6 Kitchen
7 Storage
8 Bathroom
9 WC

| 0 | 5 | 10 m |
| 15 | | 30 ft |

Villa Girasole

Ettore Fagiuoli, 1884–1961

Marcellise, Italy; 1935

Girasole means sunflower and, like a sunflower, the Villa Girasole turns its face to the sun, following it across the sky. The owner and inventor of the villa was Angelo Invernizzi, a civil and nautical engineer. Having made his fortune working in the port of Genoa, he decided to build himself a country house near his birthplace north of Verona.

To this day, the Marcellise valley is a peaceful place of vineyards, olive groves and oak woods streaked with cypresses. The romantic idea of a sunflower house suits the surroundings perfectly. To make the idea a reality, however, Invernizzi and his collaborators had to call on the technology of another world: the world of mechanized transport and heavy engineering, the world that had been celebrated a couple of decades earlier by the Futurists. In reality, the Villa Girasole is more like a travelling crane or a swing bridge than a flower.

The villa is divided into two parts. The lower part is a three-storey drum built into the hillside. This is a sizable house in its own right, containing several functionally non-specific rooms and a large belvedere looking out over the valley. It has a reinforced-concrete structure, faced with stucco and decorated in the vaguely classical Novocento style. Its main purpose, however, is to serve as the static support for the sunflower itself which, to mix metaphors, sits on its roof like a slice of cake on a cake-stand. A quadrant-shaped platform supports a two-storey, L-shaped house, and the entire assemblage is mounted on 15 wheeled bogies running on three circular rails. Two of the bogies on the outer rail are fitted with electric motors that are powerful enough to push the house through one complete revolution in about nine hours. The most extraordinary part of the mechanism is the axle or pivot around which the house revolves. This is attached to the cake, not the cake-stand, and it takes the form of a cylinder containing an open-welled spiral staircase and a lift. Far down below, in a basement chamber, lurks a large central roller bearing.

Surprisingly, the structure of both the house and the pivot is an advanced vierendeel frame in reinforced concrete, rather than steel. At the top, the hollow pivot projects above the roof of the house and is crowned by the lantern that looks exactly like the lens of a lighthouse.

Architecturally, the revolving house is quite distinct from its static base. An uncompromisingly modern building, it is clad in aluminium panels with not a classical detail in sight. Balconies cantilever out from its corners; pergolas resembling goalposts frame its roof terraces; and electrically operated shutters protect its windows.

Inside, the plan is straightforward, almost ordinary. Most rooms face inwards over the moving terrace, with circulation and service rooms on the outside of the L. Spatially, these domestic areas are tame in comparison with the exciting climb up the spiral staircase towards the light.

The idea of the sunflower might have been an afterthought. The Villa Girasole is more an engineer's toy than a poem in concrete, but it is a formidable piece of collaborative design, nevertheless. The architect, Ettore Fagiuoli, ensured that it was not only ingenious but also elegant. Currently, the villa is falling into disrepair and has not revolved for some time, but the local university has taken an interest and there are plans to renovate it.

1 Lower Level Plan

1 Hall
2 Bathroom
3 Living room
4 Study
5 Storage
6 Kitchen
7 Meeting room

2 Upper Level Plan

1 Bedroom
2 Bathroom
3 Balcony
4 Landing

3 East–West Section

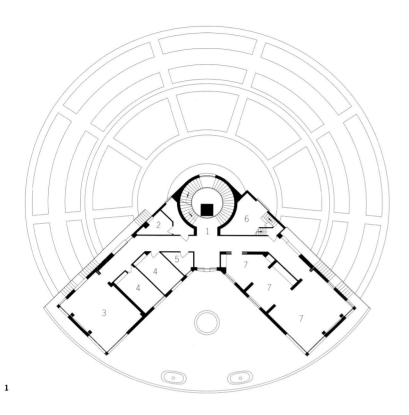

1

2

3

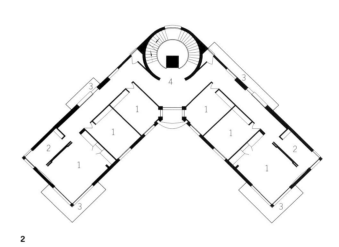

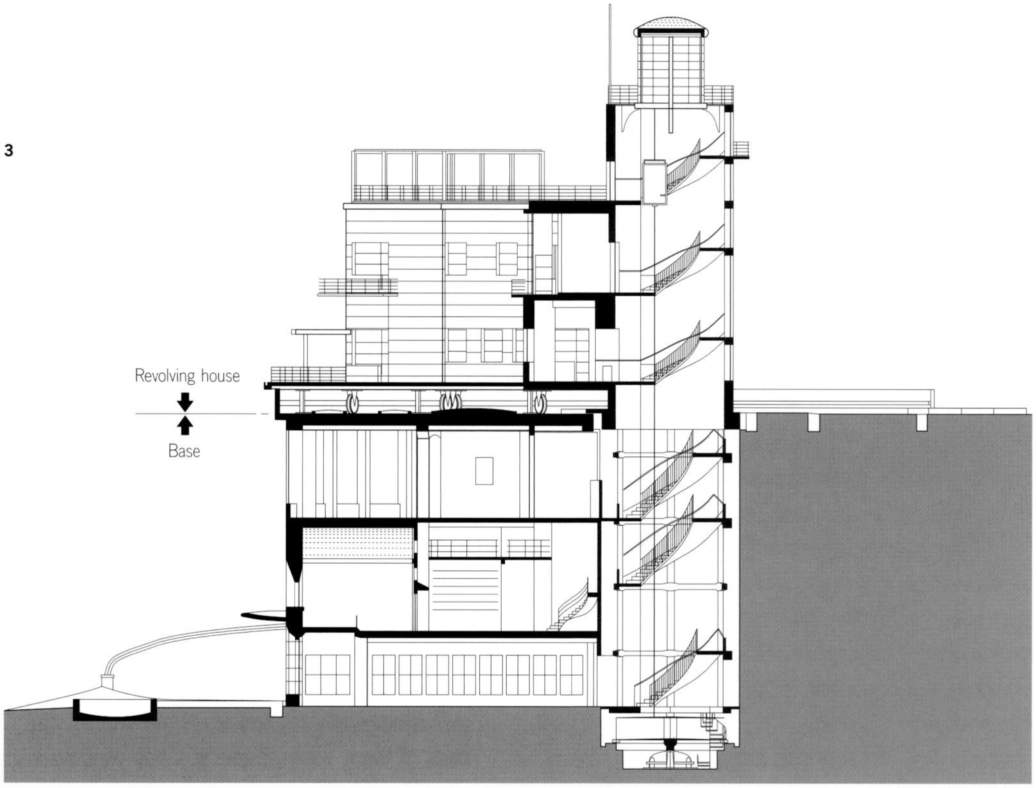

Revolving house

Base

N

0   5   10 m
15   30 ft

Sun House

Edwin Maxwell Fry, 1899–1987

Hampstead, London, UK; 1935

Sun House was one of the first truly Modernist houses to appear in London. Maxwell Fry had been introduced to the new style by his friend Wells Coates and had helped to found the famous MARS (Modern Architecture Research) group in 1932. At the time Sun House was being built, he was playing host to none other than Walter Gropius during Gropius's short sojourn in England before emigrating to the USA.

That Fry was influenced by Le Corbusier's Purist villas is obvious, but he was no dilettante. He had graduated from Liverpool University in 1924, worked for various practices including the Architects Department of Southern Railways, and designed several social-housing schemes to tight budgets using innovative construction techniques. He brought all of this practical experience to bear on Sun House, and it shows in the many clever subtleties of the plan and section.

The site slopes steeply from north to south and commands a fine view over London. Fry's first move, therefore, was to lift the main living space up onto a piano nobile, providing it with a panoramic window and a balcony the whole width of the house. A garage, a plant room and a small entrance hall are dug into the slope below, and a

retaining wall, painted dull grey, is pushed back behind the thin steel columns that support the balcony, creating the effect of pilotis. Bedrooms on the second floor also have south-facing ribbon windows, and the flat roof is a garden, as Corbusian doctrine dictates.

It is in the details that the quality of the house becomes apparent. For example, the stair that rises from the entrance hall to the piano nobile winds to the left for the top six steps, pointing the visitor straight at the living-room door. The staff domain — the kitchen and a maid's room — is two steps further up in the opposite direction. However, the kitchen reconnects with the dining room and living room over the stair — behind the visitor's back, as it were. The dining room is therefore two steps higher than the living room, creating a perfect transition within the open-plan space. The living-room balcony is not a mere ledge from which to admire the view, but a considered functional space that expands at the east end into a square external room. A thin concrete canopy propped up on a single column keeps the rain off when necessary and also shades the kitchen from the sun. At the back of living room, there is a bay window in the

corner which is big enough to sit in and perfect for reading or sewing in the constant north light. On the floor above, the master bedroom is served by a little complex of three ancillary spaces: a lobby containing a wardrobe gives access to a bathroom on one side and a covered balcony on the other, overlooking the larger living-room balcony below. The roof garden is not a token gesture, but a comfortable patio, sheltered from the wind and served by a dumb waiter from the kitchen two floors below.

This may be an early work in stylistic terms, but it is nevertheless the mature work of a master craftsman. After the Second World War, Maxwell Fry and his architect wife, Jane Drew, designed many educational buildings in west Africa, developing a special expertise in design for hot climates. In 1951 they were appointed senior architects for the new Punjabi capital of Chandigarh. The appointment of Le Corbusier as master planner was on their recommendation.

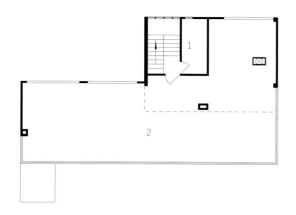

1

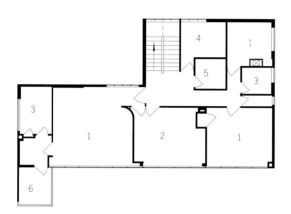

2

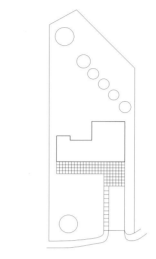

3

2   First Floor Plan

1   Bedroom
2   Dressing room
3   Bathroom
4   Sewing room
5   Dark room
6   Balcony

3   Site Plan

4

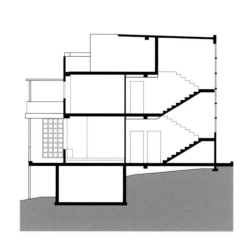

5

4   Ground Floor Plan

1   Living room
2   Dining room
3   Kitchen
4   Maid's room
5   Cloak room
6   Terrace

5   Section A–A

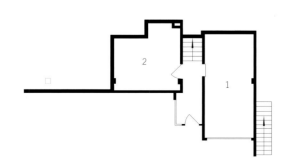

6

6   Lower Ground Floor Plan

1   Garage
2   Heating room

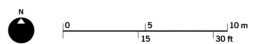

N
0   5   10 m
15   30 ft

Jacobs House

Frank Lloyd Wright, 1867–1959

Madison, Wisconsin, USA; 1936

From the late 1930s onwards, in the final phase of his long career, Frank Lloyd Wright built 26 individual, relatively cheap houses which he called Usonian houses. The name's origin is obscure, but to Wright Usonia was a kind of Utopia, an ideal America in which every family lived in a detached suburban house and owned a car. This may sound not very different from the real America, but Usonia was an America designed by Frank Lloyd Wright. The Jacobs House is the best of the Usonians and the clearest statement of Wright's solution to the problem of the small house.

The typical American suburban house is a two-storey box, often a version of a traditional Colonial or Cape Cod prototype. Placed in the middle of the site, it divides the garden and leaves useless spaces at the sides. The Jacobs House is different: L-shaped, single storey, and placed on the corner of the site with its back to the street so as to leave the garden in one piece. The internal plan is equally groundbreaking. Ten years previously, before the Depression, a professional family such as the Jacobses (he was a journalist) might have employed a maid. The kitchen would have been tucked away out of sight. But by 1938 the kitchen had become the domain of the most

important person in the home – the lady of the household, in this case Mrs Jacobs. It therefore occupies a commanding position at the centre of gravity of the plan, between the living-room and bedroom wings. The dining room, previously a kind of ceremonial space, the focus of family life and of entertaining, has disappeared, its function absorbed by the relaxed, informal living room. Wright's instinct was always to unify rather than divide space, to let it flow freely through the whole house, anchored only by the solid brick hearth.

The three-dimensional form of the house is revolutionary, too: the application of a building system rather than the adaptation of a standard type. Dimensions are controlled by a planning grid measuring 0.6 by 1.2 metres (2 by 4 feet) and a 0.33 metre (13 inch) vertical grid. (The debt to traditional Japanese architecture is obvious.) There are three types of wall – brickwork, full-height glass doors in wooden frames, and a special sandwich construction of plywood sheets faced both sides with alternating softwood and hardwood strips. Roofs are flat, on two levels with continuous clerestory lights in between, and the floor is a simple, groundbearing concrete slab, without the usual cellar. Heating is by hot-water

pipes cast into the floor slab – another innovation. This is not a building system in the industrial sense. Wright never envisaged setting up a factory to mass-produce Usonian houses. But it saved design time by combining a reference grid with a set of standard construction details, and it struck an economical balance between what Wright called 'millwork' and 'fieldwork'.

The Usonian Houses were only relatively small and cheap, built not for factory workers but for middle-class clients who knew the value, social as well as monetary, of owning a house designed by Frank Lloyd Wright. Nevertheless, Wright was one of the few great architects of the twentieth century to have direct influence on popular taste. His designs were often published in home-making and women's magazines. After the war, Usonian features such as the open plan, the built-in closets, the garden terrace and the car port became the very symbols of American suburban culture.

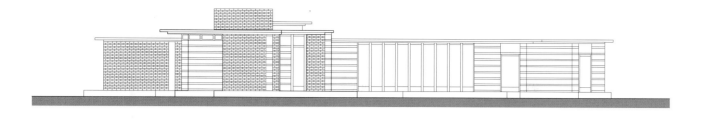

1

2   Section A–A

2

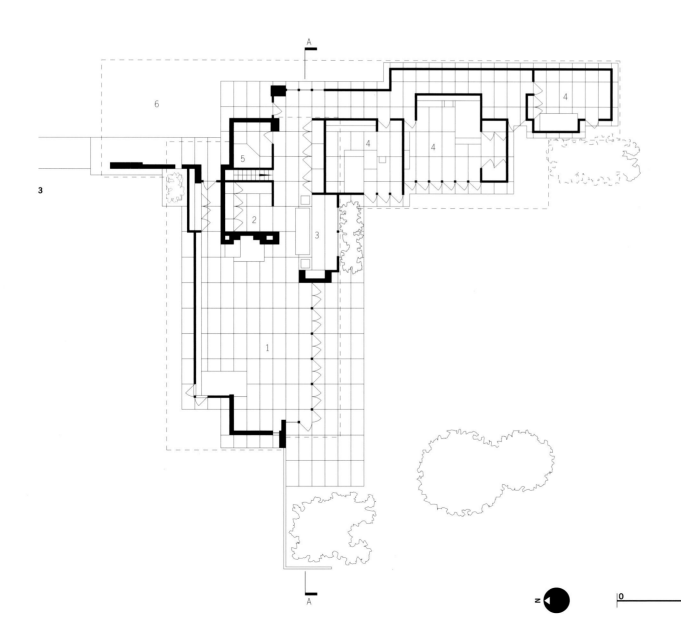

3

3   Ground Floor Plan

1   Living room
2   Kitchen
3   Dining
4   Bedroom
5   Bathroom
6   Car port

| 0 | | 5 | | 10 m |
| 15 | | | 30 ft | |

Fallingwater

Frank Lloyd Wright, 1867–1959

Bear Run, Pennsylvania, USA; 1935–37

Frank Lloyd Wright designed everything in his head, using drawings only to confirm what he had already fully imagined. He was not unduly worried, therefore, when, one day in September 1935, he heard that his client Edgar J. Kaufmann would be with him at his Taliesin office within hours and would expect to see the long-overdue sketch design for Fallingwater. No drawings yet existed. Wright sat down at his drawing board and without hesitation produced a composite plan, a section and an elevation, all fully resolved. When Kaufmann arrived and saw the design, he was thrilled. From that day on – despite terrible technical difficulties, blazing rows and huge overspending – Kaufmann remained dedicated to the project. Fallingwater was an inspiration to him for the rest of his life.

Kaufmann and his wife had been in the habit of spending their weekends at a picturesque spot near a waterfall on Bear Run, a mountain stream in the woods of west Pennsylvania. Asked to provide a replacement for their little prefabricated cabin, Wright proposed a house perched on the very rock from which they fished and swam. At first the idea seemed self-defeating; the house would surely destroy its own *raison d'être*. But Wright was confident that he could improve

on nature. His solution lay in the principle of the cantilever and in a material he had previously shunned: reinforced concrete. It would be a big, spacious house, but it would spread out not on the river bank but in the very air above the waterfall. Structurally, the terraces of the house would be like the leaves of the rhododendrons that hung over the river, or like the startling yet natural apparition of a bracket fungus. They would be anchored by an equally natural extension of the river bank in the form of walls and piers of locally quarried stone.

The vision was triumphantly realized. Far from destroying a beautiful spot, the house lifts it into a vision of the harmony of man and nature. In another setting, the great terraces might seem aggressive and boastful; here they look natural and inevitable, as though this were some unknown tribe's normal method of housebuilding. The spatial programme is conventional enough: a large, unified living space and four sizable bedrooms. But the rooms seem secondary to the complex, many-layered organism of the concrete terraces and the stones that anchor them. Sometimes rooms are carved out of the masonry, sometimes they are merely areas of terrace enclosed by minimal steel-

framed glass walls. The details are inventive but not gimmicky because they are intrinsic to the overall vision: a flight of steps descends from a hatch in the living-room floor to hover just above the surface of the stream; three tree trunks grow through the floor of the western terrace; by the hearth an uncut boulder breaks the surface of the stone-flagged floor like the rock on which the house is founded. This last detail was suggested by Kaufmann himself and, for once, wholeheartedly approved by his architect.

But there is a big price to pay, psychological as well as monetary, for building and living in an architectural masterpiece. For many years after the completion of the house, Kaufmann kept a nervous eye on the structure as it groaned and sagged. Engineers were regularly called in to survey it, and regularly they recommended propping the cantilevers up on columns. This, of course, would have destroyed the vision. Kauffman never gave in, and the house survives more or less as it was designed, now in the care of the Western Pennsylvania Conservancy.

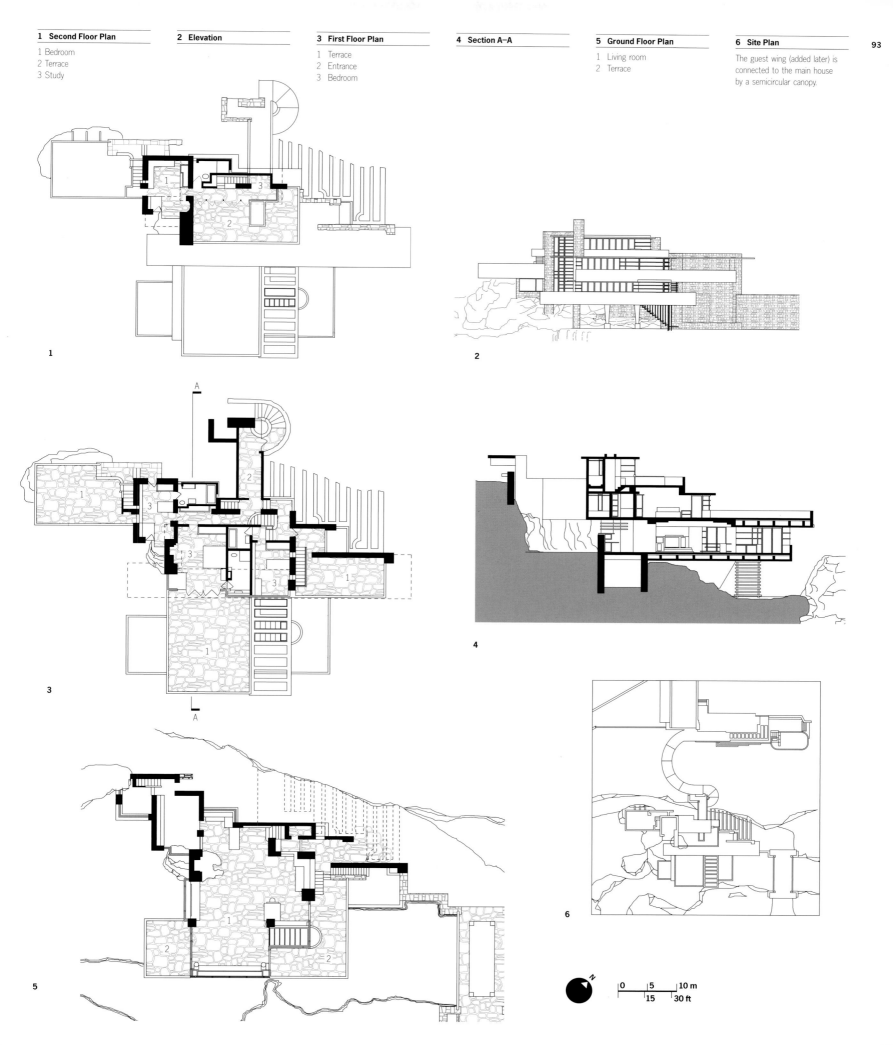

1 Second Floor Plan

1 Bedroom
2 Terrace
3 Study

2 Elevation

3 First Floor Plan

1 Terrace
2 Entrance
3 Bedroom

4 Section A–A

5 Ground Floor Plan

1 Living room
2 Terrace

6 Site Plan

The guest wing (added later) is connected to the main house by a semicircular canopy.

1

2

3

4

5

6

A

A

0   5   10 m
15   30 ft

Villa Mairea

Alvar Aalto, 1898–1976

Noormarkku, Finland; 1938–39

Alvar Aalto often said of his work, 'It all began in painting.' The painter is free to create form and space (or the illusion of form and space) without the constraints of structure and function. Aalto's architecture aspires to that freedom, avoiding anything that threatens to become a 'system'.

The Villa Mairea is like a cubist collage, freely juxtaposing objects that already carry meanings and associations. Columns are trees; a timber-boarded wall recalls an old Finnish farmhouse; a balustrade is borrowed from a Japanese temple.

Even the process of developing the design for Villa Mairea was unsystematic. Construction work had started on a different design when Aalto decided it was not good enough and should be rethought. His indulgent clients, Harry and Maire Gullichsen, had specifically encouraged him to experiment and not to worry about the possibility of failure, so they did not object.

But, instead of clearing away the old design and starting afresh, Aalto kept the outline while radically altering the plan. The new plan, though unsystematic, is nevertheless logical enough: L-shaped, with two wings — one for the family, another for the staff — divided by a secondary entrance hall and a dining-room zone. The roof

of the dining room continues out into the garden, eventually linking up with a traditional sauna by the pool that is the main feature of the courtyard.

A brief analysis of the family wing must suffice to illustrate the main characteristics of this exceptionally rich design. On the ground floor, one large space is divided in different ways to suit different uses. A change of floor finish on a serpentine line separates a sitting area focused on an elaborate corner fireplace from an area for playing music or entertaining. The entertaining space looks out on the driveway and arriving guests. A library in another corner is defined by apparently casually positioned bookcases, while a garden room in the opposite corner is walled in by painted brickwork. Forms and materials, mostly natural, are varied enough to avoid any charge of consistency, but the overall envelope is square, and it even has columns on a regular grid. Almost every column is different, however. The majority of them are circular and made of steel, but one is concrete. The steel columns may be single, double or triple, for no obvious structural reason.

On the upper floor any hint of a system evaporates. The external walls ignore the outline of the square below, leaving large areas of flat roof

as open terrace. In one corner, the organic, timber-clad form of Maire Gullichsen's studio bulges out over the edge of the square and has to be supported on a couple of external columns, one single and one double. Inside, columns emerge from the floor below, as might be expected, but their position bears no relation to the plan. One occurs in the middle of the master bedroom.

Perhaps Aalto's painterly freedom was in some way typically Finnish — representing an architecture of lake and forest rather than of city and factory — but the paintings that inspired it were modern paintings and, for all its nationalist pride, it was part of an international movement. After Villa Mairea, Modernist architecture could never again pretend to be a simple matter of structure and function.

1 Southwest Elevation

2 Southeast Elevation

3 First Floor Plan

1 Studio
2 Maire's bedroom
3 Upper hall with fireplace
4 Harry's bedroom
5 Terrace
6 Children's hall/playroom
7 Child's bedroom
8 Guest room

4 Section A–A

5 Ground Floor Plan

1 Swimming pool
2 Sauna
3 Winter garden
4 Living room
5 Library
6 Dining room
7 Entrance hall
8 Main entrance
9 Staff room
10 Office
11 Kitchen

1

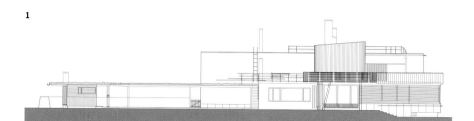

2

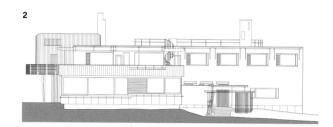

3

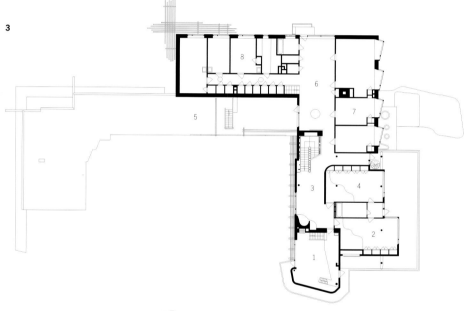

4

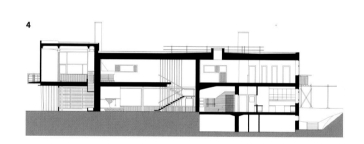

5

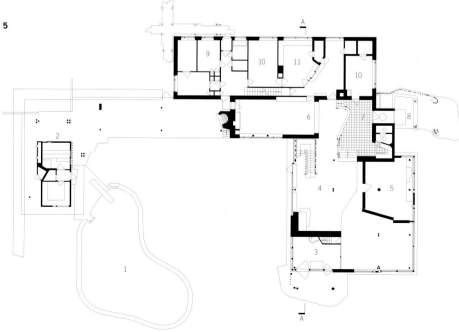

Willow Road

Ernö Goldfinger, 1902–87

London, UK; 1939

Although they were designed by a Hungarian who received his architectural education in Paris, the three houses in Willow Road, north London, completed in 1939, are in some ways a typically English compromise. Ernö Goldfinger had been a radical student, rejecting his stuffy Beaux-Arts teachers to join the studio of Auguste Perret, a pioneer of reinforced-concrete construction. But when he visited London in the 1930s, Goldfinger was much taken with the brickwork and fine proportions of Georgian street architecture. Willow Road's combination of reinforced concrete and brickwork therefore makes perfect sense. Goldfinger was never a 'white box' Modernist. Structure, materials and proportion were his preoccupations and remained so throughout his career. In 1933 he married Ursula Blackwell, whose family had made its fortune from Crosse & Blackwell soups. Willow Road was to be their family home — a sound investment of Ursula's money and an architectural marker to signal Goldfinger's arrival in a new territory.

The Goldfinger house is flanked by two smaller houses, one of which was sold, the other rented. Externally, however, the impression is of a single building, three storeys high, with a large

horizontal window at first-floor level looking north over Hampstead Heath. The façade is perfectly symmetrical, almost classical, with round concrete piloti on the ground floor supporting a brick wall above. Despite the size of the elaborate first-floor window, the impression remains of a punctured brick box rather than of a lightweight skin, although the structure behind is reinforced concrete from top to bottom.

Inside, symmetry is immediately abandoned. The entrance hall between the two garages leads to an off-centre spiral stair. This is made to work extremely hard in a very economical plan with almost no additional circulation spaces. On the first floor, the tiny landing has three doors opening directly into the dining room and studio at the front and the living room, three steps higher, at the back. These are separate rooms, but partitions can be folded back to create a single, split-level space. Adolf Loos's *Raumplan* idea was almost certainly a direct influence on this arrangement. The low ceilings of the garages and entrance hall below make space for the higher piano nobile of the dining room and study. The external wall of the sunny living room is an end-to-end, floor-to-ceiling sliding glass door opening onto a

cantilevered balcony. On the top floor, bedrooms with small, square windows face north, and the whole of the south side is occupied by the nursery and nanny's room. This can be a single space but is divisible into three by folding partitions. The flat roof allows internal bathrooms to be top-lit and there is also a big round rooflight over the spiral stair. The site slopes quite steeply to the south, away from the road, and the section takes advantage of this, with service rooms at basement or garden level at the back. The kitchen was originally sited on the ground floor at the back, with a dumb waiter to serve the other floors.

Detailing throughout is simple but exquisite. Every door handle and light fitting is carefully considered and the furniture, much of it designed by Goldfinger himself, suits the spaces perfectly. The house and its contents, including important Modernist works of art, is now owned by the National Trust and open to the public.

1 Second Floor Plan

1 Bedroom
2 Bathroom
3 Nursery

2 First Floor Plan

1 Dining room
2 Living room
3 Studio
4 Bedroom
5 Bathroom

3 Ground Floor Plan

1 Garage
2 Dining room
3 Kitchen
4 Maid's room

4 Basement Plan

1 Garden room
2 Nursery
3 Workshop
4 Boiler room
5 Fuel
6 Box room
7 WC

5 Section A–A

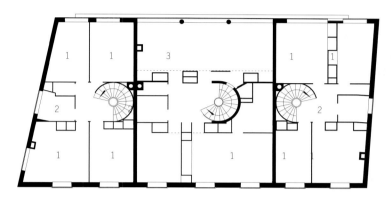

1

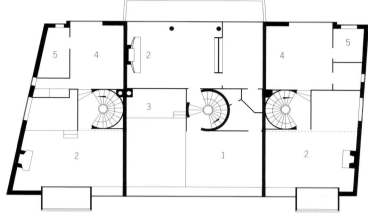

2

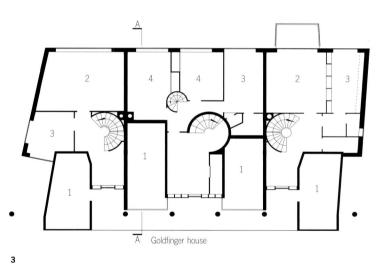

Goldfinger house

3

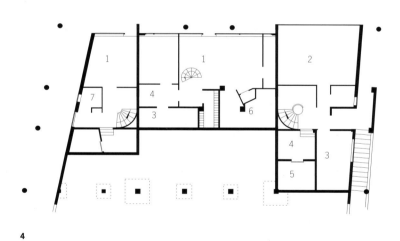

4

5

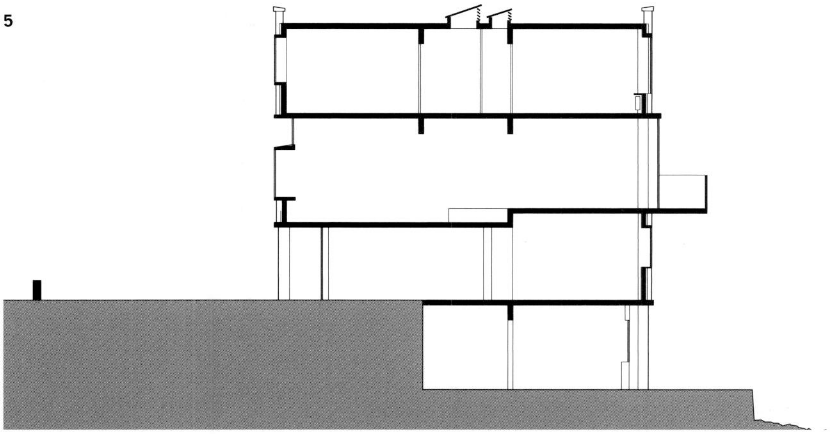

Newton Road

Denys Lasdun, 1914–2001

London, UK; 1939

Denys Lasdun is best known as the designer of the National Theatre on London's South Bank — a building loved and loathed in equal measure. The Prince of Wales likened it to a nuclear power station, but its characteristic stratified form, with open decks on several levels from which theatregoers can enjoy wide views of the River Thames, is a powerful and original urban prototype.

From the 1950s onwards, Lasdun developed his own brand of Modernism, adapting it to a range of building types, including housing for both rich and poor. Before the Second World War, however, he was still learning his craft by copying the first-generation masters, particularly Le Corbusier, whose buildings he studied first-hand in Paris. His 1935 student project for an Academy of Colonial and Dominion Scholars, for example, is clearly a version of Le Corbusier's Pavillon Suisse.

On the Modernist map of the world at this time, England remained an outlying province, with very few native practitioners. It was while working for Wells Coates, the Canadian designer of the Lawn Road flats in Hampstead, north London, that Lasdun got his first important independent commission: a house and studio in Newton Road, Paddington, for a painter called F. J. Conway.

Conway wanted a Modernist house and Lasdun's instinct was to copy Le Corbusier once again. The 1926 Villa Cook in Paris is the model: a four-storey house, roughly square on plan, with blank side walls and a roof garden. Lasdun's version is straighter and more sober — perhaps in response to a more vigilant local planning authority, or perhaps because the 23-year-old architect, not long out of college, had yet to immerse himself fully in the Modernist idiom.

The front elevation is almost identical to the Villa Cook, with two ribbon windows, a top-floor loggia and a ground floor recessed behind a single central column or piloti. But it has been tidied up and made more respectable by the application of brown tiles below and between the ribbon windows. And where the Villa Cook has a free plan, with an off-centre staircase, curved partitions and a double-height living room on one side, the Newton Road house is four-square and basically symmetrical. The front door is in the middle, right behind the column, and the entrance hall leads straight to a staircase at the back. The large living room on the first floor juxtaposes a starkly modern, full-width ribbon window with an ornate recycled baroque mantelpiece. But even this

surreal combination has a Corbusian precedent, in the roof garden of the Beistegui apartment of 1929, also in Paris. The two front bedrooms on the second floor share a ribbon window between them. A separate little staircase in the corner of this floor rises to an attic studio, with high windows facing north and a sun terrace on the south side looking out over the street through a big opening resembling an unglazed window.

The Newton Road house is set well back from its neighbours, so that most of the open space on the site is occupied by the semi-public landscaped forecourt. The main living spaces have no direct contact with the ground. What might have been a private garden at the back is occupied by a single-storey extension containing staff bedrooms. Certain features of the house, such as the placing of the living room on the piano nobile and the use of brickwork for the side walls, recall the traditional London town house. A copy of Le Corbusier it may be, but it is also the first step in the creation of an English Modernism.

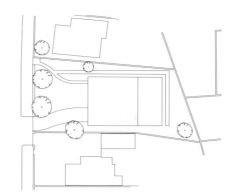

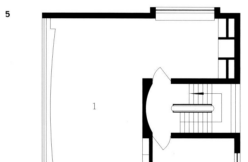

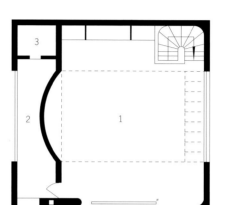

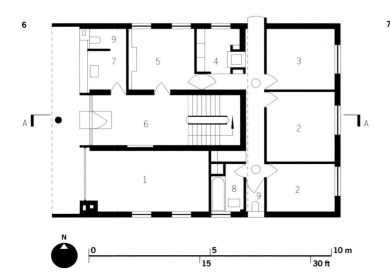

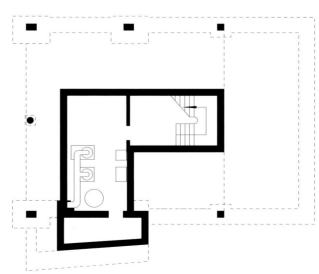

3 Third Floor Plan

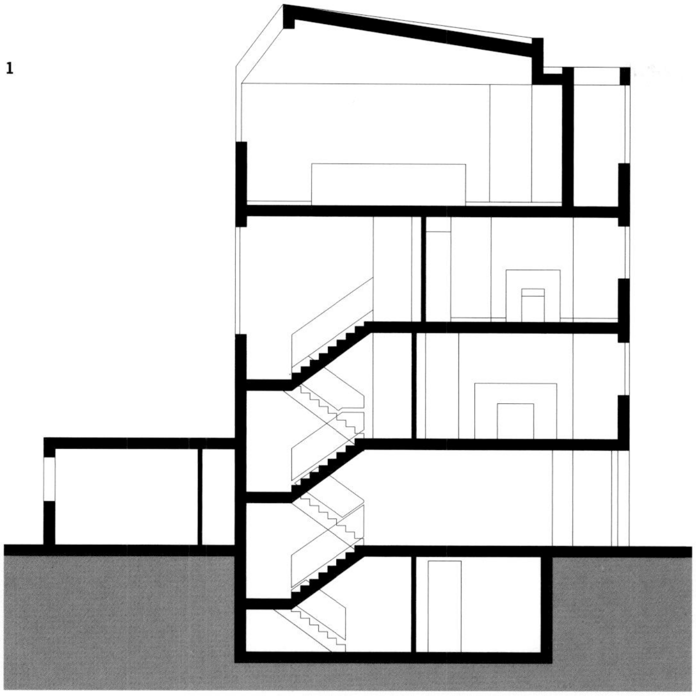

1 Studio
2 Terrace
3 Tanks

4 Second Floor Plan

1 WC
2 Bathroom
3 Bedroom
4 Pantry
5 Linen cupboard

5 First Floor Plan

1 Living/dining room
2 Study

6 Ground Floor Plan

1 Garage
2 Staff room
3 Kitchen
4 Servery
5 Servants' hall
6 Entrance hall
7 Cloakroom
8 Bathroom
9 WC

N

0   5   10 m
      15   30 ft

Casa Malaparte

Adalberto Libera and Curzio Malaparte, 1903–63 and 1898–1957

Capri, Italy; 1936–40

'A house like me' was how Curzio Malaparte's described his lonely lair on its rocky, sea-sprayed promontory on the island of Capri. Evidently, he saw himself as a mythical figure, a poet or a king. In fact, he was a journalist and a political activist but important enough to be imprisoned by the fascists before the Second World War and by the anti-fascists after the war.

Malaparte was certainly no saint, and he seems to have built the house at least partly with money that had been fraudulently claimed from a journalists' benevolent fund. Having bought the site cheaply because building on it was forbidden by the Capri authorities, he used his political influence to get the restriction lifted.

Scale and simplicity are the secrets of the building's power. Little more than a bare box, it seems a natural outgrowth of the rock it is built on, yet it commands the coastline like a fortress. The design is often attributed to the Roman Rationalist architect Adalberto Libera, but Libera's scheme was no more than a starting point. It was Malaparte himself, working with his builder, Adolfo Amitrano, who gave the building its final shape, altering it again and again during the four-year construction period.

The building's most unforgettable feature – the wedge of steps that rises to the roof terrace on the landward side – seems to be a literal quotation from the steps in front of the church of the Annunziata on Lipari, the island where Malaparte was imprisoned in 1934. For a short time during construction, the main entrance to the house was reached through a slot in the middle of the flight of steps, like a vomitorium in a Roman theatre. This arrangement had great formal and functional logic, but it was eventually rejected, possibly because such an entrance would be flooded by the sea in stormy weather.

Sealing up the vomitorium had a disastrous effect on the plan, shifting the main entrance to the ground floor on one side and squeezing the internal staircase into an awkward corner. It seems certain that Malaparte would have preferred a symmetrical arrangement, like the plan of his private suite at the other end of the building, with its twin bathrooms and T-shaped corridor. Removing the vomitorium also destroyed the relationship between the main living space and the rooftop terrace. In the house as built, the journey from one to the other is prohibitively tortuous – down 16 steps and up 48. But, for Malaparte,

the image of the house (and therefore of himself) was more important than efficient planning. The profile of the windbreak wall or 'sail' on the otherwise featureless and unfenced terrace was adjusted several times before attaining its final elegant sweep. Internal spaces are mostly small, boxy rooms, with the exception of the main living room, which is an enormous, quasi-external court, paved like a Roman street and furnished with what look like classical relics, including a big relief sculpture called *Danza* by Pericle Fazzini. Huge picture-windows frame Homeric views of the Bay of Naples.

The house first came to the attention of the general public in 1963, six years after Malaparte's death, when Jean-Luc Godard used it as the setting for his film *Le Mépris* (*Contempt*) starring Brigitte Bardot.

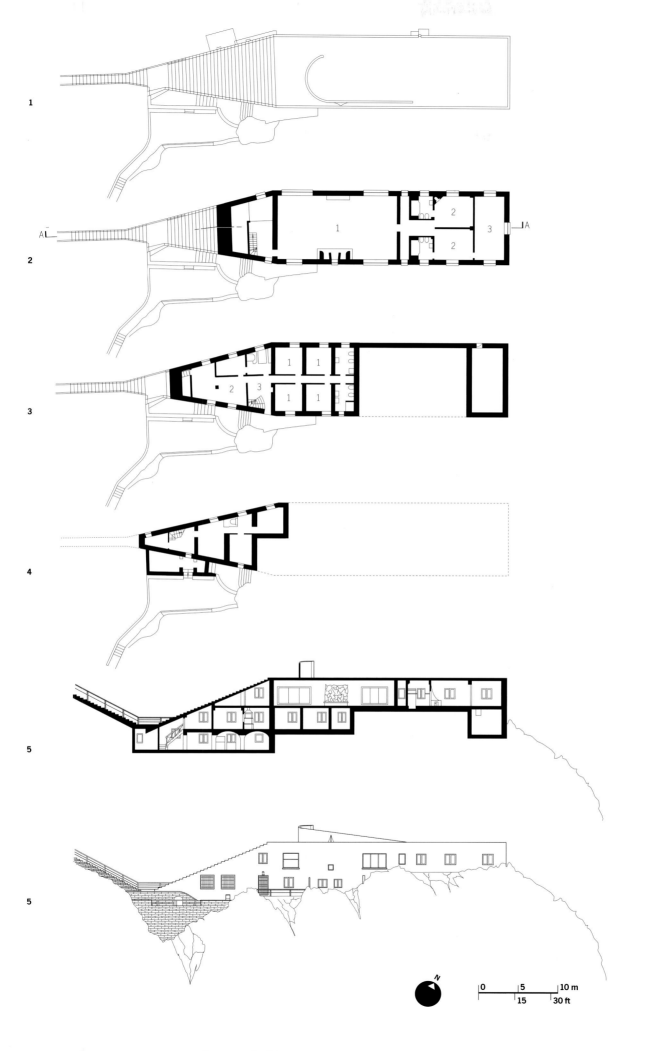

1 Roof Plan

2 Upper Floor Plan

1 Living room
2 Bedroom
3 Study

3 Lower Floor Plan

1 Bedroom
2 Kitchen and service rooms
3 Entrance

4 Cellar Floor Plan

5 Section A–A

6 Southeast Elevation

0 5 10 m
15 30 ft

Chamberlain Cottage

Marcel Breuer, 1902–81

Wayland, Massachusetts, USA; 1940

Though small and formally simple, this weekend retreat for an elderly couple is architecturally and structurally rather complex. The box containing the main living areas is clearly a Modernist form, raised above the ground like one of Le Corbusier's white cubes and cantilevering out 2.5 metres (8 feet) at one end. But it is not white and it stands not on pilotis but on a solid fieldstone semi-basement. It has no ribbon windows either, just standard steel-framed casements puncturing walls clad in Douglas fir boards like any ordinary suburban American house. The International Style is thus softened by the incorporation of natural materials and local building traditions.

Breuer was fascinated by the balloon-frame form of house construction that was, and remains, standard in the USA. This consists of lightweight panels framed in thin wooden studs at close intervals and covered with clapboards. The panels are normally continuously supported on strip foundations or basement walls, but Breuer, who had been in charge of the carpentry workshop at the Bauhaus, thought that they could be made to work harder. Braced by an inner layer of diagonal boarding, they could become storey-height beams that were capable of spanning wide openings

and cantilevering out some distance beyond their points of support. This is the secret of the 2.5 metre cantilever of the Chamberlain Cottage. There is no hidden steel or concrete frame, although the floor span has been reduced by a longitudinal beam supported on two columns in the basement. The end of this beam is indicated on the west façade by a slight stepping-down of the timber cladding.

Inside, the main box is split into broad and narrow zones by the line of the longitudinal beam, which has its counterpart at ceiling level. Kitchen, bathroom and dressing room occupy the narrow zone; living/dining room and bedroom occupy the broad zone. But the most prominent feature is the freestanding fieldstone fireplace and chimney that seems to have erupted from the basement. Breuer's liking for natural stone may have its roots in England, where, like his partner Walter Gropius, he stayed for a year on his way from Germany to the USA. Working with F. R. S. Yorke, he was involved in the design of a furniture showroom with walls of plate glass and Cotswold stone.

On the north side of the cottage, the roof and floor of the main box are extended and propped up on a wooden 'goalpost' frame to

form a generous porch, which is open-sided apart from a fly screen. The porch is accessible from the garden via a short ramp and there is enough space under the floor to store wood.

It has been suggested that this elegant cantilevered structure might have been the inspiration for Mies van der Rohe's Farnsworth House (see pages 112–13), where the idea is translated into steel. The Chamberlain Cottage therefore combines three distinct structural systems: loadbearing wall for the basement, balloon frame for the main living box, and post-and-beam for the porch. Breuer himself regarded it as the most beautiful of the 100 or so houses that he designed in his long career.

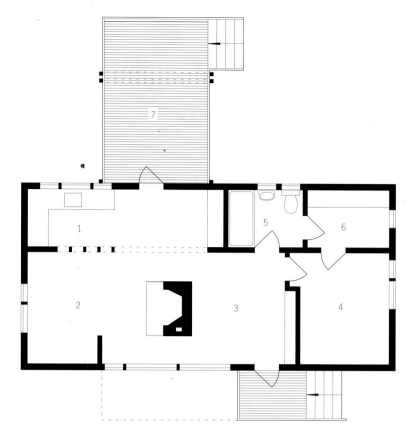

1 Ground Floor Plan

1 Kitchen
2 Living room
3 Dining room
4 Bedroom
5 Bathroom
6 Dressing room
7 Porch

2 Basement Plan

1 Workshop

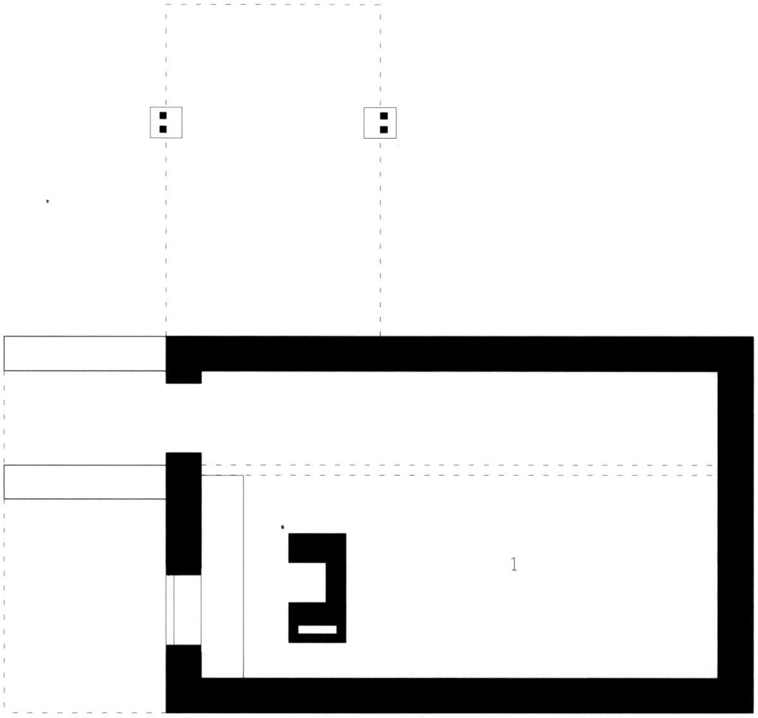

N

0   5   10 m

15   30 ft

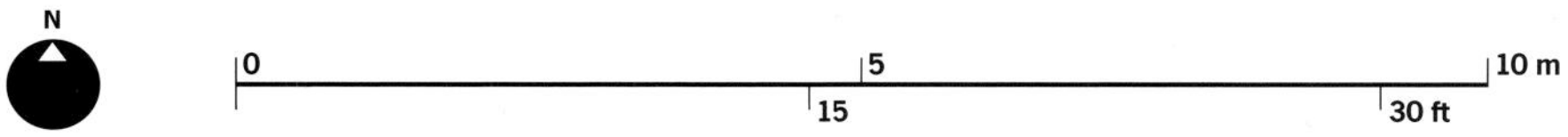

Wichita House

Richard Buckminster Fuller, 1895–1983

Wichita, Kansas, USA; 1947

In 1944, with the end of the Second World War in sight, workers in American aircraft factories saw redundancy coming and started to look for alternative employment. There was a danger that they would drift away before the job was done, but if they could be convinced that a factory was to be converted to make peacetime products the hope of postwar employment might be kept alive. And if those products were the houses that the trailer-dwelling workers desperately needed, then the incentive to stay on would be even stronger.

Who better to convince and inspire them than the futurist and inventor Richard Buckminster Fuller? In 1928 Fuller had patented the Dymaxion House, a hexagonal metal house suspended from a central mast, and in 1936 he had designed the prefabricated Dymaxion Bathroom for the Phelps Dodge Corporation. Neither of these inventions had gone into production, but from 1940 many thousands of examples of Fuller's Dymaxion Deployment Unit, which was basically a converted agricultural storage bin, had been produced for use by military personnel as radar huts. The time had come to put these three ideas together in a mass-produced house that would alleviate the inevitable postwar housing shortage.

A corner of the Beech Aircraft factory in Wichita, Kansas, was allocated to Fuller and he set about finalizing the design of what was to become the Wichita House. Propaganda was as important as actual production, so Fuller gave lectures to the employees and their wives about the new wonder house that would secure their future. It had a circular plan and a streamlined profile to reduce wind resistance and heat loss.

Fuller seems to have envisaged the Wichita House less as a building, more as a vehicle travelling through the air at high speed. A rotating roof vent resembling a big weathervane controlled the interior air flow. All mechanical services, including two Dymaxion Bathrooms, were concentrated in a central core. Otherwise, the plan was cut like a cake into five slices – living room, two bedrooms, kitchen and entrance hall – by fat, radial partitions incorporating rotating storage devices. The structure was equally revolutionary. A steel floor designed to take the weight of 120 people was suspended from a single central mast by a combination of tension wires and compression rings like bicycle wheels. The external cladding was shiny Duralumin, the same material used to make Beech aircraft, with a ribbon of

fixed Plexiglass to admit daylight. The components of the whole house could be carried on one lorry, and it was estimated that a team of six men could erect it on site in a single day.

The first of two prototypes was well received and orders started to come in at a healthy rate. But a massive investment was needed to tool up the factory and, although his colleagues in Fuller Houses Inc. were all for pressing ahead, Fuller himself got cold feet and pulled the plug.

The house of the future remained in the future. But the ploy had worked. The exodus from the factory had been brought to a halt. The house had already done its job. One of the prototypes can be seen, fully restored, in the Henry Ford Museum in Dearborn, Michigan.

2 Diagrammatic showing air-flow

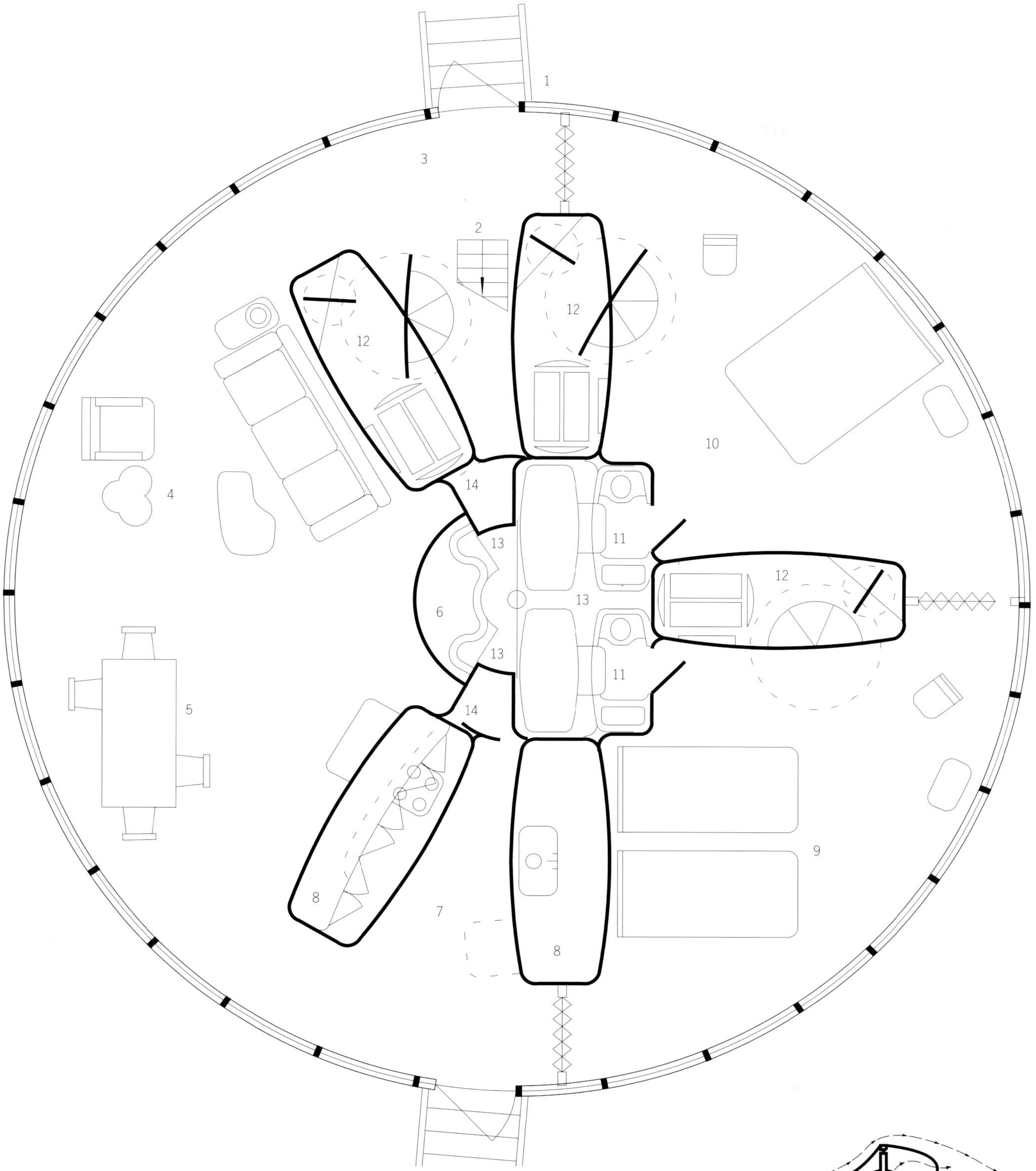

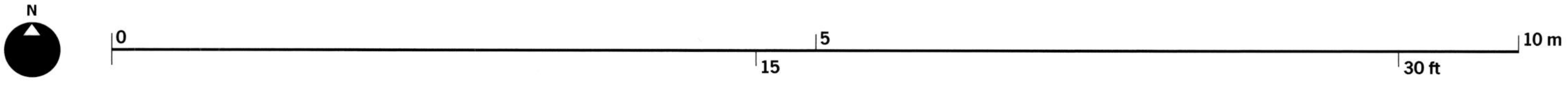

N

0   5   10 m
15   30 ft

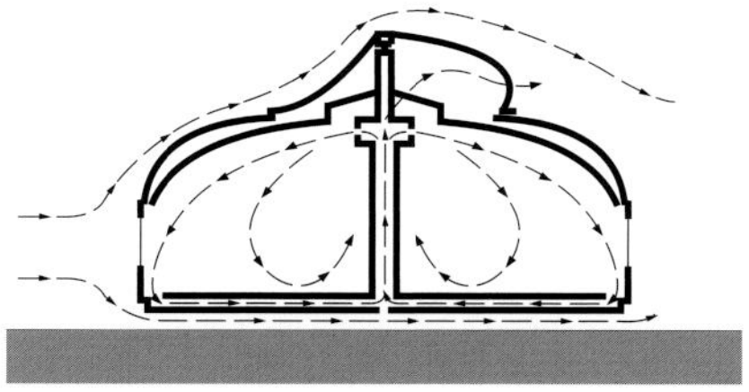

Eames House

Charles and Ray Eames, 1907–78 and 1912–88

Los Angeles, California, USA; 1949

Originally called Case Study House No. 8, the Eames House was one of the famous California demonstration houses sponsored by *Arts and Architecture* magazine in the late 1940s.

The design was well advanced when Charles Eames visited an exhibition in New York of the work of Mies van der Rohe and discovered that he had unconsciously imitated a Mies sketch for a house in the form of a glazed bridge. When he returned to Santa Monica to consult his artist wife, Ray, they decided to scrap the bridge idea and reconfigure the whole design. The result was one of the most influential houses of the twentieth century. Where the Miesian design had been assertive and monumental, cutting across the contours of the site, the new design was gentler, perhaps more feminine, staying close to an earth bank behind a row of eucalyptus trees. It was certainly not conventional, however. Its use of steel, glass and coloured panels seemed relaxed and natural, but no one had used these materials in such a way before.

Two simple two-storey boxes, one for the house and one for the studio, are separated by a small courtyard. There are double-height spaces at the outer ends of both the house and the studio, so that an alternating rhythm is set up, the courtyard counting as a third double-height space.

The entire composition is tied together by the continuous storey-height concrete retaining wall that integrates the buildings with the nearby hillside. The remainder of the structure is made of steel: a decidedly non-monumental frame, infilled with ordinary steel-framed windows and various kinds of lightweight panel.

In the hands of another designer (Mies van der Rohe, perhaps), this formula might have been worked through rigidly and dogmatically, emphasizing its symmetries and regularities, its structural articulation and its austere materials. Instead, the house is all reasonable compromise. Solid and transparent panels are arranged not according to some abstract system but to create a subtle, shifting light in the interior. The Japanese influence is obvious. And although inexpensive, industrial products such as the lattice steel beams and the trough metal decking are frankly exposed to view, there is an abundance of warm natural materials too, such as the wood-block floor in the studio and the large timber-boarded wall in the living room. The plans seem almost too relaxed. For example, the principal bedroom occupies a gallery that is open to the living room below. But what seems awkward in a drawing works well in the actual space.

The Eames House is so well known that many myths have gathered around it: that the new design cleverly reused the steelwork ordered for the original design; that the house cost much less than a standard timber-framed house; that it took only a few days to build. None of these is true. The most widely accepted myth is that the house was built from standard components ordered straight from catalogues and this is at least partly true. The windows, for example, are mostly standard units 1 metre (3 feet 4 inches) wide. In architecture it is ideas that count, not historical fact, and the Eames house remains an inspiration to any designer interested in the architectural potential of prefabrication.

1 West Elevation

2 Section A–A

3 East Elevation

4 North Elevation of House

5 First Floor Plan
1 Upper part of living room
2 Bedroom
3 Dressing room
4 Hall
5 Bathroom
6 Work room
7 Upper part of studio

6 South Elevation of House

7 Ground Floor Plan
1 Living room
2 Dining room
3 Kitchen
4 Utility room
5 Courtyard
6 Dark room
7 Studio

8 North Elevation of Studio

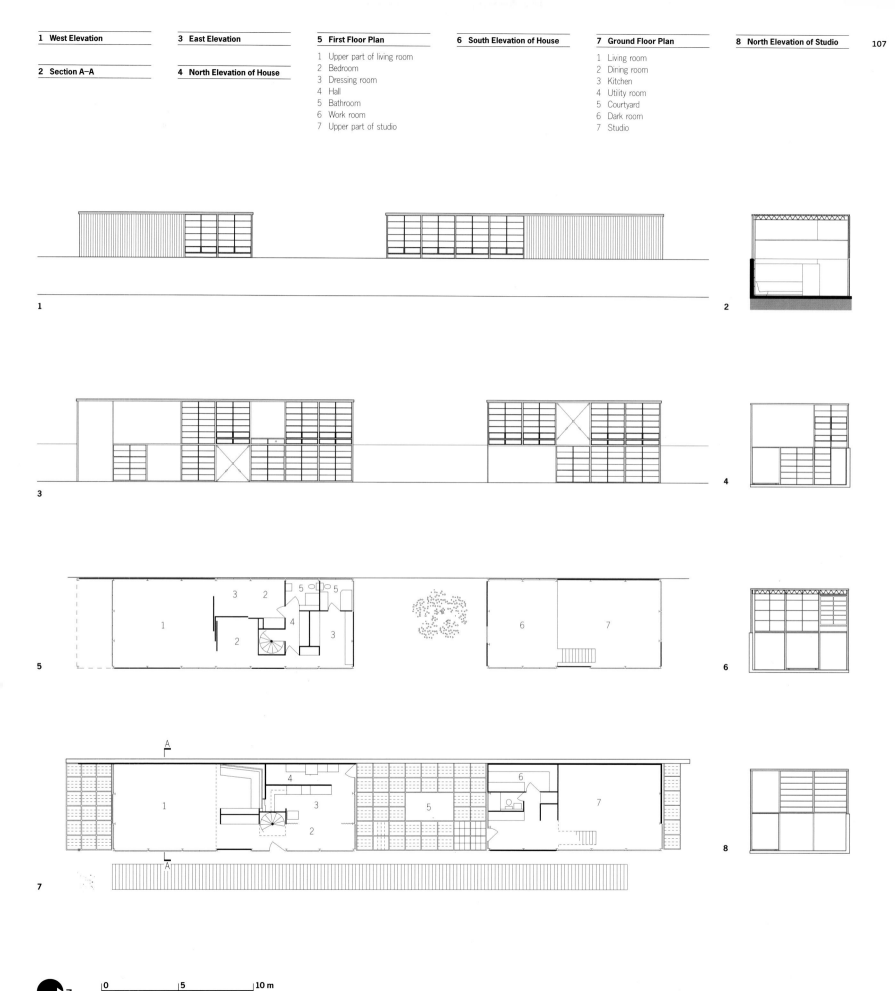

0   5   10 m
15   30 ft

Johnson House

Philip Johnson, 1906–2005

New Canaan, Connecticut, USA; 1949

The Johnson House is often compared with the contemporary Farnsworth House (page 112–13) by Mies van der Rohe. Philip Johnson was a friend and admirer of Mies and was certainly familiar with the Farnsworth House design, although in fact his own house was finished first.

Despite the obvious similarities, the two houses are fundamentally different in conception. Whereas the Farnsworth House is a composition of floating planes, the Johnson House is an earthbound box. Its most characteristic element is not the glass envelope but the cylindrical brick hearth-cum-bathroom that rises from a brick-paved floor and penetrates the roof. This heavy vertical form stakes a claim to the site and directs attention outwards to the surrounding landscape. In this respect, the house owes more to Frank Lloyd Wright than to Mies van der Rohe. Johnson described it as a camp – a fire and a ground sheet – from which to observe nature in comfort.

If it is a camp, it is an extremely civilized one. By 1949, Johnson was already an influential figure in the world of architecture, having helped to organize the 1932 International Style exhibition in New York. But he was a rich dilettante, and had only recently graduated from the architecture school at Harvard as a mature student. The house therefore had to be both a signal of his arrival as a professional architect and a luxury home for a man of taste. The 'camp' is graced by notable works of art, including Nicholas Poussin's *Funeral of Phocion* in a freestanding metal frame, as well as classic Barcelona chairs by Mies and elegant walnut storage units to divide the space.

Perhaps more importantly, the herringbone brick 'ground sheet' is underfloor heated and the glass walls protect against the New England wind and snow. In the Farnsworth House, structure is paramount, the H-section steel supports standing in for classical columns, but in the Johnson house the steel columns are merely part of the frame that holds the glass. The detailing is neat, and Miesian, but not structurally expressive. Four single-leaf doors, one in the middle of each wall, act as air vents and are said to keep the non-air-conditioned house cool on even the hottest days.

In a sense, the glass house is only half a house. Guests are accommodated in a separate structure, a kind of negative version in solid brick. It was built at the same time, but stylistically seems to belong to a different period. A triple square on plan, its interior is modulated by a shell-like structure of shallow domes merging into squashed arches and slender columns. The breakfast room in John Soane's London house was the acknowledged inspiration. It would be difficult to think of anything less like Mies, but in hindsight it makes Johnson's later Postmodernist works, such as the AT&T tower in New York, less surprising.

The guest house simplifies the glass house so that it becomes a pavilion, like a classical temple in a picturesque English garden. Its siting at the top of a steep slope has even led some to describe it as the Parthenon of a miniature Acropolis. References such as these were readily acknowledged by Johnson. In later years he bought more land around the site, expanding it from 2 to 16 hectares (5 to 40 acres), and built several more buildings – some functional, such as the studio built in 1980, and some simply to look at, such as the trompe l'oeil dwarf's palace by the lake at the bottom of the slope.

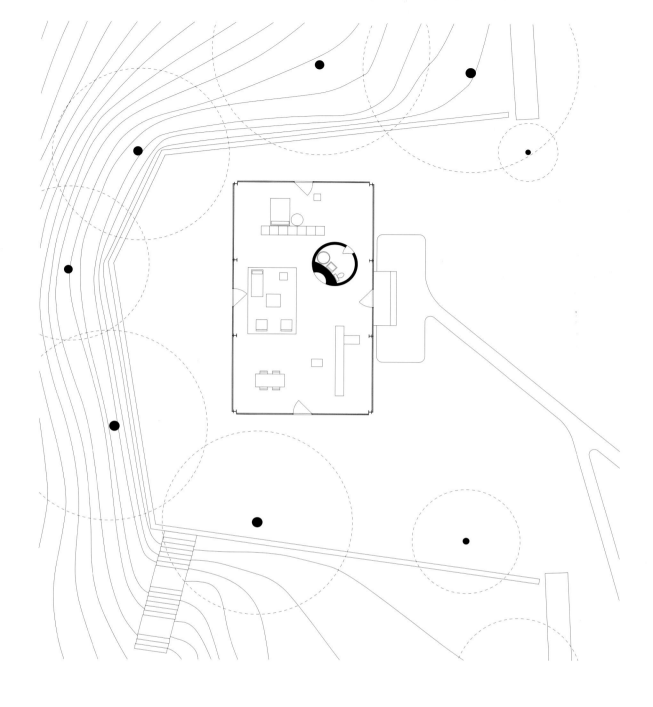

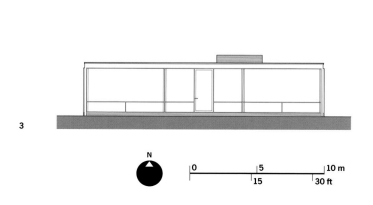

2 North Elevation

3 East Elevation

N

0   5   10 m
     15   30 ft

Rose Seidler House

Harry Seidler, 1923–2006

Turramurra, New South Wales, Australia; 1950

The award of the Sir John Sulman Medal for outstanding architectural merit to the Rose Seidler House in 1951 signalled the acceptance of Bauhaus Modernism as the basis for the development of Australian architecture.

The Rose Seidler House was in every way a foreign import. Harry Seidler himself had only recently arrived in the country. Born in Vienna in 1923, he made his way via England and Canada to Harvard, where he studied architecture under Walter Gropius. Graduating in 1945, he took a job in Marcel Breuer's New York office, where he worked on several houses, including the Chamberlain Cottage (see pages 102–103) and Breuer's own house in New Canaan, Connecticut. He became a devoted disciple, and when he finally joined his parents in Sydney, he built them a house in the Breuer style; it is an almost exact copy of a house that Seidler had designed with R. D. Thompson while in New York. Set in the Sydney suburb of Turramurra, the Rose Seidler House is an Australian house only in the sense that it stands on Australian soil.

A typical Breuer box, raised off the ground and cantilevering out over its base, the house has a U-shaped plan, with bedrooms in one wing and living rooms in the other, separated by a multi-purpose family space and an open terrace. The terrace is so much part of the overall box that it seems more like a room.

In spite of the fact that this is a recycled design, one of its most pleasing aspects is the relationship between the house and its site. A steep, north-facing slope with long views over a wooded valley was carved out and stabilized by fieldstone retaining walls that reach back into the bank like anchors. The main box hovers over this storey-height step in the land, with a car port, a studio and a small entrance hall tucked in underneath. From the entrance hall, a simple, straight stair rises right in the middle of the plan beside an open lightwell at the back of the timber-decked terrace. Straight ahead lies another favourite Breuer device: a freestanding stone fireplace and chimney, dividing the living and dining spaces. From the family room and the kitchen to the left, it is possible to step out onto the upper level of the bank.

Seidler learned his basic architectural language from Breuer, but he also learned from his mentor's mistakes. The house at New Canaan almost failed disastrously because of an over-optimistic use of cantilevering timber-framed walls. The Rose Seidler House also has timber-framed walls, but they rest on a solid reinforced-concrete slab, supported on concrete walls and slender round steel columns. Concrete cantilevered beams support an extension to the terrace, from which a long timber ramp descends to the forecourt. The elevations of the box are freely composed to suit the spaces behind, combining full-height glass panels with solid boarded areas, occasionally punctured by ordinary windows. A colourful abstract mural, painted by the architect, covers one of the walls of the terrace 'room'.

Having made his mark with this notable European/American house, Harry Seidler went on to become one of Australia's most important architects and the designer of some of its most distinguished skyscrapers.

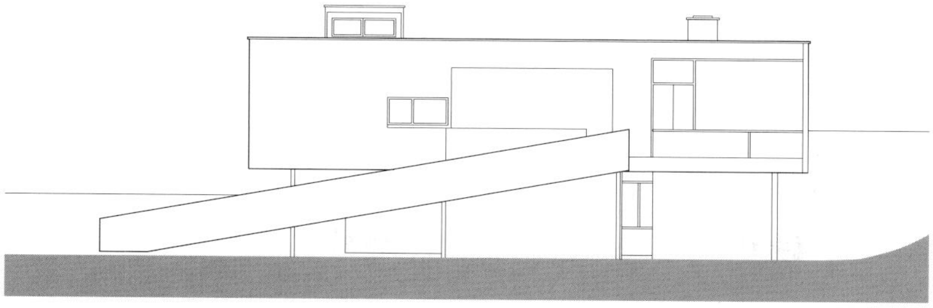

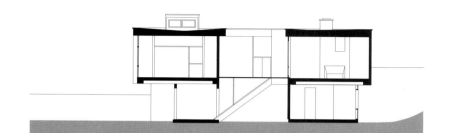

1

2

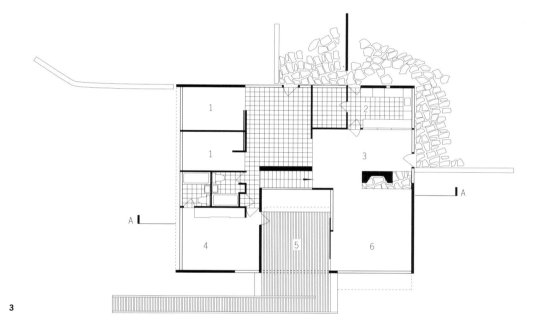

2 First Floor Plan

1 Bedroom
2 Kitchen
3 Dining room
4 Master bedroom
5 Terrace
6 Living room

3

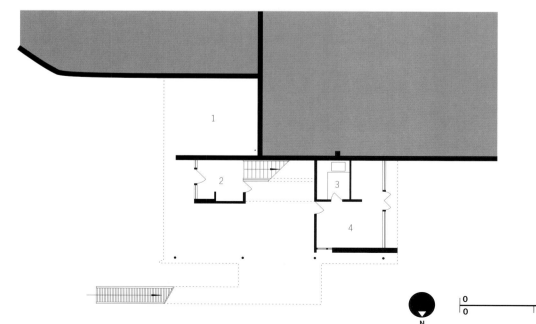

2 Ground Floor Plan

1 Car port
2 Entrance
3 Dark room
4 Studio

4

0   5   10 m
0   15   30 ft

N

Farnsworth House

Ludwig Mies van der Rohe, 1886–1969

Plano, Illinois, USA; 1945–51

It is almost certain that Mies van der Rohe and his client Dr Edith Farnsworth had some kind of romantic affair. They often visited the building site together. On one occasion, so the story goes, Mies asked Edith to stand in the raised porch of the half-finished house 'so that I can have a look at you'. She climbed up, posed and smiled. 'Good,' said Mies, 'I just wanted to check the scale.' The house was designed more for him than for her. It was his opportunity to build an architectural ideal: the perfect building, the epitome of his style. All the conditions were right: a big, flat, wooded site by a river, a simple brief, and a single, well-off client whom he could bully.

The Farnsworth House marks the end of a period during which Mies tested all the dynamic possibilities of Modernist composition, only to arrive back where he started, with the stillness and formality of the neoclassical tradition. Almost all the later Mies buildings can be seen as variations on the Farnsworth theme. The shifting asymmetries and ostentatious materials of the Barcelona Pavilion and the Tugendhat House (see pages 78–79) have been set aside; from now on, the steel frame rules like a classical order. Floor and roof are rectangular and apparently identical

flat planes supported not on but between four pairs of ordinary H-section steel columns. There are cantilevers at the ends and the floor plane is 1.5 metres (5 feet) above the flood-prone ground. A glass wall, with minimal framing, encloses about two-thirds of the space between the planes, leaving an open porch at one end. A third plane, smaller but of the same proportions as the other two, is placed alongside at low level to serve as an entrance terrace. Two short but wide flights of steps link ground to terrace and terrace to porch. Inside the house, a freestanding building-within-a-building accommodates the 'servant' spaces: a kitchen, two bathrooms and a utility room. There are no other fixed walls.

This brief description sums up the building almost completely. Everything else is refinement. For example, the apparent asymmetries of the composition – the relationship between the floor slab and the enclosing glass wall, or between the house and the terrace – turn out on closer inspection to be complex, overlapping symmetries, defined and mediated by the columns.

At the level of detail, note how the mullions, of thinnest possible steel bar, divide the big glass panes into perfect squares; how every floor, inside

and out, is paved in the same white travertine; how the hardwood flank walls of the service core stop short of the ceiling to preserve the unity of the living space.

In Mies's terms it was indeed an almost perfect building, but it far exceeded its budget and it was hard to live in. In the winter, the underfloor heating could not prevent streaming condensation. In the summer, it was unbearably hot and the mosquitoes made the porch unusable without screens that ruined the whole transparency effect. Eventually, Edith Farnsworth decided that she had been duped and refused to pay Mies's bill. He took her to court and it ended in tears.

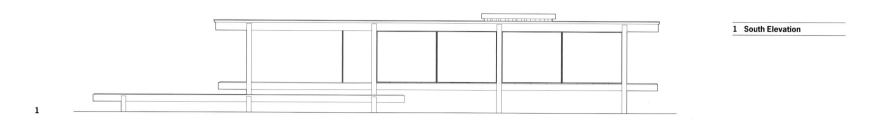

1 South Elevation

1

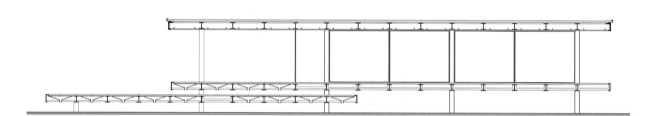

2 Section A–A (staggered)

2

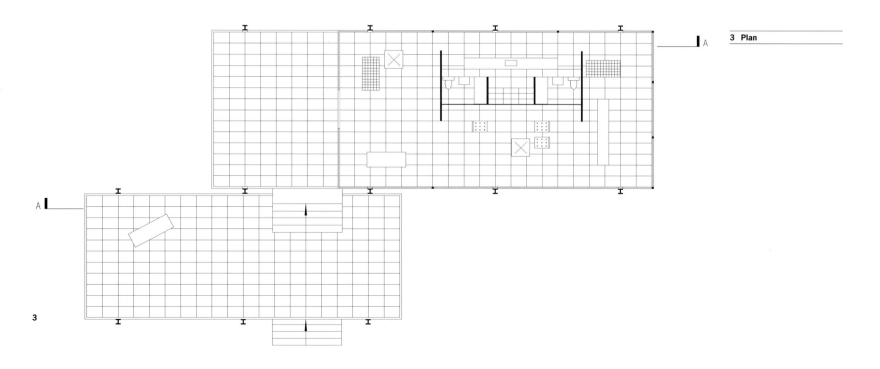

3 Plan

A

A

3

N

0   5   10 m

15   30 ft

Lina Bo Bardi House

Lina Bo Bardi, 1914–92

Morumbi, near São Paulo, Brazil; 1950–51

After graduating from the Rome School of Architecture in 1939 at the age of 25, Lina Bo went to work for the architect and designer Gio Ponti in the more progressive cultural environment of Milan. There she flourished, despite the war, and gained valuable experience in furniture and industrial design as well as architecture. She also began to contribute articles and illustrations to magazines, becoming a deputy director of *Domus* in 1944. In 1946 she married Pietro Maria Bardi, an art connoisseur and journalist, who had supported prewar rationalist architects such as Giuseppe Terragni and Adalberto Libera, and was well connected with Modernists elsewhere in Europe. In 1946 the couple emigrated to Brazil, first to Rio de Janeiro, then to São Paulo, where Bardi had been invited to set up an art museum.

The house that Lina Bo Bardi designed for herself and her husband was sited in what was then the remnants of the Mata Atlantica, the original rainforest surrounding São Paulo. It is now the wealthy suburb of Morumbi. Early photographs show the house rising above the trees on the brow of a hill like an elegant watchtower surveying a swathe of cleared land. A more domesticated version of the rainforest has since re-established

itself around the house, concealing it from view. Neighbours called it 'the glass house', a name that invites comparisons with those other world-famous glass houses built at about the same time: the Johnson House (see pages 108–109) and the Farnsworth House (see pages 112–13). Mies van der Rohe may well have been an influence, but Le Corbusier was probably the original inspiration. Bo Bardi much admired the Ministry of Education building in Rio that Le Corbusier had designed with Lucio Costa, describing it as 'a great white and blue ship against the sky'.

The main part of the house is a horizontal slice of space sandwiched between thin reinforced-concrete slabs and skewered by slender circular columns. The enclosing wall of glass and the absence of any downstand beams call to mind Le Corbusier's Domino house project. The columns are unmistakably pilotis, allowing the landscape to flow under the building, but whereas Le Corbusier in his Purist phase would have insisted on a roof garden, the roof of this house is given a subtle, painterly kink. The entrance is via a wobbly steel stair that ascends into a hole in the soffit. Inside, the main living area is almost completely open except for a kind of courtyard or lightwell that

allows the trees in the garden below to grow up into the heart of the house. There are zones allocated to different functions – a dining room, a library and a sitting area around the freestanding fireplace – but all are unified by the forest views through the glass, which surround the space like a vast mural. In theory, the glass panels slide open horizontally, but there is no balcony or veranda to encourage closer contact with the landscape; essentially this is a viewing platform.

The living area is only half of the house. The other half sits on solid ground at the top of the hill, on the north side of the living room. A row of bedrooms faces a narrow courtyard, on the other side of which is the blank wall of the staff wing. Only the kitchen crosses the divide – a territory shared by servants and mistress, and equipped with an array of well-designed labour-saving devices. However, anyone tempted to think of Bo Bardi as a mere domestic designer should look at her later buildings, especially the extraordinary inhabited bridge of the São Paulo Art Museum, completed in 1968.

1 First Floor Plan

1 Entrance
2 Library
3 Living room
4 Courtyard
5 Fireplace
6 Dining room
7 Bedroom
8 Clothes cupboard
9 Kitchen
10 Staff bedroom

11 Staff living room
12 Wardrobe
13 Veranda
14 Patio

2 Ground Floor Plan

1 Storage

3 Section A–A

4 Elevation

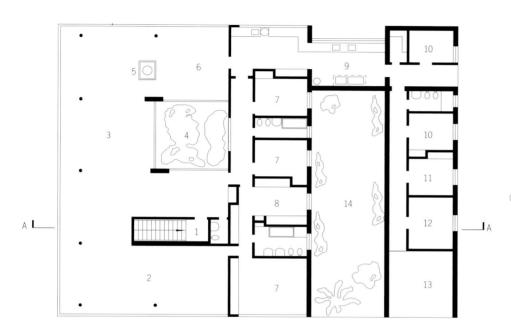

1

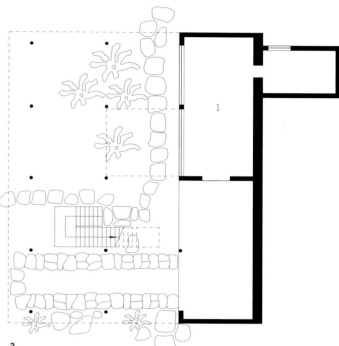

2

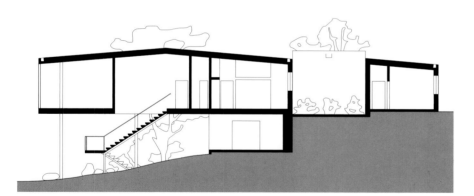

3

4

Casa Ugalde

José Antonio Coderch, 1902–81

Caldes d'Estrac, Spain; 1952

José Antonio Coderch was a leading member of Grup R, an association of progressive architects established in Barcelona after the Second World War. Although he was certainly a Modernist, and even attended CIAM meetings, he was far from being an uncritical follower of the prewar pioneers. He was too interested in vernacular architecture and the landscape of Catalonia to concern himself much with strict Rationalism or Functionalism. The Casa Ugalde is the perfect example of a Modernism that is local rather than international, that respects tradition and the special qualities of particular places.

Eustaquio Ugalde was an engineer. He fell in love with a hilltop site overlooking the sea near the village of Caldes d'Estrac, about 30 km (19 miles) from Barcelona, and asked his architect friend to build him a house there. The site — its rocks, its pine trees and especially its views — was therefore the starting point of the design. This would not be a house placed on a hill but a house growing out of the brow of a hill.

Serpentine stone retaining walls, following the contours, create an amoeba-shaped terrace covered in terracotta tiles with a swimming pool near its eastern edge. In a more traditional

Costa Brava holiday home, this terrace would form the base of a unified, rectilinear and probably pitched-roofed house. Here the house is a restless, articulated form that seems reluctant to remain confined within the boundaries of the space prepared for it. On the south side the angled box of the guestroom steps down off the edge of the terrace, supporting itself on a stone wall that forms a car port underneath. On the north side, another angled box, containing the master bedroom, steps up onto the hillside above. And on the west side a servants' wing wanders off along the contours between a narrow service yard and the footpath to the main entrance. Interiors and exteriors interpenetrate in unexpected ways. The terracotta paving continues unchanged into the main living area which, with its big windows and glass doors, seems to be part of the terrace. On the other hand, the space under the master bedroom, which is notionally outside, would be easy to enclose with glass, and the 'patio' next to it would be easy to roof over.

This is basically a two-storey house, but not straightforwardly so. Its section is as enigmatic as its plan and almost every upstairs room is on a different level. The main internal staircase, which is

of whitewashed stone like its external counterparts, rises in the living room to a head-height wooden landing suspended by balusters from the ceiling. A false ceiling corresponding to the height of this landing defines a sitting area on the other side of the living room. Like Aalto's Villa Mairea (see pages 92–93), an undoubted influence on Coderch, the house shows no congruity between upper and lower levels. The flat roofs of the living room and of the thin-edged canopy that connects the guest room to the main house are terracotta-tiled and left without balustrades so that they become another level of terrace.

If there is a single unifying theme in this loose composition of concrete and stone, it is the idea that the building is essentially a viewing place. The panorama to the south is carefully cut up and framed by horizontal and vertical planes, and by openings both glazed and unglazed, which create a kind of gallery of Mediterranean views. It would come as no surprise to an observer of Casa Ugalde to learn that Coderch was an accomplished photographer.

| **1** | **Level Three Plan** | **2** | **Section A–A** | **5** | **Section C–C** |

<table>

1 Level Three Plan

1 Master bedroom
2 Bedroom
3 Study

2 Section A–A

3 Section B–B

4 Level Two Plan

1 Master bedroom
2 Staff wing
3 Living room
4 Guest room

5 Section C–C

6 Section D–D

7 Level One Plan

1 Terrace
2 Pool
3 Guest room
4 Patio

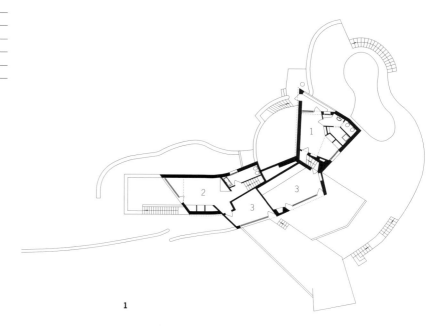

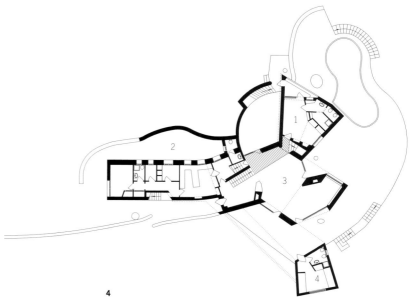

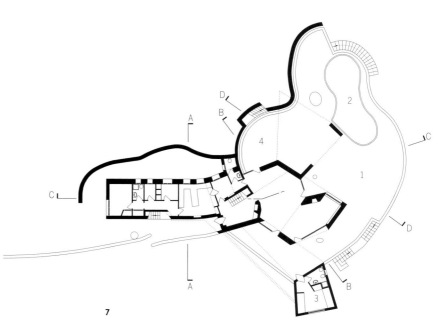

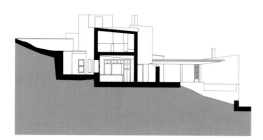

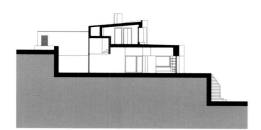

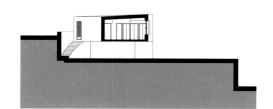

N

0 5 10 m
15 30 ft

Utzon House

Jørn Utzon, 1918–

Hellebaek, Denmark; 1952

When the time came to modernize Danish domestic architecture in the early 1950s, Jørn Utzon was well prepared. He had worked for Alvar Aalto in Helsinki during the Second World War; he had visited Frank Lloyd Wright and Mies van der Rohe while travelling in the USA on a scholarship in 1949; and he had studied non-western architectural traditions on trips to Mexico and Morocco. In 1951, he was 32 years old and married with three children. His family needed a home; since the income from his architectural practice was uncertain, it would have to be a cheap one. He found a site in the wooded grounds of a large house near Helsingor and applied for a low-interest government loan – a condition of which was that the floor area of the house should not exceed 130 square metres (1,400 square feet). He decided to dispense with a formal building contract and develop the design with a sympathetic local builder. The result was one of the first truly modern, open-plan houses in Denmark.

Single-storey and flat-roofed, with hearth and kitchen at the core of plan, the house was clearly influenced by Wright's Usonian Houses, such as the Jacobs House of 1936 (see pages 90–91), but there are key differences. The long drive ends under a pergola spanning between the garage and the north-facing brick wall of the house, which is totally blank except for the recessed panel that frames the entrance.

This is a single-aspect house and nothing is allowed to compromise the purity of the concept, so the bedrooms must do without windows and manage with rooflights. Wright would never have been so dogmatic. The big rectangular living area, with a south-facing glass wall, includes the kitchen in the southeast corner behind a freestanding brick hearth and chimney. Such openness was beginning to be popular in suburban America, but was still daringly innovative in conservative Denmark. The degree of openness is carefully controlled, however. The hearth loosely defines different types of living space – an area open to the view, a dining alcove, a cosy zone near the fireplace – and a sliding door hidden in the brickwork of the chimney can be pulled across to hide the kitchen worktop when necessary.

Dimensional coordination was a growing interest at the time among progressive architects aware of the potential of prefabrication. Wright's Usonian houses were based on a 0.6 by 1.2 metre (2 by 4 foot) planning grid, and there was much interest in the traditional Japanese house, built according to the ancient Kiwari modular system. In the Utzon house it is the humble brick that sets the module, both externally and internally. All dimensions are multiples of 120 mm (4¾ inches) (a Danish brick plus a mortar joint). Floor tiles, brick paving and timber boarding are all accommodated in the grid. Utzon disliked windows and doors, preferring uninterrupted vertical and horizontal planes. Internal doors are therefore full height and covered with the same vertical boards as the non-loadbearing partitions. A black 'shadow gap' between wall and ceiling suggests that partitions might one day be rearranged.

One other important feature of the house must be mentioned. Viewed from the south, it reads as a lightweight timber frame standing on a solid-brick platform – or, in the jargon of architectural theory, a tectonic superstructure on stereotomic base. This idea, which may have been inspired by Chinese traditional architecture, was to become a central theme in Utzon's later works, not least in the building that made him famous: the Sydney Opera House.

| 1 South Elevation | 2 Ground Floor Plan | 119 |

1 Entrance
2 Living room
3 Kitchen
4 Bathroom
5 Bedroom
6 Study
7 Garage
8 Terrace

1

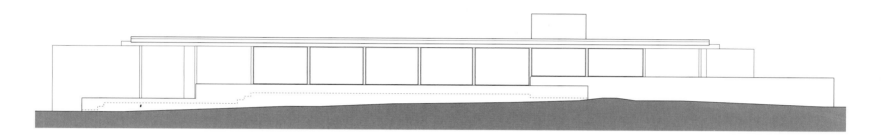

2

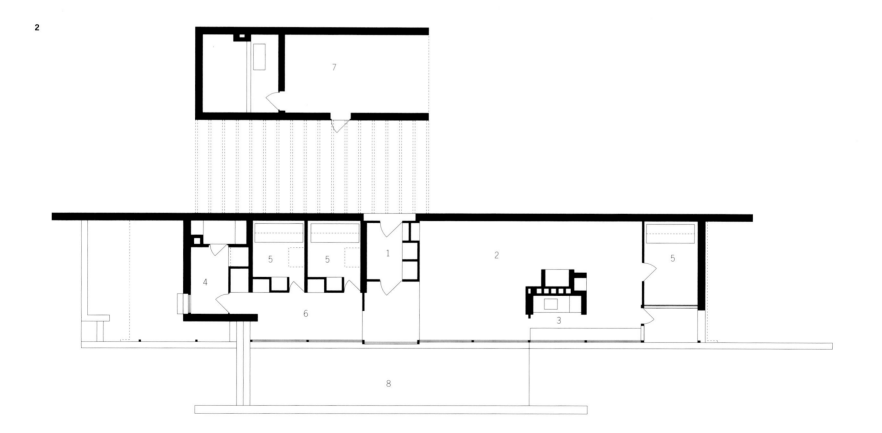

N

0   5   10 m

15   30 ft

Case Study House No. 16

Craig Ellwood, 1922–92

Bel Air, California, USA; 1953

As a designer, Craig Ellwood had a big advantage over his rivals: he never went to architecture school. One of his earliest ambitions was to be a Hollywood actor, and he got as far as doing some modelling before drifting into finance, marketing and eventually construction. All these experiences were helpful to him in his career as an architect. In the late 1940s, he worked as an estimator for the contractor Lamport Cofer Salzman (LCS). LCS built several of the famous Case Study houses sponsored by *Arts and Architecture* magazine, including the Eames House (see pages 106–107) and the house of the magazine's editor, John Entenza. This was a business contact that Ellwood exploited to the hilt when he left LCS and began designing houses on his own account.

In 1951, John Entenza asked Ellwood to put forward one of his houses for inclusion in the second stage of the Case Study programme. Ellwood chose a speculative house that had been commissioned by his former employer, Henry Salzman of LCS. The fact that a developer had commissioned such an architecturally advanced house for sale on the open market is some measure of the popularity of the Modernist style in postwar Los Angeles.

Case Study House No. 16 is essentially a simple single-storey box containing two bedrooms, two bathrooms, a kitchen and a generous open-plan living area. The box sits rather awkwardly on a cramped hillside site but is adapted to its surroundings by means of a frame, walls and roof that extend into the garden. On the north side, the thin plane of the roof sails out over a car port. On the west side a thin steel frame emerges from the fascia to support a louvred sunshade. On the south-west corner, a stone fireplace extends onto the terrace to become a barbecue. Near the main entrance, the wooden north wall of the box extends to screen the bedrooms then turns into the house's most unusual feature: a delicate, steel-framed fence of obscure glass wrapping right around the east end of the building.

As an estimator, Ellwood saw the potential benefits of prefabrication and the importance of taking into account the fluctuating costs of materials. Frequently he would obtain preliminary estimates from subcontractors and suppliers before finalizing a design. The regular, gridded or modular nature of his buildings is both practical and architectural. Case Study House No. 16 is planned on a 1.2 metre (4 foot) grid, with

steel columns and beams at 2.4 metre (8 foot) intervals. Ellwood often exposed his beams, giving the space a directional emphasis, but here — perhaps because the living room faces both west and south to take advantage of the views — the steel beams are concealed in the roof deck; their bottom flanges are visible as recessed lines in the plastered ceiling. Columns are similarly recessed into walls so that the house can be read either as a frame with infill panels or as a composition of continuous vertical and horizontal planes. External wall panels of wood or glass are all full height and full width, column to column. Internal partitions are recessed at the foot and glazed at the head to emphasize their non-loadbearing status.

Case Study 16 is the classic Ellwood house, partly because it perfectly exemplifies his mastery of clean, minimalist form, and partly because it is indisputably his own design. Later in his career, he tended to leave architectural decisions to his school-trained partners, although he always maintained an interest in the construction and marketing aspects of the practice.

In 1977, by when his style had become unfashionable, Ellwood retired from architecture to devote more time to painting in Tuscany.

1 Plan

1 Entrance
2 Dining room
3 Kitchen
4 Scullery
5 Bathroom
6 Bedroom
7 Living room
8 TV room
9 Master bedroom
10 Service yard
11 Children's play area
12 Parking
13 Living terrace
14 View terrace
15 Courtyard

1

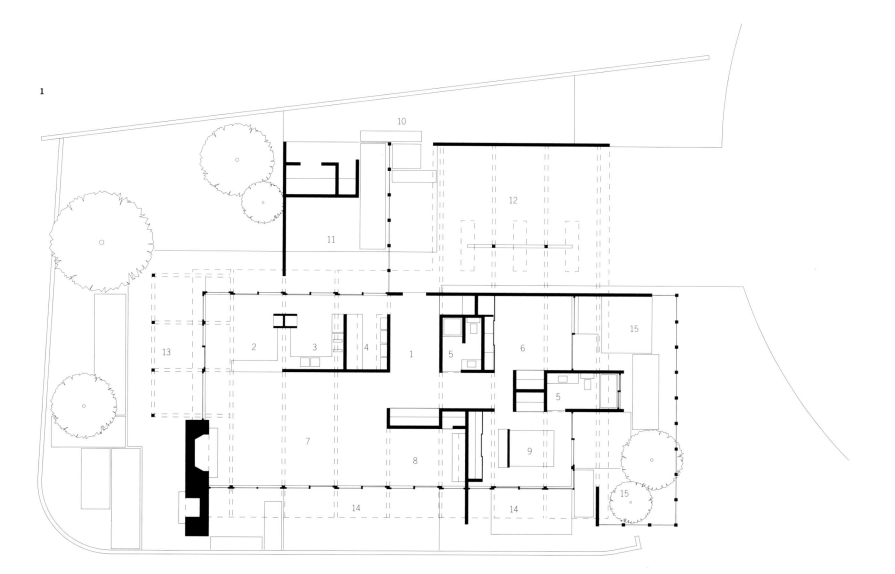

Experimental House

Alvar Aalto, 1898–1976

Muuratsalo, Finland; 1952–54

Alvar Aalto was a master of ambiguity. He deplored anything schematic or obvious, anything that could be readily explained. Many architects, especially Modernists, need to find — or, if necessary, invent — rational 'justifications' for their designs, but Aalto was content to rely on his instincts and to allow room for unpredictable interpretations. His own summerhouse on the rocky, forested island of Muuratsalo is in one sense a very simple building — a three-bedroomed cottage, planned as an L shape embracing a square courtyard — but its many ambiguities endow it with a genuine richness and complexity.

That courtyard, for example: is it really a courtyard? It has no roof, but it looks as though it could have one — or perhaps that it once had one that fell into ruin or was removed for some reason. What prompts this thought is the extraordinarily high walls that follow the profile of the longitudinal mono-pitched roof over the double-height living room, as if the whole building were one big mono-pitched block. If this were genuinely intended to be a courtyard, one would have expected more direct contact with the surrounding rooms — French windows, perhaps, and maybe a mediating veranda or colonnade.

It is true that a large window has been cut into the living-room wall, but other openings onto the courtyard are simply single-leaf doors, resembling the doors of outhouses.

One should not, perhaps, expect verandas in Finland, but it is still surprising that there is no sense of the courtyard being a common space onto which the other spaces look. So perhaps the courtyard was originally a room. What else could explain the big west-facing 'window' with its vestigial mullions? And why would that window have a stepped sill if not to accommodate some forgotten internal function? The hearth in the middle of the courtyard also seems to indicate that this might be the ruin of some kind of ceremonial hall like the council chamber of the roughly contemporary Säynatsälo Town Hall, the best known and most influential of Aalto's mature postwar works.

On the other hand, the materials suggest a different interpretation. Normally, one would expect brickwork to be painted internally and left natural externally. Here, the reverse is the case. So maybe the courtyard was always meant to be an exterior space. The brickwork, however, poses an even more puzzling question. Walls and paving alike

are 'sewn together' from rectangular patches of brickwork, all differently textured and patterned, with here and there a surprising patch of coloured ceramic tile. Are these perhaps sample panels or experiments of some kind?

Aalto did in fact — unsuccessfully — claim tax relief on his summerhouse at Muuratsalo on the grounds that it was a testbed for various building techniques, and he planned and partially executed several more experiments on the land to the east of the house. But clearly the patchwork is also intended to be a work of art, like the Modernist abstract paintings and collages that were his constant inspiration.

So the ambiguity remains, and with it a sense of freedom — freedom of invention on Aalto's part, and freedom of interpretation on our part.

1 Ground Floor Plan   **2 Section A–A**   **3 Site Plan**   **4 Section B–B**

1 Living room
2 Kitchen
3 Bedroom

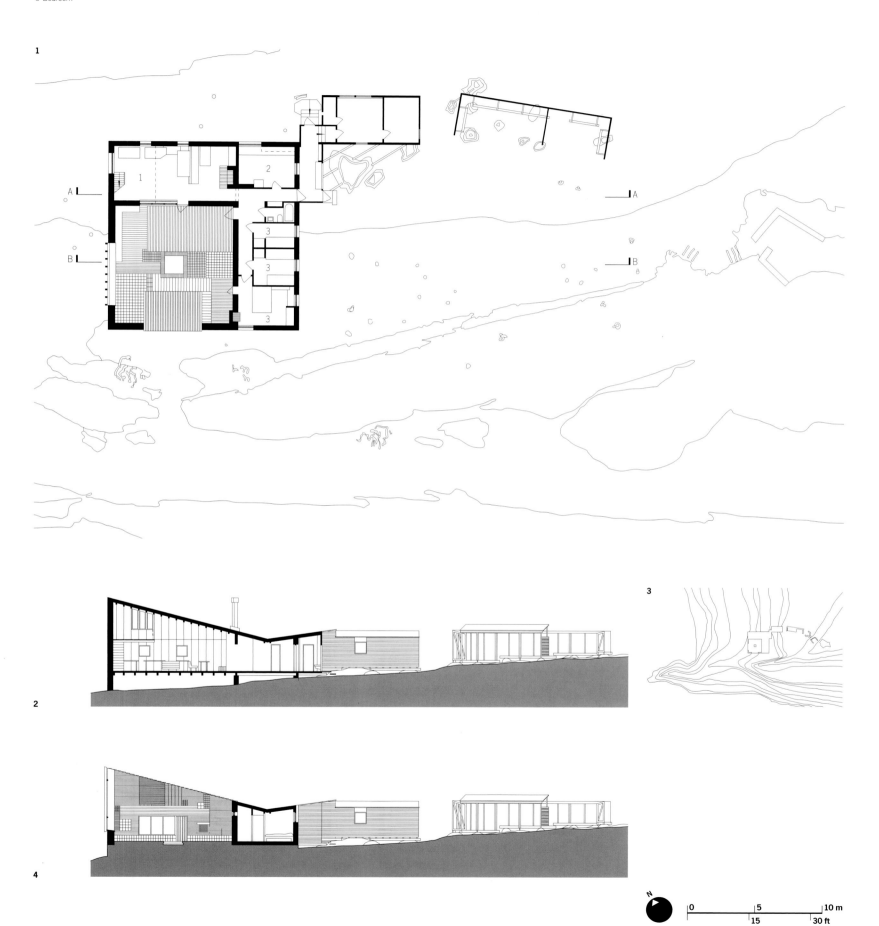

Maison Prouvé

Jean Prouvé, 1901–84

Nancy, France; 1954

Jean Prouvé began his career as an art metal worker, making furniture and fittings for famous architectural clients such as Robert Mallet Stevens and Tony Garnier. Then, in the 1930s, he himself began to dabble in the design of buildings, often in collaboration with the architects Baudouin and Lods. There was a prototype prefabricated weekend house, some rapid-erection huts for soldiers, and a group of permanent prefabricated houses in the Paris suburb of Meudon. As an architect, Prouvé was unusual because he based himself not in an office or a studio but in a workshop. An intimate knowledge of materials and manufacturing methods was the basis of his skill as a designer. Architectural theory and convention meant nothing to him. For example, the common architectural distinction between structural frame and non-loadbearing infill, displayed with such clarity in Mies van der Rohe's Farnsworth House (see pages 112–13) and its many imitators, was far too abstract an idea to appeal to Prouvé. He would never let 'architecture' get in the way of a simpler, faster, more practical solution.

Prouvé's workshop at Maxéville in Nancy was supported financially by the big aluminium smelting company L'Aluminium Français. In 1953,

wanting a bigger return on their investment, the parent company began interfering with what had previously been Prouvé's exclusive domain and he was forced out. Frustrated at losing his business, he channelled his energies into building a house for himself, using components left over from aborted projects.

The site was a narrow platform cut into a steep, south-facing slope that had been thought unsuitable for building. The house, not surprisingly, has a linear plan – basically, it is a single row of rooms with a circulation strip along the north side. What is extraordinary is the number of different buildings technologies that the house uses. The back wall, of sheet aluminium, is supported by small steel frames with wooden infill, set at right angles like fins. These form the compartments of a continuous storage wall that runs the whole length of the building. On the south side of the house, the external wall is made of three different types of loadbearing panel: full-height glass for the living room, slatted wood and glass for the bedrooms and study, and aluminium with small glass portholes for the service rooms. The end walls, however, are of heavy masonry and concrete, perhaps to give the structure lateral stability.

The west-facing flank wall of the living room is one large steel-framed glass door with a big pivot hinge. There is no structural frame, but there is a single steel roof beam to break the roof span over the wider rooms. The roof deck is very unusual: a three-layer pine lamination, in 1 metre wide sections, that curves slightly to form a shallow barrel vault over the main volume of the house, but curves the other way over the extensions beyond the roof beam. The deck supports itself without joists, and is covered in sheet aluminium. Inside, the partitions are mostly of solid wood, with round-cornered doors literally cut out of them. Finally, the bathroom walls are concrete, perhaps to give good acoustic insulation.

The Maison Prouvé sounds like a messy montage, but the various elements are so ingenious and practical that they have an elegance all their own. The house feels more like a boat or a vehicle than a building. Prouvé never intended it to last more than ten years, but the high regard in which he is held by his adopted profession has ensured its preservation.

1 Plan   **2 Front Elevation**   **3 Back Elevation**

1 Living room
2 Bedroom
3 Bathroom
4 Kitchen
5 Study

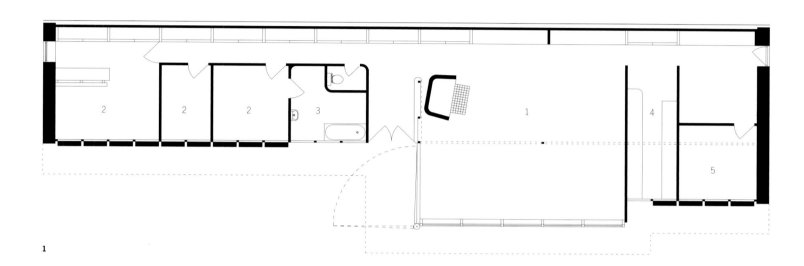

1

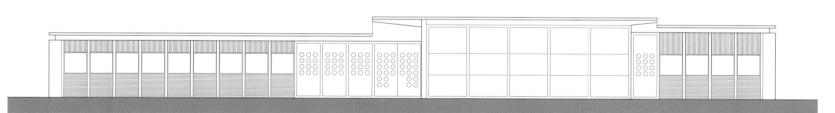

2

3

N   0   5   10 m
          15   30 ft

Bavinger House

Bruce Goff, 1904–82

Norman, Oklahoma, USA; 1950–55

There is nothing conventional about the Bavinger House. It does not even have a proper outside and inside. The space gathered up by its spiral stone wall moves smoothly from relative openness to relative enclosure. There is a glass wall that notionally divides exterior from interior, but the stone pavement is the same on both sides, the lush planting of creepers and climbers continues uninterrupted, and there is no change in the rough surface of the rubble walls. Well into the 'interior' is a large fishpond. The roof, in form like the peeled skin of an apple, is supported not by the wall but by tension cables attached to a central steel column. There are no conventional windows. Daylight is admitted by continuous ribbons of glass between roof and wall.

In the tight centre of the spiral there is something almost resembling a conventional kitchen. But where are the bedrooms? Hanging in the space above like a formation of flying saucers. If you sleep in a saucer suspended from the ceiling, what do you do with your clothes and other things? The answer is that you store them in an adjacent revolving cylindrical cupboard also suspended from the ceiling. On the plans, the saucers have conventional names such as 'parents' sleeping area' and 'play area', and certain sunken parts of the ground floor are reserved for lounging or dining. But does it really matter what happens where? This is a quasi-natural environment, an adventure playground – or perhaps a Garden of Eden, innocent of all worldly restrictions.

Yet there is a controlling geometry in the Bavinger House. The spiral is strictly logarithmic and the saucers, each provided with its own rotating cupboard, are regularly spaced off the landings of the spiral staircase. As the spiral tightens, the saucers and their satellites start to break out through the enclosing wall. The last and highest saucer, designated 'studio', becomes a projecting cylinder, like the turret of a castle.

Gene and Nancy Bavinger were artists who taught at the local university in Norman, Oklahoma, where Bruce Goff was head of the architecture department. They were the perfect clients. They were not concerned that the house took five years to build, and they did much of the work themselves, with some assistance from Goff's students. When the house was finished, it attracted crowds of curious visitors, both architects and local residents, so the Bavingers charged $1 for admission and recouped a worthwhile proportion of the building costs. The couple lived in the house for more than 40 years.

Bruce Goff was a self-taught architect who scorned any idea of stylistic continuity or development. He had a curious attitude to time, claiming to be interested not in the past or the future but only in what he called 'the continuous present'. And some of his buildings would be hard to date on their appearance alone. The Bavinger House is a good example. It is a return to nature, yet it does not seem backward-looking, and although it is a kind of fantasy, it is not exactly futuristic. In other words, like its architect, it owes nothing to anybody, except perhaps to his old friend and mentor, Frank Lloyd Wright.

1 Upper Level Plan

1 Parents' sleeping area
2 Play area
3 Child's sleeping area
4 Studio
5 Revolving cupboard
6 Bridge

2 Section A–A

3 Lower Level Plan

1 Outside terrace
2 Entrance
3 Visiting area
4 Pool
5 Fireplace
6 Kitchen
7 Breakfast area
8 Mechanical equipment area

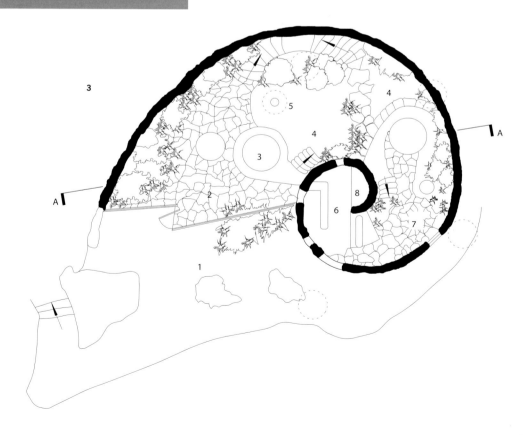

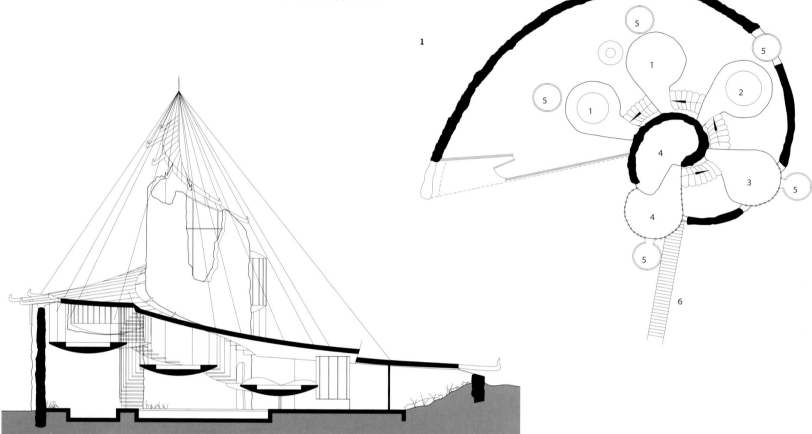

N

0   5   10 m

15   30 ft

Sugden House

Alison and Peter Smithson, 1928–93 and 1923–2003

Watford, UK; 1955

'I said that I wanted a simple house, an ordinary house, but that this should not exclude it from being a radical house.' It seems like an impossible brief, but Derek Sugden, a structural engineer who later became an acclaimed acoustician, was given exactly what he asked for. The Sugden house is ordinary in a radical way. Looked at naively, it is just a brick-built, four-bedroom suburban detached house like thousands of others. Yet it holds a firm place in the history of postwar British architecture and remains an inspiration to a certain school of earnest young architects.

But simplicity is hard to achieve, especially for architects, and the design was arrived at with some difficulty. The first sketch scheme had a butterfly roof and narrow windows. It was clearly a piece of 'Architecture'. Sugden and his wife, Jean, did not like it and said so, making Alison Smithson 'very cross'. (Sugden's account can be found in the book *Alison and Peter Smithson – from the House of the Future to a house of today* edited by Dirk van den Heuvel and Max Risselada.)

Peter Smithson smoothed things over and came back with a reworked version, without the trendy roof and windows. The Sugdens accepted it almost immediately, and the house was built without further alteration. All the 'Architecture' had apparently been taken out of the design. But the lesson the house teaches is that architecture is a matter not of form and gesture but of care and judgment. The Smithsons had recently completed the austerely Miesian Hunstanton School in Norfolk, UK, and were associated with the style known as Brutalism. Contemporary critics were nonplussed by the Sugden House, which did not seem to fit the architects' public image at all. But, for the Smithsons, Brutalism meant no more than 'directness' – the serving of everyday life directly by construction, without the intervention of self-conscious art. Getting rid of the 'Architecture', therefore, made perfect sense.

But if the Sugden House is just ordinary, why does it deserve special attention? Because, looked at another way, it isn't ordinary at all. The plan, for example, is extremely subtle. The wall dividing living and dining rooms mostly does not exist, yet its presence is suggested by the positioning of the staircase and the hearth. Ceiling heights are different on either side, which means that, upstairs, the two main bedrooms are raised two steps above the landing, emphasizing their private character. Finishes (or their absence) are subtle, too. Some wall surfaces are plastered, others left as fair-faced brick. Floor joists are all exposed downstairs and there are no loft spaces, so bedrooms have sloping, timber-boarded ceilings.

Outside, the ordinary/special conundrum is even more interesting. The local authority planners at first disliked what they called the 'arbitrary' placing of the standard steel-framed windows. They expected them to be neatly aligned or linked by decorative panels as they might have been in a conventional builder's version of the house. In fact, the window arrangement was the opposite of arbitrary. The windows were sized and positioned very deliberately to frame garden views and achieve particular spatial effects in the interior. Yet they are undeniably wrong-looking – an aspect no doubt enjoyed by the architects. One tiny detail sums up the ambiguity of the whole: the standard chimney-pots are upside down.

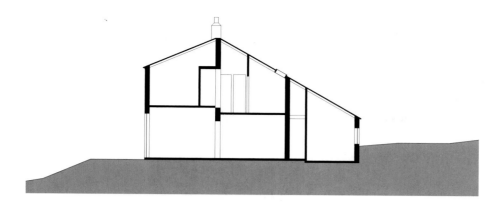

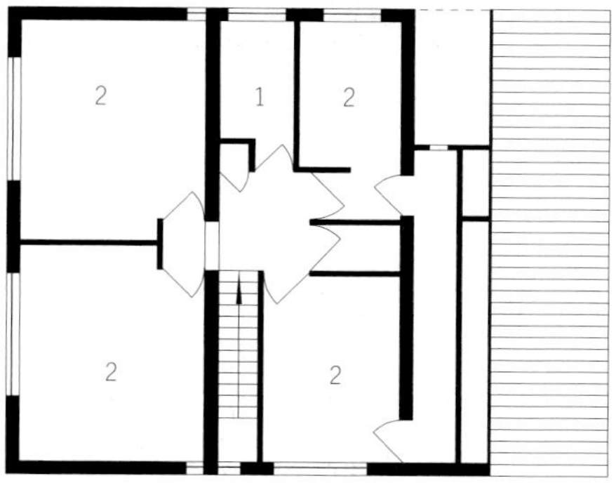

2 First Floor Plan

1 Bathroom
2 Bedroom

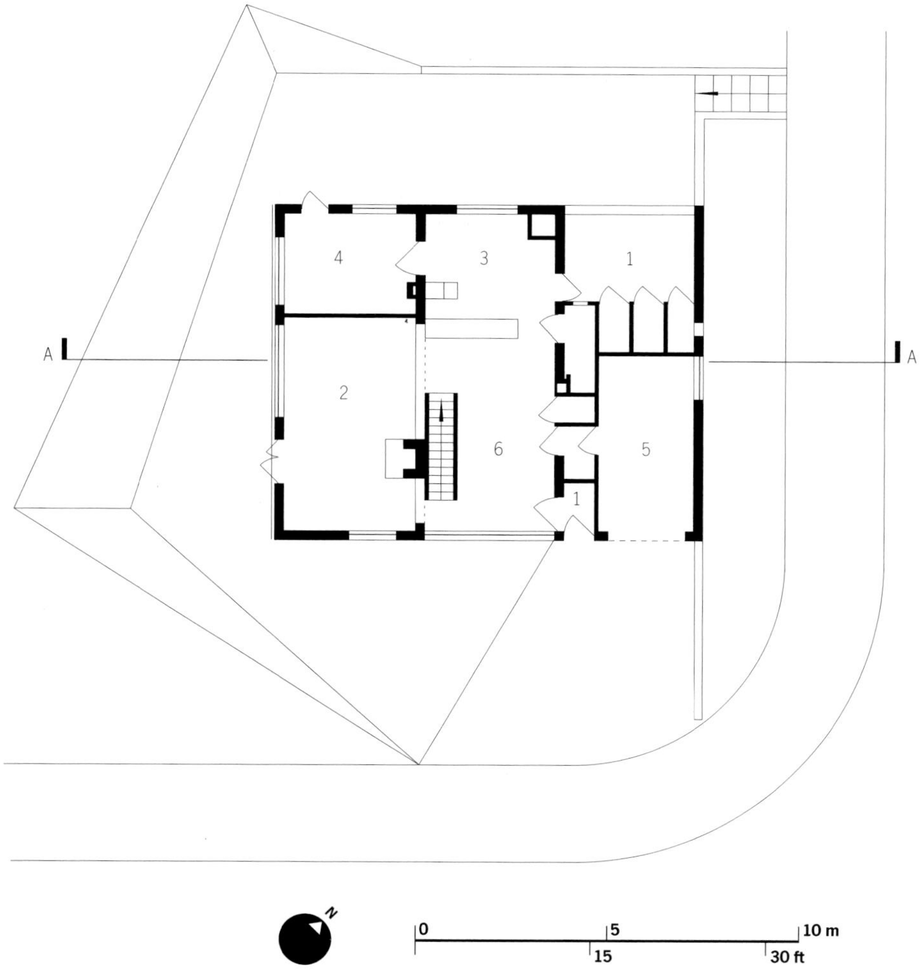

3 Ground Floor Plan

1 Entrance
2 Living room
3 Kitchen
4 Study
5 Garage
6 Dining room

0   5   10 m
    15   30 ft

Villa Shodan

Le Corbusier, 1887–1965

Ahmedabad, India; 1956

Le Corbusier was responsible for designing four buildings in Ahmedabad: two houses, a museum and the Millowners' Association Building. All his clients were members of Ahmedabad's close-knit social elite, whose wealth was based on textile manufacturing. The Villa Shodan was originally designed for the secretary of the Millowners' Association, Sri Surottam Hutheesing, a bachelor in his late forties, but Hutheesing sold the completed design to another mill-owner, Sri Shyamubhai Shodan, who was married with four children. Shodan proposed to build the villa on a different site. It seems that the prestige of owning a house designed by Le Corbusier was more important than any functional considerations.

Le Corbusier himself saw the house as a close relative of the Villa Savoye of 25 years earlier (see pages 80–81). There are similarities, such as the four-stage pedestrian ramp, the square plan and the fact that the frame of the composition contains more open space than enclosed space. But the differences are more striking. In the intervening period, Le Corbusier's architecture had undergone a transformation. Nature had replaced the machine as the source of his inspiration, and the controlled, Purist

composition of *objets types* had become a rough and rugged assemblage of concrete casts, more geological than mechanical.

Villa Shodan has a bold and aggressive form: large areas of blank concrete wall facing north, enormous crate-like brise-soleils facing south, and a parasol roof in the form of a thick, flat, cantilevered concrete slab with rounded holes in it. Although orientated carefully in relation to the path of the sun, the villa is not influenced by any features of its suburban setting. Nevertheless, it is evident that Le Corbusier had learned lessons from the verandas, shady courtyards and fretwork screens of the local domestic architecture. If the Villa Savoye was designed to catch the sun, the Villa Shodan was designed to keep it out while at the same time welcoming in every passing breeze.

The interior arrangement of the Villa Shodan is indescribably complex — many of the spaces are double- or triple-height and interlock with each other in section — but the accommodation consists essentially of a large living and dining space on the ground floor, a guest suite and study on the first floor, and two bedrooms and on the second floor. The whole concept of an 'interior' is almost irrelevant in a house with so much

inhabitable exterior space. The biggest volume in the house is the triple-height veranda or 'hanging garden' that extends from the second floor right up to the soffit of the parasol. A curious storey-height concrete table with a hole in it stands in the veranda, acting as a horizontal brise-soleil. The table is inaccessible, but two levels of roof over the bedrooms can be reached via narrow staircases. The whole multi-level veranda space resembles a functionless adventure playground until you remember that sleeping on the roof is normal in this part of India.

Whereas in the Villa Savoye the chauffeur's and maids' rooms are included in the main volume of the house, at the Villa Shodan staff are accommodated in a separate single-storey block, which also contains the kitchen.

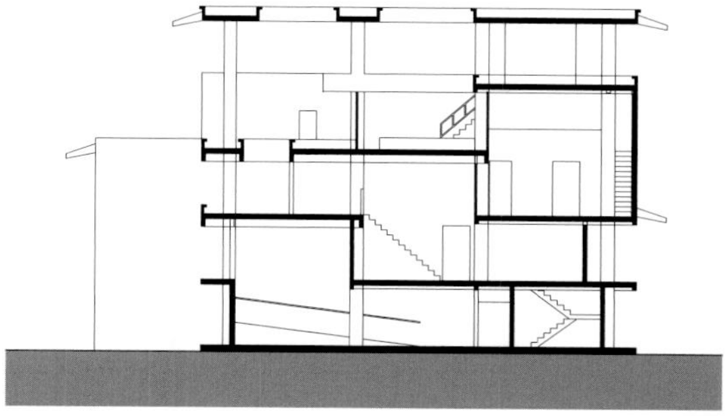

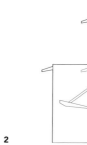

1 Section A–A

2 Northeast elevation

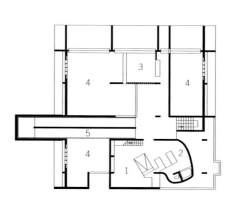

3 Fourth Floor Plan

1 Veranda
2 Water tank
3 Void

4 Third Floor Plan

1 Veranda
2 Void
3 Gallery

5 Second Floor Plan

1 Bedroom
2 Veranda
3 Void
4 Gallery
5 Ramp

6 First Floor Plan

1 Spare room
2 Bathroom
3 Study
4 Void
5 Ramp

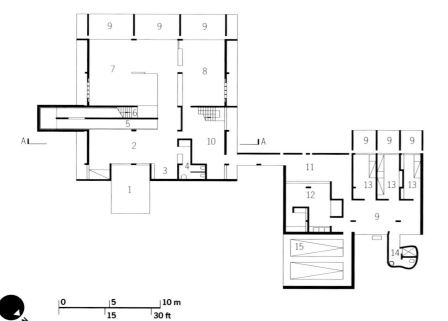

7 Ground Floor Plan

1 Entrance
2 Entrance hall
3 Cloakroom
4 WC
5 Ramp
6 Basement stairs
7 Salon
8 Dining room
9 Veranda
10 Servery
11 Kitchen
12 Larder
13 Staff room
14 WC
15 Garage

0   5   10 m
15   30 ft

Maisons Jaoul

Le Corbusier, 1887–1965

Neuilly-sur-Seine, Paris, France; 1956

Critics of architecture were at first baffled by the Maisons Jaoul. How could Le Corbusier, the prophet of the machine age and the pioneer of Purism, have designed anything so primitive? Where were the pilotis, the roof gardens, the ribbon windows? Where had these brick walls, tiled vaults and turf-covered roofs come from? And in Paris! It seemed like a betrayal of Modernism.

In an article in the *Architectural Review* of September 1955, the British architect James Stirling described it as 'disturbing to find little reference to the rational principles which are the basis of the Modern Movement'. But only a year later Stirling himself was designing blocks of flats (at Ham Common in Surrey) in the new, primitive, brick-and-concrete style.

The bafflement was not really justified. Le Corbusier had been moving in this direction ever since the completion of the Villa Savoye (see pages 80–81) in 1931. The Petite Maison de Weekend of 1937, for example, had rough stone walls and vaulted roofs covered in turf. But it is true that he seems to have regarded the Maisons Jaoul as a kind of definitive statement of his new, postwar style. The design was developed through countless versions and more than 500 drawings

were made – all this for a pair of medium-sized suburban houses. A lot of design time seems to have been wasted in trying to link the houses together, but in the final design they are separate.

House A, built for André Jaoul and his wife Suzanne, stands at the front of the site, and House B, built for their son Michel and his family, is situated behind House A and at right angles to it. The site originally sloped down to the street, so the ground-floor level is raised up half a storey with a shared garage underneath. Both houses are plain rectangles on plan, mainly two-storey with a short raised section to form a third storey. The rectangle is divided longitudinally into a wide and a narrow bay, giving three possible room widths. It is a system of a kind, applied slightly differently in each house. In the living room of House A, for example, a section of the first floor is omitted to form a double-height volume, whereas in House B this space is occupied by an extra bedroom.

The structural system may look primitive but it is actually a rather sophisticated adaptation of a traditional technique: the Catalan vault. Terracotta tiles are formed into shallow barrel vaults using adhesive mortar and no formwork. Extra layers of tiles are applied to strengthen the structure or

increase the span. Here, the vaults span between parallel concrete beams and act as permanent formwork for the concrete floors. The beams are supported by brick walls, which are treated as flat panels, unbuttressed, so that, for example, adjacent walls at the entrance end of House A do not meet at the corners. The vault's tendency to push the walls over is counteracted by horizontal steel bars at intervals across the ceiling.

With their clumsy curved roofs and their deliberately mortar-smeared brickwork, these houses are designed to look rough, even brutal. But, like every Le Corbusier building, they are also subtle and ambiguous. Inside, the spaces flow into each other and the multi-directional daylight makes the natural materials glow: brickwork, terracotta, wood, board-marked concrete and the occasional painted wall. In 1955 this was a new architecture – primitive and poetic but also modern.

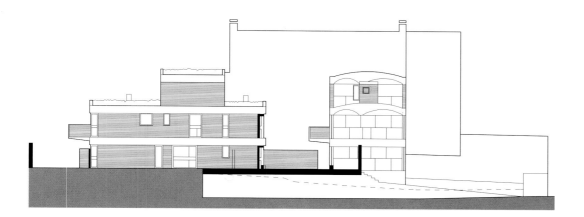

1 Northeast Elevation

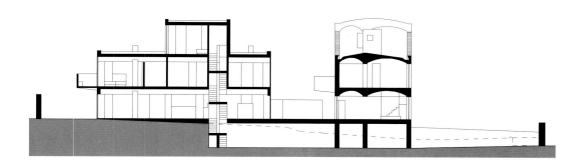

2 Section A–A

House B

House A

4

5

6

3 Ground Floor Plan

1 Entrance hall
2 Dining room
3 Living room
4 Study
5 Kitchen
6 Garage

4 First Floor Plan

1 Bedroom
2 Bathroom
3 Void

5 Second Floor Plan

1 Bedroom
2 Bathroom

0 5 10 m
15 30 ft

Case Study House No. 22

Pierre Koenig, 1925–2004

Los Angeles, California, USA; 1960

Pierre Koenig's steel-and-glass masterpiece is different from its more easterly cousins, the Johnson House (see pages 108–109) and the Farnsworth House (see pages 112–13). While they are seriously classical and slightly pompous, laden with European architectural theory, Case Study House No. 22 is relaxed and informal. It looks out over Los Angeles — a jewelled carpet in Julius Shulman's famous photograph — not in any awestruck, still less dominating way, but for the simple enjoyment of the spectacle, a pleasure that must have been shared by the young lovers who drove up to this site on balmy evenings before the house was built. This is great architecture but reticent, finding no need to draw attention to itself. Life, it seems to say, is more important. And in the late 1950s life was sweet for middle-class Angelenos like Buck and Carlotta Stahl.

Actually, at that time, sites such as this were thought inferior because they were hard to build on: too narrow, with unstable subsoil and no room for a proper yard. The Stahls may have paid over the odds for the site, but they bought it for the view, and when they briefed their architect they insisted that not the smallest slice of the 270-degree panorama should be blocked or obscured.

Koenig solved the problem by grouping the service spaces along a blank north wall facing the road and thrusting a glass-walled living room out towards the view, its last bay supported on cantilevered concrete ground beams. The decision to place the living room end-on rather than side-on to the view meant that even the bedrooms could command a piece of the panorama. The L-shaped plan also unified the open space on the site, creating a perfect semi-enclosure for a patio and a swimming pool.

The entrance to the house is completely informal. From the car port at the west end of the building, one turns left in front the bedrooms along a footpath that hops over a couple of small extensions of the pool. The 'front door' is in the inner corner of the L, but it virtually identical to the big, full-height patio doors that form most of the external wall.

The kitchen is a freestanding, cabin-like structure within the larger living room. Originally it had an illuminated ceiling and sliding doors to close it off, but it works best as an open worktop and bar. The chimney that divides the dining space from the living space is another freestanding, see-through structure.

The key to that informal quality is the steel frame. Its 30 cm (12 inch) deep beams and 10 cm (4 inch) square columns are not there to be looked at, though they are handsome enough with their neat welded joints. Rather, they stay out of the way, opening up the view and allowing the space to flow. The columns are especially discreet: 6.7 metres (22 feet) apart and scarcely thicker than the frames of the sliding doors. The beams have long, effortless cantilevers, sawn off casually just beyond the trough steel roof-decking that they support, and the decking itself is cantilevered further than it seems it should be, to shade the south- and west-facing glass.

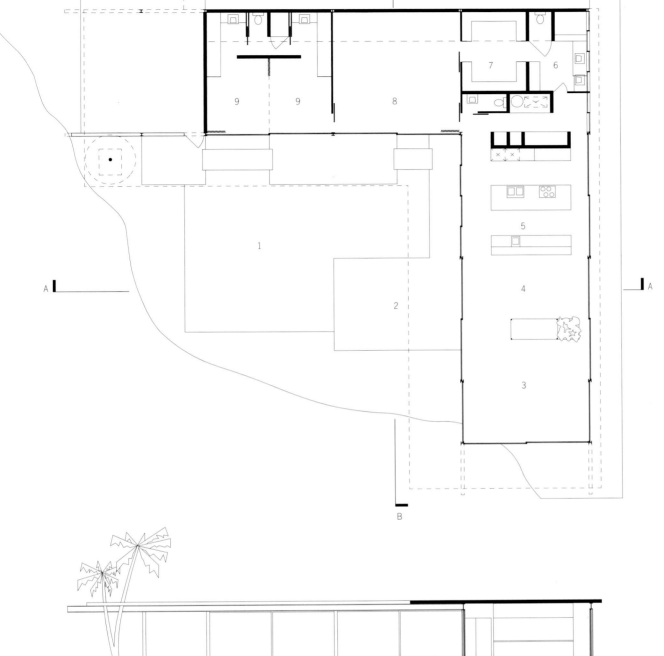

1 Ground Floor Plan

1 Pool
2 Patio
3 Living room
4 Dining room
5 Kitchen
6 Bathroom
7 Dressing room
8 Master bedroom
9 Children's bedroom

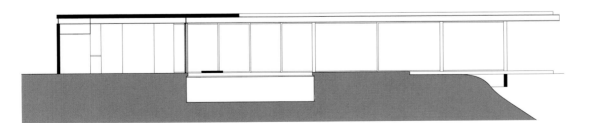

2 Section A–A
showing South Elevation

3 Section B–B
showing West Elevation

N

0   5   10 m
15   30 ft

Malin Residence

John Lautner, 1911–95

Los Angeles, California, USA; 1960

For reasons that are obscure, the Malin Residence in the Hollywood Hills is sometimes known as the Chemosphere – a suitably scientific-sounding name for a house that looks like a flying saucer. This is not a fantastical or futuristic design, however. The client, a young aircraft engineer, would have understood that the design embodies a practical solution to the challenge of building on a steeply sloping site.

Reyner Banham, in his book *Los Angeles, The Architecture of Four Ecologies*, analyses the various techniques for building houses on the valuable but difficult land in the foothills north of the city. There were two common methods. The ground could be cut and filled to create a level platform or the house could be supported on an open steel framework.

The design of the Malin Residence rejects both of these methods, instead perching the house on top of a single concrete column. The column has quite a large foot buried in the ground, but otherwise the hillside – its profile, its ground water, even its vegetation – remains undisturbed. The cost was reckoned to be about half that of the more conventional solution with retaining walls and land drains.

The house itself is octagonal and one-storey, its floor supported umbrella-fashion by diagonal steel struts. Surprisingly, the concrete column stops at the floor instead of carrying on up to support the roof. In the centre of the roof, where the column would have been, is a circular rooflight, brightening the middle of a relatively deep plan. The superstructure is made of steel and timber. Concrete might have been more consistent architecturally, but would have been too heavy and precarious in this earthquake-prone region. The steel umbrella struts support the ends of floor beams radiating from the concrete column, with tie beams around the perimeter. The roof is supported by curved portal frames of laminated wood that spring from the ends of the struts and terminate at a ring around the rooflight.

The whole interior is therefore a column-free, flexible space. Half of it is occupied by an open-plan kitchen/dining/living space, with a fireplace alcove including sitting area in the middle under the rooflight. The other half is divided like the slices of a pie into bedrooms, but with some improvised local adjustments to improve the proportions of the rooms. The treatment of the perimeter, where the saucer of the floor meets the upside-down saucer of the roof, is particularly thoughtful. Windows are raked back between the portal frames to reduce the vertigo effect, but in one section a glass panel has been cut below sill level to allow a view down to the car port below.

There remains the question of access. From above, a narrow bridge spans from solid ground to an entrance near the kitchen, where the external wall is set back to form a balcony. From below, visitors climb into an open-topped lift car which rises up the slope like a miniature funicular railway, passing under the house and arriving at the land end of the bridge.

John Lautner lived in Los Angeles most of his life and designed more that a hundred houses in southern California, yet he seems not to have had much affection for the place. He served his apprenticeship with Frank Lloyd Wright and he saw himself as an organic architect, not a superficial image-maker. Hollywood, however, knows a striking image when it sees one and the Malin Residence has appeared in several films, including *Charlie's Angels* and *Body Double*.

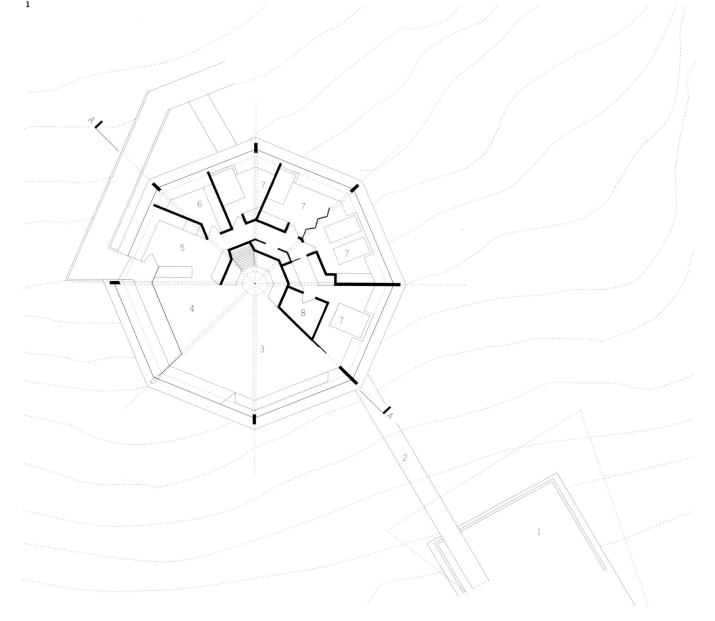

1 Plan   137

1 Carport
2 Hill-a-vator
3 Living room
4 Dining room
5 Kitchen
6 Laundry room
7 Bedroom
8 Bathroom

2

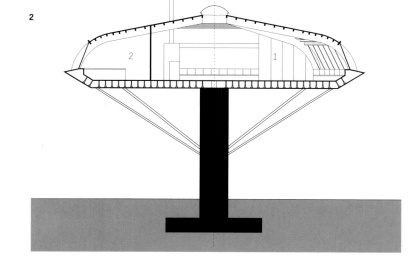

2 Section A–A

1 Living room
2 Kitchen

Esherick House

Louis Kahn, 1901–74

Philadelphia, Pennsylvania, USA; 1961

Louis Kahn designed 20 private houses but only nine of them were built. The low success rate might be explained by his tendency to exceed the design budget and to treat his clients as if they were his students. It was certainly not due to any reluctance to design small, unprofitable buildings. Kahn loved designing houses and used them as testbeds and showcases for his ideas.

The Esherick house, which was built for a single woman in a northern suburb of Philadelphia and completed in 1961, exemplifies a number of important aspects of Kahn's mature style. First, it is monumental. Its assertive, vertical posture seems somewhat formal, as if it were a public rather than a domestic building. Second, it is contained and box-like, with no extensions or projections apart from two symmetrically placed chimneys at opposite ends of the building. In contrast to the flowing space of the typical Modernist free plan, Kahn's space is essentially static. His rooms are still, silent spaces waiting to accommodate archetypal human activities: a group of friends talking, a communal meal, a solitary person reading. Third, the house is naturally lit and ventilated, using the form of the building itself rather than any mechanical equipment or attached devices to control the quality of the internal spaces. In short, this is, as the slogan has it, an architecture of 'silence and light'.

Although the house is basically a large box, a close examination of the plan reveals that it is organized into four strips, each a contained and well-proportioned rectangle: a service strip, with kitchen and laundry rooms on the ground floor and bathrooms above; a dining-room strip with the bedroom above; a circulation strip, containing the staircase and the front and back entrances with recessed balconies over; and finally the double-height, double-cube volume of the living-room strip. Conceptually, these strips can be combined in different ways. For example, the living, dining and sleeping spaces can be conceived as the main house, with the service strip added on one side. Alternatively, the three two-storey strips can be seen as the 'servant' wing to the main spatial event of the living room. The ambiguity of the external elevations, which sometimes indicate the divisions between strips and sometimes don't, seems to encourage such double readings.

Windows commonly have three functions: to admit light, to encourage ventilation and to provide a view out. Kahn designed various kinds of openings to fulfil these different functions. For example, in the living room of the Esherick House, ventilation is provided by wooden shutters on both sides of the full-height, south-east-facing, fixed-glass window. Glare from this window is controlled not by brise-soleils but by the balancing light of the other windows in the room, especially the high window above the bookcases on the opposite wall. A narrow vertical strip window in the middle of the bookcases gives a view out towards the road. In the side wall, there is a window above the fireplace, the view from which is mostly blocked by a freestanding external chimney. This is perhaps a miniature version of the monumental brick fume cupboard exhausts of the Richards Medical Research Building, which was under construction in Philadelphia at the time the house was being designed.

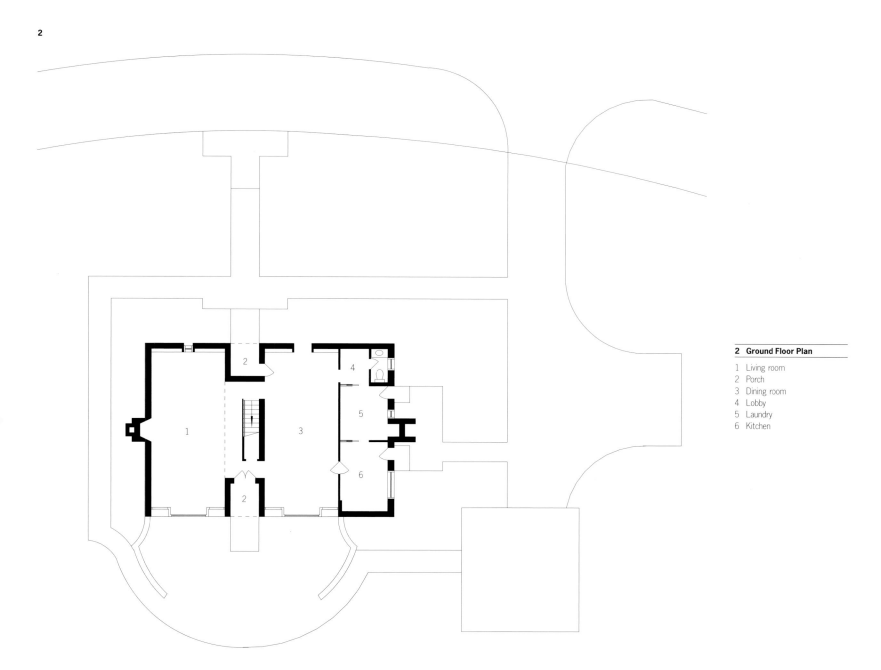

1 First Floor Plan

1 Porch
2 Upper living room
3 Study
4 Storage
5 Shower
6 Bathroom
7 Dressing room
8 Bedroom

2 Ground Floor Plan

1 Living room
2 Porch
3 Dining room
4 Lobby
5 Laundry
6 Kitchen

0   5   10 m

15   30 ft

Moore House

Charles Moore, 1925–93

Orinda, California, USA; 1962

Charles Moore was as much a teacher as an architect. During his long career he held teaching posts at Salt Lake City, Princeton, Berkeley, Yale, the University of California and Austin, Texas. And his architecture contains something of the communicativeness and gregariousness required by his second vocation. Like Robert Venturi, he was bored by po-faced Modernism and determined to make architecture enjoyable again. He travelled widely and is said to have had an elephantine memory for buildings and places.

Vernacular and Classical architecture inspired Moore at a time, in the 1960s, when function and structure were all that mattered in the schools and architectural history was a poor relation in the curriculum. His Piazza d'Italia, a kitsch Classical confection designed in 1975 for the Italian community in New Orleans, was actually not typical of his work, but it showed his contempt for the Modernist orthodoxy and it quickly became a Postmodernist icon.

Louis Kahn – the form-giver whose influence no respectable late 20th-century American architect seems to have escaped – was Moore's teacher for a while, and Kahn's Trenton Bath House of 1959 is immediately discernible in the square plan and semi-pyramidal roof of the little house Moore designed for himself in Orinda, California, three years later. Inside the house there are two more squares and two more pyramids, this time inspired not by Kahn but by John Summerson's classic essay 'Heavenly Mansions', in which he discusses the importance of the 'aedicule' in architectural history. An aedicule is a little pavilion or canopy, usually supported on four columns and often combined with other aedicules to make more substantial architectural compositions. Aedicules come in many styles – gothic, classical, Mughal, Hindu.

Moore's aedicules are lopsided pyramids, each supported on four circular wooden columns salvaged from demolition sites. The pyramids are painted white inside to reflect the daylight from rooflights at the apexes and to contrast with the dark-stained roof timbers of the outer enclosing pyramid. The aedicules therefore create special places within a larger general space. One defines the main sitting area, and the smaller, surprisingly, is an open bathroom, like a modern version of the bath in an ancient Roman villa.

The space around the aedicules is occupied by a relaxed arrangement of furniture and fittings: some museum-like display cases against the walls, a dressing space, a pair of beds separated by a tall bookcase, and a grand piano.

Solid external walls account for about half of the total enclosure. The rest is sliding doors, some solid and some glazed. There are no fixed walls or columns at the corners, so when the doors are slid back the whole house becomes an open pavilion on a circular lawn surrounded by trees.

At first sight the absence of corner columns is puzzling. A more conventional designer would have supported the main roof on perimeter columns and made the aedicules independent, lightweight structures like stage sets. But Moore insists that his salvaged wooden columns should hold up the whole building. They do so in a rather indirect way that involves a big wooden truss at roof-ridge level and rafters that lean against the entablatures of the aedicules. But this is architecture, not engineering, and structural logic is a secondary consideration. What matters is the ambition of the design, its inclusiveness and openness. This is a small house, but it makes big gestures and it refuses to be dull.

2

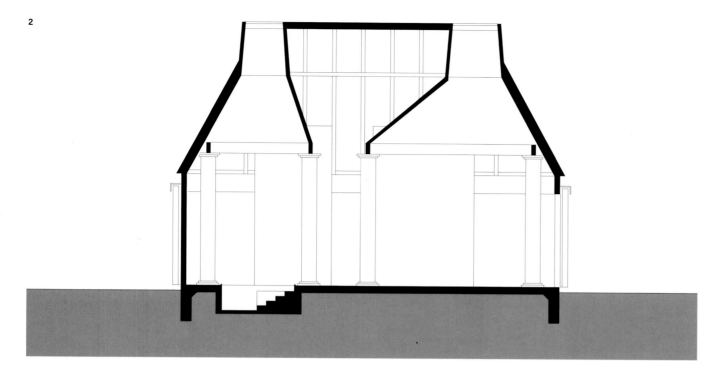

1

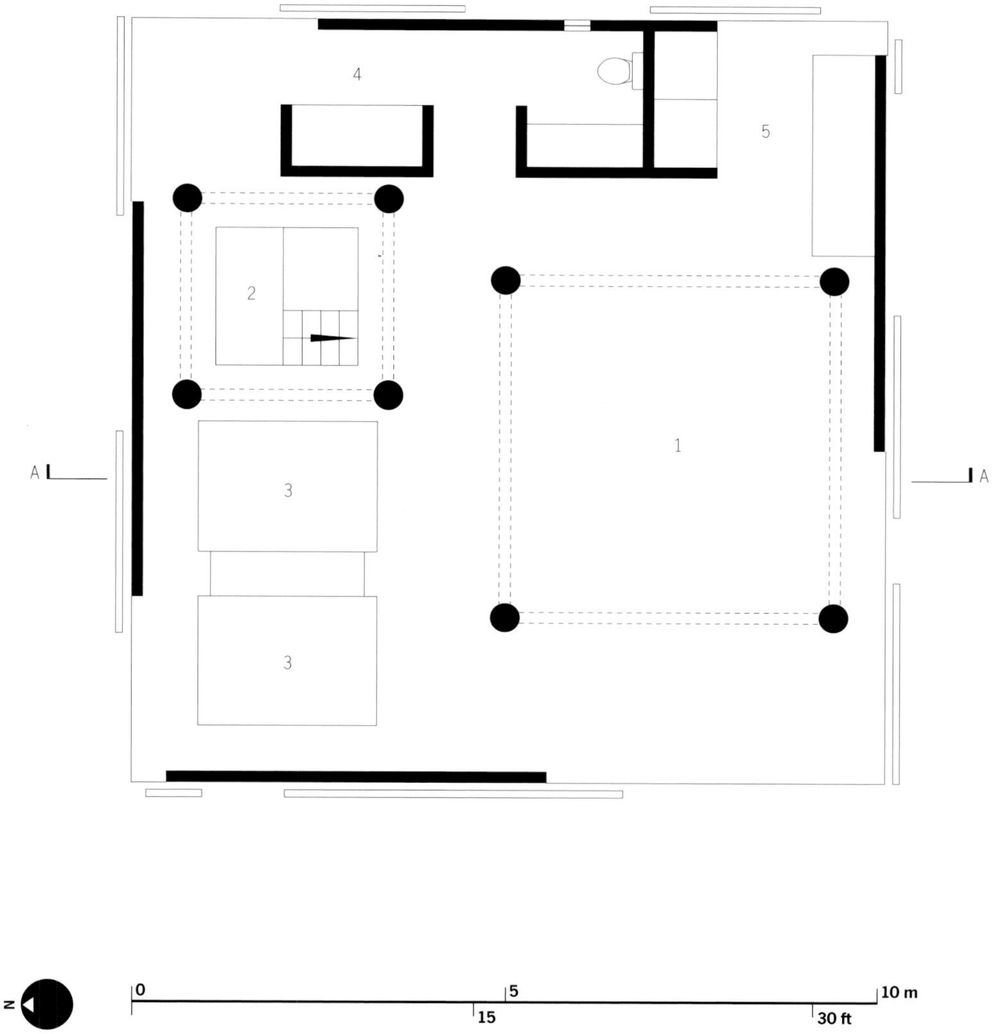

2 Plan

1   Sitting area
2   Bath
3   Bed
4   Dressing room
5   Kitchen

4

5

2

A

A

3

1

3

N

0   5   10 m

15   30 ft

Vanna Venturi House

Robert Venturi, 1925–

Chestnut Hill, Philadelphia, Pennsylvania, USA; 1962–64

Consistency is generally regarded as a virtue in architecture, especially Modernist architecture. But Robert Venturi dared to question why this should be. Why, for example, should the outsides of buildings necessarily reflect the insides? Why should buildings always be as simple as possible; why could they not also be complex? And what would a building look like that was contradictory rather than consistent?

Venturi tried to answer these questions in a book, *Complexity and Contradiction in Architecture* (1964). He found inspiration not in the Modern Movement but in the Mannerist and Baroque architecture he had studied on a fellowship at the American Academy in Rome. While writing the book, he was also designing a house for his mother on a site opposite the Esherick House (see pages 138–39) by his mentor and one-time employer, Louis Kahn. It should have been his first building but it took so long to design (his mother imposed no deadlines) that in the meantime he designed and built a small headquarters building for a visiting nurses' association. But the house absorbed most of his creative energies. The design went through at least six fully worked-out versions. It would be much more than a house;

it would be a manifesto for a new architecture, a Postmodern architecture. Although very small – it has five habitable rooms – the house looks bigger than it is. The front elevation is a wide, symmetrical gable like a classical pediment, with the main entrance in the middle. McKim Mead and White's shingle-style Low House of 1887, in Bristol, Rhode Island, is an acknowledged influence on the overall form. But this is a broken pediment, and its precedents go further back, to Vanburgh perhaps, or Michelangelo. Contradiction is immediately apparent in the distribution of doors and windows, which are balanced but arranged asymmetrically, responding to the functional requirements of the plan: a Modernist ribbon window for the kitchen on the right and a couple of square windows, for a bedroom and a bathroom, on the left.

This is not a simple rejection of consistency; it is consistent and inconsistent, symmetrical and asymmetrical, at the same time. In a consistent building, everything has its place and relates consistently to everything else. Here, elements jostle one another, competing to occupy the same space. The porch, the staircase and the fireplace all want to be at the centre of the composition. Somehow, they come to an accommodation.

The result is a new hybrid form, less mechanistic, more human. Where the staircase is squeezed by the chimney, for example, the few steps that are left stranded form a handy shelf for things that are waiting to be taken upstairs.

Inside, it is apparent that the external walls, front and back, are more like screens than walls – or, rather, they are both screens and walls. The all-glass east wall of the living room is recessed, forming a covered yard screened by the back wall, and there are smaller versions of this device for the bedrooms on the other side of the house. The room upstairs, lit by a central lunette window, is set back behind the parapet of the back wall, forming a long narrow balcony. Again, the effect is to make the wall seem like a screen. 'Layered' was the word that Venturi used to describe this treatment of surfaces and spaces, thus coining one of the architectural clichés of century.

Complexity and Contradiction in Architecture was enormously influential and became the foundation of the architectural movement known as Postmodernism. The Vanna Venturi House can reasonably claim to be the first Postmodern building. The critic Frederick Schwartz goes so far as to call it the first Postmodern anything.

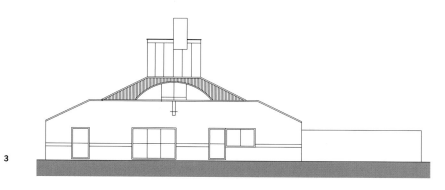

1   Long Section

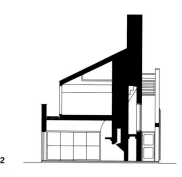

2   Cross Section

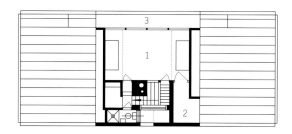

3   Rear Elevation

4   Front Elevation

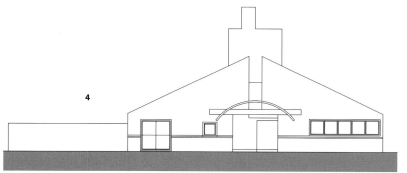

5   First Floor Plan

1 Bedroom
2 Storage
3 Terrace

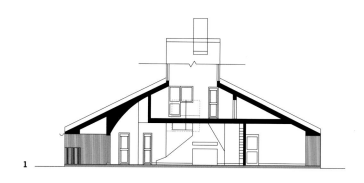

6   Ground Floor Plan

1 Living room
2 Bedroom
3 Kitchen
4 Yard

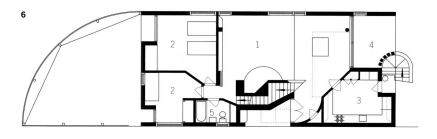

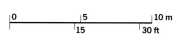

0   5   10 m

15   30 ft

Creek Vean House

Norman Foster and Richard Rogers, 1935– and 1933–

Cornwall, UK; 1966

Throughout the 1970s and 1980s, Richard Rogers and Norman Foster were rivals for the title of chief High Tech architect. The contest eventually culminated in the building of the two masterpieces of the high-tech style, Rogers's Lloyds Building in the City of London and Foster's Hong Kong and Shanghai Bank in Hong Kong, both finished in 1987. But in the 1960s Rogers and Foster, with their wives Su and Wendy, had been partners in a practice called Team 4. The house in Creek Vean, Cornwall, was not their first job, but it was the job that made their names. The client was Su's father, Marcus Brumwell, the retired boss of an advertising agency and an art lover. The great Dutch abstract painter Piet Mondrian had once borrowed money from him and paid him back with a painting. It was that painting that was to pay for the house. With a sympathetic client, a reasonable budget and a fantastic site, it was a dream job for the struggling young practice.

The house stands almost at the top of a steep riverbank. A winding footpath connects a car-parking space at the top to a boathouse standing in the water below. On the way, the path passes over and through the house, first hopping onto its roof via a little metal bridge, then slicing it in two with a flight of grass-covered steps. On one side lies the single-storey bedroom and studio block, on the other the two-storey living and dining block. A glance at the plan is enough to reveal the other main determinant of the design: all rooms look out over the river, and the walls that divide them are splayed out as if straining for an even wider angle of view. A narrow corridor runs along the back of the single-storey block with a totally blank external wall, which is converted into an art gallery by a sloping glass roof. The walls of the bedrooms and studio slide aside to allow more room to view the paintings on special occasions. The two-storey wing is a more assertive, boxlike form with an all-glass, south-west-facing wall. Kitchen and dining room are on the ground floor, with the living room above on a kind of bridge across the double-height space.

The surprising thing about this house, in view of the future careers of its designers, is that it is not at all High Tech. The main material is loadbearing concrete block, fair face inside and out — just the kind of heavy, site-crafted material that Rogers and Foster later rejected in favour of lightweight, prefabricated metal and glass components. The ground-hugging form of the single-storey block, and its placing just below the top of the hill, seem more reminiscent of Frank Lloyd Wright than, say, the Eameses or Craig Ellwood, while the two-storey block has a vaguely Corbusian look. But there were some technical innovations. The roof planting, though common today, was very rare and rather daring then, and the glass in the gallery rooflight was fixed using a new material called neoprene. Neoprene gaskets had been used only once before in England, in the Cummins Engine factory at Darlington, Co. Durham, by the American architects Roche and Dinkeloo. And it was this factory that inspired Team 4's next major building, the Reliance Controls factory in Swindon, Wiltshire, a brilliantly simple construction regarded as the first example of the British High Tech style. When that building was finished, the road ahead was clear for both architects, and they went their separate ways.

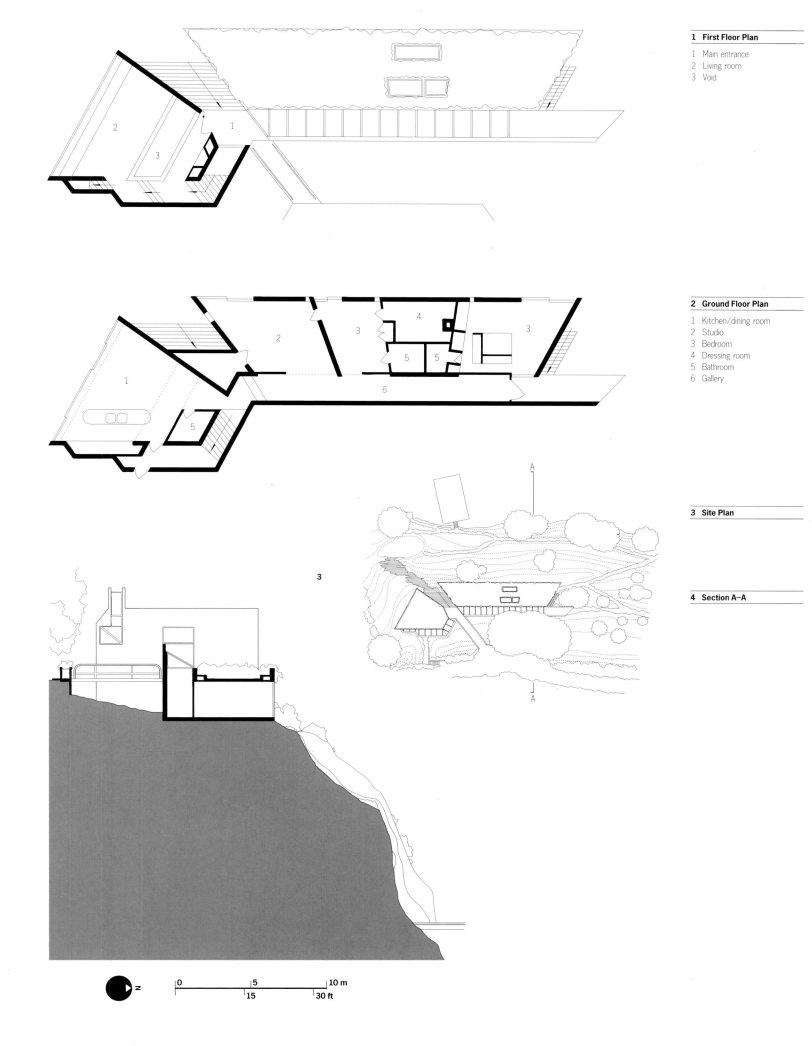

1   First Floor Plan

1   Main entrance
2   Living room
3   Void

2   Ground Floor Plan

1   Kitchen/dining room
2   Studio
3   Bedroom
4   Dressing room
5   Bathroom
6   Gallery

3   Site Plan

4   Section A–A

0   5   10 m
15   30 ft

Hanselmann House

Michael Graves, 1934–

Indiana, USA; 1967

Michael Graves began to attract critical attention in the late 1960s as a member (with Eisenmann, Gwathmey, Hejduk and Meier) of the so-called New York Five. It was a somewhat artificial grouping, formed precisely in order to attract critical attention, but its members did share certain attitudes to modern architecture, in particular a love of the Purist Modernism of Le Corbusier combined with a complete disregard for the socialist ideals inherent in that style.

Graves and his colleagues were interested in form and space, not the future of society. Their houses, published in detail in the 1975 book *Five Architects*, superficially resembled Le Corbusier's houses of the 1920s and 1930s, except that they were mostly constructed of steel and wood rather than reinforced concrete and stuccoed blockwork. The Hanselmann House is typical of the New York manner even though it was built in Indiana.

Since it is a representation of an earlier, geometrical style, the Hanselmann House is both figurative and abstract. It is hard to say which of these principles is dominant, though the question becomes important in view of the future direction of Graves's career. Part of the composition is certainly abstract, and to a radical degree, since it does not physically exist. Notionally, the form of the house is a double (near) cube, but only one of the cubes has been built. The 'presence' of the other is indicated only by the positioning of the entrance steps far away from the built cube at the end of a long bridge. The original design included a small studio to one side of the bridge and a flimsy steel frame outlining the missing cube, but these were never constructed.

The entrance is on the first floor, a piano nobile containing the living room, dining room and kitchen. Downstairs is the children's territory, with four bedrooms and playroom. A separate staircase leads to the parents' bedroom and study on the top floor. The plan is a perfect square, divided structurally into nine smaller squares by four internal columns that sometimes merge with walls.

In the Villa Stein–de Monzie (see pages 54–55), Le Corbusier took a regular, classical framework and modernized it by removing parts of the walls and floors and introducing asymmetrical curved elements. Graves does the same, carving into the sunny, southern corner of his cube to create ambiguous inside/outside spaces such as the extraordinary roof terrace on the top floor, which is equipped with walls and windows like a proper room and lacks only a roof. It has its own balcony overlooking the entrance bridge, and on the other side it looks down into the living room.

Derivative and formalistic it may be, but the Hanselmann House is definitely a Modernist composition. Nobody could have predicted in 1967 that Graves would soon adopt a new style which rejected abstraction and enthusiastically embraced figuration. By 1980, his Portland Building was recognized as the prime example of Postmodern Classicism. Five years later he was designing buildings for Walt Disney with the Seven Dwarves as caryatids and Dopey installed in the pediment like a god.

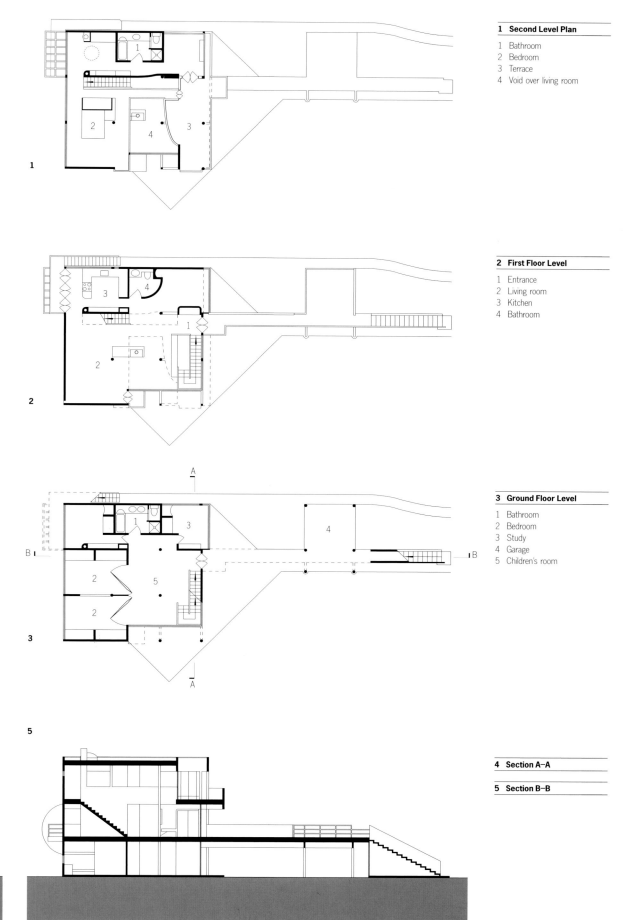

1 Second Level Plan

1 Bathroom
2 Bedroom
3 Terrace
4 Void over living room

1

2 First Floor Level

1 Entrance
2 Living room
3 Kitchen
4 Bathroom

2

3 Ground Floor Level

1 Bathroom
2 Bedroom
3 Study
4 Garage
5 Children's room

3

4 **5**

4 Section A–A

5 Section B–B

N

0		5		10 m
	15			30 ft

San Cristobal

Luis Barragán, 1902–88

Mexico City, Mexico; 1968

To describe Luis Barragán as a Mexican Modernist is accurate enough but misses an essential quality of his work, especially his late work. He loved the vernacular domestic architecture of his homeland – its massive walls, small windows and tangled gardens – but he was also profoundly influenced by Le Corbusier, whose work he studied on a trip to France in 1932. The two tendencies are represented respectively by the private houses and gardens he designed in Guadalajara in the 1920s and the economical apartment buildings he designed in Mexico City in the 1930s. In his work after the Second World War the two strands come together in a personal style to which critics often apply words such as 'emotional', 'surreal' and 'mythical'. The San Cristobal house and stud farm for the Folke Egerstrom family in a suburb of Mexico City is a good example.

Even the site layout has surreal overtones. A dwelling place for human beings is placed next to a dwelling place for horses, the plans echoing one another as if there were no essential difference between these two types of animal. The human house is a composition of stuccoed cubic forms perforated by squareish windows and divided into two main blocks by an entrance hall. Internally, the plan is unremarkable; the main interest lies in the relationship between internal and external spaces. The living room, for example, looks out over the paddock to the north through a big full-height window, but it is also linked by means of a single narrow door to a perfectly square patio enclosed by high walls on three sides. The external space between the house and the road is divided by a long plain wall, with a garden on one side and a service yard on the other. A flat-roofed veranda on the garden side of the wall offers a shady refuge for swimmers in the pool at its southern end.

On the wider, northern part of the site, the dividing wall/veranda/pool arrangement is repeated on a larger scale for horses, but this time the dividing wall is a row of back-to-back stables, the veranda has a pitched roof, and the pool is made monumental by a waterfall that arcs out of a cavity in a thick, blood-red wall. The architectural temperature has risen considerably. It is like the stage set for an elemental drama.

The place of the house in the human version of the composition is taken by a hay barn, but its high, massive wall, painted shocking pink, is anything but agricultural. It is a backdrop against which to view the beautiful thoroughbreds hitched to two outsize wooden rails placed-off centre in the paddock. A longer, lower and even more shockingly pink wall runs along the west side of the paddock right up to and (conceptually at least) through the house. Opposite the horse pool, two openings in this wall lead to a small exercise field.

That Barragán was a lover of horses – and that in some mythical way the horse represented for him an aspect of humanity – is obvious. It is rare for architecture to communicate an idea such as this so unambiguously. The human house is painted a neutral, passive cream; the sexy reds, pinks and purples are reserved for the realm of the horse. But perhaps there is another way to interpret San Cristobal: that this is simply one dwelling, designed for the two animals combined, as horse and rider.

1 Ground Floor Plan

1 Living room
2 Dining room
3 Bedroom
4 Kitchen
5 Swimming pool
6 Garage
7 Flat

2 Section A–A

4 North Elevation

3 West Elevation

5 East Elevation

6 Section B–B

7 Site Plan

1 Haybarn
2 Field
3 Patio paddock
4 Stable
5 Stamping ground
6 Horse pool
7 Garden
8 Egerstrom house
9 Swimming pool
10 Entrance

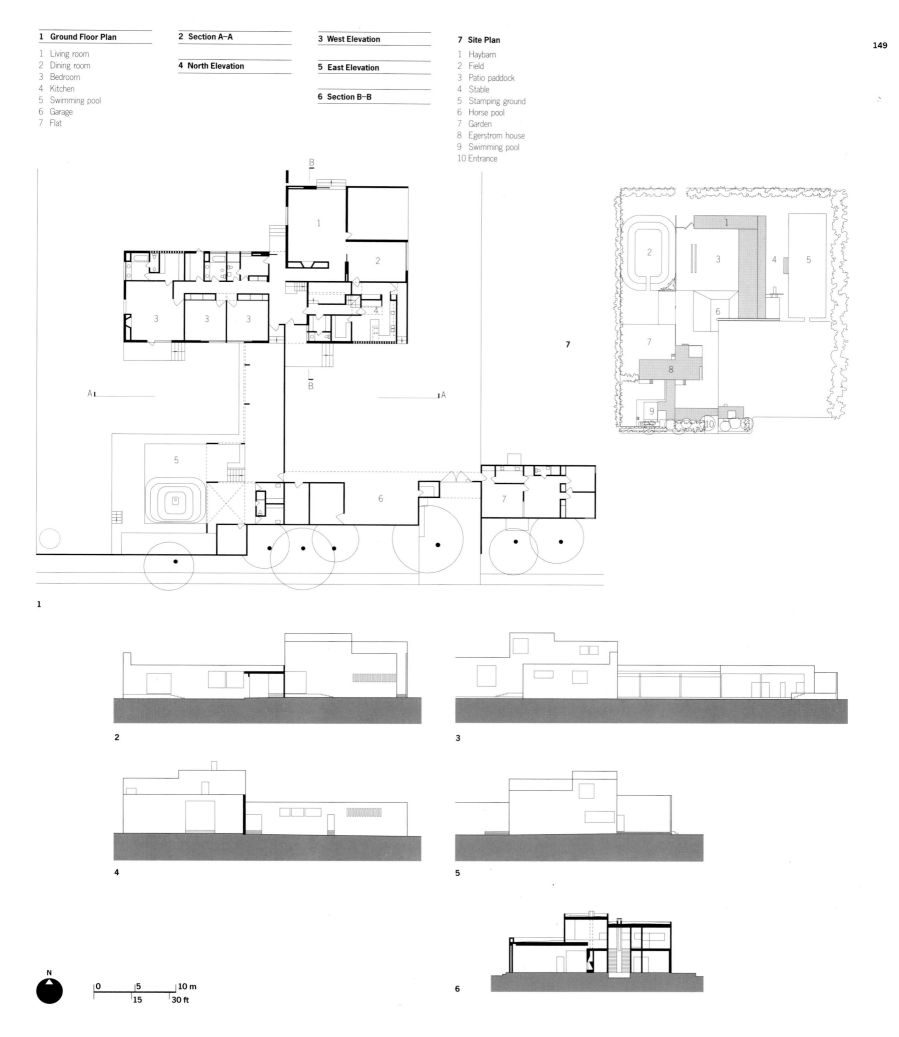

1

2

3

4

5

6

N

0   5   10 m
  15   30 ft

Bawa House

Geoffrey Bawa 1919–2003

Colombo, Sri Lanka; 1958–69

Geoffrey Bawa was not only a Modernist but also a regionalist. He trained at the Architectural Association in London but built most of his buildings in his native Sri Lanka. Perhaps this makes him a 'critical regionalist', although by the time Kenneth Frampton popularized the term in the early 1980s, Bawa was well into the mature phase of his career, having already completed the Sri Lanka parliament building, the Triton Hotel at Ahungala and much of Ruhunu University. Bawa's architecture is sometimes described as 'vernacular' on account of its pitched roofs, verandas and courtyards, but he was equally fluent in the abstract language of European Modernism.

Geoffrey Bawa's own house in Colombo (he also owned a country estate at Lunuganga) combines the two aspects of his work in a literal way. A small, three-storey Corbusian villa faces onto the street, proudly proclaiming its modernity, while behind the villa stretches a woven mat of interconnecting roofed and unroofed single-storey spaces contained by a boundary wall. Something essentially European has been grafted onto something essentially Sri Lankan. But it had not been designed this way; it evolved gradually over a period of almost 40 years.

There were originally four bungalows on the site, arranged in a row along a cul-de-sac. Bawa bought number three first and acquired the others as they became vacant, adjusting the overall plan with each new addition. When the site was complete, he demolished the first house and built the new frontage. It would be hard now to retrace the outlines of the original bungalows.

The Corbusian villa has most of the required features: a garage (which, in Bawa's time, accommodated two gleaming but immobilized vintage cars), a roof garden, and a second, higher roof garden accessible only by an external stair, just like Le Corbusier's original Maison Citrohan project. Immediately behind the villa, and partly tucked underneath it, a self-contained guest suite occupies about a third of the single-storey part of the house. Even this small dwelling has been given four courtyards, or roofless rooms, for its enclosed living spaces to look out on. When, nearing the end of his career, Bawa had dissolved his practice, he converted the guest house into a studio and started up again on a smaller scale.

The main part of house is entered via a long, roofed passageway that terminates in a miniature pool framed by columns recycled from old Chettinad houses. From this pausing place, a cross axis leads to the heart of the house: a square vestibule with the master bedroom on the right, the sitting room and dining room on the left, and a veranda straight ahead, furnished as a study and completely open to a courtyard beyond. The distinction between inside spaces and outside spaces is practically irrelevant, which makes perfect sense in this hot, rainy climate, although some of the rooms are fitted with air conditioning.

Bawa rarely used any ornament in his buildings, but he enjoyed the idea of bricolage, the recycling of ready-made objects such as the Chettinad columns (there is another in the dining room). He also liked to incorporate works by his artist friends, such as the doors decorated by Donald Friend and Ismeth Raheem. With its compressed plan, toplit spaces, bricolage and art works, this house recalls the work of the English architect John Soane.

1 Second Floor Plan

1 Roof garden

2 First Floor Plan

1 Bedroom
2 Bathroom
3 Living room

3 Ground Floor Plan

1 Entrance
2 Garage
3 Pool
4 Sitting room
5 Veranda
6 Vestibule
7 Master bedroom
8 Dining room
9 Kitchen
10 Bathroom
11 Guest suite
12 Living room
13 Bedroom

4 Section A–A

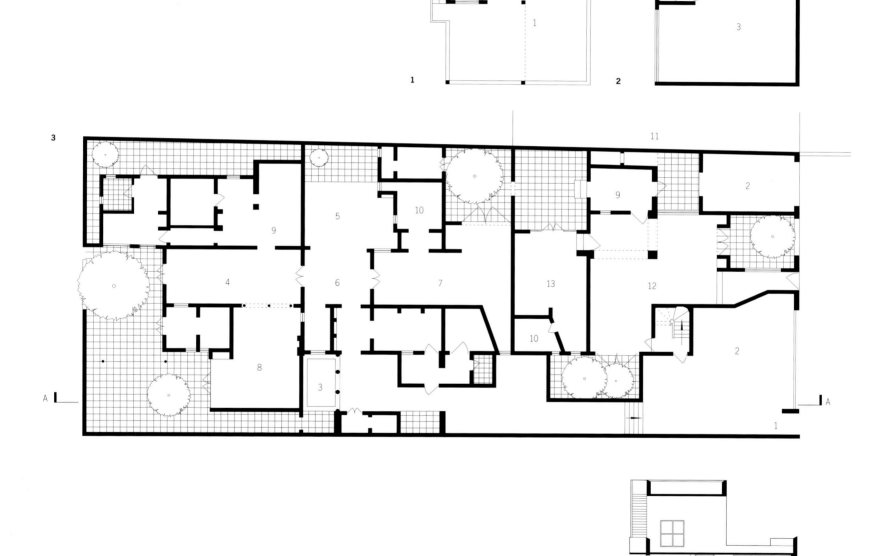

N

0   5   10 m
15   30 ft

Tallon House

Ronnie Tallon, 1927–

Foxrock, Dublin, Ireland; 1970

Scott Tallon Walker evolved from the practice founded by Michael Scott in 1928. It was Scott who brought Modernism to Ireland in a group of Dutch- and German-influenced prewar buildings, including two hospitals, his own house at Sandycove in Dublin, and the Irish Pavilion at the 1939 New York World Fair.

Scott was a larger-than-life figure who in the 1920s combined the practice of architecture with a successful career as a professional actor. His name is still revered in Irish architectural circles, but there is doubt about the authorship of certain postwar projects usually attributed to him. For example, the Busaras (bus station) in Dublin of 1953 was actually designed by a team of young architects led by Wilfrid Cantwell and including Kevin Roche, who later found fame in the USA.

By the late 1960s, it had become clear that it was not Scott but his new partners, Ronnie Tallon and Robin Walker, who were setting the design agenda of the practice. Both were totally committed followers of Ludwig Mies van der Rohe, and they set about transforming the character of several important Dublin institutions by the scholarly and craftsman-like application of Miesian architectural principles. The Bank of Ireland

Headquarters completed in the early 1970s, for example, is like a scaled-down version of Mies's Federal Centre in Chicago, and the site occupied by Radio Telefis Eireann was developed over many years according to a master plan reminiscent of the Illinois Institute of Technology campus.

It is not surprising, therefore, that the house Ronnie Tallon designed for himself and his family in the Dublin suburb of Foxrock should be a version of Mies's Farnsworth House (see pages 112–13). Several features fix the Farnsworth connection: the steel frame, the glass walls, the way the house is lifted off the ground as if to avoid a possible flood, and the entrance platform with its two flights of hovering steps. But this is not a slavish copy and there are key differences.

Despite the glass walls of the Tallon House, the space is much more contained than at Farnsworth, with solid walls at the ends (before the extensions were built) and no cantilevers. Hollow-section columns and beams, welded together seamlessly, frame the whole house both structurally and visually. The covered terrace at one end of the Farnsworth House has been redistributed as continuous decks along the long sides, between the columns and the sliding-glass

walls. Materials are different too, with wood in place of travertine for the decks, and concrete bricks for the end walls, perhaps inspired by the steel-framed brick walls at the Illinois Institute of Technology teaching buildings. Inside, the plan is as uncompromising as Farnsworth, perhaps more so, since this is a permanent home for a family, not just a country retreat for a single woman. Basically it is one big space. No partitions meet the glass walls, so none of the main living spaces is completely enclosed, not even the bedrooms. Uncompromising indeed, but spatially liberating.

The original house was completely resolved, perfectly proportioned and, it might be thought, impossible to extend. Eventually family pressures, especially a demand for more bathrooms, necessitated changes, and after much agonizing Ronnie Tallon came up with a plan. He might simply have added an extra bay, preserving the logic of the design but sacrificing its proportional perfection. Instead, he built narrower extensions at each end, set well back, so that, visually and conceptually, the original house still survives.

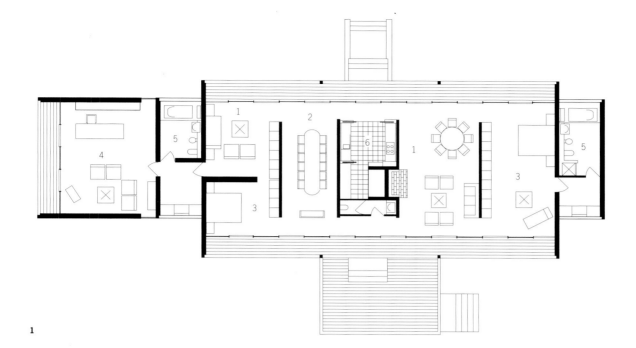

1

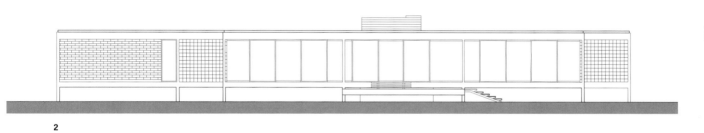

2 Front Elevation

2

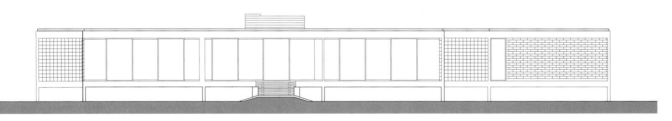

3 Back Elevation

3

4

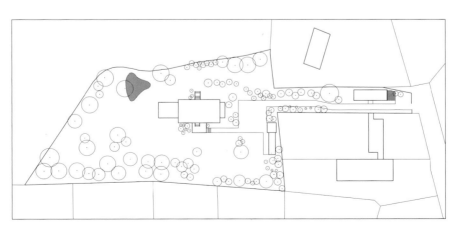

4 Site Plan

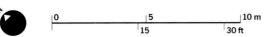

Fathy House

Hassan Fathy, 1899–1989

Sidi Krier, Egypt; 1971

Closeness to nature, respect for tradition, care for humanity and a striving for spirituality: these are the qualities that Hassan Fathy cherished in his architecture. Fathy was not a Modernist, and he cared little about technology, efficiency or progress. His most famous project is the village of New Gourna near Luxor. It was built in the late 1940s to accommodate a community of mostly poor people who had been relocated to prevent them from robbing the ancient tombs near their old village. A western Modernist might have designed an efficient mass-housing scheme with standardized living units, possibly multi-storey, possibly of reinforced concrete. Fathy made a special house in the traditional style for every family and developed a simple mud-brick building method that the inhabitants could understand.

Fathy's architecture is not, however, merely a continuation of an Egyptian vernacular. He was a cosmopolitan intellectual, learned in western as well as eastern literature and philosophy, and he drew influences from many different traditions. Medieval Cairo was a constant inspiration, and he had an intimate knowledge of the whole history of Islamic architecture, but he also studied the tombs and temples of the pharaohs. He used his

knowledge of mathematics and music (he played the violin) to invest simple domestic structures with the dignity of harmonic proportions. He was inventive, certainly, especially in the devising of new construction methods suitable for common materials and simple tools, but his spatial language was based on traditional forms and types.

Some of those traditional forms and types are present in the house that he designed for himself at Sidi Krier on the Mediterranean coast. A rough, austere structure of rendered mud brick, it looks like an old building but is not in any respect a pastiche. Somehow it escapes the curse of shallowness and obviousness that afflicts most modern efforts to reinterpret traditional forms.

Freestanding and isolated, the Fathy House is nevertheless compact and inward-looking, as one would expect in a society that puts such a high value on the privacy of family life. The main entrance is in the middle of the west wall, facing the sea. To the left of the entrance hall lies a square, high-walled courtyard with a central fountain and a loggia on one side. Beyond the courtyard is the *qa'a*, the multi-purpose main room of the house, flanked by two *iwans*, or alcoves that serve as bedrooms. To the right

of the entrance hall are the service spaces: a kitchen, a bathroom and a yard from which steps rise to the roof terrace. The plan is very simple, yet it creates a spatial sequence of great subtlety. Although most of the spaces are unified and symmetrical, they are grouped asymmetrically, avoiding any abstract, diagrammatic quality. Only the courtyard and the *qa'a* share an axis to emphasize their importance.

This is an entirely arcuated structure. There are no columns or beams, only thick walls supporting domes and vaults. Windows and doors mostly have either round or pointed arches. Even narrow spaces such as the entrance hall are covered by elliptical vaults, and important spaces such as the *qa'a* and (surprisingly) the bathroom are graced by beautiful domes of different types: a beautifully proportioned pendentive dome for the *qa'a* and a hemisphere on corner squinches for the bathroom.

The house was built in 1971 – but the date seems irrelevant to such timeless architecture.

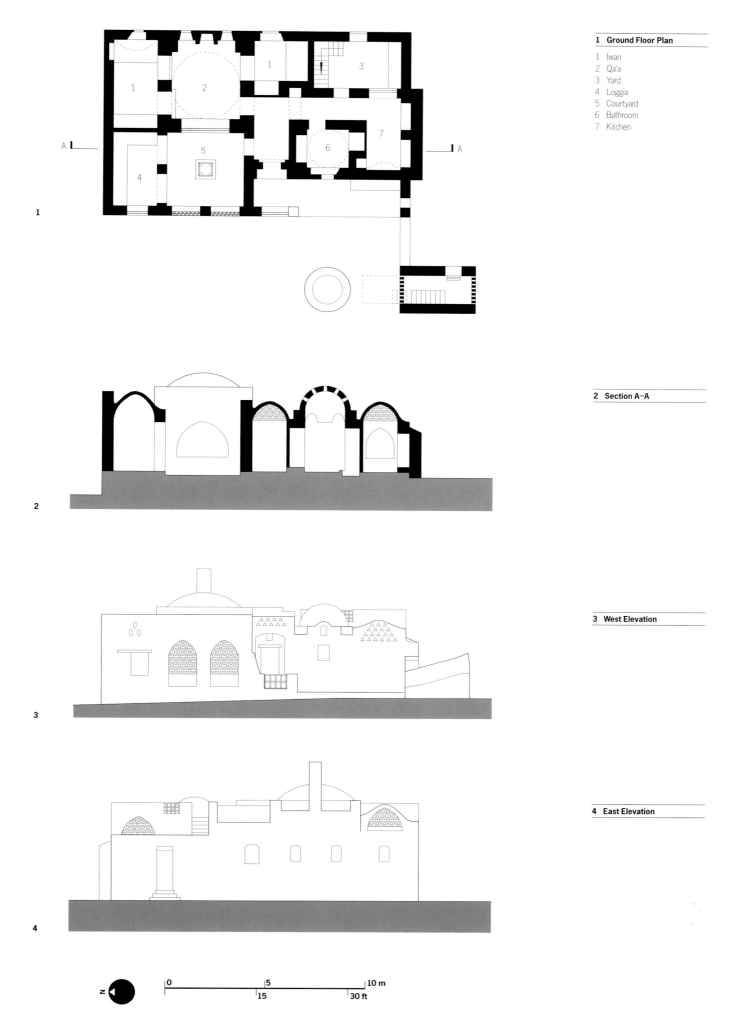

1   Ground Floor Plan

1   Iwan
2   Qa'a
3   Yard
4   Loggia
5   Courtyard
6   Bathroom
7   Kitchen

2   Section A–A

3   West Elevation

4   East Elevation

0   5   10 m
15   30 ft

Cardoso House

Alvaro Siza, 1933–

Moledo do Minho, Oporto, Portugal; 1971

As a building type, the weekend retreat in the countryside poses a special design problem: how to accommodate the needs of leisured clients – the swimming pool, the sunbathing terrace, the ensuite bathrooms – without destroying the picturesque rural character of the site that was the reason for choosing it in the first place. We no longer have the confidence to build luxurious villas in 'unspoiled' beauty spots. One way to solve the problem, in areas where tourism has taken over from agriculture, is to convert an existing farm building that has fallen into disuse. Barns, byres, sheds and stables that would once have been left to rot are now considered beautiful and worth preserving. They provide the perfect camouflage and help to assuage the guilt of urban invaders.

In Portugal in 1964 this was a new idea. Architects were expected to design bright new buildings, not to tinker around with old sheds. But Alvaro Siza was a 'topological' designer, interested in the special qualities of particular places. When asked to design a holiday house in an old vineyard in the village of Moledo do Minho near Oporto, he decided that two existing storage buildings were essential to the character of the site and must be kept. They were squat, solid structures, one

single-storey and one two-storey, on either side of a yard at the north end of the site. Their rubble-stone walls and traditional Portuguese tiled roofs seemed to grow naturally out of the retaining wall that separated the vineyard from the sunken lanes around it. The brief was rather demanding, however. The two-storey building could easily be converted into a two-bedroomed house, but five bedrooms, a living room and a kitchen would somehow have to be squeezed into the single-storey shed.

Siza's design is radical but discreet: the shed becomes the living room and kitchen, and the bedrooms are accommodated in a new single-storey triangular wing. On plan, the extension is about twice as big as the existing building, but it has been half buried to reduce its bulk. A stone retaining wall forms the support for a ribbon of windows topped by a flat, zinc-covered roof.

The relationship between the new wing and the old shed is more a collision than a smooth transition. The acute-angled corner of a bedroom thrusts itself into the living room, taking with it the flight of steps necessitated by the change of floor level, and there is a similar spatial overlap at the extension's other end. The master bedroom and its large bathroom occupy the eastern corner

of the triangle, where a little terrace, like a sunken balcony, is sheltered by a big roof overhang. Apart from the stone retaining wall, the structure of the new extension is unlike that of the old buildings. Walls between bedrooms are loadbearing, but the roof is supported at the corners on wooden posts. An ingenious eaves detail reduces the roof edge to the slimmest possible profile. Windows are a curious compound of the modern and the traditional: a continuous ribbon but made of traditional wooden sashes modelled on an sample taken from the one of the old buildings. The horticultural effect – a greenhouse, perhaps – is heightened by the fact that the roof is at the same level as the supports for the nearby vines. A swimming pool on the south part of the site has an irregular geometry and is made of rough stone, just like the existing buildings. It might be taken for a converted animal dip.

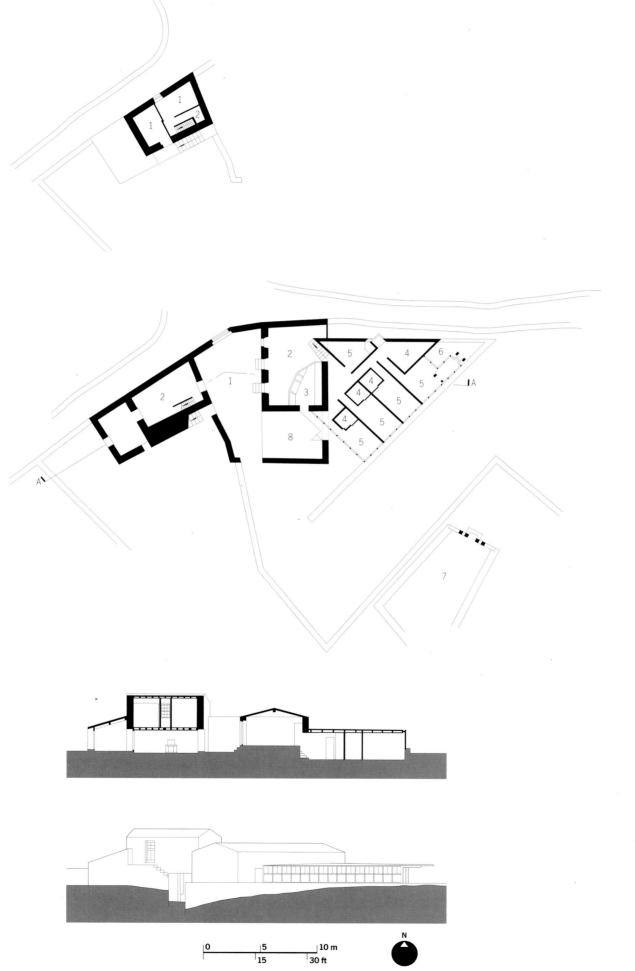

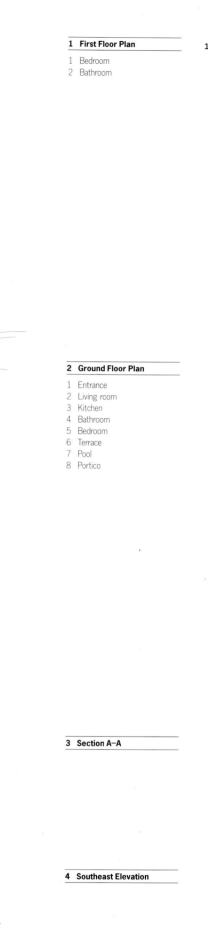

1 First Floor Plan

1 Bedroom
2 Bathroom

2 Ground Floor Plan

1 Entrance
2 Living room
3 Kitchen
4 Bathroom
5 Bedroom
6 Terrace
7 Pool
8 Portico

3 Section A–A

4 Southeast Elevation

Fisher House

Louis Kahn, 1901–74

Philadelphia, Pennsylvania, USA; 1973

'I always start with squares,' said Louis Kahn. Even a cursory survey of the plans of his best-known buildings, from the Trenton Bathhouse of 1955 to the government complex in Dhaka of the 1980s, will confirm the truth of the remark. Sometimes the whole building is square (the Exeter Library at Exeter, New Hampshire), but more often squares are clustered or grouped (the towers of the Richards Medical Research Building in Philadelphia). The Fisher House is the simplest expression of the idea: two cubes, one for the living room and one for the bedrooms, touching at an angle, as if by accident, like dice thrown on a table. Actually, they are not perfect cubes, and the living-room 'cube' is not even square on plan, but they are near enough to be perceived as such.

Putting the living room into a separate block is an instance of another Kahn preference. He disliked buildings that were unified forms divided up inside to make usable spaces. Ideally, he wanted every space, or room, to have its own form. This was seldom practical or economical in a large building, but in a private house the ideal could be approached. The living room of the Fisher House fills the form it occupies despite the fact that it shares it with a kitchen. This is

because the kitchen also has its own form – a cube within a cube. The space of the living room continues over and around it. In the two-storey bedroom block it is harder to maintain the formal integrity of every room. This cube has to be divided up. Nevertheless, each space is complete and coherent. The two east-facing bedrooms on the upper floor, for example, are (almost) perfect squares, each a quarter of the larger square, or an eighth of the larger cube.

Kahn loved stone, the material of the ancient ruins he had so much admired during his sojourn in Rome. In Pennsylvania, it was cheaper to build in wood, and for the Fisher House Kahn was happy to adopt the traditional platform frame technology. But the site sloped down to a river and there was requirement for basement storage. So Kahn got his stone after all, using uncoursed rubble as a base for the timber frame and bringing it right up into the living room in the form of a semi-cylindrical chimney and fireplace.

For Kahn, space and light were one and the same thing, and orientation was a precise art. The living room looks out to the north over a river through an elaborate corner window that incorporates a built-in desk. Smaller windows in

the north-west and south-west walls soften the glare and admit occasional shafts of afternoon and evening sunlight. As in the Esherick House (see pages 138–39), ventilation is provided by separate wooden shutters, here deeply recessed so that they do not project when open. The dining room, behind the stone chimney, was originally to have been a rather dark, secluded space with only a small window, but the clients insisted on a view out and a larger window was installed some months after completion.

The Fishers had waited almost seven years for their house, always taking second place as Kahn busied himself with what he regarded as his more important commissions, but they seem to have loved it all the same, taking the trouble to clean and re-treat its red-cedar cladding regularly for years afterwards.

1

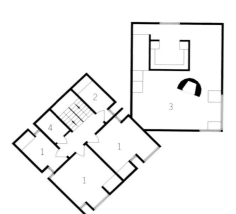

1 First Floor Plan

1 Bedroom
2 Bathroom
3 Void
4 Storage

2

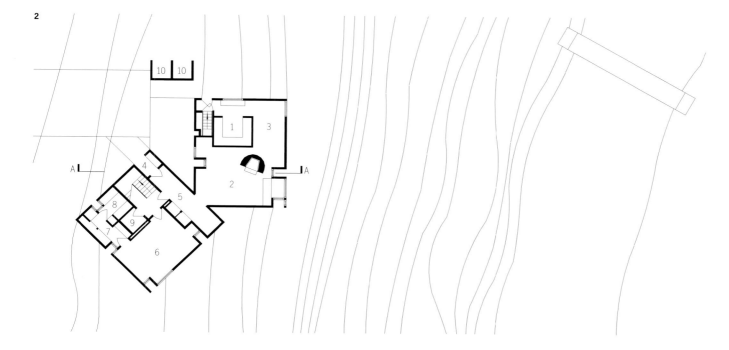

2 Ground Floor Plan

1 Kitchen
2 Living room
3 Dining room
4 Entrance
5 Hall
6 Bedroom
7 Dressing room
8 Bathroom
9 WC
12 Storage

3

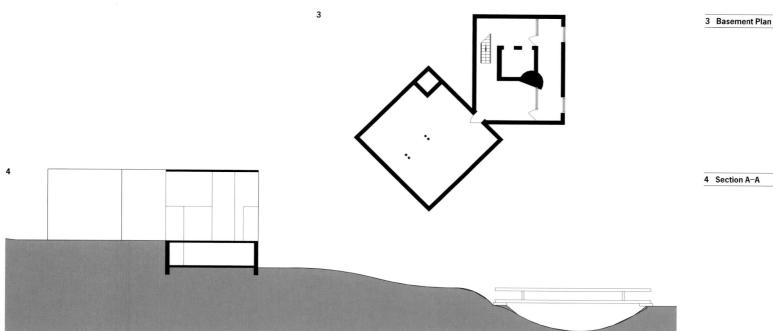

3 Basement Plan

4

4 Section A–A

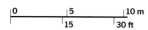

House VI

Peter Eisenman, 1932–

Cornwall, Connecticut, USA; 1973

There is some doubt about whether House VI is a house at all in the sense of a building designed to be lived in. It represents the culmination of the first creative phase of Peter Eisenman's career, during which he developed an almost purely conceptual architecture. His early houses were composed of what he called 'formal universals' – which were meaningless in themselves and had nothing to do with ordinary concepts such as function and context, but were nevertheless in some way essentially architectural. According to Eisenman, House VI it is not really even an object in the sense of the end of a process. Rather, it is a record of a process. That process is kind of a game in which a combination of formal universals is transformed and made complex by a sequence of moves governed by unwritten rules. Rectangular planes, cubic voids and linear elements (don't say 'walls', 'rooms' or 'columns') are shifted, divided, duplicated, subtracted, rotated and extended, step by step, until the architect decides the process has gone far enough – at which point the resulting composition is called a house.

And somebody has to live in it – in this case, New Yorkers Suzanne and Dick Frank, an art historian and a photographer, who commissioned it as a weekend cottage. Their experience is related in fascinating and occasionally hilarious detail in Suzanne Frank's book *Peter Eisenman's House VI: The Client's Response*, published in 1994.

Presented with the first sketch scheme, the Franks were basically sympathetic to Eisenman's artistic aims. They were willing to accept, were even delighted by, the focal point of the house, which was a conjunction of two staircases. One, to be painted green, was a regular flight of steps giving access to the first floor in the ordinary way. The other, at right angles to it and to be painted red, extended from the first floor to the roof, but would be unusable since it was upside down.

The Franks were less happy, however, about the fact that Eisenman had provided only one small bedroom but had made the ground-floor living space double-height. This seemed a waste of space. The double-height living room would have to go. Eisenman agreed very reluctantly, but compensated for his loss by removing sections of the floor next to the staircases to create visual connections between the two levels. More controversially, he insisted that the new bedroom over the living room should have an open slot cut into the middle of its floor. Amazingly, the Franks agreed, exchanging their double bed for two single beds to preserve the conceptual purity of the design. Similarly, although they insisted that there should be space for a dining table to seat six, they had to accept the presence of an intrusive column which became, as it were, an extra dinner guest.

Ordinary practicalities were also somewhat neglected in the construction of the house. The basic structure is a standard American timber frame, sheathed in plywood and rendered, but Eisenman's detailing was over-optimistic, and the contractor was unprepared for the complexity of the junctions. As a result, the render cracked, the roof leaked and the timber began to rot. When they made visible ad hoc modifications to keep the interior dry, the Franks were accused of cultural vandalism. Yet, despite all the trials they had to endure, the Franks stayed loyal to the house and continued to enjoy its special qualities: the warm daylight blended by a combination of windows, rooflights and translucent 'Kalwall' panels, the exciting internal views, and the supremely elegant external form.

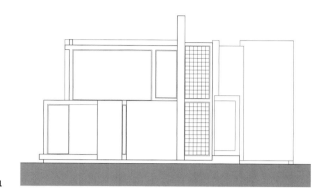

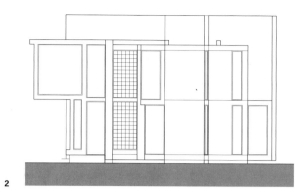

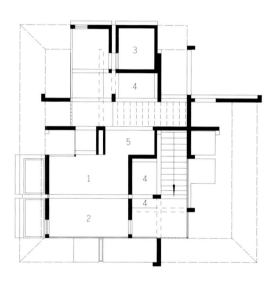

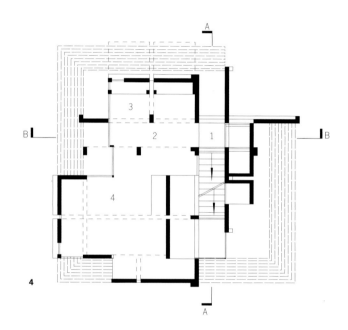

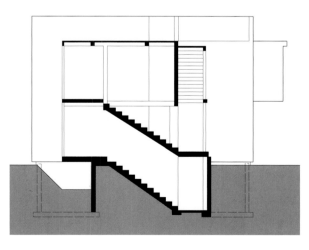

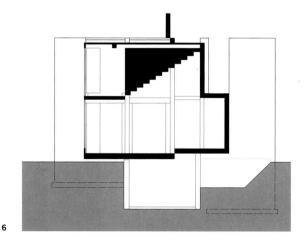

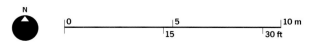

Douglas House

Richard Meier, 1938–

Harbor Springs, Michigan, USA; 1973

White is Richard Meier's favourite colour. But this is more than just a personal preference. It says a lot about Meier's basic approach to architecture: he wants his buildings to contrast with their surroundings and with nature in general, rather than blend in with them or grow out of them; he wants to minimize visual distractions so that the observer can concentrate on what Le Corbusier called 'the masterly, correct and magnificent play of forms in light'; and he regards 'materiality' – the enjoyment of the specific qualities of different building materials – as not particularly important. Whether the material is wood, metal or concrete does not matter, as long as it is painted white. Meier's buildings tend to stand up straight and make themselves known, like the classical temples in 18th-century English gardens. These temples were placed in such a way that they would not contradict the landscape but affirm it and enhance it, and make its forms, colours and textures more clearly visible. And so it is with Meier's buildings.

The Douglas House is the perfect example. It stands proudly among conifers on a steep, west-facing shore of Lake Michigan, and its presence transforms that shore, giving it scale and, in the fullest sense, significance. It makes the landscape mean something in human terms. At first sight, the house seems a rather complicated object. The elevation to the lake is crisscrossed by lines like those in a Mondrian painting, except that they are white rather than black and there are no primary colours. A pair of metal flues, artfully placed off centre, are the focal point of the composition, like the flèche of a church or the clock tower of a town hall. There are open terraces at the south end of the house and on the roof, and most of what isn't open is enclosed by glass. Everything else is made of a flat, white material which, on close inspection, turns out to be ordinary painted wooden siding, fixed vertically and flush, with joints suppressed.

The basic diagram of the house is simple enough: a three-storey box, standing on a solid basement plinth, is divided vertically into a 'private' bedroom zone facing the slope and a 'public' living zone facing the lake. The wall that divides the zones is a continuous plane from top to bottom, with a big rooflight above it and horizontal windows cut into it to allow views over the living spaces from the bedroom corridors. On the public side, sections of floor are omitted to create double- and triple-height spaces, and the relationships between enclosed rooms and open terraces are altered by shifting the non-loadbearing external walls at each level. Often these cuts and shifts follow curved profiles that are reminiscent of certain forms in Le Corbusier's Purist villas. We are reminded that Meier was a member of the celebrated New York Five, who in the 1960s revived interest in those early Modernist masterpieces, imitating their forms if not their materials or their utopian politics.

The house is entered at roof level via a long bridge from a parking space cut into the slope. An ordinary double-flight staircase in the northeast corner links all the levels. Another staircase, external and projecting out towards the lake, links the open terraces on the opposite corner. From the lowest landing it is possible to climb down a vertical ladder fixed to the cliff face of the plinth to a footpath that leads to the beach.

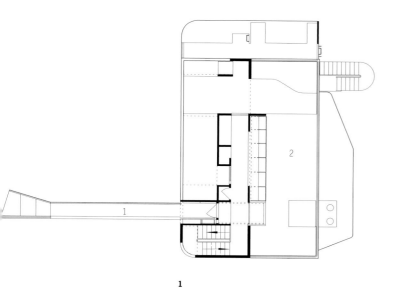

1

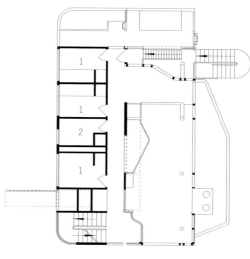

2

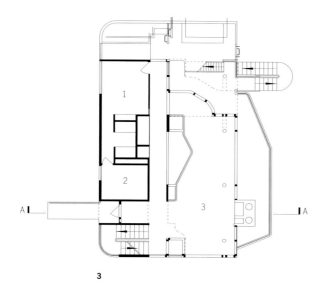

A — — A

3

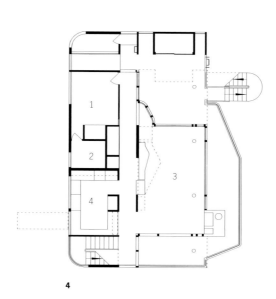

4

5

6

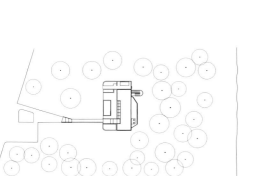

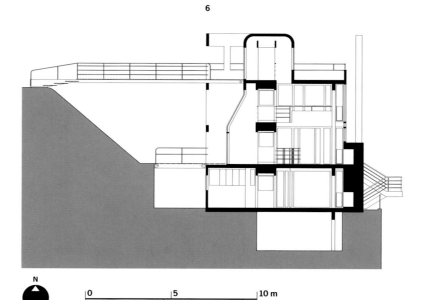

N

0	5	10 m
15	30 ft	

Dickes House

Rob Krier, 1938–

Luxembourg; 1974

'It is my aim to rehabilitate an architecture that has become dishonoured and disgraced,' says Rob Krier in his 1985 book, *Architectural Composition*. The dishonouring has been at the hands of developers and bureaucrats for whom the poetry of architecture means nothing and the European city is merely a site to exploit for maximum profit.

Rob Krier and his younger brother Leon made their reputations as anti-Modernist urban planners more through polemical writings and paper projects than actual buildings. In recent years, however, Leon's association with the Prince of Wales has led to the completion of several phases of the Poundbury housing development in Dorchester, and Rob's partnership with Christoph Kohl has produced live master plans in a number of German, Austrian, French and Dutch cities. The majority of these plans aim to recover the definition and containment of public space that is characteristic of the pre-industrial city. Modernist urban space, functionally zoned, indeterminate and designed according to abstract criteria, is rejected. The components of the anti-Modernist city are traditional types: streets and squares shaped by continuous walls of apartment blocks and punctuated by monuments.

In view of these later developments, it is interesting to look back at the Dickes house in Luxembourg, designed by Rob Krier in the mid 1970s. At first sight it does not look traditional in any way. In fact, it could almost be taken for a Corbusian villa. Its overall form is abstract and geometrical, a pure cube without any conventional tectonic expression. There is very little articulation of the walls, no visible roof or cornice, no columns apart from a single fat pillar completely without ornament, and no windows of the ordinary kind. And yet this little house is the product of a traditional typological design method.

In *Architectural Composition* Krier catalogues systematically the spatial and architectural potential of every regular geometrical plan-form: the rectangle, the circle, the octagon, the T-shape, even the triangle – and, of course, the square. Each type has its subtypes. A subtype of the square is the L-shape. As a square/L-shape, the plan of the Dickes House is therefore not a response to particular circumstances but a choice from a pre-existing range of possibilities. In one respect, though, the design does respond to a special requirement. Apparently, Mrs Dickes had been troubled by a persistent voyeur and had

developed a dislike of windows. Outward-facing windows are therefore replaced by glass curtain walls in the re-entrant corner. But the re-entrant corner is also, of course, what makes the plan a standard L-shaped variant of the square type.

Within its geometric frame, the plan is actually rather free and accommodating. There is a full basement, containing a garage and utility rooms, two main living floors and an additional multi-purpose room at the top opening onto a roof terrace. The shape and placing of the staircase is rather surprising. One expects it to be placed symmetrically, perhaps in the corner diagonally opposite to the fat column, but instead it is placed against a side wall, which it pushes out, creating a slight bulge on the exterior. No room is a straightforward rectangle. Each has to negotiate its space with its neighbours.

Krier's drawings of the house include a distorted perspective of the living room populated by four figures. Recalling certain German Expressionist paintings of the 1920s, it reminds us that, despite his geometrical and typological obsessions, Krier's vision is essentially poetic.

1 First Floor Plan

1 Bathroom
2 Bedroom

2 Ground Floor Plan

1 Entrance
2 Living room
3 Kitchen
4 Terrace

3 Basement Plan

1 Garage

4 Roof Plan

5 Second Floor Plan

1 Terrace
2 Study

6 Section A–A

7 South Elevation

8 East Elevation

9 North Elevation

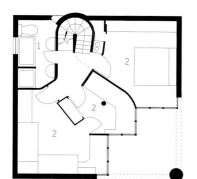

1

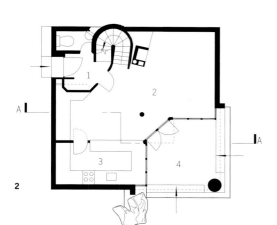

2

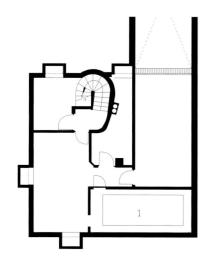

3

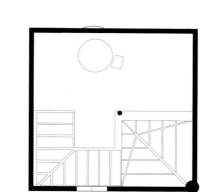

4

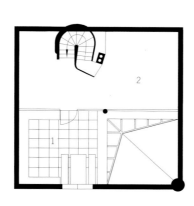

5

6

7

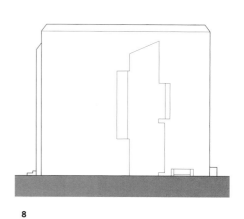

8

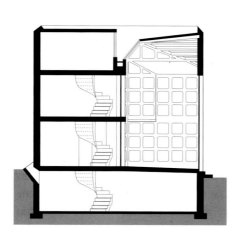

9

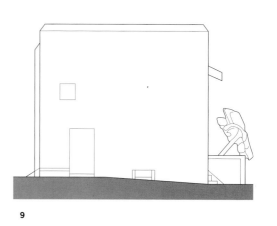

N   0   5   10 m
     15   30 ft

Capsule House K

Kisho Kurokawa, 1934–

Karuizawa, Japan; 1974

In the early part of his career, Kisho Kurokawa was a member of an influential group of young Japanese architects known as the Metabolists. The Metabolists saw cities not as static monuments such as Paris or Berlin, or as mechanistic utopias like Le Corbusier's Ville Radieuse, but as living, changing organisms like Tokyo. The idea was that cities should be in constant flux, renewing their components in the same way that animal bodies renew their cells. The urban cells would be houses or apartments – 'living capsules', in the jargon of the time – which would be mass-produced and attached to a more permanent infrastructure of roads and towers. When the capsules wore out or became obsolete, they would be replaced. The Archigram group in London were developing similar projects at about the same time, notably Peter Cook's Plug-in City, but Kurokawa was the first to realize the vision in the Nagakin Capsule Tower, constructed in central Tokyo in 1973. Capsule House K is an application of the capsule concept to a single house – a summer retreat for Kurokawa himself.

The steeply sloping site, almost a cliff, is approached from above. A concrete tower built into the slope corresponds to the 'infrastructure' and has a parking space on top. It also contains the main living rooms, on two levels. A steep, straight stair leads down from the car park to the first level, which has a fireplace and raised circulation gallery. A separate spiral stair continues down to a cosy lower room with a big circular window looking out towards distant hills.

Four capsules cantilever out from the tower without any visible means of support. In fact, each is fixed by just four 25 mm (1 inch) high-tensile steel bolts. The capsules are roughly the size and shape of shipping containers and in fact they were made in a container factory. They have trussed-steel frames, insulated and fireproofed with sprayed asbestos, and are clad in rusty-red Cor-ten steel panels. Three of them are provided with round, bulging windows that resemble the doors of washing machines.

In the Nagakin tower, the capsules were fundamentally hotels rooms with built-in beds, baths and desks. Here, two of the capsules are bedrooms with bathrooms, one is a kitchen and the last is a traditional Japanese tea ceremony room, complete with tatami mats and bamboo ceiling. Like the bedroom capsules, the tea room has a circular window, but in this context its meaning is totally changed because the *ensoudoko*, or circular window, shuttered by miniature paper shoji screens, is a traditional tea-house form.

The tea room is one of several surprisingly old-fashioned features of the Capsule House, such as the timber-boarded lining of the main living room, the rubble-stone chimney and the crazy paving of the rooftop car park. None of these would have been allowed in any building by the High Tech followers of Archigram and the Metabolists, who later enthusiastically developed the capsule concept in buildings such as Lloyds in London and the Hong Kong and Shanghai Bank in Hong Kong. But Kurokawa is a more subtle and flexible designer, fascinated by the differences between western and Japanese cultures, and prepared to juxtapose them in provocative ways. Some would even claim him as a Postmodernist.

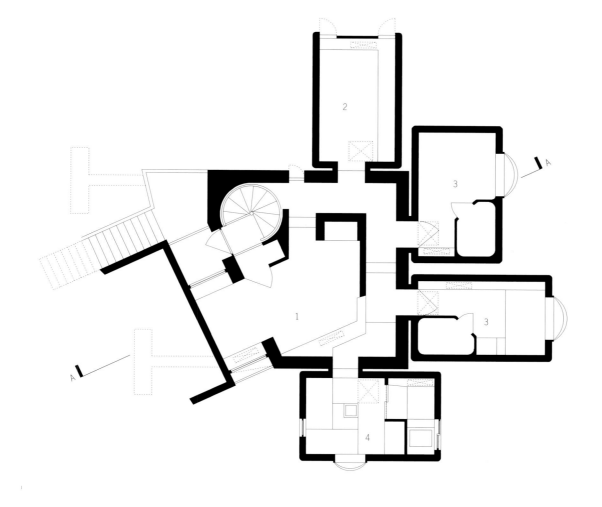

1 Living room
2 Kitchen
3 Bedroom
4 Tea room

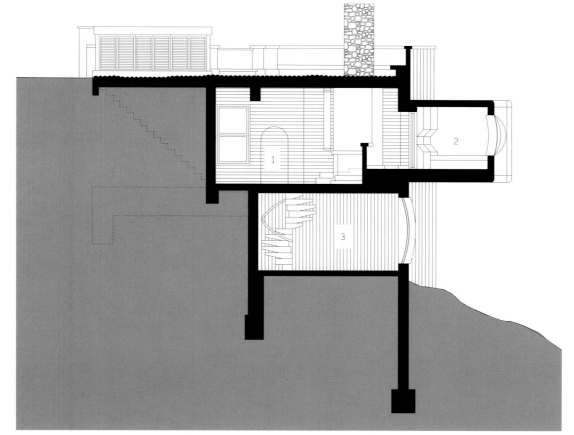

2 Section A–A

1 Living room
2 Bedroom
3 Lower living room

Bofill House

Ricardo Bofill, 1939–

Montras, Spain; 1976

The Catalan architect Ricardo Bofill was never a Modernist in the true sense. Even in his early projects of the 1960s, a search for a new complexity was evident, in particular a liking for clusters of articulated cubes. The 1968 El Castell apartment building on the outskirts of Barcelona, for example, is an eight-storey pile of room-size boxes reminiscent of Moshe Safdie's Habitat building at the 1967 Expo in Montreal. In the Xanadu Holiday apartments in Alicante of 1971, the boxes were organized into a symmetrical pyramid or pagoda form and dressed up in vernacular details such as pitched, pantiled roofs and arched windows.

These projects were followed in 1975 by the competition-winning (but ultimately unbuilt) project for the reconstruction of Les Halles, the old market buildings in the centre of Paris. There, at last, Bofill could be seen committing himself to a thoroughly Beaux Arts plan that is the very opposite of Modernist. From then on, during the next 20 years, his style became baroque to the point of megalomania in enormous monumental housing projects for French suburbs and new towns such as Saint-Quentin-en-Yvelines, Marne-la-Vallée and Cergy Pontoise.

The holiday house at Montras that Bofill built for his own family in 1973 occurs at a pivotal point in this stylistic swing. It is both cubic and classical, combining the compositional method of El Castell with the monumentality (on a small scale) of the later urban plans.

The site was a ruined country house in wooded hills not far from the Costa Brava. Laid out on a rectangular paved platform like a temple precinct, this is a house not for an individual or a couple but for an extended family. The main three-storey block at the east end is for the grandparents, while children and grandchildren are accommodated in a row of separate blocks, resembling little houses, extending westwards. In between lies a swimming pool overlooked by a dining room. This is the meeting place for the whole family – the public square, so to speak, of this miniature urban composition.

So the Bofill House is rather like a small hotel or holiday village, except that the private suites are not chalets or huts but solid brick boxes. There are five altogether. The first, which is connected to the dining room, houses the kitchen on the ground floor, with a bedroom above; the next two contain double-height bedrooms; and

the two at the end, one turned at right angles to close the vista, have bedrooms on both levels, with external staircases.

The grandparents' house is a more complex, three-storey, L-shaped structure, with the lowest floor below the level of the paved platform. The angle of the L is occupied by a quarter-pyramid of external steps, giving direct access to the top-floor living room and forming the sloping ceiling of the double-height spaces below. Next to the steps, another quarter-pyramid, this time a negative version, is dug into the slope like a little theatre. This is where monumentality asserts itself, but curiously these very formal landscape devices do not line up with the axis of the paved platform.

The fully Beaux Arts manner that Bofill went on to develop is not clearly evident in the house at Montras. It is foreshadowed nevertheless in details such as the mirrored external staircases and cypress-flanked entrances to the brick boxes. With their windowless walls and tall, thin doorways, these little houses might almost be tombs.

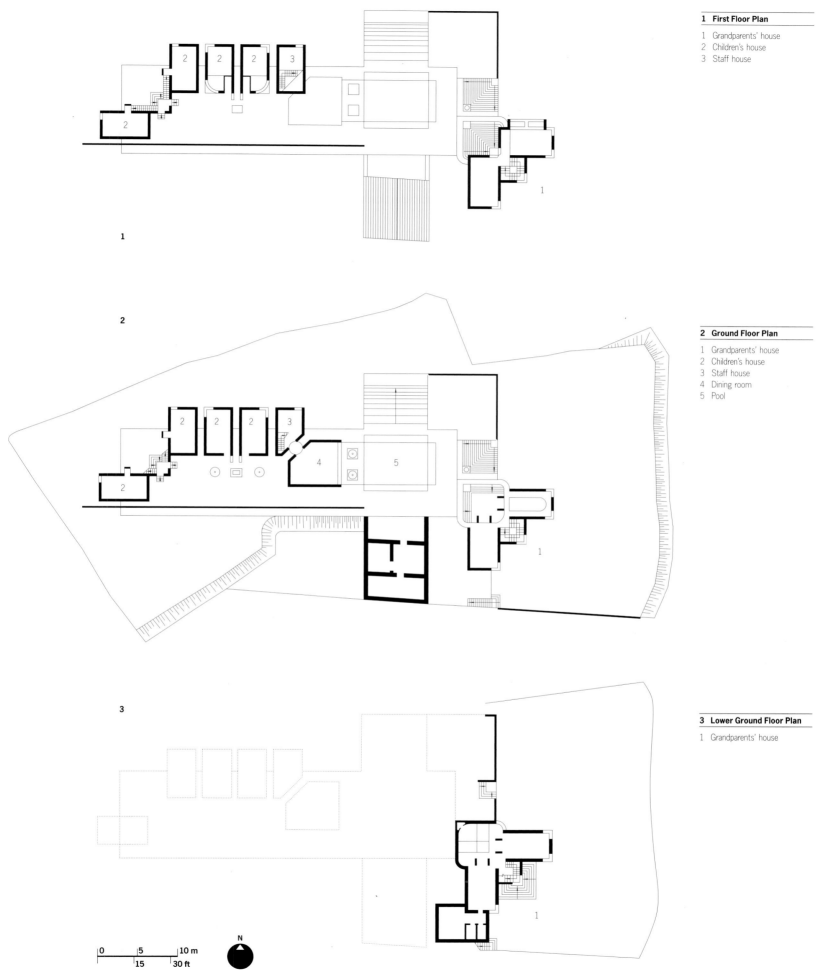

1   First Floor Plan

1   Grandparents' house
2   Children's house
3   Staff house

2   Ground Floor Plan

1   Grandparents' house
2   Children's house
3   Staff house
4   Dining room
5   Pool

3   Lower Ground Floor Plan

1   Grandparents' house

Kalmann House

Luigi Snozzi, 1932–

Brione sopra Minusio, Ticino, Switzerland; 1976

In the 1970s and 1980s, Luigi Snozzi belonged to the so-called Tendenza, a group of like-minded architects practising in the Italian-speaking Swiss canton of Ticino. Other members included Mario Campi, Aurelio Galfetti and Mario Botta. The Tendenza architects were basically Modernists, but their Modernism was tempered by the ideas of Italian theorists such as Giorgio Grassi and Aldo Rossi. Grassi and Rossi were the inheritors of the prewar Rationalist tradition. They had begun to question certain aspects of Modernism, such as the idea that function should be the prime generator of form, stressing instead the continuity of traditional building types. And since traditional types are culturally specific, this also implied a new respect for the character of particular places. The idea that Modernism could be an 'international style' no longer seemed tenable.

The Kalmann House on Lake Maggiore is a good example of this new, tempered Modernism. Though at first sight perfectly abstract, an artificial form standing proudly in contrast to an Alpine landscape, on closer inspection it turns out to be intimately related to its site. It is not just a three-storey box perched on a steep slope; it is a subtle response to that slope in respect of its size, its

gradient, its orientation, its views, the character of little stream that runs by it, and the structure necessary to stabilize it. The slope faces east, but the best views over the lake are to the south and south-west. To do justice to the view, the house would ideally spread itself east–west, but the slope is too steep and narrow to allow this. The house therefore has to be end-on to the view. This inevitable eventuality is clearly reflected in the treatment of the three-storey box, the south end of which is almost completely open, with the glass wall set back to create a terrace and a balcony. The box takes on a vaguely anthropomorphic aspect, as if it were a figure looking out with shaded eyes towards the lake in the distance.

The entrance on the north-east corner is reached via steps and ramps from the road below, but the original idea was to approach from further up the road via a narrow bridge over the stream (as shown in the plan). This arrangement would have been physically easier and psychologically far more satisfying, but it was never realized. From the small entrance hall, a straight stair of two superimposed flights rises on the dark, west side of the house, dug into the slope. The first flight lands beside the living room, which is divided

into sitting and dining zones by a freestanding fireplace. The second flight lands on an internal balcony overlooking a double-height space with a view out straight ahead through the full-height glass wall. The staircase has now emerged out of the ground and can be lit by a long window facing the slope. There are two bedrooms at this level, sharing a single bathroom.

The house has one more important item of accommodation. The living room opens onto a long narrow terrace that curves around to the right, along the contour, terminating in a pergola from which the best views of the lake can be had.

The formal subtleties of this raw concrete box are now apparent: the way the wall facing the slope curves in anticipation of the curve of the inner wall of the terrace; the way the internal bedroom balcony, overlooking the double-height space, passes through the glass wall to become the external viewing balcony; the way the straight, outer wall of the terrace enters the open end of the box and turns into its east-facing wall. It is still a box, but a box designed for this specific site.

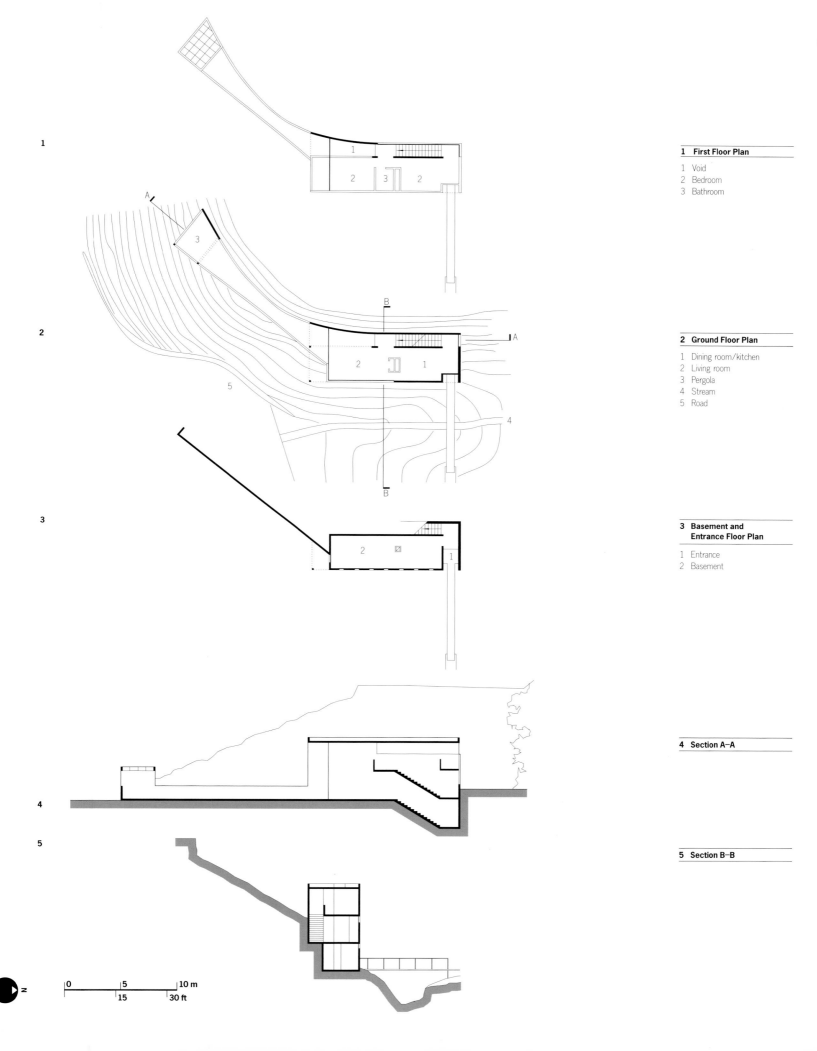

1

2

3

4

5

1 First Floor Plan

1 Void
2 Bedroom
3 Bathroom

2 Ground Floor Plan

1 Dining room/kitchen
2 Living room
3 Pergola
4 Stream
5 Road

**3 Basement and
   Entrance Floor Plan**

1 Entrance
2 Basement

4 Section A–A

5 Section B–B

N

0   5   10 m
  15   30 ft

Dominguez House

Alejandro de la Sota Martinez, 1913–96

Pontevedra, Spain; 1976

Alejandro de la Sota Martinez was born in Galicia, north-west Spain, and studied mathematics at the University of Santiago de Compostela. In the 1930s he sided with Franco in the Spanish Civil War but also found his true vocation and attended the architecture course at the Escuela Superior de Madrid. For a large part of his subsequent career he was a public-sector architect working for the Spanish postal service, but he also became an influential teacher, and is now regarded as one of the fathers of modern Spanish architecture. Outside Spain, he is chiefly known for two works of the early 1960s, the government building in Tarragona and the Gimnasio Maravillas in Madrid. In the 1990s, certain progressive European architects rediscovered these buildings, seeing in their toughness and inventiveness a way out of the cul-de-sacs of Postmodernism and High Tech.

The Dominguez house, on the outskirts of de la Sota's home town of Pontevedra, displays that characteristic toughness and inventiveness. The design is governed by a single, strong idea: the division of everyday life into two realms, the active and the contemplative. Inward-looking spaces in which to rest and think are separated from outward-looking spaces in which to be busy

and sociable. This turns out in practice to mean little more than a conventional division between waking and sleeping, but the normal pattern is reversed, with the living rooms upstairs and the bedrooms downstairs, and the separation is more radical than usual. Between the zones, a notional ground floor (actually raised slightly above street level) is open to the fresh air apart from a small entrance hall containing the main staircase and lift.

Above, a square, flat-roofed box containing the living spaces is supported on nine columns. This, the architecture seems to say, is the real house, the part to which guests might be invited and in which most of the action takes place. It is a Corbusian box on pilotis, like the Villa Savoye (see pages 80–81), with large windows and a garden on the roof. Inside, the plan is fairly conventional. A big living/dining room takes up half the space, leaving the other half for a kitchen and a small library on either side of a service core.

Downstairs in the underworld, things are a lot more congested. There are five bedrooms and one of them is planned as a small dormitory to accommodate four children. Every bedroom has its own bathroom and the dormitory has two. In addition, there is a staff flat behind the garage.

We are in a notional basement, but the sloping site has been moulded in such a way that most rooms have windows. This subterranean part of the house is much more complex than its serene other half. The main bedroom floor is split-level, with an enormous wine cellar under its upper part and large playroom half a level above that.

Conceptually, the house is more like a landscape than a building. The flat roofs become terraces at various levels, with flights of steps between. The main materials are brick and concrete, their weight and texture contrasting with the smooth metal and glass box hovering above. The two worlds meet on a steel-framed platform that rises up and attaches itself to the superstructure to become a living-room terrace.

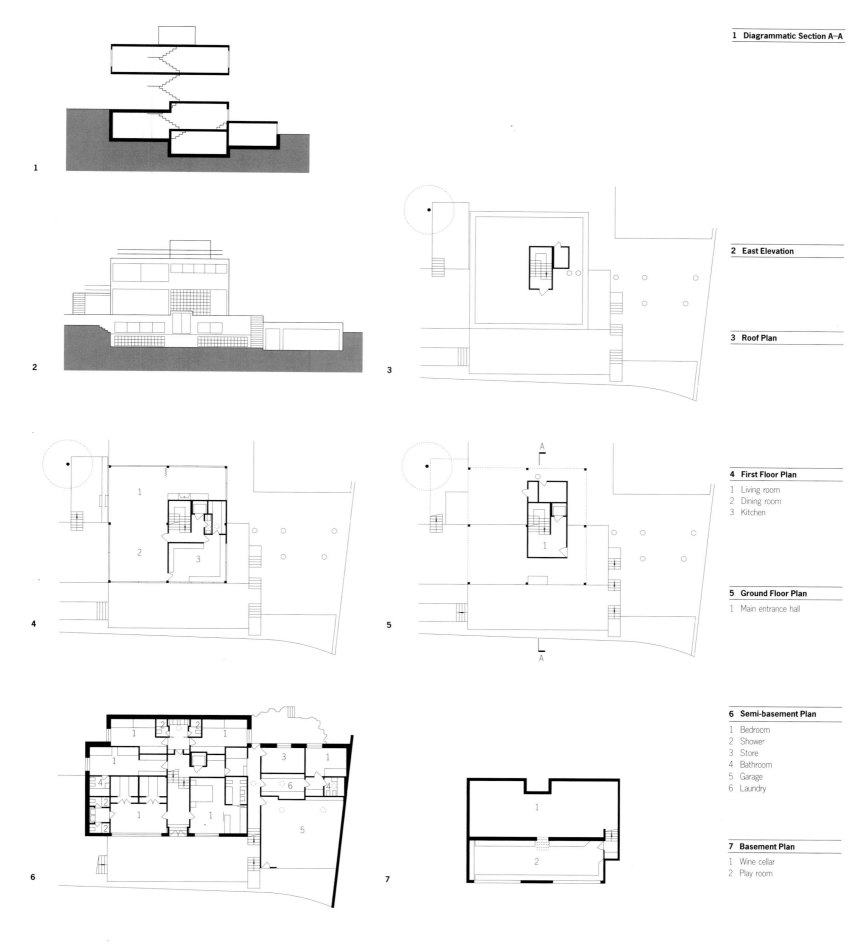

2 East Elevation

3 Roof Plan

4 First Floor Plan

1 Living room
2 Dining room
3 Kitchen

5 Ground Floor Plan

1 Main entrance hall

6 Semi-basement Plan

1 Bedroom
2 Shower
3 Store
4 Bathroom
5 Garage
6 Laundry

7 Basement Plan

1 Wine cellar
2 Play room

0   5   10 m
15   30 ft

Hopkins House

Michael and Patty Hopkins, 1935– and 1942–

London, UK; 1977

At the start of his career, Michael Hopkins worked with Norman Foster on the design of a couple of early High Tech buildings: the elegant, American-style temporary office building for IBM at Cosham in Hampshire and the frameless-glass-walled Willis, Faber & Dumas offices in Ipswich, Suffolk, perhaps the best British building of the 1970s.

By 1976, Hopkins and his architect wife, Patty, were ready to set up their own practice. They decided to build themselves a house in Hampstead, north London, that would be big enough to accommodate their office and would also serve as an architectural demonstration piece.

Conceptually, the Hopkins House has much in common with those early classics, especially the IBM building, but a more obvious inspiration is the 1949 Eames House in California (see pages 106–107), an assemblage of off-the-shelf industrial components, including steel lattice trusses. But whereas the Eames House is relaxed and informal, with its coloured infill panels and its occasional natural materials, the Hopkins House is obsessively strict. Two materials – steel and glass – predominate, and no more than half a dozen standard details are enough to describe every joint and junction in the building.

The secret of the design's simplicity is the very small structural grid – only 4 x 2 metres (13 x 6½ feet) – which obviates the need for any secondary or intermediate members. The troughed metal decking of the floor and roof spans directly onto the diminutive lattice trusses, which in turn rest their minimal load on steel columns 60 mm (2½ inches) square. Most joints are site-welded rather than bolted – not easy to make but very simple in appearance. The front and back walls of the two-storey box are all glass, in horizontal sliding panels with no vertical frames, and that includes the front door.

The original design was even simpler, with glass walls all around, but the side walls close to the site boundaries had to be changed to profiled metal sheeting to satisfy fire regulations. Such a light structure might today be criticized for its low thermal capacity, tending to be hot in summer and cold in winter, but the compact volume cuts heat loss and the large areas of opening window encourage through ventilation. The ducted warm-air heating system is said to be very effective.

The plan is open and adaptable to an extreme degree. Prefabricated melamine-faced partitions with full-height doors enclose some of the private spaces, but elsewhere venetian blinds, neatly fitted between columns, are enough to separate, say, a working space from a lounging space. An open spiral staircase near the middle of the plan is the only means of vertical circulation.

It is surprising to come across such an uncompromisingly modern, industrial-looking structure in the traditional north London suburb of Hampstead. Perhaps its very low profile enabled it to slip beneath the radar of the local planners. The site is actually 3 metres (10 feet) below street level, so the entrance is on the first floor, across a little perforated metal bridge. Visually, the house is single storey and apparently consisting of no more than six sheets of glass.

The British High Tech style, which flourished in 1970s and 1980s, produced a very small number of houses. The Hopkins House is the most important of them, representing the clearest statement of High Tech principles: prefabrication, flexibility, visible structure and truth to materials.

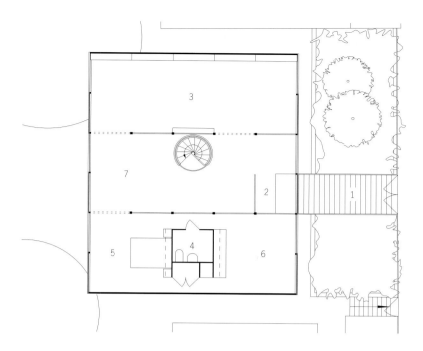

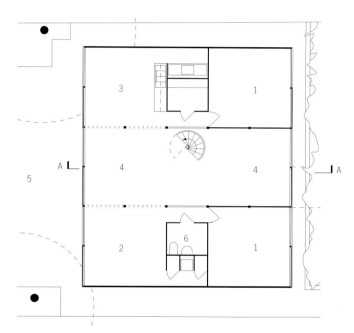

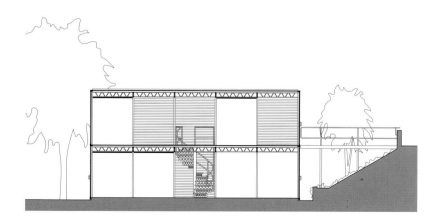

1 Street Level Plan

1 Entrance bridge
2 Entrance
3 Studio
4 Shower room
5 Bedroom
6 Dressing room
7 Kitchen/dining room

2 Garden Level Plan

1 Bedroom
2 Living room
3 Kitchen
4 Dining room
5 Garden
6 Shower room

3 Section A–A

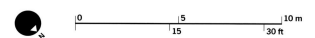

Rudolph Apartment

Paul Rudolph, 1918–97

New York City, New York, USA; 1978

In 1965 Paul Rudolph rented an apartment in a traditional five-storey terraced house in Manhattan, near the United Nations Plaza. Ten years later, a slump in property prices enabled him to buy the whole building. He let the lower floors and set about converting and extending the top floor. This would be no ordinary penthouse but a four-storey-high structure – a house on top of a house. It became, as many architects' own houses do, a testbed for formal and spatial ideas, embodying Rudolph's late Modernist style in its purest form.

In buildings such as the Yale School of Architecture (1964) and the Government Center in Boston (1971), Rudolph developed a method of composition that involved the combining of cubic forms and spaces into articulated clusters or mega-structures. The New York apartment is like a miniature mega-structure. Rectilinear volumes of various sizes overlap and interpenetrate, vertically and horizontally, to create an interior of surprising vistas, ambiguous boundaries and hidden light sources, all contained in a space between the party walls that is just 6 metres (20 feet) wide. It has often been compared with the early 19th-century house/museum in London of John Soane, an architect with a similar liking for intricate spatial

arrangements. Conceptually, this is not so much a four-storey apartment as a single high space with platforms and bridges at various levels. Almost every room looks up or down into another room, through a hole or a slot or a Plexiglass floor. The split-level living room and library is overlooked by a gallery, which is an extension of the dining room, and the dining room is in turn overlooked by the bedroom, through slots around the lowered floor. Complete privacy is virtually impossible. One detail seems to indicate that the design of the house is some kind of voyeuristic game: the Jacuzzi in the main bedroom has a transparent bottom that is visible from the guest bedroom below.

The habit of conceiving space in cubic volumes extends to the various terraces and balconies at both ends of the plan; steel-framed pergolas bedecked with trailing plants convert the terraces into notional rooms. The main structure is also steel-framed, which makes the separate wall and floor planes look like prefabricated elements. Finishes are eccentric, not to say kitsch. Steel columns are either chrome-plated or covered in silver Formica. Elsewhere, the colour scheme is entirely monochromatic, with many highly polished surfaces, of marble, glass and plastic.

Although he was always acknowledged as an accomplished and original designer, Paul Rudolph never won the unqualified admiration of his fellow architects. He took Modernism's abstract language and made it into a clever game, but perhaps his interpretation lacked intellectual depth. When Robert Venturi and Denise Scott-Brown were looking for a Modernist building to compare unfavourably with their Postmodernist Guild House old people's home in Philadelphia, they chose Rudolph's Crawford Manor in New Haven, a high-rise building answering a similar brief. They mocked it for its misplaced heroics, its meaningless articulation and its dry expressionism. Whereas their own Guild House, they implied, stood at the fresh beginning of a new movement, Crawford Manor stood at the decadent end of an old one. Unluckily for Rudolph, the book in which the critique appeared, *Learning from Las Vegas*, was to become one of the most influential architectural texts of the late 20th century.

1

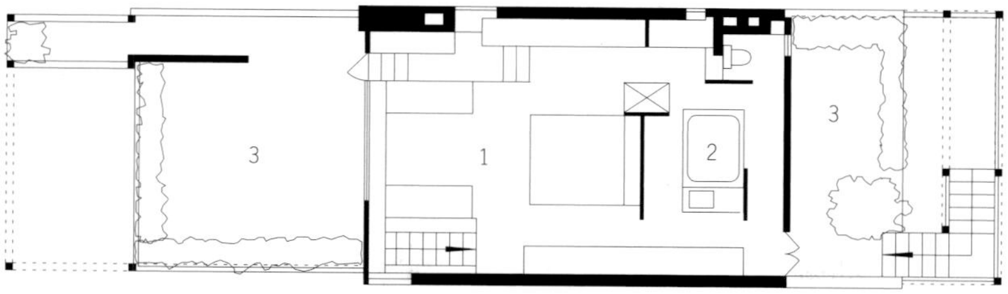

1 Master Bedroom Level Plan

1 Master bedroom
2 Bathroom
3 Terrace

2

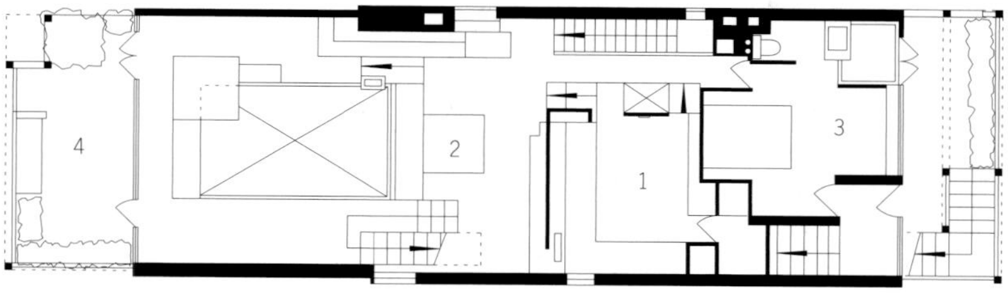

2 Kitchen/Dining Level Plan

1 Kitchen
2 Dining room
3 Bedroom
4 Terrace

3

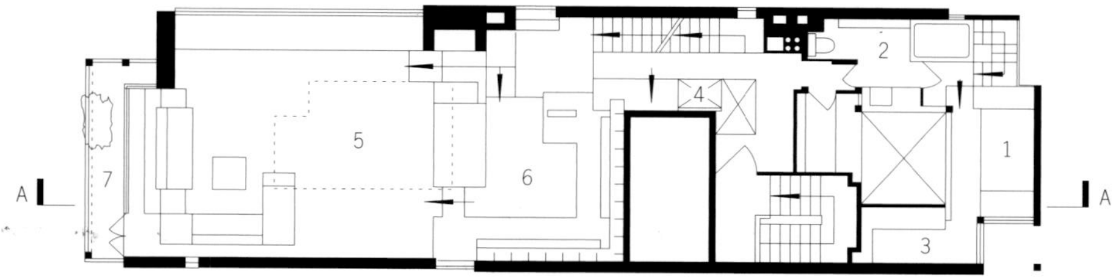

3 Living & Library Level Plan

1 Guest bedroom
2 Bathroom
3 Closet
4 Elevator
5 Living room
6 Library
7 Terrace

4

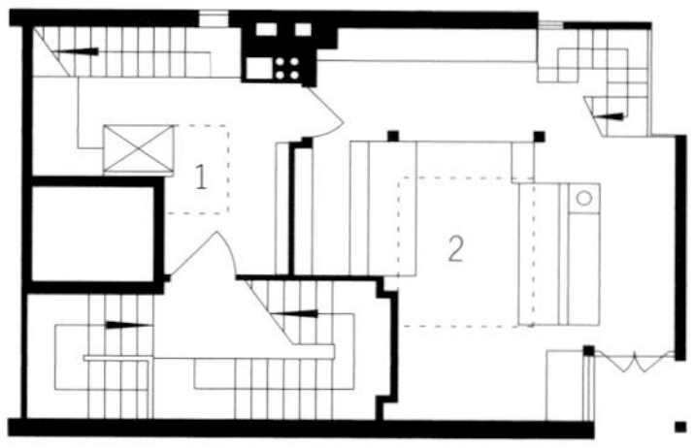

4 Entry Level Plan

1 Entrance lobby
2 Guest living room

5

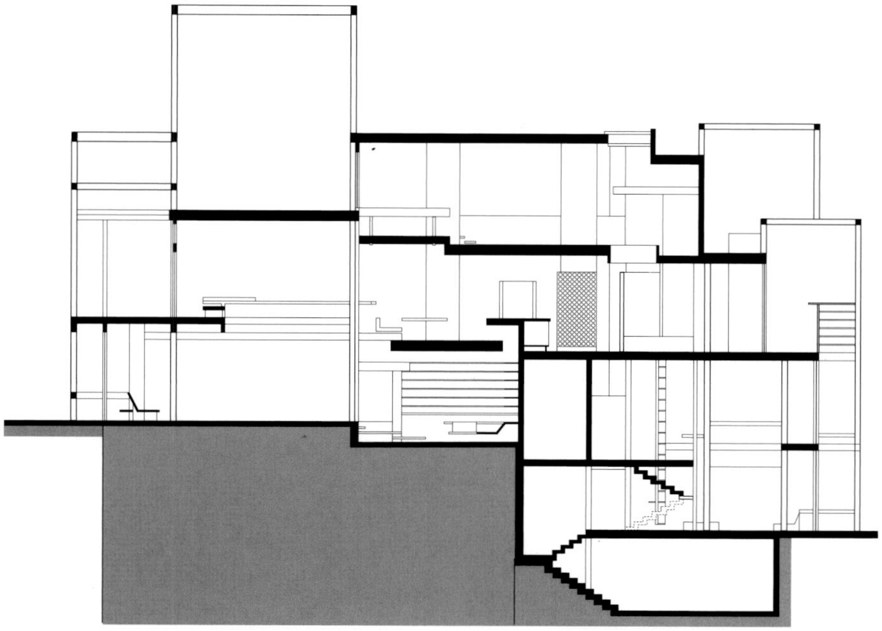

5 Section A–A

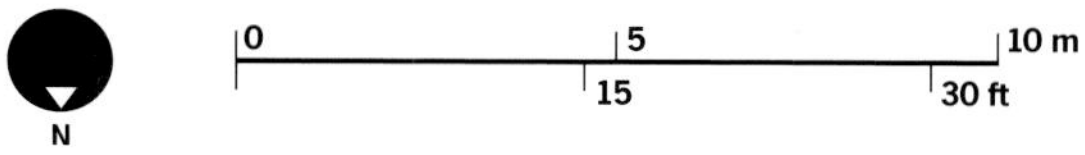

0 5 10 m
15 30 ft

N

Glass Block Wall–Horiuchi House

Tadao Ando, 1941–

Osaka, Japan; 1977–79

Critics often emphasize the Japanese qualities of Tadao Ando's buildings – their calm simplicity and subtle daylighting – but there is also evidence of a strong western influence, most obviously the architecture of Louis Kahn. Ando's exquisite reinforced-concrete walls can be justified as earthquake-resisting structures, but the smooth finish and careful organization of the marks made by formwork is surely borrowed from buildings such as the Salk Institute and the Kimbell Art Museum. The preference for unambiguous cubic enclosures is Kahnian too. Ando's is mainly an architecture of static, introverted rooms rather than of free-flowing spaces. This is especially so in his early urban houses. A favourite plan form is the rectangle divided into three parts, with the middle part left open as a courtyard and the main source of daylight. In the Azuma House of 1976 the courtyard is crossed by a bridge at first-floor level, and in the slightly later Ishihara House it is lined with glass blocks so that the occupied spaces are denied a clear view of even this confined external space.

In the Horiuchi House the concrete walls, the tripartite rectangle, the courtyard, the bridge and the glass blocks are all present, but in a new combination that achieves a more satisfying balance. The bridge has moved to one side of the courtyard and the glass blocks have been put to better use as a translucent screen between the courtyard and the city street.

In his own descriptions of the house, Ando makes much of the symbolic importance of this screen. If the introverted plan is a rejection of the visual chaos of the surrounding city, the screen is an attempt to come to terms with it. Leaving the courtyard completely open to the street would have made it into a semi-public space, perhaps even a small urban square. On the other hand, a solid-concrete screen would have represented a forbidding gesture to passers-by. The steel-framed, glass-block screen is a judicious compromise. Light and shade become a kind of currency of exchange between the house and the street. In the morning, the partial shadow falls in the courtyard; in the evening, it falls in the street. Sunshine is filtered both ways, and at night the house glows.

This is a corner site with quite a steep slope, and there is enough height for access to a basement garage on one side. Above this is the living room on the ground floor and the master bedroom on the first floor. The kitchen/dining room is on the other side of the courtyard, with children's bedrooms above and a traditional tatami room in a semi-basement below. The link between living and dining rooms is a stark, narrow corridor between concrete walls, but on the first floor this become a 'bridge' between open balconies. The walls flanking the courtyard are almost all glass.

Ando rarely refers specifically to traditional Japanese architectural forms, but there is one curious feature of this house that may have an historical source and a symbolic meaning. The courtyard edges of the roofs and floors are supported by a pair of round concrete columns, kept well away from the glass external walls, inside on the ground floor and outside on the first-floor balconies. Each might be a version of the massive wooden post in a traditional Japanese farmhouse, called the *daikokubashira*, which symbolizes the authority of the head of the household.

1 Section A–A	2 Elevation

3 Second Floor Plan

1 Bedroom

4 First Floor Plan

1 Living room
2 Dining room
3 Bedroom
4 Cupboard

5 Ground Floor Plan

1 Garage
2 Tatami room
3 Bathroom

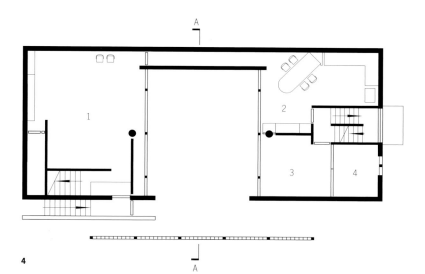

3

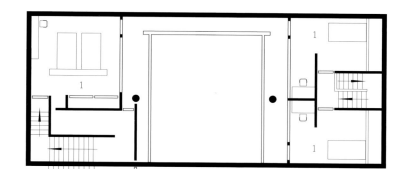

1

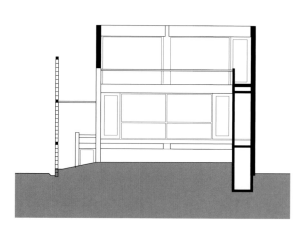

4

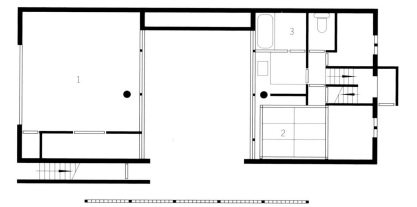

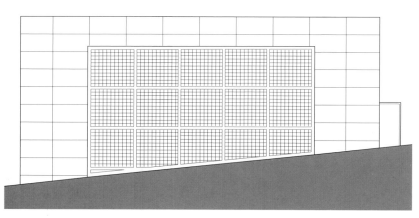

2

5

0   5   10 m

15   30 ft

N

House at Regensburg

Thomas Herzog, 1941–

Regensburg, West Germany; 1977–79

'Sustainability' is the watchword of responsible builders everywhere now that the ice-caps are measurably melting and it has become clear that carbon-dioxide emissions are to blame. The architectural profession first started to think seriously about low-energy building after the oil crisis of the early 1970s. The result was a rash of experimental houses, many of them built in a folksy or rustic style to proclaim their 'alternative', anti-industrial ideology. Thomas Herzog was an early pioneer of low-energy architecture in West Germany, the country that adopted the creed most enthusiastically in the years that followed, turning it into a new orthodoxy. But he did not adopt the folksy style, seeing no reason to break the continuity of the Modernist tradition.

The house at Regensburg, Herzog's first low-energy house, is anything but folksy or rustic. It is a new invention, a logical design owing more to science than to sentiment. Mostly made of wood – not a typical Modernist material – its pure prism form and rational plan make it almost machine-like. The triangular shape was designed to collect free solar energy and use it to heat the house. The 'passive' energy principle is now well established but it was a relatively new idea

in 1977. Of course, the conservatory had been around since Victorian times, but always as an addition to a conventional house. Herzog found this 'add-on' approach unsatisfactory. He wanted to integrate energy-saving features into a new, environmentally responsive architecture. So instead of a two-storey house with a conservatory attached we have – well, a two-storey house with a conservatory attached, except that both elements share the same roofline, a long mono-pitch, the hypotenuse of the triangle, reaching right down to the ground.

Energy saving is by no means the only architectural theme of the house. Regularity and flexibility are just as important. The plan is not a collection of rooms but a system for apportioning space, an abstract grid, the cells of which can be combined in different ways, horizontally and vertically. Between the high north wall and the sharp point of the triangle on the south side, the space is divided into four zones or strips: a service strip containing mainly bathrooms, storerooms and a kitchen; a wider strip containing the main living spaces; a narrow covered walkway outside the glass wall that separates the living spaces from the conservatory; and, finally, the

conservatory itself. In the other direction, east to west, these strips are divided equally into six bays, each 3.6 metres (12 feet) wide. A number of different tunes might be played on this instrument. The one Herzog has chosen omits the upper floor in one single and one double bay to create a double-height spaces for the living room and entrance hall respectively, each with a spiral staircase. It also omits the conservatory roof over two separate bays, one to accommodate a beautiful existing beech tree and the other to create a patio next to the dining room.

Wood, a sustainable resource, is used in various forms: in laminated beams and columns, in veneered chipboard and plywood sheets for the internal walls, and in horizontal boards for the external cladding, which is an early exercise in the now familiar 'rainscreen' principle. Windows are double-glazed, solid walls are highly insulated (for 1977) and the roof is covered in high-tech titanium-zinc sheeting.

1 Upper Floor Plan

1 Gallery
2 Apartment
3 Guest room

2 Lower Floor Plan

1 Plant room
2 Sleeping area
3 Entrance/hall
4 Living area
5 Deck
6 Fern greenhouse
7 Shady court
8 Covered patio
9 Sunny court
10 Mediterranean greenhouse

3 Section A–A

4 Section

1 Winter day
2 Winter night
3 Summer day
4 Summer night

5 Site Plan

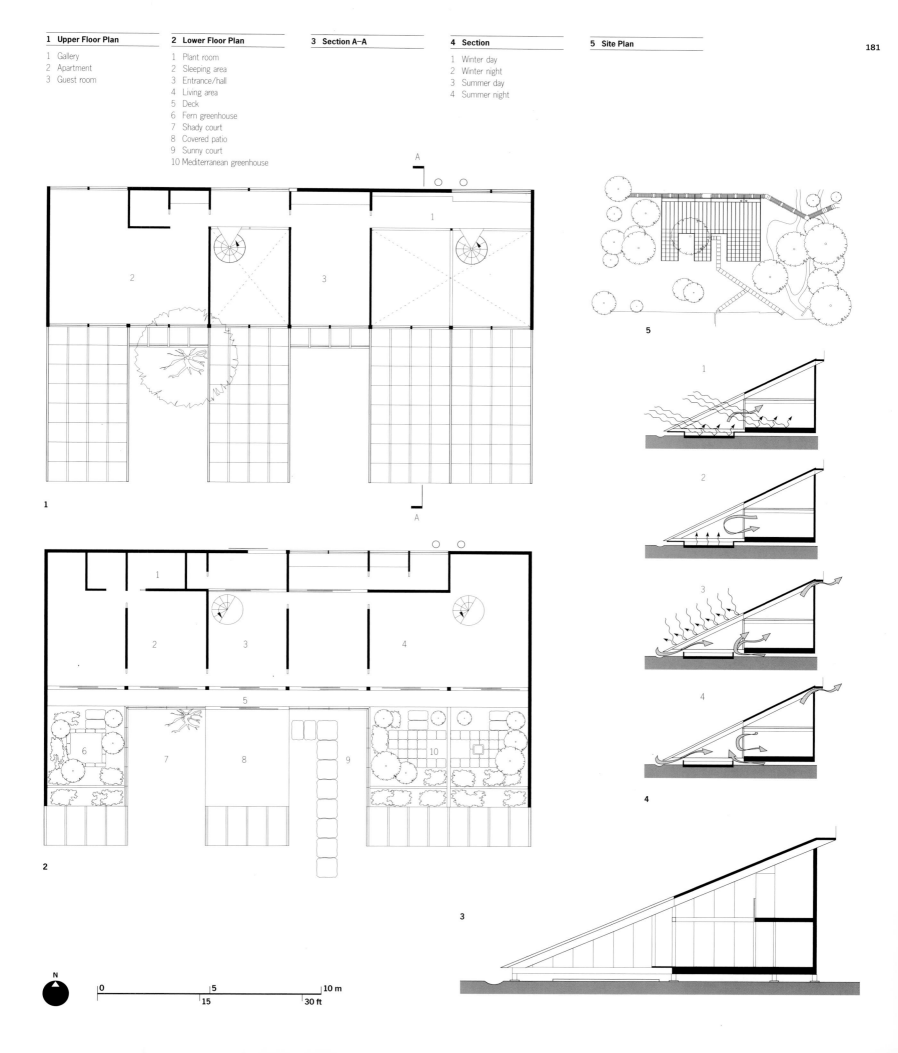

Casa Rotunda

Mario Botta, 1943–

Stabio, Switzerland; 1980–82

Most modern architects begin the process of designing a house by analysing the site and the client's brief. Looking at the many houses that Mario Botta has designed in the Ticino canton of Switzerland – that hothouse of contemporary architecture – it is clear that his method is rather different. He starts not with a quasi-scientific investigation but with the bold assertion of a simple geometrical form.

In the case of the Medici home at Stabio, known as the Casa Rotunda, that geometrical form is a cylinder, squat and solid in grey concrete blockwork. It isn't that the form ignores the site – far from it. The form is a considered response to the topography and the surrounding buildings. Viewed against the hillside to the west, which is dotted with villas of every type and style, the Casa Rotunda stands out like a smart-suited gentleman among poolside loungers. And the man has a frown on his face.

This earnest, formal architecture is implicitly critical of the undisciplined, unprincipled products of capitalist culture. What it proposes is a return to the good manners and dignified bearing of the traditional European city. Botta does not make explicit use of columns, capitals and entablatures

(though he comes close in the staircase enclosure of this house) but he is, nevertheless, unmistakably a child of the classical tradition.

Having proposed a solid cylinder, there is really only one way to proceed. Nothing can be added without spoiling the purity of the form, so it must be developed and made habitable by subtraction, by carving out the space and the openings to light the space. The first carver's stroke cuts the cylinder in half, making a slot in the roof and the second floor through which daylight can enter into the middle of the plan. On the south side the slot divides to form a horizontal window for the first-floor living space and two entrances at ground level. On the north side, the slot is closed by the narrow apse of the staircase, standing like a fat column in a kind of stepped niche. This is the overtly classical feature mentioned above: the blockwork at the top of the apse is corbelled out to form a capital.

Inside, the ground floor is entirely taken up by an open porch and a car port, flanking the entrance hall and staircase. These spaces are relatively shady, but the first floor is brightly lit by the big south-facing window and by the rooflight high overhead, visible through the slot in the floor

above. The plan is open but the functional areas – living room and study on one side, dining room and kitchen on the other – are well defined, as much by light as by partitions. On the top floor, galleries on either side of the slot in the floor give access to the bedrooms and bathrooms and allow views down into the living space.

Early in his career, Botta collaborated with two giants of twentieth-century architecture, Le Corbusier and Louis Kahn. There are echoes of both in his work, but perhaps neither influence is as strong as the spell cast by the city in which he trained: Venice. It is perhaps impossible to live and work in that beautiful place without becoming convinced that most modern architecture is corrupt and worthless, and that what is needed is a revival of the formal and the monumental.

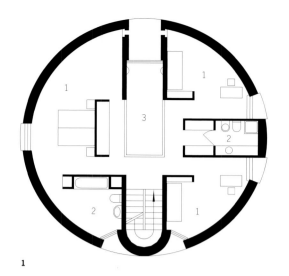

1

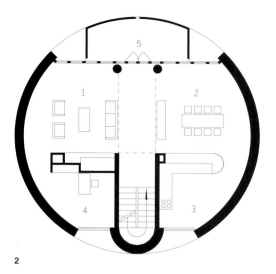

2

1 Second Floor Plan

1 Bedroom
2 Bathroom
3 Void

2 First Floor Plan

1 Living room
2 Dining Room
3 Kitchen
4 Study
5 Balcony

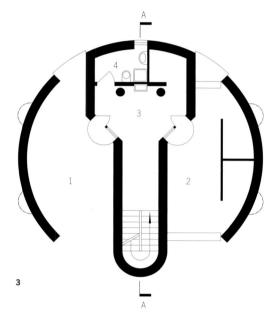

3

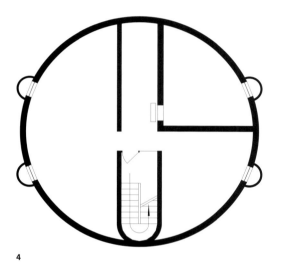

4

3 Ground Floor Plan

1 Porch
2 Car port
3 Entrance hall
4 Cloakroom

4 Basement Plan

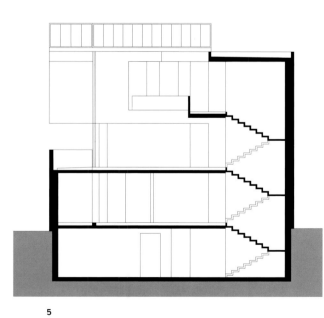

5

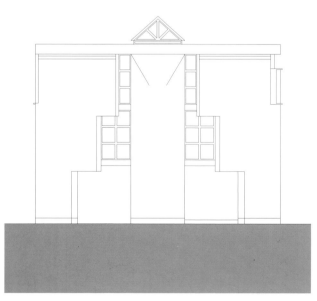

6

5 Section A–A

6 North Elevation

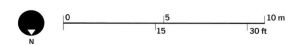

House at Santander

Jerónimo Junquera and Estanislao Pérez Pita, 1943– and 1943–99

Santander, Spain; 1984

Jerónimo Junquera and Estanislao Pérez Pita are associated with the so-called Madrid School, which includes Rafael Moneo and Alberto Campo Baeza. In the 1980s, these serious-minded architects came to be much admired by certain northern European and American critics because they represented an alternative to the frivolities of Postmodernism then prevailing. The complexity and subtlety of their work also seemed more interesting than the reductive and picturesque tendencies of Italian Neo-rationalism. It was said that the Madrid architects – and Junquera and Pérez Pita in particular – were more Nordic than Latin, more influenced by Alvar Aalto than Le Corbusier.

Junquera and Pérez Pita's architecture is additive and inclusive rather than reductive and simplistic. Their method is to propose a series of ideal concepts in response to the requirements of the project under headings such as structure, space, services, climate and culture. These ideas are then combined, adjusted and reconciled to one another, in the process losing their ideal quality but creating a rich and satisfying whole.

The method is well illustrated by the holiday home for Junquera and his family built on a coastal site near Santander in northern Spain.

Spatially, it is a house within a house. The most important habitable space – the double-height living room overlooked by a first-floor gallery – is surrounded by secondary spaces, some of which have a quasi-external character. This arrangement immediately suggests a regular, nine-square structural grid. A further concept is introduced to deal with questions of orientation and climate. On the south and west sides, the concrete frame is mostly infilled with glass, allowing for sea views, while creating a conservatory for shelter on this rainy, windswept site. The other two external walls are solid and pierced by relatively small windows. These walls are expressed as separate elements, masking the concrete frame rather than infilling it, thus emphasizing their sheltering function. They are even equipped with rudimentary cornices, as if they had been left over from some older, classical building. The concept for services and circulation is equally clear. Bathrooms are arranged back to back and one above the other on the east side of the plan, alongside the simple, single-flight stair.

Once the main concepts, each conforming to a simple geometry, have been established, it remains to reconcile them. First, the nine-square grid is subtly adjusted by increasing the size of

the central square. This creates a hierarchy of square and rectangular spaces that can be more easily adapted to different uses. It means, for example, that the elements of the service and circulation 'core' can all be accommodated in a single bay, and the central square bay can be combined with an adjacent rectangular bay to create a more spacious living room. In the ideal plan there is no room for a kitchen, so the car port added to the side of the house is extended and part of it adapted for this purpose.

The house-within-a-house concept is by now thoroughly compromised. The building has become a free cluster of spaces screened by an L-shaped, double-height conservatory. Even this relationship is further adjusted by extending the upper floor into the conservatory to form balconies with serpentine edges. Large openings between house and conservatory can be closed by roller shutters when the house is unoccupied. When all the necessary adjustments have been made, the whole composition becomes complex and ambiguous. But the underlying discipline is still apparent, giving the house an earnest, purposeful character, making it not only a comfortable holiday home but also a serious piece of architecture.

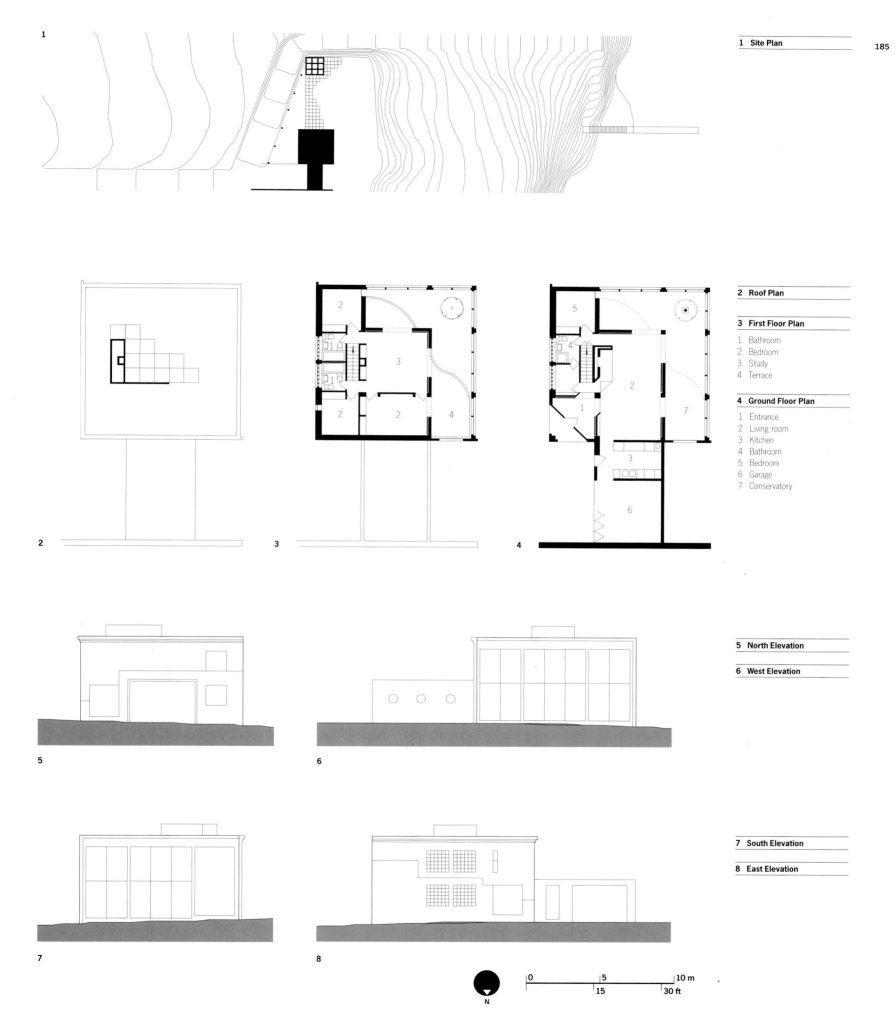

1   **1**   Site Plan

2   Roof Plan

3   First Floor Plan

    1   Bathroom
    2   Bedroom
    3   Study
    4   Terrace

4   Ground Floor Plan

    1   Entrance
    2   Living room
    3   Kitchen
    4   Bathroom
    5   Bedroom
    6   Garage
    7   Conservatory

5   North Elevation

6   West Elevation

7   South Elevation

8   East Elevation

0   5   10 m
15   30 ft

N

Roof Roof House

Ken Yeang, 1948–

Kuala Lumpur, Malaysia; 1984

One way to cool a building in a tropical climate is to install air conditioning. There are some practical objections to this method: air conditioning wastes energy, pollutes the atmosphere, is expensive to run and may simply replace one kind of discomfort with another. But there is also a cultural and architectural objection: air conditioning effectively cancels out climate, a traditional determinant of architectural style and one of the factors that bind a building to the place in which it is built and the society that it serves.

In the 1980s and 1990s, as worries about global warming grew and the idea of a single international Modernist style suitable for all places began to seem culturally insensitive, architectural opinion turned against the high-tech, mechanical solution and became interested again in traditional climate-modifying devices such as verandas. All the talk was, and is, of 'passive' climate control. The Malaysian architect Ken Yeang's Roof Roof House (presumably so-called because it has, in a sense, two roofs) is an early example of passive energy-saving design in a truly demanding location: a residential suburb of Kuala Lumpur.

Yeang trained in England, at the Architectural Association in London and at Cambridge University,

where he completed a PhD thesis on ecological architecture. He is therefore a thoroughly western designer with no interest in a revival of traditional Malaysian architectural forms. His architecture is regionalist only in the sense that it responds to specific local conditions, especially climate. He was later linked with the concept of the 'Bioclimatic Skyscraper' — the subject of a book published in 1996, in which he used his own projects as examples — but in 1984 he was still developing his ideas and using his own house as a testbed.

The design of the Roof Roof House is essentially Modernist, a Corbusian villa adapted for the heat and humidity of Kuala Lumpur by modern equivalents of the veranda, the wind tower and the fountain. The most obvious climate-modifying feature is the big curved concrete pergola that casts shifting, stripey shadows over the roof terrace below. But the house itself is also conceived as a kind of environmental filter. External doors are designed to be left open, sometimes behind special security grilles, to promote through ventilation. The swimming pool — the equivalent of a fountain in a courtyard — is positioned in such a way as to cool the prevailing southerly and south-easterly breeze before it

enters the house through the patio doors of the living room. A north-west-facing louvred opening in the middle of the roof terrace draws the air up through both levels of the house like a miniature wind tower. There are veranda equivalents too, in the shady circulation space that surrounds the main living area and in the balcony-cum-cloister around the pool. If the living room looks small on the plan, it is because it is merely an annexe of the true external living room beside the pool. Another balcony, shared by the two bedrooms on the opposite side of the building, makes an entrance porch below big enough to shade a car.

This is a feature-packed house on a very small scale and has been criticized for its cramped interior. But what use is an interior in this climate? Far better to provide plenty of shady external spaces. Dwellers in temperate climates tend to think of external spaces as extensions of internal ones. In the Roof Roof House, that relationship is reversed. Where interior spaces are fully enclosed — in the bedrooms, for example — air conditioning has been installed to avoid discomfort.

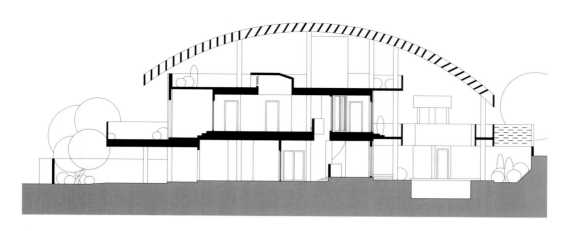

1

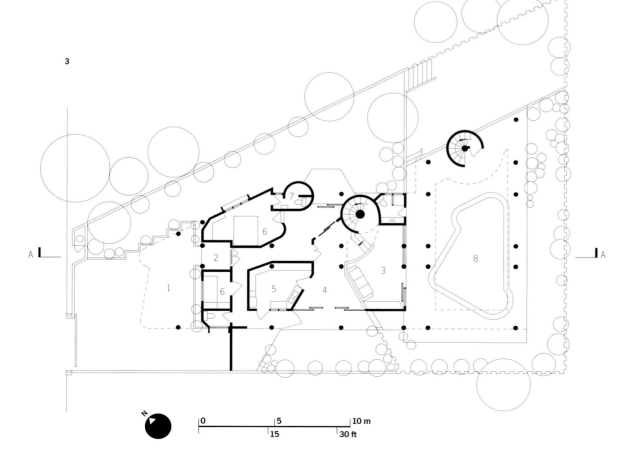

2

3

0   5   10 m
15   30 ft

Magney House

Glenn Murcutt, 1936–

Bingie Point, New South Wales, Australia; 1982–85

Glenn Murcutt is an artist in corrugated iron. The material that roofs the nondescript suburban houses of many an ordinary Australian town becomes in Murcutt's hands a poetic expression of a society and a landscape. The thin, curved, overhanging roof of the Magney House at Bingie Point, Moruya, on the south coast of New South Wales, could be the architectural symbol of the Aboriginal injunction to 'touch the earth lightly'.

Mies van der Rohe was an early influence on Murcutt but, whereas Mies's designs are universal, Murcutt's are responses to specific site conditions, in particular climate. He points out that human beings adjust their clothing in response to the weather and he believes that buildings should do the same.

The overhanging roof is no mere elegant architectural gesture; it is a precisely angled peaked cap, shading the glass north wall of the house in midsummer but letting in the winter sun to bounce off the curved plaster ceiling and flood the interior with light. Below the fixed-glass, high-level windows, the wall is made of sliding glass panels shaded by external adjustable louvres. On the other side of the house, the external wall is similarly divided into upper and lower zones,

but this time the lower zone is solid and clad in corrugated iron. The corrugations run horizontally, as is always the case in Murcutt's buildings.

Where most people regard corrugated iron as simply a cheap cladding material for factories and sheds, Murcutt sees it as an echo of the horizontality of the Australian landscape, reflecting the light of the sky and the light of the land in a shimmering silver surface. Above the solid wall, a strip of patent glazing is angled slightly to accommodate a continuous ventilator at sill level. At the ends of the building the roof is like an asymmetrical pair of wings – recalling a bird that has just alighted or is set to take off.

If this is a poetic and a practical building, it is also an extremely rational one. The plan is uncompromisingly linear. A circulation route runs from end to end under the dip of the roof, dividing a narrow 'servant' strip from a wide living strip. There are neither kitchens nor bathrooms in the ordinary sense, but rather an array of facilities – sinks, cookers, wall cupboards, toilets, shower cubicles – all lit by the high-level patent glazing. There is just one viewing window, cut into the wall over the main kitchen sink, perhaps at the insistence of the client. Bedrooms and living

rooms all face north, benefiting from the filtered sunshine and the view over the ocean from this open hillside. One of the six structural bays of the original house (a seventh has since been added) is left open to form a covered patio, a meeting place between the parents' and children's zones.

The division of the external walls into upper and lower zones is carried through to the internal partitions, which are solid plastered brick below door-head height and frameless glass above. The ceiling of the next-door room is therefore always visible, which unifies the interior space but also reduces privacy, or the feeling of privacy. This is a comfortable home, but it is also a piece of architecture, and sometimes relaxed domesticity must be sacrificed to graceful refinement.

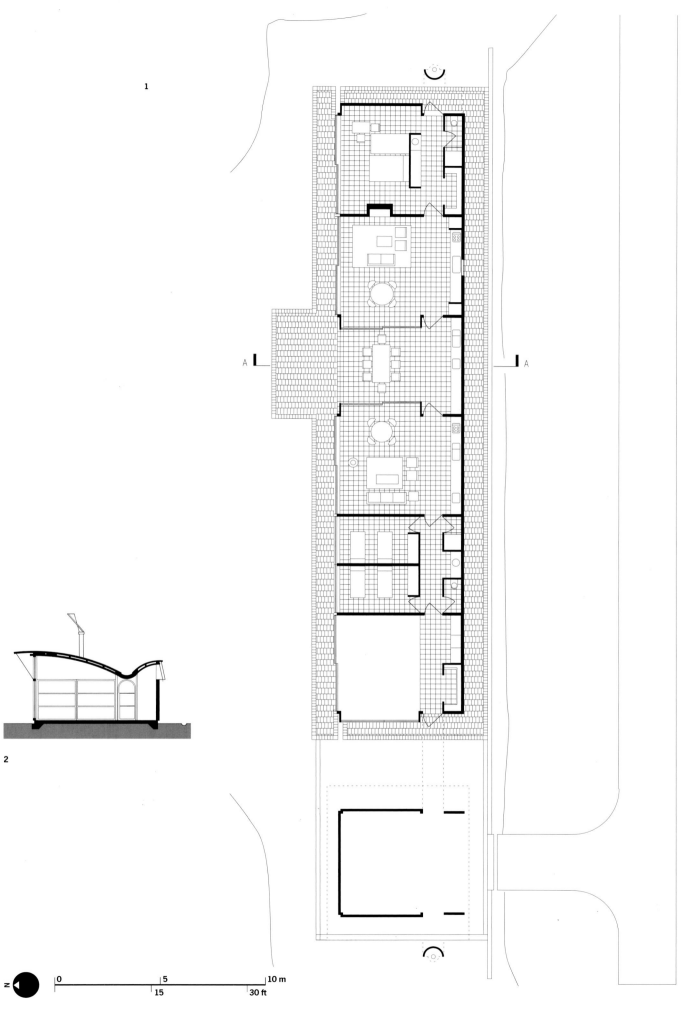

Casa Garau Agustí

Enric Miralles, 1955–2000

Barcelona, Spain; 1985

'Deconstructivist' is a convenient stylistic label that many would apply to Enric Miralles. But it is not quite accurate. Miralles was an architect with an international reputation and must have been familiar with the work of Bernard Tschumi, Zaha Hadid, Peter Eisenman and other participants in the famous 1988 exhibition of Deconstructivist architecture at MoMA in New York. But he was also a Catalan and the inheritor of a vigorous local architectural tradition that included José Coderch – who in the Casa Ugalde (see pages 116–17) broke formal conventions long before anyone had heard of Jacques Derrida – and, further back, Antoni Gaudí, who reinvigorated the Gothic tradition by freeing it from geometrical regularity. Miralles's interpretation of Deconstructivism was inspired more by particular conditions – climate, site, programme, materials – than by philosophical ideas. It may seem chaotic and confusing, but it is not wilful or arbitrary.

The Casa Garau Agustí occupies a narrow suburban site, sloping longitudinally to the south-west with striking views across a shallow valley. Two zigzag walls define the footprint of the house, one placed close to the north-west site boundary and mostly blank to preserve privacy in relation to the house next door, the other more open, facing the garden. The dual demands for privacy and openness are possible explanations for the folds in the walls. Most folds have a window on one side and a blank wall on the other. Windows in the garden wall mostly face south towards the view, while windows in the boundary wall mostly face north, away from the neighbour. There are, however, some exceptions to this rule. A less imaginative architect would have imposed it rigidly, probably letting it congeal into a regular saw-tooth plan, but Miralles's plan remains free and spontaneous, defying any trite logic.

The house occupies the site not as a single serrated form but as a collection of forms, like a small group of people standing in the garden, perhaps talking to one another and most, but not all, looking at the view.

Inside, the key space is the staircase that both divides and unifies the house. In conventional houses, entrance halls and staircases are often combined, but here the entrance opens directly onto a staircase landing, with six angled steps down to the living room on the left and a straight flight up to the first floor on the right. The first-floor landing, far from being a mere circulation space, is perhaps the most important room in the house: the library. A straight wall of books anchors a tapering space opening out to the view and extending onto a cantilevered balcony.

Interior spaces connect in ways other than via the staircase. For example, a north-facing study or sitting room on the first floor unexpectedly overlooks the living room below, becoming a kind of secret spying place. And the client's pottery studio, with the children's bedrooms above, occupies a semi-detached wing that seems to turn around and look at the rest of the house like an animal looking at its own body.

One might assume that such playfulness would be possible only in the special conditions of the one-off house, but Miralles went on to apply his strange collage style to much bigger buildings, including a national gymnastics training centre in Alicante and the Scottish Parliament building in Edinburgh. He died in 2000, aged only 46.

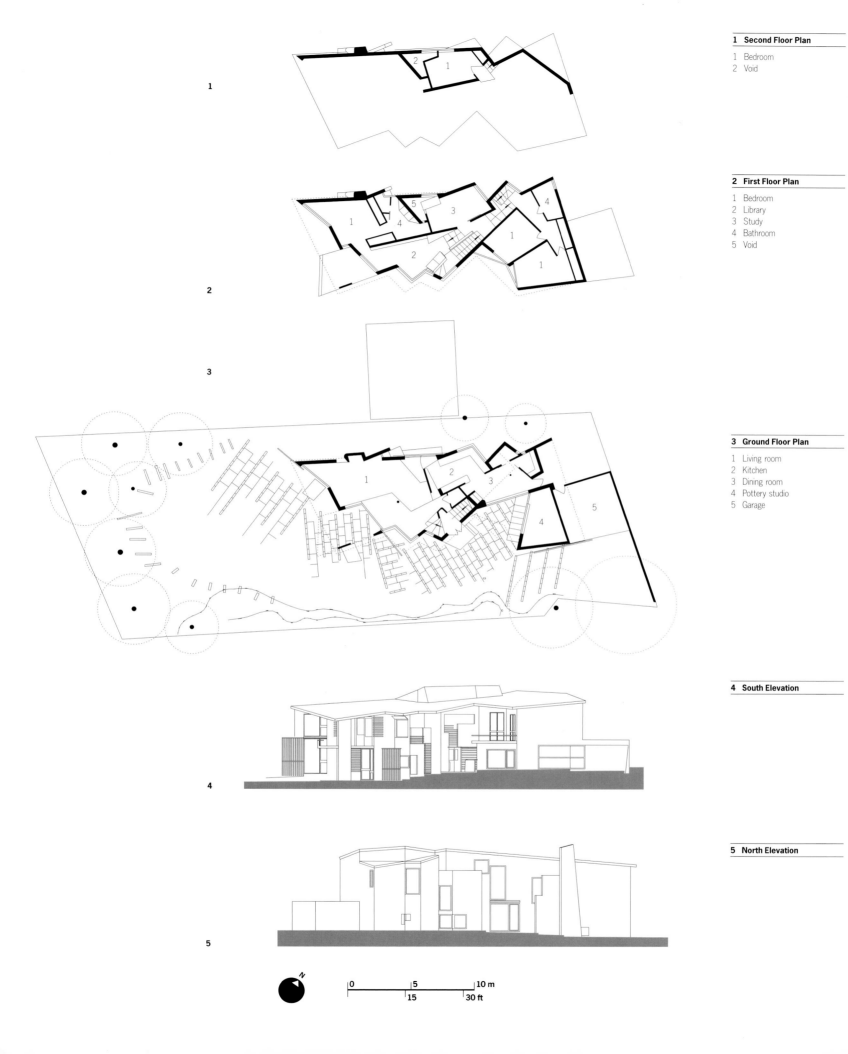

1

1 Second Floor Plan

1 Bedroom
2 Void

2

2 First Floor Plan

1 Bedroom
2 Library
3 Study
4 Bathroom
5 Void

3

3 Ground Floor Plan

1 Living room
2 Kitchen
3 Dining room
4 Pottery studio
5 Garage

4 South Elevation

4

5 North Elevation

5

N

0   5   10 m
    15   30 ft

Winton Guest House

Frank Gehry, 1929–

Winton Guest House, Wayzata, Minnesota, USA; 1983–87

Frank Gehry absorbs influences like a sponge: from nature, especially fishes; from painting, including old masters such as Giovanni Bellini, as well as personal friends such as Ed Moses; from literature, including the works of Marcel Proust and Anthony Trollope; from other architects, especially Alvar Aalto; and from sculptors such as Claes Oldenberg, who helped to design the huge pair of binoculars in front of the Chiat/Day building in Venice, California. In the case of the Winton Guest House, the acknowledged inspiration was the Italian artist Giorgio Morandi, who obsessively painted hundreds of small, grey still-lifes of bottles and jugs on table tops. Gehry's influences are often transformed out of all recognition – so, in the same way that none of his buildings looks exactly like a Bellini Madonna or an Aalto summer house, so the Winton Guest House looks nothing like a Morandi still-life, except in the general sense that it is a collection of objects.

The Winton Guest House is definitely more sculpture than architecture, however, and there is a reason for this. It shares its site in Wayzata, Minnesota, with a Miesian house designed by Philip Johnson in 1952. The Wintons bought the house in the 1960s. By the 1980s, they had five children and a growing tribe of grandchildren, and the house could no longer accommodate them all. A guest house would help to keep the family together. At first they asked Johnson to design it, but he declined. Then they read an article about Frank Gehry in the *New York Times Magazine*, visited a few of his buildings, liked what they saw and duly commissioned him. Their brief was flexible as far as accommodation was concerned. Gehry's main problem was the proximity of Philip Johnson's earnest Miesian exercise. A lively piece of sculpture on the lawn would be different enough not to compete with it, he reasoned.

There are six objects in the collection. In the middle stands a kind of chimney like a cooling tower or pottery kiln. This is sometimes referred to as the living room but, since almost every other room opens onto it, it seems more like an entrance hall. It is a high space with windows in its upper walls through which the sky and nearby trees can be glimpsed. The cosy part of the living space is a separate brick box resembling a primitive cabin with a fireplace and a real chimney.

Two more objects each accommodate a bedroom and a bathroom, but are totally different in form and materials. One is a simple shed with a mono-pitch roof, clad in black sheet metal. The other is roughly triangular in plan, but with one curved wall and a curved roof. Clad in slabs of local limestone, this is the least architectural of all the objects, although it has a perfectly ordinary wooden-framed window in one side.

The last two objects are joined in an oblique and odd way. A long box clad in plywood panels contains the garage and a very small kitchen. A staircase in the corner leads up to a sleeping loft housed in another box on the roof, a corner of which is propped up on a single column.

The allusion to Morandi suggests that the house should be seen as a serious work of art open to many subtle interpretations. But it is also vaguely reminiscent of a toy village, a makeshift camp, an adventure playground or a bouncy castle – a place for children as much as for art lovers.

1 Site Plan

1 Original house
2 Guest house

2 Ground Floor Plan

1 Garage
2 Kitchen
3 Living room
4 Bedroom
5 Fireplace alcove
6 Bathroom

3 Section A–A

4 North Elevation

5 West Elevation

1

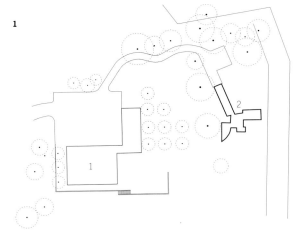

2

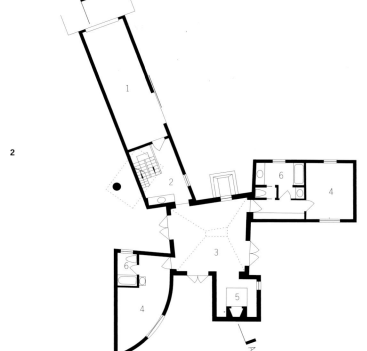

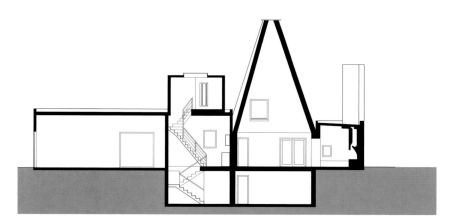

3

4

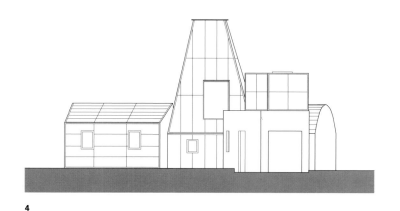

5

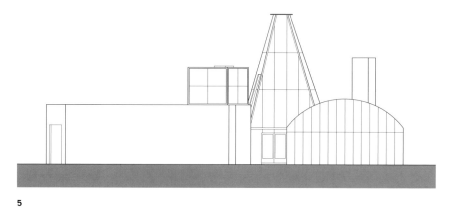

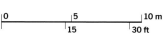

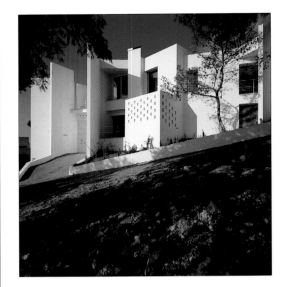

Cap Martinet

Elías Torres and José Antonio Martínez Lapeña, 1944– and 1941–

Ibiza, Spain; 1987

In cold climates, houses tend to be box-like enclosures designed to keep out the wind and build up the warmth inside. In warm climates, they are more usually assemblages of open forms – terraces, verandas, balconies and belvederes – to keep off the sun and encourage the cooling breeze. In this house on the Mediterranean holiday island of Ibiza, the distinction between inside and outside has almost been abolished.

The major part of the structure is a flat platform with an irregular outline, built out from the top of the sloping site to open up the views of the sea. Some parts of this platform happen to be covered by flat roofs and enclosed by a combination of solid walls and glass sliding doors, but essentially it is one subdivided space rather than a collection of rooms. This impression of continuity is created by the angled walls, which define space in a loose way but also seem to invite movement. They do not curve or lean or slope, but in plan they fold and kink freely, extending out onto the open terraces and even beyond the edge of the platform.

Most of the house is on platform level. From a first glance at the plan, it is difficult to distinguish one functional space from another,

or even to discern the line of the external wall. On closer inspection, however, it becomes clear that the house is equipped with all the usual 'rooms', though many are defined only by movable screens and small differences of ceiling height.

The main entrance is at the top of the site, where a flat roof spanning onto a rubble-stone boundary wall forms a kind of porte-cochère or shaded parking space. The entrance leads into a generous hall space, from which a staircase with a rooflight above it descends to the lower level. To the right are the kitchen, dining room and living room; to the left are the master bedroom, the study and a utility room. This might be the description of any ordinary house, but the spaces are positioned and divided in subtle ways that suit their functions. For example, the privacy of the bedroom is preserved by tucking it away behind the staircase, while the relatively public study can be opened to the view from the front door. At the heart of the house lies the dining space, enclosed only by venetian blinds and a large built-in cabinet.

Three more major rooms should be included in the description of this level, even though they are not actually covered by roofs. The main, south-facing terrace is the largest uninterrupted

space in the house. It has walls and windows of a kind, but the windows are unglazed and the walls serve only to frame the views and cast useful shadows. Narrow openings on either side lead to two more terrace rooms, one associated with the kitchen and the other, rather secluded, resembling an external study. Children's bedrooms and a polygonal garage occupy the space underneath the platform.

There are many delicate and pleasing details, such as the triangular chimneys and minimal balustrades, but perhaps the cleverest are the tiny bathroom courtyards, which make it possible to have proper windows without sacrificing privacy.

1 Section A–A

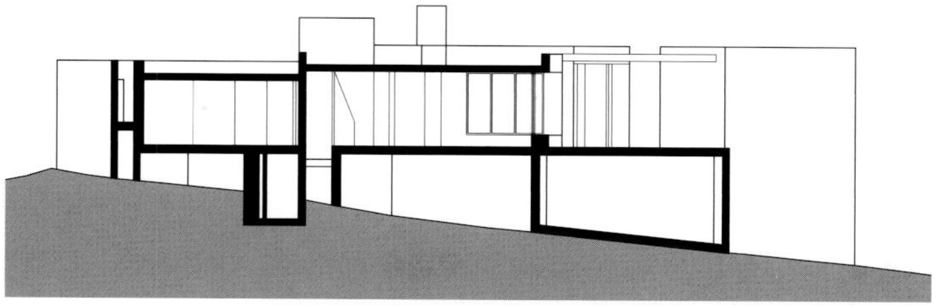

2 Section B–B

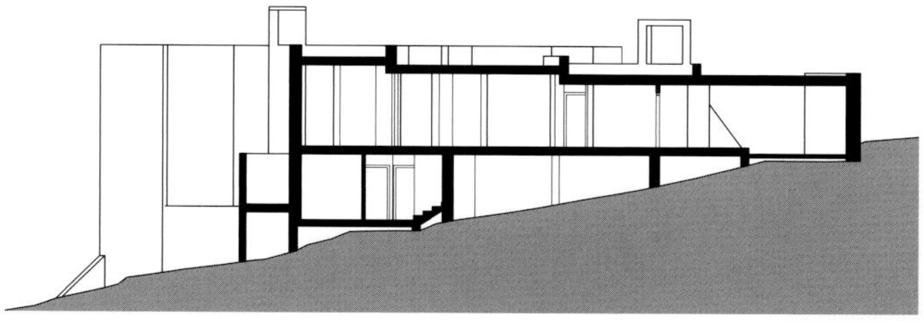

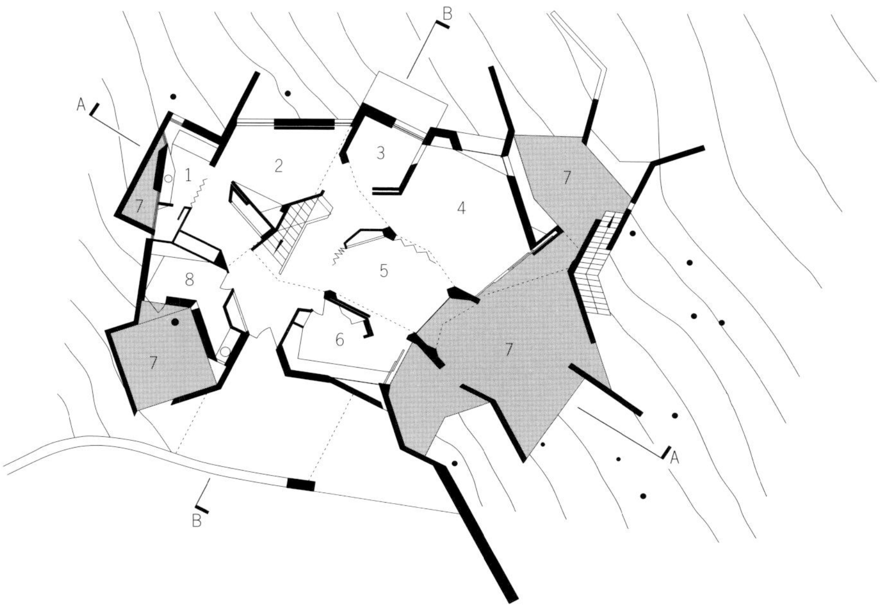

3 Upper Level

1 Bathroom
2 Bedroom
3 Study
4 Living room
5 Dining room
6 Kitchen
7 Terrace
8 Utility room

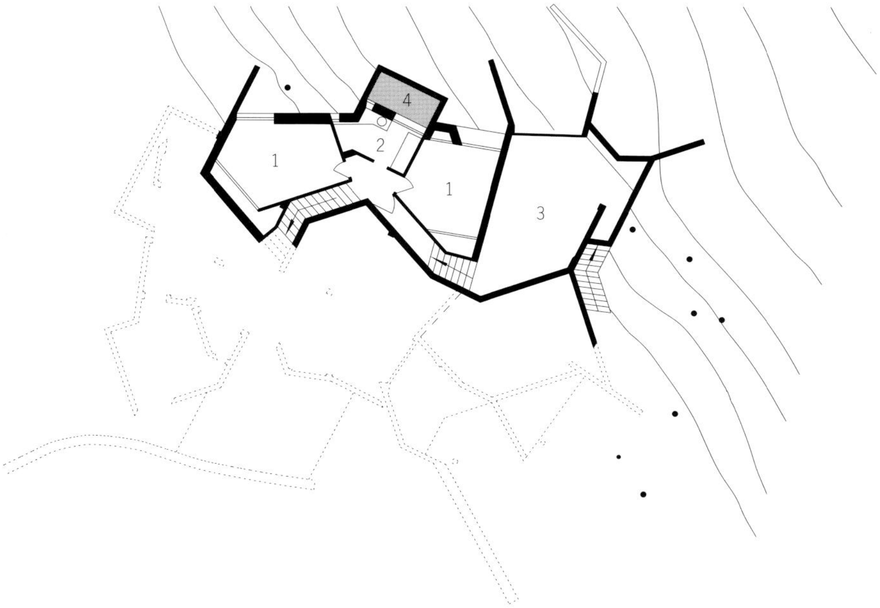

4 Lower Level

1 Children's bedroom
2 Bathroom
3 Garage
4 Terrace

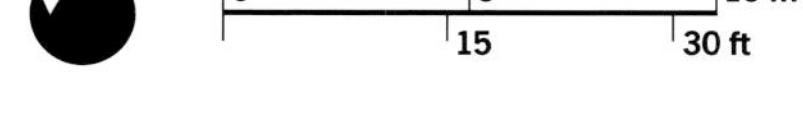

1

2

3

4

0   5   10 m
15   30 ft

House at Koramangala

Charles Correa, 1930–

Bangalore, India; 1985–89

The Indian architect Charles Correa is of the generation that could not help but be influenced by Le Corbusier. In later life, however, he has become more interested in reinterpreting the vernacular architecture of the Indian subcontinent. In 1986, Correa completed a housing project in Belapur near Mumbai (Bombay) that ingeniously achieved high density without rising to more than two storeys and without any party walls. Each house had room to expand, and the development was leavened by a hierarchical network of private, communal and public spaces. According to Correa, Indians need more than just rooms to live in; they need a range of spaces for different activities at different times of day and in different seasons.

While working on Belapur, Correa was also building a house for himself and his family at Koramangala in Bangalore. The projects have much in common: a certain looseness or indeterminacy; the use of common materials such as brick and tile that small builders understand; and a pleasure taken in spaces that are 'open to the sky' – to use a favourite Correa phrase. In the middle of the house lies a square courtyard, a roofless room surrounded by a tiny cloister with a column in each corner. Too small to house any activity other

than circulation, this courtyard is nevertheless the spiritual as well as the spatial centre of the house. A Champa plant, taking the place of the traditional Hindu Tulsi, or sacred tree, almost fills it. The entrance to the courtyard is at the corner, from a subtly offset intermediate space, which in turn is connected to a covered footpath leading across a paved court to a roofed porch on the street. This entrance route illustrates an important general characteristic of the house: although it is placed more or less in the middle of its plot, with garden all around, it is experienced not as an object but as a sequence of contrasting spaces.

The rooms opening off the courtyard have designated functions – office, studio, living room, dining room – but they could be used differently in response to an alteration in the work/life balance. This is not to say that they are all the same. Different orientations and adjacent gardens give each a special character. The east-facing studio, for example, opens onto a *kund*, or sacred well, assembled from blocks of granite. As a room, it is every bit as important as the studio itself. The south-facing living room, on the other hand, opens onto a deep veranda, which is shared with the master bedroom next door.

The indeterminate character of the building might be explained by the many changes made to the plan during construction while family members hesitated and changed their minds about the move from Mumbai to Bangalore. Only the central courtyard remained as a constant reference point. The result is hardly rational or economical. The two first-floor rooms, for example, are completely separate, each occupying a little house of its own at different corners of the main house. But then the design is not aiming at rationality. It is more like a cluster of houses grown up over time than a single dwelling designed all at once. More specifically, it is like is one of the neighbourhood clusters at Belapur.

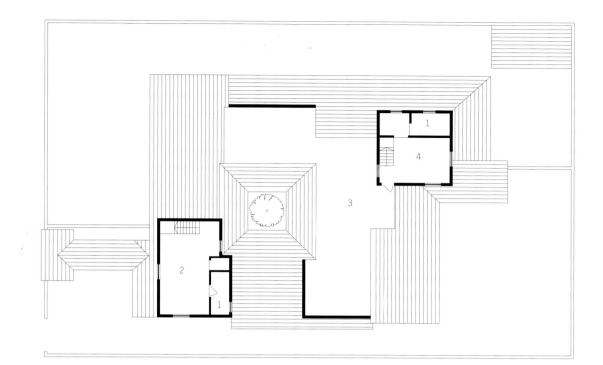

1 First Floor Plan

1 Bathroom
2 Studio bedroom
3 Terrace
4 Bedroom

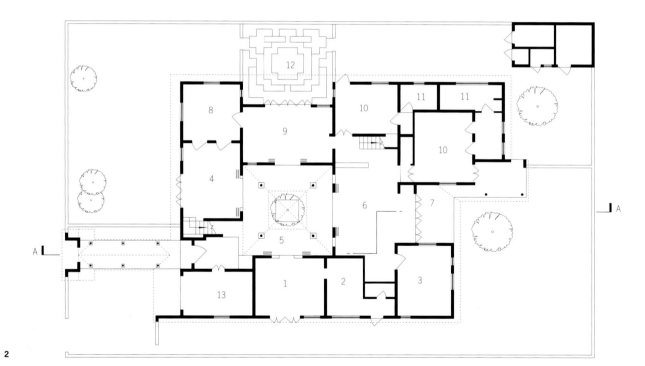

2 Ground Floor Plan

1 Dining/conference room
2 Kitchen
3 Weaving room
4 Office
5 Courtyard
6 Living room
7 Veranda
8 Own room
9 Studio
10 Bedroom
11 Bathroom
12 Kund
13 Garage

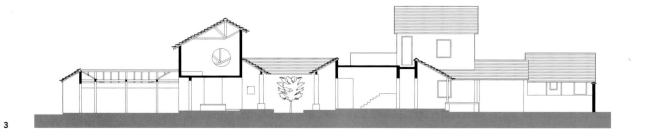

3 Section A–A

Zuber House

Antoine Predock, 1936–

Phoenix, Arizona, USA; 1989

Although born in Missouri, Antoine Predock is spiritually a child of the desert. He began his architectural training at the University of New Mexico and his practice is based in Albuquerque. He also studied at Columbia University and won a Rome Prize fellowship in the 1980s, but the East Coast and European intellectual traditions were not for him. When he toured Europe, he did so on a motorbike, and the thrill of riding fast through a strange landscape seems to have been more important than the cultural monuments he occasionally stopped to sketch.

If there is cultural flavour to Predock's architecture, it comes from Mexico and Spain, not New York or Paris. But, for him, architecture is principally a physical and emotional pursuit. The fundamental conditions of existence in the desert – the dusty earth, the glaring sky, the baking sun, the freezing nights – give birth to a 'regionalism' that is based on landscape and climate rather than culture. Not surprisingly, Frank Lloyd Wright is a powerful background presence (for a time, Predock worked as an apprentice in the office of Wright's associate, Charles Adams), but Louis Kahn and Luis Barragán are also acknowledged as influences.

The Zuber House occupies a sloping site in the desert not far from Phoenix, Arizona. It is a solid, fortress-like structure of grey concrete and reddish blockwork that tones in with the rough, rocky ground roundabout. A lightweight, transparent building in this climate would be foolish. Windows must be relatively small and set deep in the walls to reduce the glare, and there must be weight in the structure to absorb the daytime heat and hold it through the cold nights.

The clients required a luxurious house, but in functional terms their brief was quite simple: a few large, connected spaces for entertaining, a master bedroom and a secluded study. They might easily have been arranged in a monolithic block, but Predock loosens the composition to make space for shady courtyards. A long main block runs parallel to the contours, with the garage at one end, the visitors' entrance at the other, and the main entertaining spaces in between. A second block at right angles contains the bedroom, with its attendant dressing rooms and bathrooms at first-floor level, and the study dug into the slope at the back. But it is the third, courtyard element that transforms the spatial feel of the house. The courtyard is L-shaped and

divided into three sections. The first is open to the slope at the back of the site, the second, at the hinge of the L, is tucked under the bedroom, and the third is almost totally enclosed by walls but open to the sky. Each of these three sections is provided with a pool. In the third section, adjacent to the study, the pool completely fills the space and spills over a weir into the diamond-shaped pool under the bedroom.

The bedroom is perhaps the heart or command centre of the house. It looks out in all directions: east and west along the slope, north over the water-filled courtyard at the back, and south over the city of Phoenix in the distance. It even peeps under the shallow barrel-vault roof into the dining room below. From one of the two angled towers that visually buttress the barrel vault, a steel-framed bridge emerges with no other functional justification than to provide for the exciting spatial experience of being suspended above the desert on a starry night.

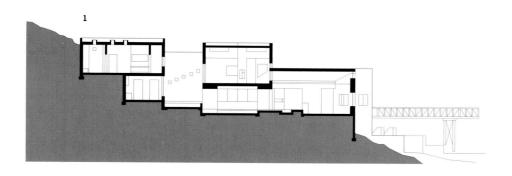

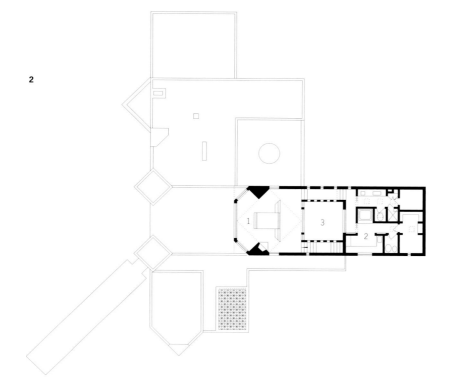

2

2 First Floor Plan

1 Bedroom
2 Dressing room
3 Court below

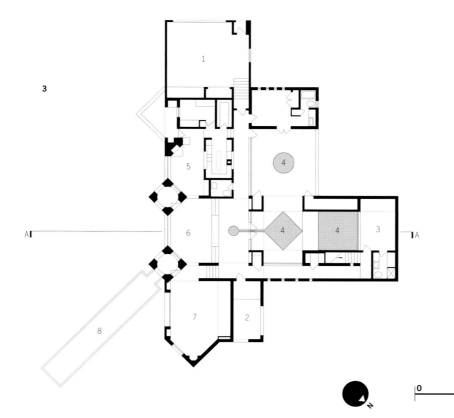

3

3 Ground Floor Plan

1 Garage
2 Visitors' entrance
3 Study
4 Courtyard
5 Kitchen
6 Dining room
7 Living room
8 Bridge

Neuendorf House

John Pawson and Claudio Silvestrin, 1949– and 1954–

Mallorca, Spain; 1990

John Pawson and Claudio Silvestrin are frequently classified as minimalists. Minimalism signifies different things in different contexts – for example, the sculptures of Donald Judd or Dan Flavin have little in common with the music of Philip Glass or Steve Reich. In architectural terms, minimalism tends to mean not just an economy of means or an absence of ornament but a devotion to calm emptiness, even when it seems to conflict with the normal requirements of everyday life. So, in minimalist dwellings, televisions are kept in cupboards and windows remain curtainless, while the interiors of minimalist art galleries are plain to the point of sensory deprivation. Pawson and Silvestrin have designed their fair share of both.

Some interior features of the Neuendorf House, a holiday home for a German art dealer, meet expectations, but its exterior seems more Surrealist than minimalist. Far from discreet, it is a monumental presence among the Mallorcan olive groves, a reddish rendered box perched on high ground. Two long projections anchor the box to its site: a plain unbuttressed wall with a level top, rising out of the ground as the land falls away, and a narrow rectangular pool emerging like a tongue from a mouthlike opening in the south-east wall.

These forms are purely geometrical, showing no marks of their construction, and making no concessions to the local vernacular apart from the red earth mixed into the stucco. Thus they are rather scaleless and dreamlike, prompting the question: is this a house or a fortress?

Familiar things such as cars are kept at a distance so as not to break the spell. Visitors enter by a stepped path beside the long wall, passing a sunken tennis court on the right before arriving at a narrow, full-height slot in the wall of the house. The slot is a gate to a different world. A courtyard, stone paved and unplanted, frames a square of pure blue sky. The enclosed part of the house is L-shaped on plan, embracing the courtyard and completing the larger square of the box. It is a familiar form in the Modernist canon. Other examples include Alvar Aalto's summer house in Finland (see pages 122–23), and Jørn Utzon's Courtyard Houses at Fredensborg in Denmark, but this two-storey version creates a shadier courtyard that feels almost urban.

The courtyard is in effect the living room. The only other communal space is the dining room and kitchen on the ground floor, directly opposite the courtyard entrance, which has no

windows onto the surrounding countryside, only two large square openings onto the courtyard, closed by panels that slide into the walls and external shutters. An immovable stone table stands at one end on axis with a fireplace and a low stone wall hiding a kitchen worktop at the other. A compact stone staircase rises to the master bedroom, which also has a fixed layout. Bed, wardrobe, bath, shower, basin and other fixtures are all arranged on major and minor axes. The day-lighting in this room is more subtle. A row of ten small windows in the outward-facing wall is balanced by a band of rooflights over the courtyard wall. Other bedrooms are reached by an open gallery overlooking the courtyard.

If these interiors feel like rooms in an old castle, then the pool is the drawbridge. Looking out through the opening where the portcullis would be is a hallucinatory experience: the pool apparently hovers above the ground where it reaches out beyond the terrace. In fact, there are rooms underneath the pool, reached via a narrow flight of steps to one side. Although practically invisible to the houses's inhabitants, these rooms provide an element essential to all minimalist architecture: a place to put all the clutter.

1 Ground Floor Plan

1 Storage
2 Fireplace
3 Kitchen/dining room
4 WC
5 Courtyard
6 Office/studio
7 Pool
8 Tennis court

2 First Floor Plan

1 Master bedroom
2 Master bathroom
3 Bedroom

3 Section B–B

4 Section A–A

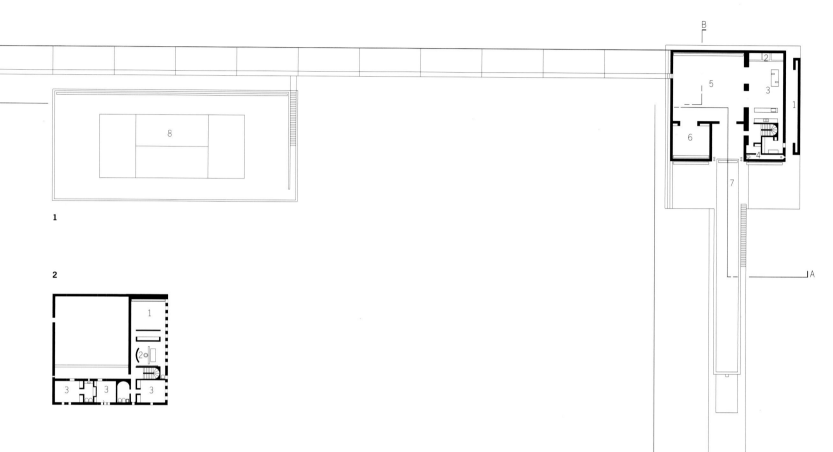

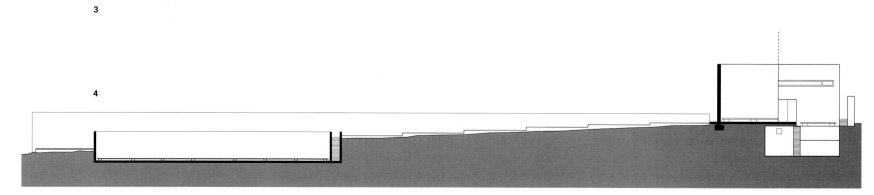

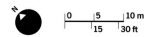

Villa Busk

Sverre Fehn, 1924–

Bamble, Norway; 1987–90

Several of Sverre Fehn's later buildings – the Glacier Museum at Fjaerland and the Aukrust Museum at Alvdal, for example – are long, low, linear structures, resembling the hulls of ships.

In the Villa Busk, the ship has somehow got itself stranded high up on an outcrop of rocks overlooking Oslo's fjord. Fehn loves wooden ships and sketches them obsessively, so the metaphor seems apt, though it cannot be taken too far. The solid-concrete wall that anchors the structure to the rock, fitting itself to the irregularities of the terrain like a castle rampart, is anything but lightweight and floatable. And then there is the four-storey tower, square on plan with a spiral stair in a corner turret, that seems to come from a different narrative altogether – a fairy tale, perhaps. It is a tower from which to survey the horizon and dream of long voyages.

Fehn himself has spoken of the tower in these terms, and it is no accident that it houses the children's bedrooms, with a study or playroom in a glazed belvedere at the top. The whole house is a primitive mark on the landscape, a vertical and a horizontal stroke, a standing and a reclining figure. It joins the earth and the sky and it speaks to the horizon, telling a story of journeyings and homecomings. Fanciful, perhaps, but it is worth mentioning that Christian Norberg Schulz, who constructed a body of architectural theory on the writings of the existentialist philosopher Martin Heidegger, was Fehn's friend and compatriot. Heidegger would have approved of the Villa Busk.

The main, horizontal part of the house has a simple plan, with domestic spaces ranged along one side of a corridor. The corridor is a quasi-external space, with a mostly glazed outer wall and a stone-paved floor. A little pitched roof supported on wooden posts covers it as if it were a separate building, and at the southwest end it does indeed break free, extending itself for two bays as an open porch. The strip between the corridor and the concrete wall is sliced up into conventional functional zones – entrance hall, living room, kitchen, dining room, bedroom – but there is also an indoor pool at the northeast end, and a courtyard resembling a roofless room in the middle. At the southwest end, the floor suddenly steps up half a storey onto a natural rock platform. There is nothing in the plan to signal this violent shift, no recesses or articulations apart from the ten steps in the corridor. It is as if the whole building has been forcibly kinked to fit the shape of the ground. Spatially, though, it makes sense, lifting the living room above the activities of the entrance hall and kitchen. In the far corner of the living room there is a beautiful hearth like an open cube from which rises a big rectangular chimney. Another flight of steps, tucked away behind the kitchen, leads down to a basement recording studio under the courtyard.

What gives the house an extra spatial dimension, however, is the cross axis set up by the tower on the southeast side and the porch, with its cubic storeroom, on the northwest side. It is possible to walk straight through the house from the main entrance, across the hall, onto the glazed bridge, into the children's tower, down the spiral staircase, out of the door at the bottom and along the path to the shore of the fjord and the waiting boat.

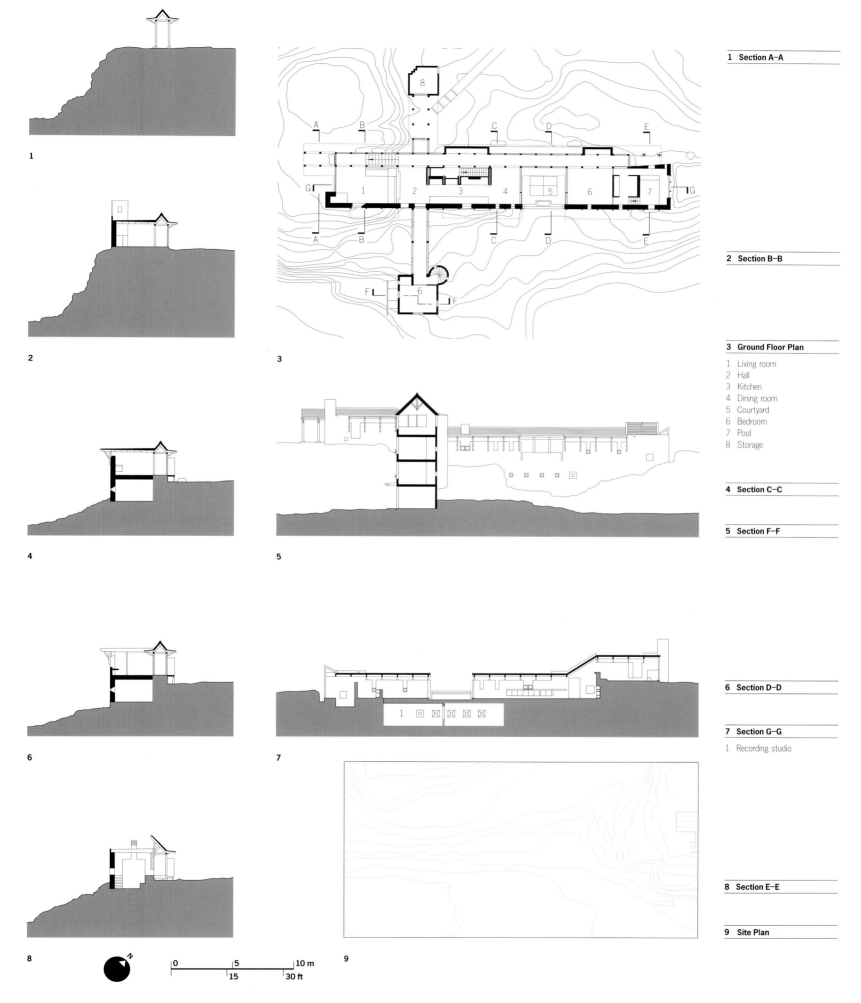

1 Section A–A

2 Section B–B

3 Ground Floor Plan
1 Living room
2 Hall
3 Kitchen
4 Dining room
5 Courtyard
6 Bedroom
7 Pool
8 Storage

4 Section C–C

5 Section F–F

6 Section D–D

7 Section G–G
1 Recording studio

8 Section E–E

9 Site Plan

1

2

3

4

5

6

7

8

9

0   5   10 m
15   30 ft

Casa Gaspar

Alberto Campo Baeza, 1946–

Zahora, Cadiz, Spain; 1991

Alberto Campo Baeza is a purist, but not in the Corbusian sense. Le Corbusier's Purist paintings contain ordinary objects such as tables, books and wine bottles. His buildings likewise accommodate and celebrate the trappings of daily life, from kitchen utensils to cars. Traditional ornament may have disappeared but life goes on. Campo Baeza's purism is of a different order. His buildings seem to want to have nothing to do with everyday life. They refuse even to acknowledge the surrounding landscape and the neighbouring buildings.

For Campo Baeza, the important things are those that are omnipresent, inescapable and immaterial — namely, gravity, light, space and time. In his book *La Idea Construida* he writes, 'Gravity constructs space; light constructs time, makes time meaningful. The central concerns of architecture are how to control gravity, and how to relate to light.' According to your point of view, this is either profound or blindingly obvious, but it at least has the virtue of simplicity, as does another Campo Baeza slogan, adapted from Mies van der Rohe: 'More with less.'

The Casa Gaspar is the perfect illustration of these principles. It is inward-looking to an extreme degree. Almost all contact with the outside world

is prevented by a wall 3.5 metres (11 feet) high. If the house were in the middle of a city, this would be no surprise, but the site is in an orange grove and the views (potentially) are of trees and fields. This is not the sort of environment that people usually want to be cut off from. Fortunately, the client valued privacy above all else and was therefore in sympathy with Campo Baeza's architectural instincts.

The house's alienation from its surroundings is emphasized by its abstract geometry. The 3.5 metre wall forms an enclosure that is perfectly square, like a Platonic geometrical figure fallen from heaven. The square is divided into three equal strips by two more 3.5 metre walls, and only the central strip is roofed over. Two lower walls divide the square in the other direction, this time into unequal strips in a 1/2/1 proportion. The dividing walls therefore form a cross in a square.

Over the rectangular intersection of the cross, the roof is raised to a height of 4.5 metres (15 feet) to form the main living room. Two bedrooms, a kitchen and a bathroom occupy the low-roofed sections at each end, and each of these rooms, except the bathroom, opens onto its own private corner patio. The 'patio' next to

the bathroom is the garage. This leaves a large rectangular patio on both the east and west sides of the living room.

As a plan it is perfectly logical and works well, but its rigid symmetries seem to derive more from a geometrical game than from any consideration of human use. The house is not, however, devoid of sensual appeal. Far from it. Campo Baeza heightens the sense of pure space by painting everything white and removing all constructional detail. For example, the four windows in the living room are all single sheets of glass installed without frames into plain, square openings. The placing of the windows in the corners of the room so that the patio walls pass through the glass to become the walls of the living room is a masterstroke.

But the point of all this simplification is to concentrate attention on the light. In other Campo Baeza houses, such as the Turegano House of 1988, direct sunlight is used to animate surfaces and unify space. Here the light is almost all reflected and re-reflected from the walls and paving of the patios. It changes constantly during the day but remains always subtle and a little mysterious, as if not of this world.

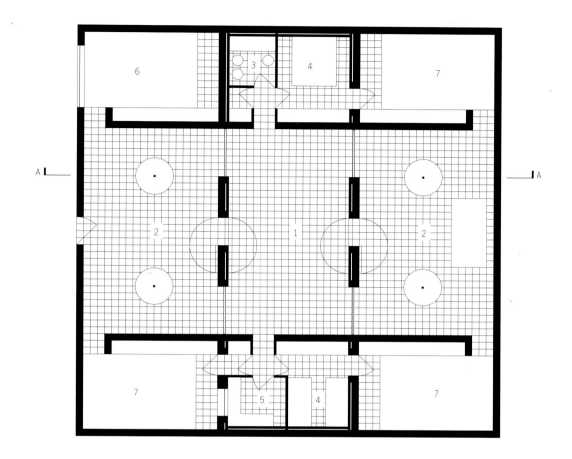

1

2

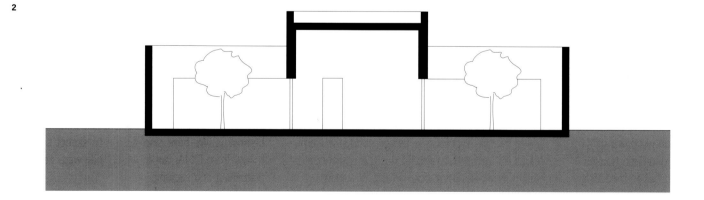

2 Section A–A

N

0   5   10 m

15   30 ft

Villa Dall'Ava

Rem Koolhaas, 1944–

St Cloud, Paris, France; 1991

'It is about its relationship with its neighbours, its context . . . It is not an object.' These statements are to be found among the notes printed, as if scrawled in Biro, on the plans of the Villa Dall'Ava published in Rem Koolhaas's and Bruce Mau's book *S,M,L,XL*. Such apparent sensitivity is ironic given that the construction of the house was long delayed by the neighbours' objections, which could only be overruled by taking the case all the way to the French Supreme Court. Nevertheless, a close scrutiny of the design will show that the statements are broadly true, especially if the reference to 'neighbours' includes the two Le Corbusier villas nearby and the Eiffel Tower, clearly visible on the horizon to the east.

The site is a walled garden in mature, suburban St Cloud. It slopes steeply down to the road and is flanked by two detached houses, one set further back than the other. Immediately, then, the reason for the villa's roughly S-shaped plan is evident, with one wing brought forward to line up with the house on the south side, another standing back as if to acknowledge the other neighbour, and a link block between them. But this arrangement is also a response to the view, the offset ensuring that the rear wing, which houses

the master bedroom, can see past the front wing, which houses the apartment of the daughter of the family. The slope is dealt with straightforwardly, too. The lowest of the three storeys is at ground level at the front and at basement level at the back. It contains the entrance hall, service spaces, a library and a studio, and where it emerges from the ground it is clad in black, rubble-patterned stone to show that it is essentially a substructure. The middle floor contains the dining, kitchen and living spaces and its walls are mostly of glass, so that spatially it is part of the garden. The bedrooms are on the top floor, at either end of the swimming pool.

Yes, a swimming pool occupies the top storey of the link block and is accessible only from the roof. At this point, the design suddenly seems a lot less straightforward. To put the enormous weight of a swimming pool on top of a glass-walled living room is an architectural solecism. But this is typical of Koolhaas and OMA (the Office for Metropolitan Architecture), who love to break every rule, reinvent every traditional form, reject every convention. The swimming pool is actually supported on a row of quite fat columns disguised by the wooden storage wall that divides

the living room from the long ramp. The ramp, which links the entrance hall directly to the main living space at the back, is perhaps a nod to the Corbusian neighbours – a sign that this house is meant to be as new and as different as the Villa Stein (see pages 54–55) and the Villa Savoye (see pages 80–81) were in their day.

There are many other strange details. The daughter's bedroom, for example, is supported by a cluster of thin, randomly angled columns, which is all the more strange since the parents' bedroom seems to require no such support. The materials are also unusual, often deliberately cheap and crude, such as the sheets of translucent plastic that form the internal kitchen wall, and the corrugated aluminium sheets that clad the two bedrooms. We have since come to expect such things from OMA, but in 1991 they were new, disturbing and exciting.

1 Roof Terrace Plan

1 Swimming pool

2 Second Floor Plan

1 Bedroom

3 First Floor Plan

1 Living room
2 Kitchen
3 Dining room
4 Void

4 Ground Floor Plan

1 Entrance
2 Service room
3 Studio
4 Garage

5 Section A–A

6 Section B–B

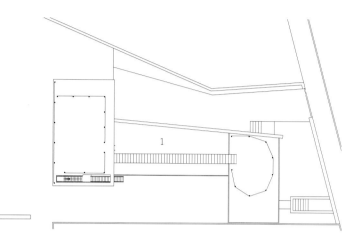

1

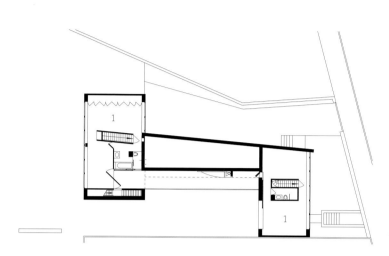

2

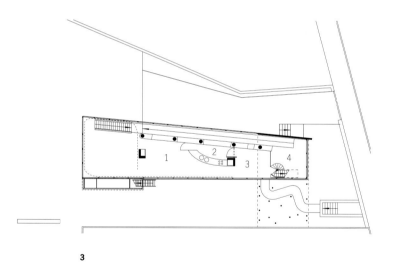

3

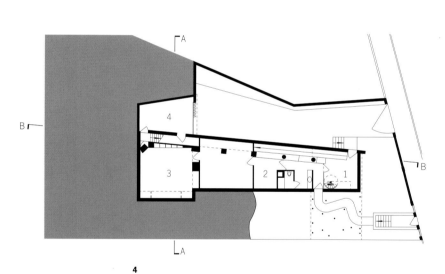

4

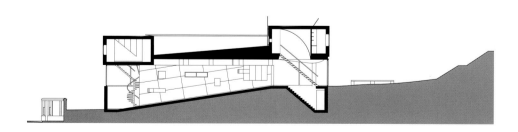

5

6

Charlotte House

Günter Behnisch, 1922–

Stuttgart, Germany; 1993

Until the fall of the Berlin Wall in 1989 and the subsequent style battles over the development of the 'new' capital, the office of Behnisch and Partner dominated the progressive, Modernist wing of West German architecture. It designed mainly public and social buildings, including the stadiums for the 1972 Munich Olympics and the Federal Parliament building in Bonn, which was commissioned in 1983 and completed just in time for it become redundant. The practice combines a tectonic sensibility based on steel and glass with the 'organic' tradition of Häring and Scharoun to create an architecture of great spatial freedom. In educational buildings of the 1980s and 1990s, such as the Albert Schweitzer Special School of 1991 in Bad Rappenau, the Behnisch manner converged with the Deconstructivist style that had emerged elsewhere in Europe and in the USA.

There is nothing Deconstructivist about the Charlotte House, however. Designed for Günter Behnisch's daughter and her two sons, it stands in an ordinary residential street in Stuttgart and fulfils the normal expectations of a detached suburban villa. A compact, economical form based on a square plan is made distinctive by a barrel-shaped, metal-clad roof. The roof form emerged

not so that the house would stand out among its neighbours but for the opposite reason: to reduce its height by allowing use of the loft space.

Two aspects of the plan are unusual. First, the half-cylinder of the roof space, which contains three bedrooms and two bathrooms, is double-height with high-level sleeping platforms accessible by ladder from two of the bedrooms. This part of the house was designed for easy conversion into a self-contained flat with external staircase access. Second, there is a swimming pool and sauna in the basement, opening onto a sunken area of garden. The client has difficulty walking so there is a lift, and circulation spaces tend to be open and generous. The ground floor is dominated by a single, large, south-facing space combining entrance hall, dining room and kitchen. A terrace or deck extends in front of the dining room, over the sunken garden, displacing the main entrance to the west side of the house.

This has been described as a 'solar-powered' house, although the architects tend to play down the importance of this aspect of the design. For some architects, energy saving is an excuse to create unusual forms, making the most of conservatories, trombe walls and south-facing roof

slopes covered with solar panels. The Charlotte House is not of this type. It uses both passive and active energy-saving techniques but in an unobtrusive way. As it happens, the curved form of the roof does allow solar collectors to be mounted at the optimum angle, but this is not its main justification. The south-facing wall is almost all glass, making good use of passive solar heat gain in the winter, but there is no hint of a greenhouse. And the external louvres that shade the glass in summer are not very different from traditional shutters. The north elevation at the back is timber-clad with small windows to reduce heat loss in winter, but again there is nothing surprising or undomestic about it.

In form and character this is not a typical Behnisch building, but its quiet competence and practicality make it a worthy addition to the practice's oeuvre.

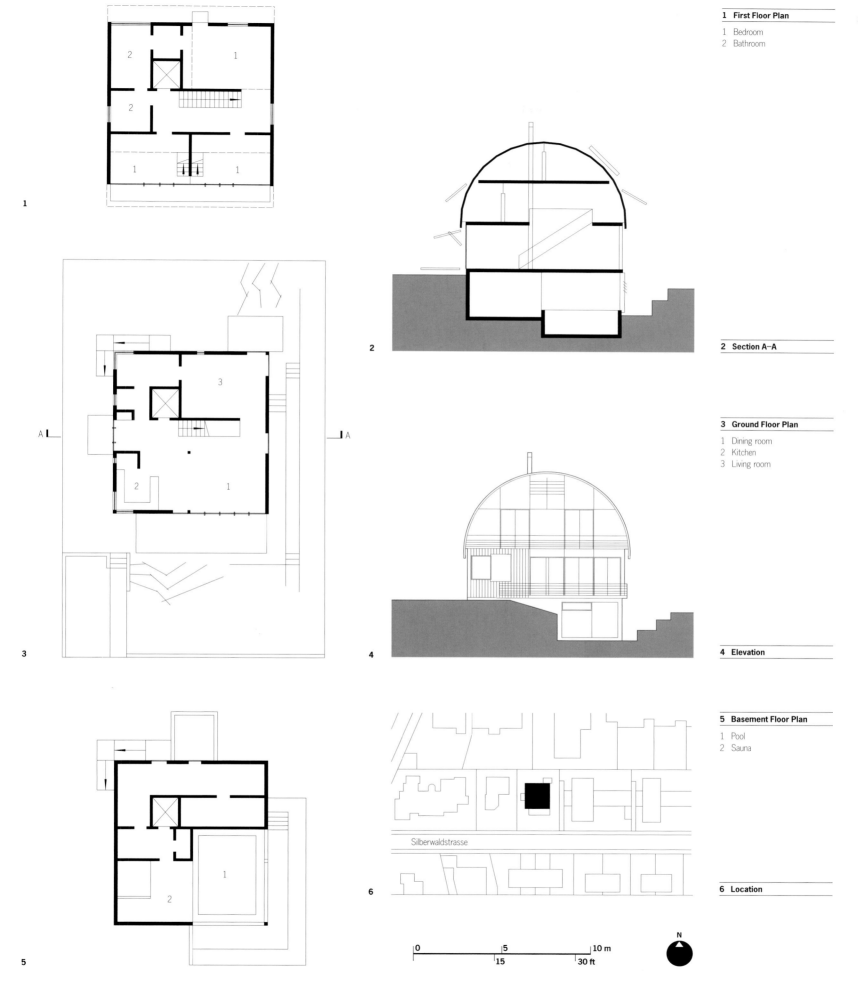

1 First Floor Plan

1 Bedroom
2 Bathroom

2 Section A–A

3 Ground Floor Plan

1 Dining room
2 Kitchen
3 Living room

4 Elevation

5 Basement Floor Plan

1 Pool
2 Sauna

6 Location

Silberwaldstrasse

0   5   10 m
  15   30 ft

N

Truss Wall House

Eisaku Ushida and Kathryn Findlay, 1954– and 1953–

Tsurukawa, Tokyo, Japan; 1993

Modern students of architecture are taught that 'context' should be an important aesthetic determinant of design, and most modern buildings try to fit into their surroundings in a sympathetic way. But what if the context is an unplanned and unlovely suburban mess such as the Tsurukawa district of Tokyo? How does a conscientious architect respond sympathetically to something he or she hates? In the case of Ushida Findlay, the answer is by ignoring it and thereby making a silent comment on it. The Truss Wall House is a detached house crammed onto a small site, just like its neighbours. But, whereas the neighbours are the product of a building industry that cares more about production and profit than space and light, the Truss Wall House is very definitely a piece of architecture. The only things in its surroundings that it responds to positively are the sky above and the hills in the distance.

It is an organic house, not in the sense that a Frank Lloyd Wright house is organic, but in that it is like an animal's remains – a skull, perhaps, or a shell. And, just as skulls and shells evolved to protect soft vulnerable organs from a potentially harmful natural environment, so the Truss Wall House evolved to protect its inhabitants from

a potentially harmful urban environment. Noise and lack of privacy were the main problems. The elevated commuter railway line into the centre of Tokyo is right opposite the house, and the site is too small to put any distance between the house and the street. It therefore looks inwards and upwards, turning its flowingly curved but mainly blank sides to the world outside. Its few windows are either very small, like portholes, or hidden behind a fold of the exoskeleton.

There are three main levels: bedrooms in the semi-basement, main living area on the raised ground floor, and garden on top. The whole point of the design is that space flows continuously from room to room, from level to level, and from inside to outside. The living area and roof garden, for example, somehow contrive to be a single continuous space, even though one is inside and one outside, and one is above the other. From the semicircular lounge area, space flows out through the only large window in the house onto a patio shielded from the street by a sweep of white wall. From here it flows up a broad flight of steps and into a sack-shaped roof garden with bone-like balustrades. These spaces are organic in another sense. The architects say that they correspond

to the invisible shapes that human bodies make in the air when they walk or climb or dance. Early twentieth-century artistic and photographic experiments, such as those of the Italian Futurists and Edward Muybridge, were an inspiration.

The name Truss Wall refers to the patented form of construction. Shaped vertical steel trusses were linked by reinforcing bars, covered with wire mesh and filled with concrete to form insulated cavity walls. Three-dimensional CAD models were used instead of ordinary working drawings, and a special 'see-through' isometric drawing was developed to capture the spatial complexities.

Eisaku Ushida and Kathryn Findlay are a Japanese–Scottish partnership. Both worked for Arata Isozaki and have taught at UCLA and Tokyo University. They ran offices in Tokyo, London and Glasgow until 2004, when their practice went into voluntary liquidation. No doubt they will be back.

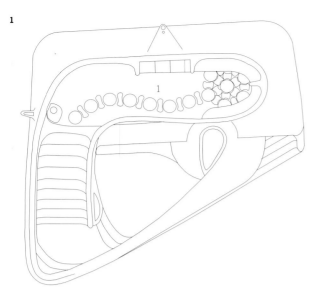

1 Roof Plan

1 Roof terrace

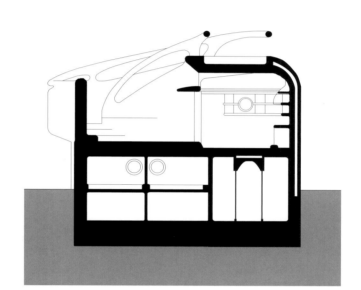

2 Raised Ground Floor Plan

1 Kitchen
2 Living/dining room
3 Terrace

3 Section A–A

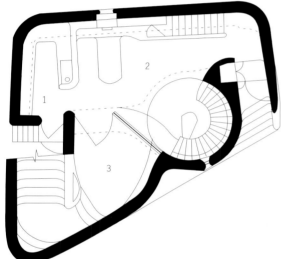

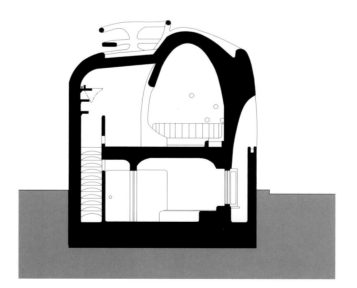

4 Semi-basement Plan

1 Bedroom
2 Bathroom

5 Section B–B

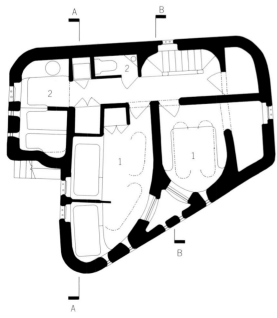

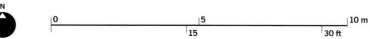

N

0   5   10 m
   15   30 ft

Cho en Dai House

Norman Foster, 1935–

Kawana, Japan; 1994

British High Tech, which flourished mainly in the 1980s, was a fiercely honest, rather literal-minded style. More concerned with flexibility than settled spatial arrangements, it rejected natural materials such as wood and brick in favour of bolt-together components of metal and glass. Not surprisingly, it produced few houses, although they include one or two interesting specimens such as the Hopkins House (see pages 174–75). Norman Foster was a leading exponent of the High Tech style, but when he was asked to design a house for a wealthy Japanese businessman he reverted to the more classical manner of Mies van der Rohe. And behind Mies, of course, stood that constant source of inspiration for Modernists of all kinds: the traditional Japanese house.

The first and perhaps most inspired design decision was the client's choice of site: a clifftop on the east side of the Izu peninsula, about 135 km (80 miles) from Tokyo, with spectacular sea views framed by pine trees. But this is not a cliff-hanging house. Its relationship to the site is mediated by an artificial landscape designed by Shigemi Komatsu. Concrete retaining walls, raw but smooth in the manner of Louis Kahn or Tadao Ando, divide up the ground into big level terraces finished in exposed aggregate concrete paving or red volcanic gravel. Three ancient stone lanterns and an exquisite late Edo tea house turn the terraces into an austere garden. The geometry, however, is relentlessly rectilinear. Four flights of steps, straight and in line, descend from the car park to the perfect paved rectangle on which the house stands.

There are instant reminders here of Mies's Farnsworth House (see pages 112–13): single-storey, flat-roofed, framed in white-painted steel, its floor slab hovering a metre or so above the ground with an intermediate entrance platform. The influence is obvious, but there are also important differences. The frame, for example, has round columns instead of H-sections, and the roof cantilevers out at the sides instead of the ends. The roof beams are tapered, which is structurally expressive and gives them a vaguely Japanese look, but the wooden-decked raised terrace is wafer thin and has no visible means of support. External walls are mostly glass, as you would expect, but all the panels slide open like shoji screens, and there is a narrow clerestory running right round the building. The least Miesian features are the smooth, aluminium-clad boxes that appear to have been parked on the terrace and plugged into the main volume. These pseudo-prefabricated modules contain bathrooms, a kitchen, air-handling plant and storage space. High Tech has evidently not been abandoned entirely. The 'served and servant' strategy leaves the interior space between the columns completely clear. Sliding partitions divide it up into two double and two single bays, almost arbitrarily designated as living room, dining room, entrance hall and bedroom.

A complicated array of shading devices (not to mention air conditioning) ensure that the Cho en Dai house does not suffer, as the Farnsworth House famously did, from solar heat gain. The roof over the main living spaces is like a machine for modifying natural light and heat. Rows of shallow-pitched glass panels can be shaded if necessary by horizontal external roller blinds. Inside, the ceiling is formed from big motorized louvres, so that daylight and sunlight can be controlled as precisely as in any museum.

A smaller, three-bay version of the main house accommodates guests on an adjacent site.

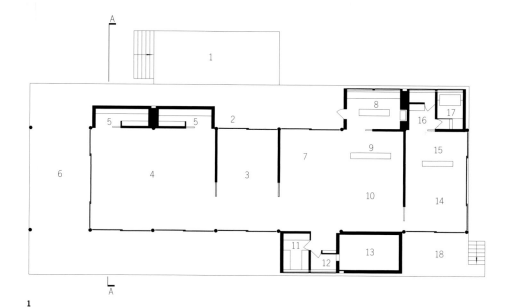

1 Main House

1 Entrance platform
2 Main entrance
3 Entrance lobby
4 Living room
5 Storage
6 External terrace
7 Dining area
8 Kitchen
9 Bar
10 Seating
11 Laundry
12 Guest washroom
13 Air-handling plant
14 Bedroom
15 Dressing area
16 Bathroom
17 Japanese bath
18 Private terrace

1

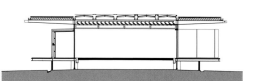

2 Guest House

1 Entrance platform
2 Main entrance
3 Living room
4 Dining room
5 Kitchen
6 Guest bedroom
7 Guest bathroom
8 External terrace
9 Swimming pool

2

3

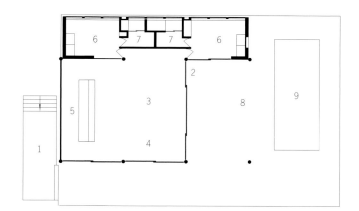

3 Section A–A

4

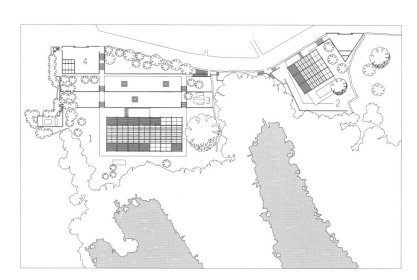

4 Site Plan

1 Main house
2 Guest house
3 Tea house
4 Car park

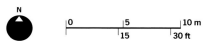

Marika—Alderton House

Glenn Murcutt, 1936—

Yirrkala, Eastern Arnheim Land, Northern Territory, Australia; 1994

Designed for the artist Banduk Marika, her English partner and their children, this house by the sea in the Northern Territory presented a multiple challenge to Australia's best-known architect.

Glenn Murcutt is a specialist house designer working almost exclusively in Australia, yet this was his first commission from an Aboriginal client and his first building in a truly tropical location. The problems were both technical and cultural: how to create a tolerably comfortable domestic environment in temperatures that never fall below 25°C (77°F) and often soar into the 40s, while keeping out the poisonous spiders and biting reptiles and avoiding culturally alien technologies such as air conditioning. The site was liable to be battered by hurricane-force winds and surge tides, and there was no skilled building labour available in the local community.

A long-house on stilts, in steel and wood, was Murcutt's answer; not an enclosed, protected volume but a shaded platform equipped with every kind of grille, baffle and brise soleil. The house opens up in all directions. There are big sliding doors at the entrance and all the 'windows', none of which is glazed, hinge upwards to a horizontal position, supported on gas lifts like those that raise the hatches of hatchback cars. The simple pitched roof overhangs the platform generously all round, and extra-generously on the northern side. Even on the supposedly shady southern side, there are deep vertical fins where the window mullions would be, to keep out the low morning and evening sun.

Having kept the sun out, the next priority is to catch every passing breeze. Through ventilation is maintained even when the house is securely closed up at night. There are swivelling roof vents to take the warm air out, and continuous insect-screened slots at floor level to let the cool air in. Fittings such as the cupboards in the living room and the beds in the children's rooms are lifted up off the floor to ensure a free flow of air. All rooms except showers and toilets are open to the high underside of the roof.

This is an entirely prefabricated building, made by a couple of yacht builders in Gosford near Sydney. The components were transported 3,200 km (2,000 miles) to the site by truck and boat before being assembled by the same two craftsmen. The steel frame uses the slender round sections familiar from other Murcutt houses, with large triangular stiffening webs to resist the hurricane-force winds. Steel rafters support wooden purlins, which in turn support Murcutt's trademark galvanized corrugated-iron roofing. Floors, partitions and external walls are of plywood or hardwood, painted or stained.

This is an economical building, almost agricultural in character, but its neat details and excellent workmanship make it a worthy partner for the many more expensive houses in the Murcutt oeuvre. Indeed, in its use of materials and its response to climate, it is perhaps the clearest statement of his architectural credo. It might also reveal the deepest source of his inspiration. When he was a young child, Murcutt lived with his family in the forests of New Guinea. His father, a gold prospector, built the house they lived in, which was raised up on stilts and roofed with corrugated iron. Legend has it that, on one occasion, Murcutt's mother had to defend the house from hostile natives by firing a rifle over their heads.

1 Living room
2 Bedroom
3 Bathroom

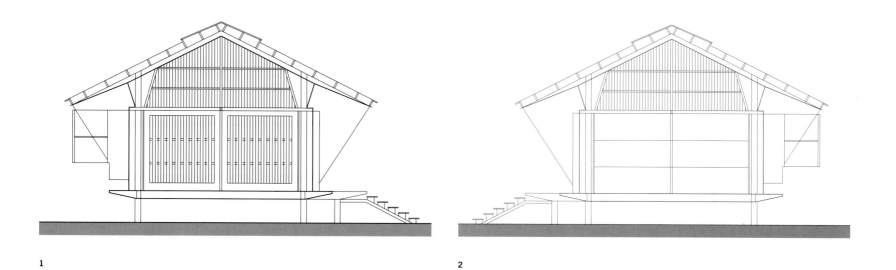

1

2

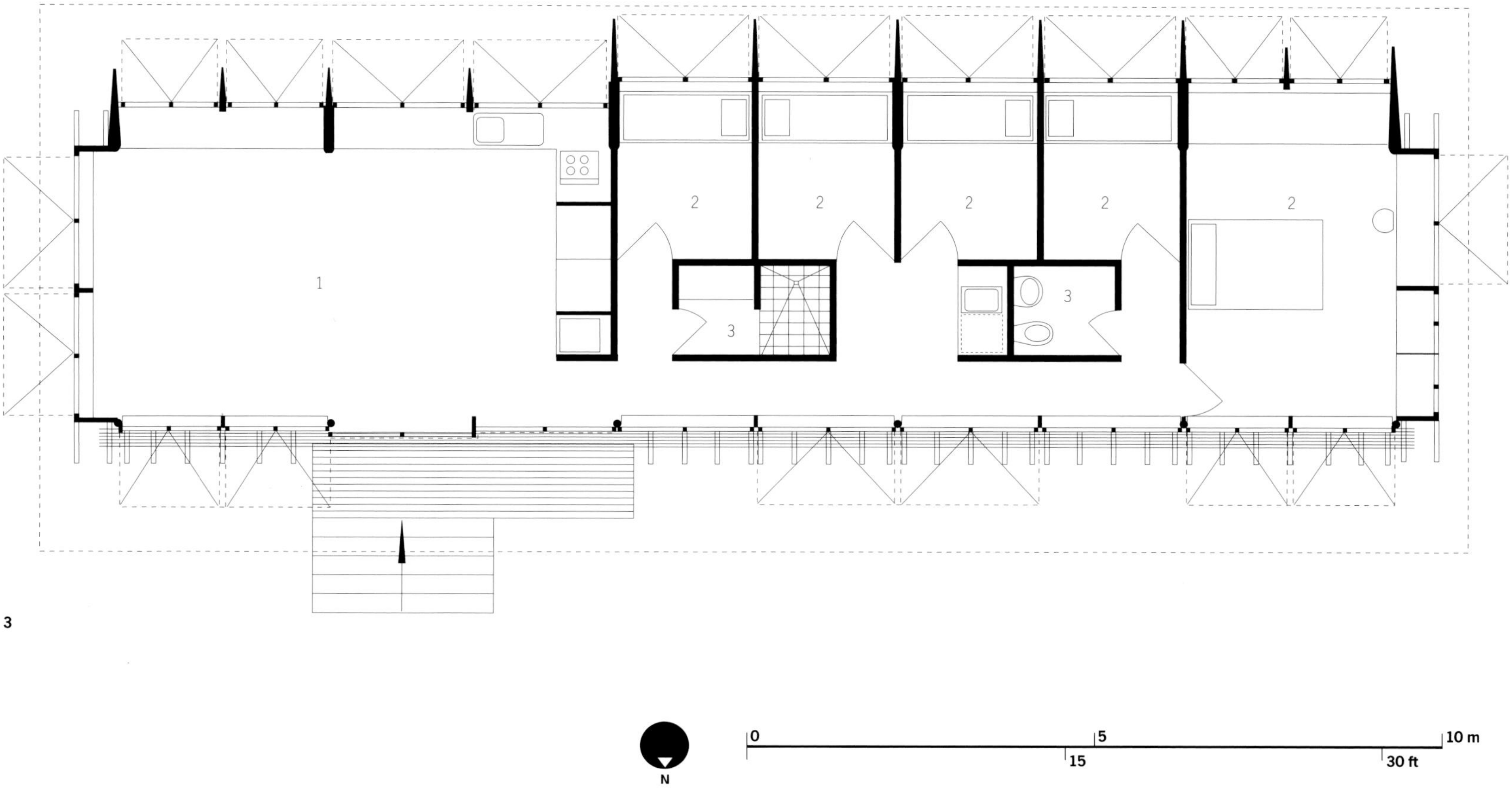

3

N

Marshall House

Barrie Marshall, 1946–

Phillip Island, Victoria, Australia; 1995

The Marshall House is long, low, black, secretive and rather scary. Its designer likens it to a Stealth bomber. Actually, it is a beach house. When architects design houses for themselves, there is always a hidden agenda. It is never just a matter of building something comfortable and cheerful to live in. Only an architect would think of living in a beach house that looks like a weapon of mass destruction. The architect in question is Barrie Marshall, a partner in Denton Corker Marshall, a large Melbourne-based practice with branches all over the world, which none the less remains 'studio-based' and design-conscious. The Marshall House is proof of that.

Marshall briefly considered building an ordinary wooden house on the site, but changed his mind when he realized that the last thing the landscape of Kitty Miller's Bay needed was an object standing in it. The house would have to be part of the landscape, resembling a dugout or a bunker (the military metaphors are unavoidable). In fact, the impression of being buried in the ground is an illusion. What appear to be natural sand dunes are really 'berms' – artificial banks piled up against concrete walls forming a square courtyard. This courtyard is the most important

space in the house, although it is difficult to determine exactly what its function is. It must occasionally become a car park, but, like some ancient temple precinct, it seems more ceremonial than functional.

The access road enters through a breach in the eastern berm. Three openings in the wall directly opposite indicate the presence of a generous garage and store room. The courtyard will not be a car park for long. From the southern wall to the left, a vertical steel blade reaches out like a robotic welcoming arm to indicate the position of the main entrance to the house.

The house itself occupies the long, relatively narrow space between the courtyard's south wall and another parallel concrete wall facing the sea. Blade-like devices – of which this extra wall is an example – are something of a Denton Corker Marshall trademark. Like a breakwater on the beach, it is buried in the sand at one end and forms a tapering retaining wall at the other. Dune grass grows on the roof of the house, reinforcing the retaining-wall illusion.

Inside, the plan is straightforward enough, with the living room at one end, the master bedroom at the other, and a circulation strip on

the courtyard side to link the two. Proportions are generous, especially around the kitchen/dining/ entrance area, which is provided with a big bay window projecting into the courtyard and a recessed porch, almost like a classical temple, facing the sea. Windows in the two concrete walls are sized and positioned to suit the spaces behind and the orientation. Those facing the courtyard on the north side are relatively few and small to keep out the sun and wind; those facing south frame wide-angled views of the sea.

The most extraordinary thing about the Marshall House is its austere character. To build a beach house out of rough, in situ concrete is daring enough, but this concrete is black, inside and out. Other finishes, such as the cold terrazzo of the floors and the unpainted steel of the doors and partitions, do nothing to soften the effect. Yet there is decoration of a kind. There are Kahn/ Ando-style dots in the concrete; the vertical daywork joints have been carefully positioned; and the gargoyles that drain the roof are set into little triangular cutouts. But none of these details does much to cheer things up. Only the flue from the living-room fireplace strikes a lighter note, emerging from its berm at a jaunty angle.

1 Ground Floor Plan   **2 Elevation to beach**   **3 Section A–A**

1 Living room
2 Dining room
3 Bedroom
4 Bathroom
5 Courtyard
6 Garage

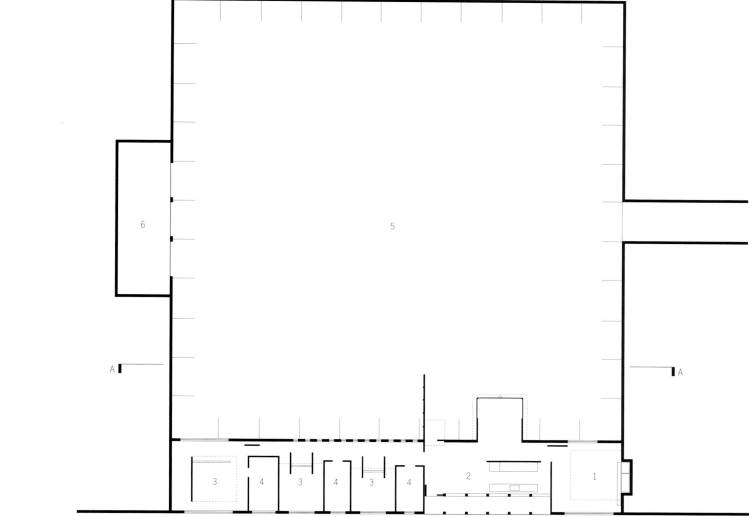

1

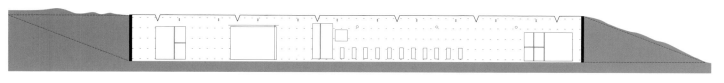

2

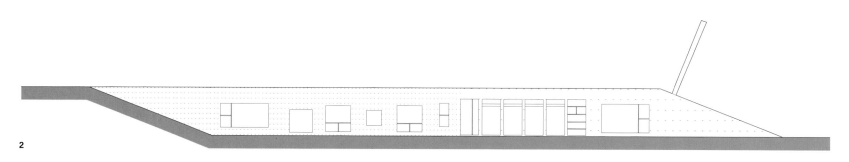

3

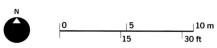

N

0   5   10 m
  15   30 ft

Furniture House

Shigeru Ban, 1957–

Tamanashi, Japan; 1996

Shigeru Ban is most widely known for his paper buildings such as the Japanese Pavilion at the 2000 Expo in Hanover, the main structure of which was a curvaceous grid-shell made of cardboard tubes. There have been paper houses, a paper art gallery, and even a paper church. In 1994 the United Nations High Commission for Refugees commissioned Ban to design paper emergency shelters for use after the Rwandan Civil War, and in 1995 his 'paper loghouses' accommodated victims of the Kobe earthquake.

The idea for the Furniture House originated in a paper building. In 1991, Ban designed a little freestanding pavilion to house the library of a poet. Its structural frame was a lattice of cardboard tubes braced by steel wires. The bookcases were structurally independent of the frame, but were insulated and weatherproofed so that they formed the external walls of the building. Ban realized that the vertical elements of the frame were redundant. With a few modifications, the roof could be supported by the bookcases.

The first Furniture House is a minimalist composition with a plan like a Mondrian painting in a square frame. All the basic spatial requirements of a luxury one-bedroomed Japanese house,

including a tatami room and a terrace with a view of Mount Fuji in the distance, are sandwiched between a flat floor and a flat ceiling, and separated by storage units.

The idea of using storage units to divide space is not new, but here there are no ordinary solid walls; all the walls are either cupboards or bookcases. Floor-to-ceiling glass and glazed sliding doors complete the external enclosure. Between the living room and the terrace, the doors can be slid right back so that they disappear completely. The thin steel frame that supports the roof in the corner of the terrace is the only structural element that is not a piece of furniture, although even this has a shelf attached to it.

Storage units were standardized and prefabricated from sheet materials in the familiar 'flat-pack' way. All are 2400 mm (95 inches) high, 900 mm (35 inches) wide and either 450 mm (18 inches) deep in the case of bookcases or 750 mm (30 inches) deep in the case of cupboards. They rest on a floor of plain concrete covered by plywood and they support a roof structure of timber joists and boards. But all is not what it seems. The units are screwed together for structural continuity but they are also reinforced

by 100 x 50 mm (4 x 2 inch) timber frames fixed to the backs. In the external walls, this frame is filled with insulation and covered with a plywood board to which the cladding is fixed. The plywood gives lateral bracing and is essential for earthquake resistance. So this structure is not very different from the 'two by four' platform frame used in many ordinary houses in Japan. The great advantage of the furniture concept is that each unit can be handled on site by just one person. It is a new way of thinking rather than a new technology. The boundaries between structure and furniture, permanent and temporary have been redrawn.

There have since been several more furniture houses, including a two-storey version that adds useful new components to the system, such as an air-conditioning cupboard and a storage staircase.

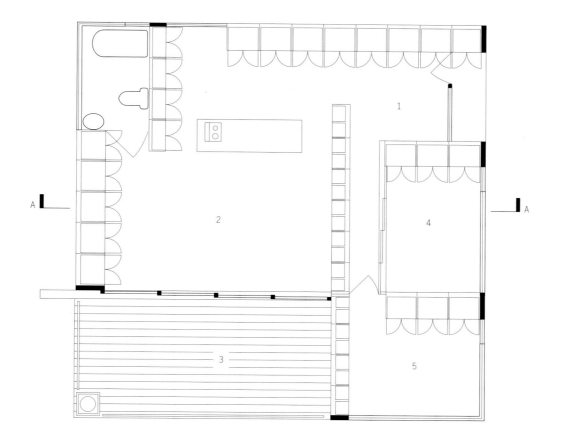

1

2

3

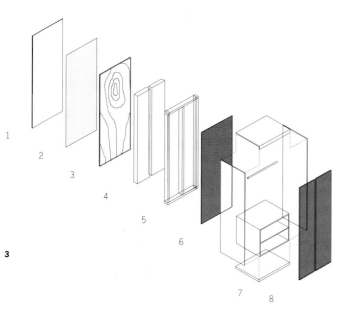

4

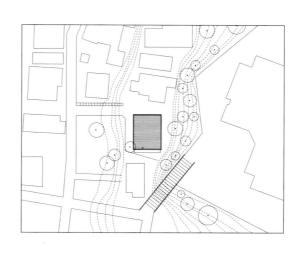

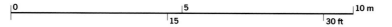

0   5   10 m
15   30 ft

N

Double House

Bjarne Mastenbroek and Winy Maas, 1964– and 1959–

Utrecht, The Netherlands; 1997

Any architect about to design a building will usually undertake some kind of systematic analysis of the site, the budget, the space requirements, the relevant building regulations, and so on. The Dutch practice MVRDV has transformed this common-sense procedure into a philosophy and a style. Their designs do more than simply take account of quantifiable factors; they become the visible and tangible expression of them. They become what the practice calls 'datascapes'. A good example is the project called 'Pig City', which translates the economic, regulatory and spatial logic of organic pork production into a perfectly rational but deeply surreal proposal for multi-storey pig farms.

But statistics are never politically neutral. They have to be evaluated and interpreted. Conflicting interests must be reconciled. A 'datascape' is therefore as much a social map as a mathematical diagram. The Double House in Utrecht might be interpreted as a map of the relationship between its co-owners. Having purchased a large plot of land with views over a beautiful park on the outskirts of Utrecht, the first owners soon realized that they could not afford to develop the site to its full potential. They found a

development partner, who would also become a close neighbour, but the two families could not decide, for example, which would have the easier access to the garden or the better view over the park. The architect Bjarne Mastenbroek was called in to help, and he in turn invited Winy Maas of MVRDV to collaborate on the project. The resulting house has a characteristic MVRDV combination of originality and literal-mindedness.

The first design move was to define a relatively tall and shallow building envelope that would admit lots of daylight while maximizing the area of garden at the back. The next question was how to divide the volume between the two partners. A straight party wall would deprive both households of the expansiveness and wide views that the site seemed offer. Putting one dwelling above the other would mean that only the lower dwelling had direct access to the garden. The answer was obvious but novel: vary the position of the party wall on each floor. The solution is hard to understand on plan but easy to appreciate in section. Each house has a straightforward staircase roughly in the middle of its half of the building envelope. The party wall can occupy any position between the two staircases, judiciously

sharing out the space between the dwellings. This arrangement is much easier to draw than it is to build, since the party wall cannot perform its normal structural function of transmitting floor loads straight to the ground. Remarkably, there are no internal columns. Instead, steel trusses and props are hidden in the internal and external walls, catching each other at various levels in a complex three-dimensional frame. Despite this, there are large areas of glass in the front and back elevations, often extending across the full height and width of a room. Otherwise the external walls are finished in flat, flush panels that emphasize the abstract box of the building envelope and reject any tectonic expression of structure or construction.

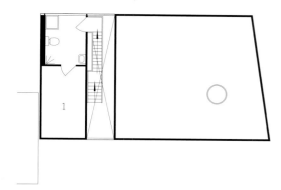

1

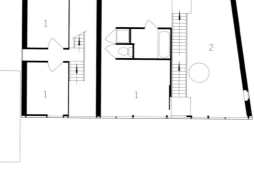

2

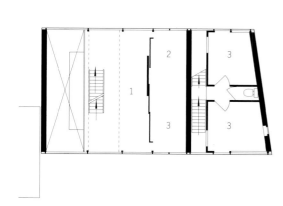

3

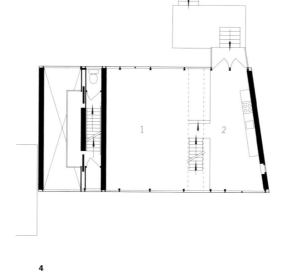

4

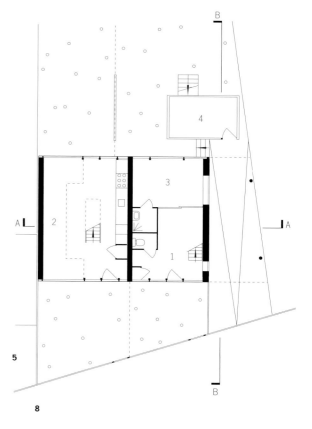

5

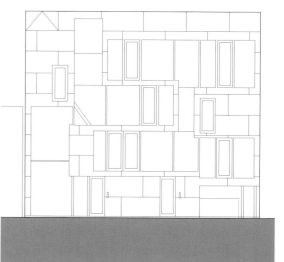

6

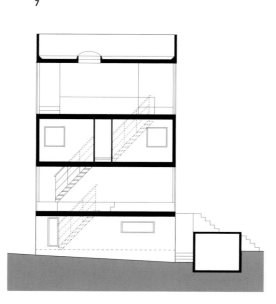

7

8

N

| 0 | 5 | 10 m |
| 15 | | 30 ft |

M House

Kazuyo Sejima and Ryue Nishizawa/SANAA, 1956– and 1966–

Tokyo, Japan; 1997

Basements are usually secondary spaces for storage or mechanical plant. In the M House, the basement is the main living area. In fact, it is most of the house. The need for both privacy and sound insulation was the main reason for the unusual arrangement

In this part of Tokyo, near the centre of the city, houses are large and expensive but packed tight, with very little space between public streets and private living spaces. Fences are high and curtains are always drawn. The clients for the M House were musicians and this was to be a workplace as well as a house, so street noise was also a potential problem. Sinking the house into the ground and introducing three linear lightwells solved two problems at once, creating an inward-looking but nevertheless light and airy interior. The lightwells at either end of the house are little more than narrow yards, but the central well is more like an external hall — a rather grand, high space, roughly a double square in height and a triple square in length. Its walls are made of translucent glass, its floor is a wooden deck on the same level as the floors of the adjacent rooms, and a metal pergola forms a kind of ceiling. A single tree at one end is its only adornment.

The central well divides the plan into two zones: an L-shaped living and dining space and a rectangular working space subdivided into music room and study. Only a narrow corridor across the end of the well connects the two zones. This is a very straightforward plan that totally fills the site. But there are more spaces to accommodate: a garage and three bedrooms, including a tatami room for guests. These occupy three separate, storey-height, steel-framed bridges of equal width, spanning across the basement from front to back at street level. The basement spaces are in effect double-height, so that they contain the bridges. A straight steel staircase descends from the ground-floor entrance hall in the gap between the garage and guest-room bridges. A similar staircase occupies the gap between the bedroom bridge and the wall of the central well.

Everything is perfectly regular; in geometrical terms, the layout could hardly be simpler. As the plans show, this is not much more than a row of linear spaces — ten altogether — of different widths like the stripes of a bar code. But there is a hidden complexity. Spaces can be read in various combinations. The living room, for example, might be just the strip of floor implied by the soffit

of the garage bridge overhead, or it might include the gaps on either side of the bridge, and the dining space beyond, and its gap, and its lightwell. Daylight adds another layer of complexity. It is almost always indirect and usually comes from at least two directions at different intensities, subtly moulding every form it illuminates.

Kazuyo Sejima is famous for her minimalist detailing. There are no projections or recesses, no cover strips or flash gaps. Every element is understated, fitting perfectly into its allotted zone. Nothing is 'expressed'. Such apparent simplicity is hard to achieve. The front wall of the house is a single plane of perforated metal, interrupted only by the front door and the garage door. But there is subtlety even here. Where the wall crosses the upper part of the central well, it is backed by a large window of translucent polycarbonate. At night, it glows softly.

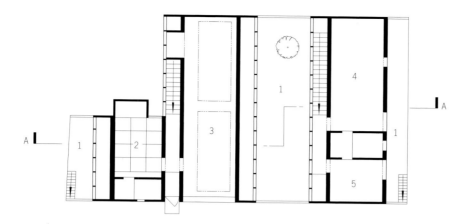

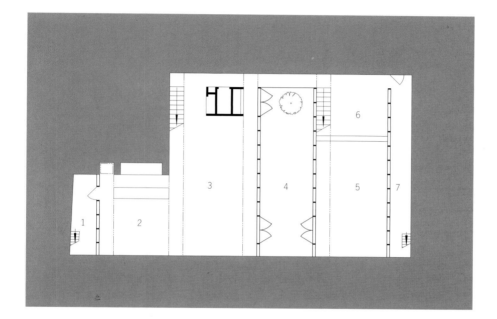

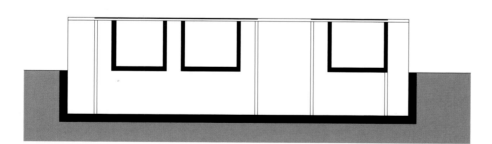

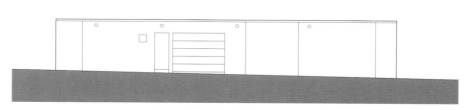

1 Entry Level Plan

1 Void
2 Guest room
3 Parking
4 Master bedroom
5 Children's room

2 Lower Level Plan

1 Lightwell 1
2 Dining room
3 Living room
4 Lightwell 2
5 Studio
6 Study
7 Lightwell 3

3 Section A–A

4 Elevation

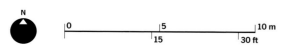

N

0   5   10 m
15   30 ft

Bordeaux House

Rem Koolhaas, 1944–

Bordeaux, France; 1998

The Bordeaux House delights in overturning every architectural convention. Take columns, for example – those most conventional of architectural forms, the very symbols of architecture itself. Apart from one or two almost invisible steel posts in the basement, there is nothing in this large house that could reasonably be described as a column, still less a loadbearing wall. Buildings are normally expected to consist of solid bases and lighter superstructures; this one is upside down. A vast concrete box hovers, apparently unsupported, over an open space casually defined by glass walls. Beams usually support their loads from beneath; here, a single steel beam, almost one storey high, sits on top of the building, looking more like a sky-sign than a piece of functioning structure. And so it goes on through every element and every detail, each one a kind of conjuring trick.

Yet this is also, in its way, a practical design that more than adequately serves the needs, both physical and psychological, of its wheelchair-bound owner and his family. Each of the three storeys is a different world. The first is a semi-basement, dug into the crown of the hill, with one glass wall facing an entrance courtyard. Inside, the space is cave-like, each room separately carved out of the ground and finished in grey plaster as if awaiting primitive paintings. The main staircase to the next level is a kind of animal orifice that emerges, surprisingly, in the open air of the ground-floor terrace. A strange sloping and sliding door opens into a glass-walled living space. On the southern side, the glass wall can slide out onto the terrace, opening up one space while simultaneously screening the other. Above, the rough, unpainted soffit of the concrete box bears down almost oppressively on the space, leading the viewer's gaze out over the valley of the Garonne and the city of Bordeaux in the distance.

The top floor, inside the concrete box, is a mostly enclosed world of interlocking spaces, some of them open to the sky. Only the master bedroom at the east end is allowed to survey the landscape through the open end of the box. The children's bedrooms have little portholes, tapered and angled to focus like lenses on key points in the rooms – a pillow, a bath, a writing desk.

But the most important space in the whole house is the lift – not a conventional one, of course, but a whole room, furnished as a study, that rises and falls on an hydraulic column like a car lift in a garage. This is the key that unlocks the space, for ambulant and wheelchair-bound occupants alike. In the basement it is part of the kitchen and opens into a wine cellar; on the ground floor it commands the living room; on the top floor it becomes an alcove in the master bedroom. But it also a room in its own right, three storeys high with a floor-to-ceiling bookcase.

And the mysterious hovering box? One end of it rests on a squat steel portal; the other hangs from the sky-sign beam, which in turn is supported by the concrete sleeve of a spiral staircase. Where it passes through the open terrace, this staircase is in danger of being mistaken for a column, so it is dematerialized by a cladding of reflective chrome. This 'column' is some way off the centre of the cantilevered beam, which is therefore balanced by a tension rod anchored to the ground in the courtyard.

1 Northeast Elevation

2 Second Floor Plan

1 Parents' Bedroom
2 Bathroom
3 Lift
4 Bedroom
5 Bathroom

3 Section A–A

4 First Floor Plan

1 Living room
2 Dining room
3 Terrace
4 Study
5 Lift

5 Section B–B

6 Ground Floor Plan

1 Main entrance
2 Kitchen
3 Laundry
4 Lift
5 Wine cellar
6 TV room
7 Staff quarters

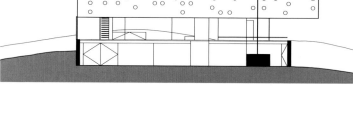

1

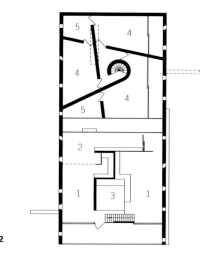

2

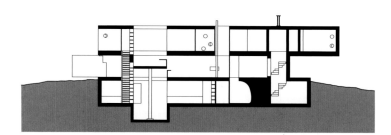

3

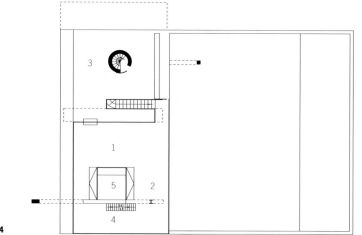

4

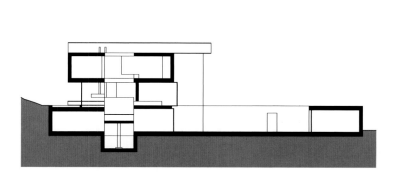

5

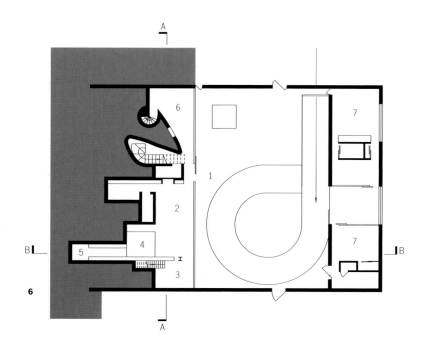

6

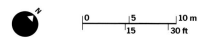

0   5   10 m
15   30 ft

Möbius House

Ben van Berkel and Caroline Bos, 1957– and 1959–

Utrecht, The Netherlands; 1998

The principle of the Möbius strip is usually demonstrated by taking a narrow piece of paper, twisting it once and joining the ends. The paper no longer has two sides, but only one. It has become a puzzling and paradoxical three-dimensional form with no inside or outside. The Möbius House does not at first look anything like a Möbius strip, unless it is a Möbius strip that has been flattened and creased, then pulled apart again. One of the primary conditions of the existence of any building, namely gravity, makes the whole idea of an inhabited Möbius strip somewhat problematic. And, in any case, the architects, Ben van Berkel and Caroline Bos, have confused the picture by saying that the design is actually based on a different form known as a 'double-locked torus'. The practice's website shows a computer model of this form, which is curvaceous and organic, like a loop of intestine. An animated version of the model even shows a slight swelling travelling peristaltically along it.

The house does not look any more like a double-locked torus than a Möbius strip. It is crystalline rather than amoebic and more crumpled than swelling. But the models are inspirational at a conceptual rather than a formal

level. They are invoked in order to escape from architectural convention and to undermine normal expectations of what a house should be. They also introduce a dynamic element into the design. The clients are a husband and wife who both work at home but separately, meeting only at certain times of the day. The house is therefore conceived not as a collection of static spaces, but as a spatial loop around which the diurnal pattern of human use — working, living, sleeping — travels like the swelling in the double-locked torus. And since there are two people, with different daily routines, there must be two possible routes — hence 'double-locked'.

The plans are hard to interpret, but a basic circulation route can be readily discerned. Beginning in the ground-floor entrance hall on the south side, we immediately ascend the dog-leg staircase straight ahead and rise to the first floor, where a kinked corridor and landing ends in another stair. This we descend to a lower-ground-floor level, doubling back under the landing before climbing a ramp up to our starting point in the entrance hall. It is not quite a Möbius strip, but it is a three-dimensional figure of eight and it provides some unusual spatial experiences on the

way. The route passes spaces with conventional names — studio, bedroom, living room — but this is very far from being a conventional corridor arrangement. The Möbius motif has been applied to the enclosing elements as well as the space enclosed. Stiff ribbons of concrete and glass fold over and around each other to create interconnecting spaces with many views through, under, over and across. There are no windows as such, only walls of glass, so the spaces connect as much with the surrounding landscape as with each other. The large, open site on the outskirts of Utrecht was landscaped by Adriaan Geuze as an extension of the house.

In 1998, van Berkel and Bos founded UN Studio. UN stands for 'united net' and refers to a collaborative mode of practice that includes builders, quantity surveyors and project managers as well as architects and designers of various kinds. It is a sensible idea. If you are going to design buildings like the Möbius house, it is as well to be on good terms with the other members of the building team.

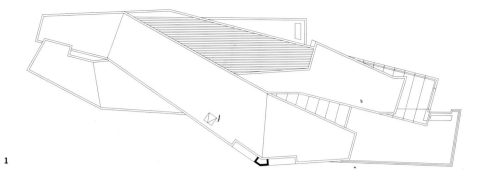

1

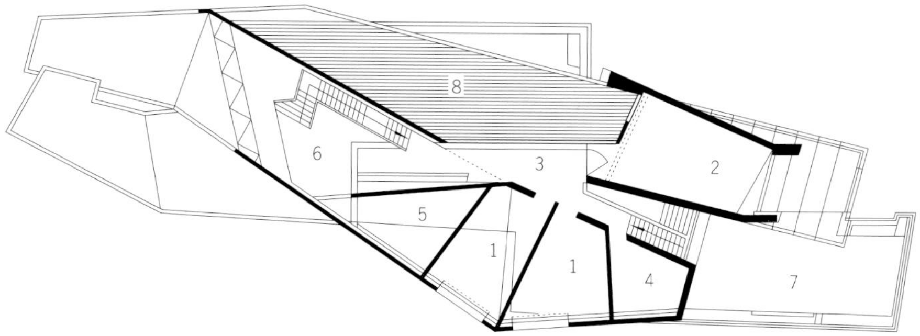

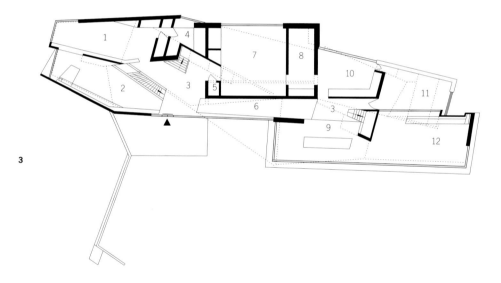

2

2 First Floor Plan

1 Bedroom
2 Studio
3 Circulation
4 Bathroom
5 Storage
6 Open space
7 Upper part of living room
8 Roof garden

3

3 Ground Floor Plan

1 Bedroom
2 Studio
3 Circulation
4 Bathroom
5 Toilet
6 Ramp
7 Garage
8 Storage
9 Meeting room
10 Kitchen
11 Verandah
12 Living room

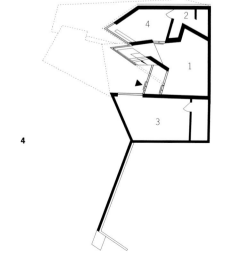

4

4 Basement Plan

1 Circulation
2 Bathroom
3 Storage
4 Guest room

Aluminium House

Toyo Ito, 1941–

Setagaya-ku, Tokyo, Japan; 2000

Whereas western cities carry the past with them in the form of boulevards, monumental buildings and piazzas, Japanese cities live always in the present. They are somehow more abstract, more like rippling networks of change than fixed, resistant hierarchies. It is said that the average life of a building in Tokyo or Osaka is just 20 years.

The architecture of Toyo Ito seems to be in tune with this evanescence and reconciled to its consequences. The Mediatheque in Sendai, which since its completion in 2000 has quickly come to be regarded as Ito's masterpiece, is a large public building displaying strikingly new forms, yet it is in no way monumental. It is a non-hierarchical system: a stack of floors linked by hollow glass columns and contained by almost invisible walls. Ito himself compares it to an aquarium, but it is the container rather than the contents that seems to float. It could reproduce and extend itself to the horizon – or it could disappear overnight.

In Ito's smaller buildings, such as the Aluminium House in the Setagaya-ku district of Tokyo, the evanescent quality turns into a kind of elegant modesty. The house is made of aluminium and glass, not wood and paper, but it seems nevertheless to owe its ancestry to the traditional

Japanese house – that architectural paragon with which early European and American Modernists were besotted. It has the same combination of ordinariness and extreme refinement. At first, it looks like a negligible piece of street furniture – a substation, perhaps, or a parked vehicle – but on closer inspection its quiet politeness becomes apparent and it suddenly turns into architecture.

The external form of the house is very simple: a small box on top of a large box, with a projecting sunshade across the front and a pergola over a car port at the side. The plan, however, is rather subtle. Most of the living spaces, including a small tatami room, are on the ground floor, arranged around a double-height space like a tiny courtyard. This space is lit by south-facing windows on the upper level so that it acts like a lantern, brightening the whole interior, and also like a chimney, improving natural ventilation by the stack effect. Upstairs there is only a guestroom and a bathroom, with access to a roof terrace.

The house was assembled rather than built, but it was assembled piece by piece on the site, not in panels or volumetrically in a workshop. Internal walls and ceilings are painted plasterboard, and the floors are wood strip, but otherwise glass

and extruded aluminium are the main materials. Columns, beams, floor decks, external walls, window frames, door frames, and shutters – all are aluminium. For this kind of house, architectural convention would normally dictate that there be a visible structural frame infilled with lightweight panels, but Ito rejects this idea. It is perhaps too obvious, too hierarchical, too western. There are linear aluminium members, cruciform in section, that function as columns, but they are hidden in the thickness – just 70 mm (3 inches) – of the external wall. The external walls themselves are made of aluminium channels 300 mm (12 inches) wide, sprayed internally with insulating foam. It is more like precision engineering than house-building. Even a simple form such as this requires a surprisingly wide-ranging set of components, including several different kinds of rubber gasket to stop the whole thing rattling in the breeze.

1 Ground Floor Plan	2 First Floor Plan	3 East Elevation	4 Section B–B	5 South Elevation	6 Section A–A

1 Ground Floor Plan
1 Entrance
2 Tatami room
3 Living room
4 Bath
5 Internal courtyard
6 WC
7 Bedroom
8 Kitchen

2 First Floor Plan
1 Upper part of internal courtyard
2 Bedroom
3 Roof terrace

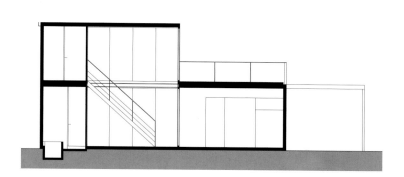

6

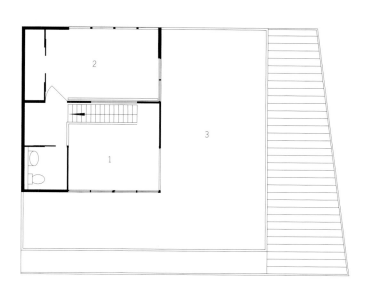

2

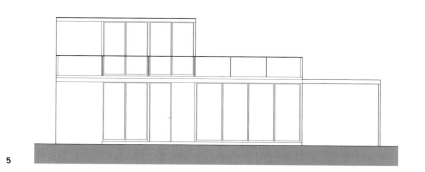

5

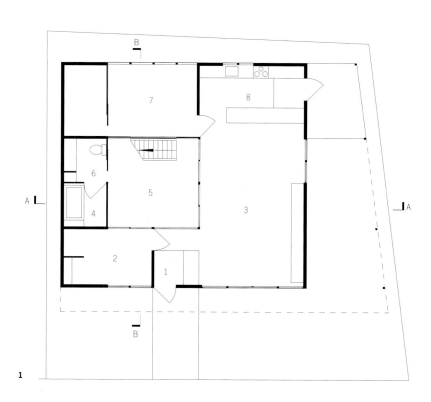

1

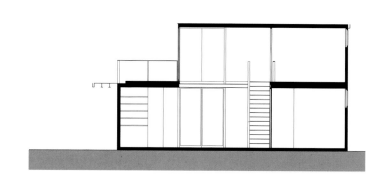

4

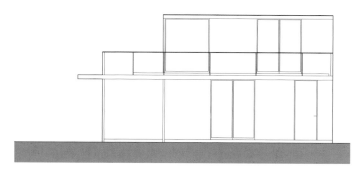

3

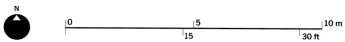

N

0	5	10 m
15		30 ft

House at Moledo

Eduardo Souto de Moura, 1952–

Moledo, Portugal; 2000

Eduardo Souto de Moura is associated with the Oporto school of Portuguese architects, led by Alvaro Siza. He was taught by Siza and worked in his practice from 1974 to 1979. He is therefore the inheritor of a particular, regional brand of Modernism that remained faithful to the cause through the Postmodernist years, finally to be rediscovered and celebrated internationally in the 1990s. But Souto de Moura is by no means a second-hand Siza. His architecture is simpler, cleaner and more abstract, though no less interested in the special qualities of particular places. He is well known for his houses, which can be seen as a set of variations on a theme. That theme owes something to Mies van der Rohe but is also influenced by later artists, in particular the American sculptor Donald Judd. The house at Moledo is simple to the point of minimalism, but true simplicity, as most architects know, is not easy to achieve. It is hard won, the result of a long process of analysis, refinement, selection and difficult decision-making.

For Souto de Moura, the characteristics of the site are more important than the client's requirements, especially when, as at Moledo, the brief is an utterly conventional list of rooms and the site is demanding: a large tract of steep hillside overlooking the Atlantic coast, terraced for agriculture, with steps about 1.5 metres (6 feet) high retained by rubble-stone walls. Souto de Moura had dealt with a similar site for an earlier house at Baião, but at Moledo the terracing was awkwardly spaced, the steps too shallow and low to provide a comfortable platform on which to build. He therefore persuaded the client to pay for the total remodelling of the hillside, with fewer, larger steps. The repositioning of the retaining walls took several years and in the end proved more expensive than the house itself.

Given the straightforward brief, the steps and the view, the obvious solution would have been to construct a single-aspect house on one of the steps, with its back against a retaining wall. A more subtle version might have pushed the house back into the retaining wall, leaving the step as a terrace in front.

Souto de Moura went further. He built the house into the step but left a gap behind, really no more than a narrow lightwell, and made the back wall all glass, looking out onto a natural rocky slope. This completely transforms the interior, in particular the quality of the daylight. All the glare and gloom that is usually associated with single-aspect rooms is banished by the 'fill-in light' from the lightwell. And the corridor that serves the bedrooms in this simple, linear plan becomes not a dim tunnel relying on borrowed light but a little canyon between the wood-veneered internal walls and the rocky slope.

The front wall is all glass too, in wood-framed sliding doors, but, curiously, there is little sense of spatial flow or inside/outside ambiguity. The completely regular plan — simply a row of rooms — seems to emphasize containment rather than openness. This impression is reinforced by the extensions of the retaining walls, which overlap the glass at each end of the façade, screening the kitchen, bathroom and service rooms. External materials are brought inside but transformed, as if tamed for domestic use. The beautiful cyclopean granite wall in the living room, for example, is like a smoothed-out version of the rocky slope. Floors are mostly of wooden boards and ceilings are one continuous plain plaster surface, unifying all the spaces. There is no separate front door, just a patch of stone paving on the terrace in front of the living room to indicate, minimally, the preferred point of entry.

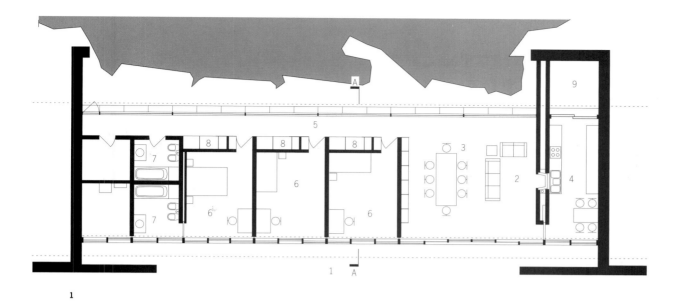

1

1 Ground Floor Plan

1 Terrace
2 Living room
3 Dining room
4 Kitchen
5 Corridor
6 Bedroom
7 Bathroom
8 Wardrobe
9 Yard

2

2 West Elevation

3

3 Section A–A

0   5   10 m
15   30 ft

Father's House

Ma Qingyun, 1965–

Xi'an, Shaanxi, China; 2000

MADA s.p.a.m. (it stands for strategy, planning, architecture, media) is one of the new generation of architectural practices that has grown up, fit and healthy, in the development hot-house of modern, free-market China. Founded in 1999 and based in Shanghai, the practice has already built a few important public buildings, including the library of Zhejiang University and a large cultural centre on the banks of the Yangtze River at Ningbo. Ma Qingyun is MADA's dynamic young principal. In 1999, he designed a house for his father near Xi'an, the ancient capital of Shaanxi province and home to the famous Terracotta Army.

The site is an often mist-shrouded hillside at the foot of the Qinlin mountain range. The house looks perfectly at home here, although it is an abstract box displaying no immediately recognizable Chinese features. It does, however, make extensive use of a local building material: rounded stones from the bed of the nearby Shaanxi river. These are said to have been gathered by local inhabitants over a period of years. They are stacked, without any visible mortar, to form the infill walls in a dark grey, reinforced-concrete frame. The texture they create has an extraordinary, almost hallucinatory quality, like

petrified frogspawn or the warty skin of a reptile. But it is the frame that dictates the form of the house. Its square plan is echoed by a square entrance court, which is paved with 'napped' versions of the flint-like wall stones and contains a reflecting pool.

The front façade of the house is a stark rectangle, divided into three bays and two storeys by the thick, dark lines of the concrete columns and beams. All six openings are completely filled by sliding/folding shutters covered in woven bamboo. When the shutters are open, an inner complexity is revealed. The real walls, set back from the shutters by the depth of a balcony, are all glass, in black metal frames.

There are two balconies on the upper level, but they are each only half a bay wide, and the rest of this in-between space is double-height. Inside, one of the bays of the full-width main living room is also double-height, with the staircase rising in one corner. A curious boxy form, resembling a chimney breast, hangs from the ceiling, stopping some distance from the floor, to demarcate a dining area at the other end of the room. And everything — walls, floor, ceiling, doors — is covered in woven bamboo.

Other rooms are treated similarly. Openings, whether internal or external, are always full-height and all windows are shuttered. The palette of colours and materials is very restricted — concrete, stone and bamboo, inside and out — and the interior undoubtedly looks best as it is shown in most photographs, without furniture. On the north side of the house, another courtyard, long and narrow, is entirely filled by a swimming pool.

Is this house really Chinese? Perhaps not. To European eyes, it is strongly reminiscent of certain buildings by the Swiss architects Herzog and de Meuron and Peter Zumthor. The ghost of Louis Kahn also seems to be present. It is no surprise, therefore, to learn that Ma Qingyun studied for his master's degree at the University of Pennsylvania.

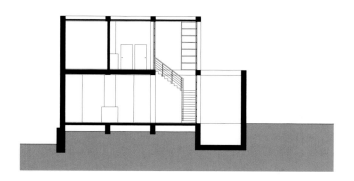

1

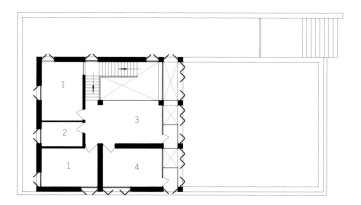

2

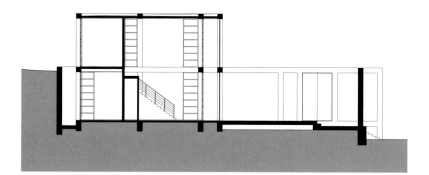

3 First Floor Plan

1 Guest room
2 Bathroom
3 Study
4 Master bedroom

3

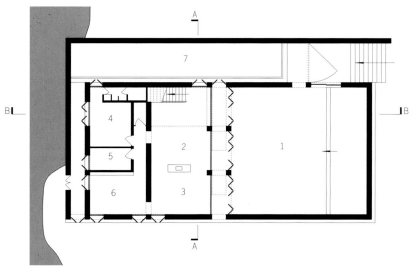

4 Ground Floor Plan

1 Courtyard
2 Living room
3 Dining room
4 Guest room
5 Bathroom
6 Kitchen
7 Swimming pool

4

0   5   10 m

15   30 ft

N

Further Reading

General Histories

Banham, Reyner, *Theory and Design in the First Machine Age* (Oxford: Architectural Press, 2nd Edn. 1962)

Benevolo, Leonardo, *A History of Modern Architecture, Volumes 1 & 2* (Cambridge, Mass.: MIT Press, 1971)

Collins, Peter, *Changing Ideals in Modern Architecture 1750–1950* (Montreal: McGill–Queens University Press, 2nd Edn. 1998)

Curtis, William, *Modern Architecture Since 1900* (London: Phaidon Press, 3rd Edn. 1996)

Frampton, Kenneth, *Modern Architecture: A Critical History* (London: Thames and Hudson, 3rd Edn. 1992)

Giedion, Sigfried, *Space, Time and Architecture* (Cambridge, Mass.: MIT Press, 5th Edn. 1967)

Hitchcock, H. R. and Johnson, Philip, *The International Style: Architecture Since 1922* (New York: Museum of Modern Art, 1932)

Jackson, Lesley, *Contemporary* (London: Phaidon Press, 1994)

Jencks, Charles, *Modern Movements in Architecture* (Harmondsworth: Penguin, 2nd Edn. 1985)

Jencks, Charles, *Language of Post Modern Architecture* (London: Academy Editions, 6th Edn. 1991)

Pevsner, Nikolaus, *Pioneers of Modern Design from William Morris to Walter Gropius* (Harmondsworth: Penguin, 2nd Edn. 1991)

Weston, Richard, *Modernism* (London: Phaidon Press, 1996)

Weston, Richard, *Plans, Sections and Elevations: Key Buildings of the Twentieth Century* (London: Laurence King, 2004)

Books about Twentieth-Century Houses

Armesto, Antonio, and Padro, Quim, *Casas Atlanticas: Galicia y Norte de Portugal/ Atlantic House: Galicia and Northern Portugal* (Barcelona: Gili, 1996)

Barreneche, Raul A., *Modern House 3* (London: Phaidon, 2005)

Benton, Tim, *The Villas of Le Corbusier 1920–1930* (New Haven and London: Yale University Press, 1987)

Boissiere, Olivier, *Twentieth-century Houses: Europe* (Paris: Terrail,1998)

Dunster, David, *Key Buildings of the Twentieth Century, Vol. 1: Houses 1900–1944* (London: Architectural Press, 1985)

Dunster, David, *Key Buildings of the Twentieth Century, Vol. 2: Houses 1945–1989* (London: Butterworths, 1990)

Frampton, Kenneth, *The Twentieth-century American House: Masterworks of Residential Architecture* (London: Thames and Hudson, 1995)

Guell, Xavier, *Casas Mediterraneas: Costa Brava/ Mediterranean Architecture: Costa Brava* (Barcelona: Gili, 1986)

Guell, Xavier, *Casas Mediterraneas/ Mediterranean Houses: Costa Brava 2* (Barcelona: Gili, 1994)

Hess, Alan, *Frank Lloyd Wright: the Houses* (New York: Rizzoli, 2005)

Jackson, Neil, *The Modern Steel House* (London: Spon, 1996)

McCoy, Esther, *Case Study Houses 1945–1962* (Los Angeles: Hennessey & Ingalls, 1977)

McGrath, Raymond, *Twentieth-century Houses* (London: Faber 1934)

Melhuish, Clare, *Modern House 2* (London: Phaidon, 2000)

Pople, Nicolas, *Experimental Houses* (London: Laurence King, 2000)

Rowe, Colin, *Five Architects: Eisenman, Graves, Gwathmey, Hejduk, Meier* (New York: Oxford University Press, 1975)

Saito, Yutaka, *Louis I. Kahn: Houses 1940–1974* (Tokyo: TOTO, 2003)

Sudjic, Deyan, and Beyerle, Tulga, *Home: the Twentieth-century House* (London: Laurence King in association with Glasgow 1999, 1999)

Tinniswood, Adrian, *The Art Deco House: Avant-garde Houses of the 1920s and 1930s* (London: Mitchell Beazley, 2002)

Welsh, John, *Modern House* (London: Phaidon, 1995)

Weston, Richard, *The House in the Twentieth Century* (London: Laurence King, 2002)

Yorke, F. R. S., *The Modern House* (London: Architectural Press, 1951)

Zabalbeascoa, Anatxu, *Houses of the Century* (London: Cartago, 1998)

Monographs about architects

Aalto, Alvar Reed, Peter, *Alvar Aalto: Between Humanism and Materialism* (New York: Museum of Modern Art, 1998)

Ando, Tadao Futagawa, Yukio, *Tadao Ando* (Tokyo: A.D.A. Edita, 1987)

Asplund, Erik Gunnar Holmdahl, Gustav (ed.), *Gunnar Asplund Architect 1885–1940* (Stockholm: Byggförlaget, 1981)

Ban, Shigeru Bell, Eugenia (ed.), *Shigeru Ban* (London: Laurence King, 2001)

Barragán, Luis Riggen Martínez, Antonio, *Luis Barragán* (New York: The Monacelli Press, 1996)

Bawa, Geoffrey Robson, David, *Geoffrey Bawa: the Complete Works* (London: Thames and Hudson, 2002)

Behnisch, Günter Blundell Jones, Peter, *Günter Behnisch* (Basel: Birkhauser, 2000)

Behrens, Peter Anderson, Stanford, *Peter Behrens and a New Architecture for the Twentieth Century* (Cambridge, Mass. and London: MIT Press, 2000)

Bo Bardi, Lina *Lina Bo Bardi* (Milan: Charta [for] Instituto Lina Bo e P. M. Bardi, 1994)

Bofill, Ricardo James, Warren A. (ed.), *Ricardo Bofill, Taller de Arquitectura: Buildings and Projects 1960–1985* (New York: Rizzoli, 1988)

Botta, Mario Pizzi, Emilio, *Mario Botta: The Complete Works Volume 1: 1960–1985* (Zurich: Artemis, 1993)

Breuer, Marcel Driller, Joachim, *Breuer Houses* (London: Phaidon, 2000)

Buckminster Fuller, Richard Pawley, Martin, *Buckminster Fuller* (London: Trefoil, 1990)

Campo Baeza, Alberto Pizza, Antonio, *Alberto Campo Baeza: Works and Projects* (Barcelona: Gili, 1999)

Coderch, José Antonio Pizza, Antonio, and Roviro, Josep M. (eds.), *Coderch 1940–1964: In Search of Home* (Barcelona: Collegi d'Arquitectes de Catalunya, 2000)

Connell, Amyas Sharp, Dennis (ed.), *Connell Ward & Lucas: Modern Movement Architects in England 1929–1929* (London: Book Art, 1994)

Correa, Charles Frampton, Kenneth (ed.), *Charles Correa* (London: Thames and Hudson, 1996)

De la Sota, Alejandro Alejandro de la Sota et al., *The Architecture of Imperfection* (London: AA Publications, 1997)

Eames, Charles and Ray Kirkham, Pat, *Charles and Ray Eames* (Cambridge, Mass.: MIT Press, 1995)

Eisenman, Peter Dobney, Stephen (ed.), *Eisenman Architects: Selected and Current Works* (Victoria: The Images Publishing Group, 1995)

Ellwood, Craig Jackson, Neil, *Craig Ellwood* (London: Laurence King, 2002)

Fathy, Hassan Steele, James, *An Architecture for the People: the Complete Works of Hassan Fathy* (London: Thames and Hudson, 1997)

Fehn, Sverre Norberg-Schulz, Christian, and Postiglione, Gennaro, *Sverre Fehn: Works, Projects, Writings, 1949–1996* (New York: The Monacelli Press, 1997)

Foster, Norman Jenkins, David (ed.), *Norman Foster: Works, Vols. 1–4* (Munich and London: Prestel, 2002–2005)

Frey, Albert Rosa, Joseph, *Albert Frey Architect* (New York: Rizzoli, 1990)

Gehry, Frank Dalco, Francesco, and Forster, Kurt, *Frank O. Gehry: The Complete Works* (New York: The Monacelli Press, 1998)

Graves, Michael *Michael Graves: Selected and Current Works* (Mulgrave: Images, 1999)

Goff, Bruce De Long, David G., *Bruce Goff: Toward Absolute Architecture* (New York:

Architectural History Foundation; Cambridge, Mass. and London: MIT Press, 1988)

Goldfinger, Ernö Warburton, Nigel, *Ernö Goldfinger: the Life of an Architect* (London: Routledge, 2003)

Gray, Eileen Constant, Caroline, *Eileen Gray* (London: Phaidon, 2000)

Greene, Charles and Henry Bosley, Edward R., *Greene & Greene* (London: Phaidon, 2000)

Gropius, Walter Isaacs, Reginald, *Gropius* (Berlin: Gebr. Mann Verlag, 1983)

Herzog, Thomas *Thomas Herzog: Architektur + Technologie* (Munich and London: Prestel, 2001)

Hopkins, Michael and Patty Davies, Colin, *Hopkins: the Work of Michael Hopkins and Partners* (London: Phaidon, 1993)

Ito, Toyo Maffei, Andrea (ed.), *Works, Projects, Writings: Toyo Ito* (Milan: Electa Architecture, 2002)

Johnson, Philip Jenkins, Stover, and Mohney, David, *The Houses of Philip Johnson* (New York and London: Abbeville Press, 2001)

Johnson, Philip Whitney, David, and Kipnis, Jeffrey (eds.), *Philip Johnson: the Glass House* (New York: Pantheon, 1993)

Kahn, Louis Ronner, Heinz and Sharad, Jhaveri, *Louis I. Kahn Complete Work 1935–1974* (Basel, Birkhäuser, 2nd Edn. 1987)

Koenig, Pierre Steele, James, and Jenkins, David, *Pierre Koenig* (London: Phaidon, 1998)

Koolhaas, Rem Koolhaas, Rem and Mau, Bruce, *Small, Medium, Large, Extra-Large* (Rotterdam: 010 Publishers, 1995)

Krier, Rob *Rob Krier on Architecture* (London: Academy Editions, 1982)

Kurokawa, Kisho *Kisho Kurokawa: From Metabolism to Symbiosis* (London: Academy Editions, 1992)

Lasdun, Denys Curtis, William, J. R., *Denys Lasdun: Architecture, City, Landscape* (London: Phaidon, 1994)

Lautner, John Hess, Alan, T*he Architecture of John Lautner* (London: Thames and Hudson, 1999)

Le Corbusier Benton, Tim, *The Villas of Le Corbusier, 1920–1930* (New Haven and London: Yale University Press, 1987)

Le Corbusier and Pierre Jeanneret Boesiger, M., Bill, M., Stonorov, O., (eds.), *Oeuvre Complète in 8 Volumes: 1910–1929; 1929–1934; 1934–1938; 1938–1946; 1946–1952; 1952–1957; 1957–1965* (Zurich: Girsberger 1929–1970)

Le Corbusier Curtis, William J. R., *Le Corbusier: Ideas and Forms* (London: Phaidon Press, 1986, reprinted 2001)

Loos, Adolf Gravagnuolo, Benedetto, *Adolf Loos Theory and Works* (Milan: Idea Books, Wien, 1982)

Loos, Adolf Schezen, Roberto, *Adolf Loos:*

Architecture 1903–1932 (New York: The Monacelli Press, 1996)

Lutyens, Edwin Weaver, Lawrence, *Houses and Gardens by E. L. Lutyens* (London: Country Life, 1913)

Maas, Winy *Reading MVRDV* (Rotterdam, NAi, 2003)

Mackintosh, Charles Rennie Steele, James, *Charles Rennie Mackintosh Synthesis in Form* (London: Academy Editions, 1994)

Marshall, Barrie Beck, Haig, and Cooper, Jackie, *Denton Corker Marshall: Rule Playing and the Ratbag Element* (Basel: Birkhauser, 2000)

Maxwell Fry, Edwin Hitchens, Stephen (ed.), *Fry Drew Knight Creamer: Architecture* (London: Lund Humphries, 1978)

Meier, Richard Ockman, John (ed.), *Richard Meier Architect* (New York: Rizzoli International Publications Inc., 1984)

Melnikov, Konstantin Starr, S. Frederick, *Melnikov, Solo Architect in a Mass Society* (Princeton: Princeton University Press, 1978)

Mies van der Rohe, Ludwig Lambert, Phyllis (ed.), *Mies in America* (Montreal: Canadian Centre for Architecture, 2001)

Mies van der Rohe, Ludwig Neumeyer, Fritz, *The Artless World: Mies van der Rohe on the Building Art* (Cambridge, Mass.: MIT Press, 1991)

Mies van der Rohe, Ludwig Riley, Terence, *Mies in Berlin* (New York: Museum of Modern Art, 2001)

Miralles, Enric Tagliabue, Benedetta, *Enric Miralles: Works and Projects 1975–1995* (New York: The Monacelli Press, 1996)

Moore, Charles Johnson, Eugene J. (ed.), *Charles Moore: Buildings and Projects 1949–1986* (New York: Rizzoli, 1986)

Murcutt, Glenn Fromonot, Françoise, *Glenn Murcutt Buildings and Projects 1962–2003* (London: Thames and Hudson, 2003)

Neutra, Richard MacLamprecht, Barbara, *Richard Neutra Complete Works* (Cologne: Taschen, 2000)

Pawson, John Sudjic, Deyan, *John Pawson: Works* (London: Phaidon, 2005)

Predock, Antoine Collins, Brad (ed.), *Antoine Predock: Houses* (New York: Rizzoli, 2000)

Prouvé, Jean Sulzer, Peter, *Jean Prouvé: Complete Works* (Basel: Birkhauser, 2005)

Rietveld, Gerrit Kueper, M. and Van Zijl, I., *Gerrit Th. Rietveld: The Complete Work:* 1888–1964 (Amsterdam: Architectura and Natura, 1993)

Rogers, Richard Powell, Kenneth, *Richard Rogers Complete Works Volumes 1 & 2* (London: Phaidon Press, 1994–2001)

Rudolph, Paul Monk, Tony, *The Art and Architecture of Paul Rudolph* (Chichester: Wiley/Academy, 1999)

Scharoun, Hans Blundell Jones, Peter, *Hans Scharoun* (London: Phaidon Press, 1995)

Schindler, Rudolph Steele, James, *R. M. Schindler* (Cologne: Taschen, 1999)

Seidler, Harry *Harry Seidler: Selected and Current Works* (Mulgrave: Images, 1997)

Sejima, Kazuyo, and Nishizawa, Ryue/SANAA *Kazuyo Sejima + Ryue Nishizawa: Recent Projects* (Berlin: Aedes, 2000)

Siza, Alvaro Cianchetta, Alessandra, and Molteni, Enrico, *Alvaro Siza: Private Houses 1954–2004* (Milan: Skira, 2004)

Smithson, Alison and Peter Webster, Helen (ed.) *Modernism Without Rhetoric* (London: Academy Editions, 1997)

Snozzi, Luigi Lichtenstein, Claude, *Luigi Snozzi* (Basel: Birkhauser, 1997)

Souto de Moura, Eduardo Esposito, Antonio, and Leoni, Giovanni, *Eduardo Souto de Moura* (Milan: Electa, 2003)

Torres, Elías, and Lapeña, José Antonio Martínez Buchanan, Peter, and Quetglas, José M., *Lapeña/Torres* (Barcelona: Gili, 1990)

Ushida, Eisaku, and Findlay, Kathryn *Ushida Findlay* (Barcelona: Gili, 1998)

Utzon, Jørn Weston, Richard, *Utzon* (Hellerup: Edition Bløondal, 2002)

Van Berkel, Ben, and Bos, Caroline Betsky, Aaron, et al., *Un Studio Un Fold* (Rotterdam, NAi, 2002)

Venturi, Robert Constantinopoulos, Vivian, *Venturi Scott Brown and Associates on Houses and Housing* (London: Academy Editions, 1992)

Voysey, Charles Hitchmough, Wendy, *C. F. A. Voysey* (London: Phaidon, 1995)

Wright, Frank Lloyd McCarter, Robert, *Frank Lloyd Wright* (London: Phaidon Press, 1997)

Wright, Frank Lloyd Levine, Neil, *The Architecture of Frank Lloyd Wright* (Princeton: Princeton University Press, 1996)

Wright, Frank Lloyd, Aalto, Alvar and Eames, Charles and Ray McCarter, Robert, Steele, James and Weston, Richard, *Architecture in Detail: 3 Twentieth Century Houses* (London: Phaidon Press, 1999)

Yeang, Ken Yeang, Ken, *The Skyscraper Bio Climatically Considered* (London: Academy Editions, 1996)

Monographs about individual houses:

Casa Ugalde Montaner, Josep M., *Coderch: Casa Ugalde* (Barcelona: Collegi d'Arquitectes de Catalunya, 1998)

Barnsdall House Steele, James, *Barnsdall House: Frank Lloyd Wright* (London: Phaidon, 1992)

Bauhaus Staff Houses Thoner, Wolfgang, *The*

Picture Credits

Bauhaus Life: Life and Work in the Master's Houses Estate in Dessau (Leipzig: Seemann, 2003)

Bavinger House Goff, Bruce, *Bavinger House, Norman, Oklahoma, 1950, Price House, Bartlesville, Oklahoma, 1957–1966/ Bruce Goff* (Tokyo: A.D.A. Edita, 1975)

Casa Malaparte Talamona, Marida *Casa Malaparte* (New York: Princeton Architectural Press, 1992)

Eames House Steele, James, *Eames House: Charles and Ray Eames* (London: Phaidon, 1994)

Fallingwater *McCarter, Robert, Fallingwater: Frank Lloyd Wright* (London: Phaidon, 1994)

Farnsworth House Vandenberg, Maritz, *Farnsworth House: Ludwig Mies van der Rohe* (London: Phaidon, 2003)

Gamble House Bosley, Edward R., *Gamble House: Greene and Greene* (London: Phaidon, 1992)

Hill House Macaulay, James, *Hill House: Charles Rennie Mackintosh* (London: Phaidon, 1994)

Johnson House Whitney, David, and Kipnis, Jeffrey eds, *Philip Johnson: the Glass House* (New York: Pantheon, 1993)

Lina Bo Bardi House Bo Bardi, Lina and Carvalho Ferraz, Marcelo, *Casa de Vidro: Sao Paulo, Brasil, 1950–1951* (Lisbon: Blau, [1999])

Melnikov House Pallasmaa, Juhani, with Gozak, Andrei, *The Melnikov House, Moscow (1927–1929): Konstantin Melnikov* (London: Academy Editions, 1996)

Robie House *The Robie House of Frank Lloyd Wright* (Chicago & London: University of Chicago Press, 1984)

Schröder House Mulde, Bertus and van Zijl, Ida, *The Rietveld Schröder House* (New York: Princeton Architectural Press, 1999)

Tugendhat House Hammer-Tugendhat, Daniela, & Tegethoff, Wolf (eds.), *Ludwig Mies van der Rohe: the Tugendhat House* (Vienna: Springer, 2000)

Vanna Venturi House Schwartz, Frederic ed., *Mother's house: the evolution of Vanna Venturi's house in Chestnut Hill* (New York: Rizzoli, 1992)

Villa Mairea Weston, Richard, *Villa Mairea: Alvar Aalto* (London: Phaidon, 1992)

Villa Savoye Sbriglio, Jacques, *Le Corbusier: la Villa Savoye* (Basel: Birkhauser, 1999)

Villas La Roche-Jeanneret Sbriglio, Jacques, *Le Corbusier: les villas La Roche–Jeanneret* (Basel: Birkhauser, 1997)

Willow Road Powers, Alan, *2 Willow Road, Hampstead* (London: National Trust, [1996])

Wittgenstein House Wijdeveld, Paul, *Ludwig Wittgenstein, architect* (London: Thames and Hudson 1993)

Work by Luis Barragán is © Barragan Foundation, Switzerland/DACS, 2006. Work by Peter Behrens is © DACS, 2006. Works by Le Corbusier are © FLC/ADAGP, Paris and DACS, London 2006 Work by Jean Emile Victor Prouvé is © ADAGP, Paris and DACS, London 2006. Work by Gerrit Rietveld is © DACS, 2006. Works by Frank Lloyd Wright are ARS, NY and DACS, London 2006

10t Colin Davies
10bl Richard Weston
10br Michael Freeman
11t Colin Davies
11b Pavel Stecha
12t Ezra Stoller/Esto
12b Fondation le Corbusier
13tl © Crown copyright.NMR
13tr Richard Bryant/Arcaid
13b Marcell Seidler/Harry Seidler and Associates
14tl Nick Dawe/Arcaid
14tr Bildarchiv Foto Marburg
15tl Fondation le Corbusier
15tr Ezra Stoller/Esto
15b Colin Davies
16 Hans Werlemann/OMA
17t Roberto Schezan/Esto
17b Richard Weston
18t Courtesy, The Estate of R. Buckminster Fuller
18b Martin Charles
19t Courtesy of Mr & Mrs Whitney
19b Colin Davies
22 Bildarchiv Foto Marburg
24 © Crown copyright.NMR
26tl Courtesy of Mr & Mrs Whitney
26tr Martin Charles
28 Richard Weston
30 Richard Weston
32 Richard Weston
34 Fondation Le Corbusier
36 Martin Charles
38 Frank den Oudsten, Amsterdam
40 Colin Davies
42 Scot Zimmerman
44 Richard Weston
46 Fondation le Corbusier
48 Fondation le Corbusier
50 Richard Weston
52 Alexander Hartmann
54 Archipress/Lucien Herve
56 Colin Davies
58 Bildarchiv Foto Marburg
60 Margherita Spiluttini
62tl Hans Engel
62tr Bildarchiv Monheim/AKG Images, London
64 Richard Bryant/Arcaid
66 Kari Haavisto
68 Michael Freeman
69 permissions courtesy Dion Neutra, Architect © and Richard and Dion Neutra Papers, Department of Special Collections, Charles E. Young Research Library, UCLA
70 Philippe Garner
72 Nick Dawe/Arcaid
74 Pavel Stecha
76 Alexander Hartmann
78 Pavel Stecha
80 Colin Davies
82 Photo by Albert Frey/Albert Frey Collection/Architecture & Design Collection, University Art Museum, University of California, Santa Barbara
84 Hans Scharoun Archive
86 Colin Davies
88 Colin Davies
90 Paul Rocheleau
92 Richard Weston
94 Richard Weston
96 Nick Dawe/Arcaid
98 Courtesy of RIBA
100 Wolfgang Voigt
102 Ezra Stoller/Esto
104 Courtesy, The Estate of R. Buckminster Fuller
106 Colin Davies
107 © 2006 EAMES OFFICE LLC (www.eamesoffice.com)

108tl Norman McGrath
108tr Paul Rocheleau
110 Marcell Seidler/Harry Seidler and Associates
112 Colin Davies
114 Courtesy of the Instituto Lina Bo e P.M. Bardi
116 Marte Catalan
118 Jan Utzon
120 Michael Freeman
122 Richard Weston
124 Martin Charles
126 © J. Paul Getty Trust. Used with permission. Julius Shulman Photography Archive. Research Library at the Getty Research Institute (2004.R.10)
128 Colin Davies
130 Roger Last/Bridgeman Art Library
132 Roberto Schezen/Esto
134 © J. Paul Getty Trust. Used with permission. Julius Shulman Photography Archive. Research Library at the Getty Research Institute (2004.R.10)
136 © J. Paul Getty Trust. Used with permission. Julius Shulman Photography Archive. Research Library at the Getty Research Institute (2004.R.10)
138 Roberto Schezen/Esto
140 All Reproduction Rights Reserved by the Morley Baer Photography Trust ©2006. Courtesy, Special Collections, University Library, University of California Santa Cruz
142 Richard Bryant/Arcaid
144 Richard Einzig/Arcaid
146 Tom Yee/House & Garden © 1973 Condé Nast Publications Inc.
148 Barragan Foundation
150 Richard Bryant/Arcaid
152 Courtesy of Scott Tallon Walker Architects
154 Aga Khan Trust for Culture
156 Luís Ferreira Alves
158 Roberto Schezan/Esto
160 Paul Rocheleau
162 Ezra Stoller/Esto
164 Archives Krier Kohl Architects
166 Tomio Ohashi
168 Photos by Serena Vergano
170 Eduard Hueber
172 Fundacion Alejandro de la Sota, Madrid
174l James Mortimer
174r Matthew Weinreb
176 Peter Aaron/Esto
178 Courtesy of Tadao Ando
180 Richard Schenkirz
182 Botta Archive
184 Miguel de Gúzman García-Monge
186 T.R. Hamzah & Yeang Sdn Bhd
188 Max Dupain and Associates Pty Ltd. Photo by Eric Sierins
190 Hisao Suzuki
192 Grant Mudford
194 Lluis Casals
196 Courtesy of Charles Correa Associates
198 Tim Hursley
200 Richard Bryant/Arcaid
202 Sverre Fehn
204 Hisao Suzuki
206 Hans Werlemann/OMA
208 Behnisch & Partner, Stuttgart
210 Ushida Findlay
212 Colin Davies
214 Reiner Blunck
216 John Gollings
218 Hiroyuki Hirai
220 Christian Richters
222 The Japan Architect Co., Ltd.
224 Colin Davies
226 Christian Richters
228 Tomio Ohashi
230 Luís Ferreira Alves
232 MADA s.p.a.m., China

All drawings, based on architects' original designs, by Adrian Scholefield and Gregory Gibbon with Sam Austin, Mike Court, Katie Collins, Gemma Murphy, Olly Moore, Alastair Gambles, Christopher Richards, Sam Utting, Wesley Whittle and Robin Jackson.

Index

Numbers in **bold** denote main entries; numbers in *italics* refer to pictures.

About the CD

The attached CD can be read on both Windows and Macintosh computers. All the material on the CD is copyright protected and is for private use only. All drawings in the book and on the CD were specially created for this publication and are based on the architects' original designs. Drawings for buildings marked with asterisks in the list below are © DACS 2006. Drawings of works by Luis Barragán are © Barragán Foundation, Switzerland /DACS 2006. Drawings of works by Peter Behrens are © DACS 2006. Drawings of works by Le Corbusier are © FLC/ADAGP, Paris and DACS, London 2006. Drawings of works by Jean Emile Victor Prouvé are © ADAGP, Paris and DACS, London 2006. Drawings of works by Frank Lloyd Wright are © ARS, NY and DACS, London 2006.

Drawings are by Adrian Scholefield and Gregory Gibbon with Sam Austin, Mike Court, Katie Collins, Gemma Murphy, Olly Moore, Alastair Gambles, Christopher Richards, Sam Utting, Wesley Whittle and Robin Jackson.

The CD includes files for all of the plans, sections and elevations included in the book. The drawings for each building are contained in a numbered folder as listed below. They are supplied in two versions: the files with the suffix '.eps' are 'vector' Illustrator EPS files but can be opened using other graphics programs such as Photoshop; all the files with the suffix '.dwg' are generic CAD format files and can be opened in a variety of CAD programs.

The generic '.dwg' file format does not support 'solid fill' utilized by many architectural CAD programs. All the information is embedded within the file and can be reinstated within supporting CAD programs. Select the polygon required and change the 'Attributes' to 'Solid', the colour information should be automatically retrieved. To reinstate the 'Walls'; select all objects within the 'Walls' layer/class and amend their 'Attributes' to 'Solid'.

All the drawings are to the same scale of 1:200.

The numbered folders correspond to the following buildings:

1. Behrens House, Peter Behrens
2. Orchards, Edwin Lutyens
3. Hollybank, Charles Voysey
4. Hill House, Charles Rennie Mackintosh
5. Gamble House, Charles and Henry Greene
6. Robie House, Frank Lloyd Wright
7. Villa Schwob, Le Corbusier
8. Villa Snellman, Eric Gunnar Asplund
9. Villa Henny, Robert van 't Hoff
10. Barnsdall House, Frank Lloyd Wright
11. Ennis House, Frank Lloyd Wright
12. Schröder House, Gerrit Rietveld
13. Villas La Roche–Jeanneret, Le Corbusier
14. Pavillon de l'Esprit Nouveau, Le Corbusier
15. Lovell Beach House, Rudolph Schindler
16. Bauhaus Staff Houses, Walter Gropius
17. Villa Stein–de Monzie, Le Corbusier
18. Weissenhof House, Le Corbusier
19. Wolf House, Ludwig Mies van der Rohe
20. Moller House, Adolf Loos
21. Lange House, Ludwig Mies van der Rohe
22. Wittgenstein House, Ludwig Wittgenstein
23. Melnikov House, Konstantin Melnikov
24. Lovell Health House, Richard Neutra
25. E1027, Eileen Gray
26. High and Over, Amyas Connell
27. Müller House, Adolf Loos
28. Houses at Am Rupenhorn, Hans Luckhardt
29. Tugendhat House, Ludwig Mies van der Rohe
30. Villa Savoye, Le Corbusier
31. Aluminaire House, Alfred Lawrence Kocher and Albert Frey
32. Schminke House, Hans Scharoun
33. Villa Girasole, Ettore Fagiuoli
34. Sun House, Edwin Maxwell Fry
35. Jacobs House, Frank Lloyd Wright
36. Fallingwater, Frank Lloyd Wright
37. Villa Mairea, Alvar Aalto
38. Willow Road, Ernö Goldfinger
39. Newton Road, Denys Lasdun
40. Casa Malaparte, Adalberto Libera and Curzio Malaparte
41. Chamberlain Cottage, Marcel Breuer
42. Wichita House, Richard Buckminster Fuller
43. Eames House, Charles and Ray Eames
44. Johnson House, Philip Johnson
45. Rose Seidler House, Harry Seidler
46. Farnsworth House, Ludwig Mies van der Rohe
47. Lina Bo Bardi House, Lina Bo Bardi
48. Casa Ugalde, José Antonio Coderch
49. Utzon House, Jørn Utzon
50. Case Study House No. 16, Craig Ellwood
51. Experimental House, Alvar Aalto
52. Maison Prouvé, Jean Prouvé
53. Bavinger House, Bruce Goff
54. Sugden House, Alison and Peter Smithson
55. Villa Shodan, Le Corbusier
56. Maisons Jaoul, Le Corbusier
57. Case Study House No. 22, Pierre Koenig
58. Malin Residence, John Lautner
59. Esherick House, Louis Kahn
60. Moore House, Charles Moore
61. Vanna Venturi House, Robert Venturi
62. Creek Vean House, Norman Foster and Richard Rogers
63. Hanselmann House, Michael Graves
64. San Cristobal, Luis Barragán
65. Bawa House, Geoffrey Bawa
66. Tallon House, Ronnie Tallon
67. Fathy House, Hassan Fathy
68. Cardoso House, Alvaro Siza
69. Fisher House, Louis Kahn
70. House VI, Peter Eisenman
71. Douglas House, Richard Meier
72. Dickes House, Rob Krier
73. Capsule House K, Kisho Kurokawa
74. Bofill House, Emilio Bofill
75. Kalmann House, Luigi Snozzi
76. Dominguez House, Alejandro de la Sota Martinez
77. Hopkins House, Michael and Patty Hopkins
78. Rudolph Apartment, Paul Rudolph
79. Glass Block Wall–Horiuchi House, Tadao Ando
80. House at Regensburg, Thomas Herzog
81. Casa Rotunda, Mario Botta
82. House at Santander, Jerónimo Junquera and Estanislao Pérez Pita
83. Roof Roof House, Ken Yeang
84. Magney House, Glenn Murcutt
85. Casa Garau Agustí, Enric Miralles
86. Winton Guest House, Frank Gehry
87. Cap Martinet, Elías Torres and José Antonio Martínez Lapeña
88. House at Koramangala, Charles Correa
89. Zuber House, Anton Predock
90. Neuendorf House, John Pawson and Claudio Silvestrin
91. Villa Busk, Sverre Fehn
92. Casa Gaspar, Alberto Campo Baeza
93. Villa Dall'Ava, Rem Koolhaas
94. Charlotte House, Günter Behnisch
95. Truss Wall House, Eisaku Ushida and Kathryn Findlay
96. Cho en Dai, Norman Foster
97. Marika–Alderton House, Glenn Murcutt
98. Marshall House, Barrie Marshall
99. Furniture House, Shiguru Ban
100. Double House, Bjarne Mastenbroek and Winy Maas
101. M House, Kazuyo Sejima and Ryue Nishizawa/ SANAA
102. House in Bordeaux, Rem Koolhaas
103. Möbius House, Ben van Berkel and Caroline Bos
104. Aluminium House, Toyo Ito
105. House at Moledo, Eduardo Souto de Moura
106. Father's House, Ma Qingyun